'*I AM NOW CHANGING MY ACCENT TO SOUND MORE AFRICAN.*'

THE COMMUNICATION OF NON-EUROPEAN OTHERNESS IN GUIDED TOURS FOR SCHOOL CLASSES IN GERMAN AND BRITISH MUSEUMS

DISSERTATION

ZUR ERLANGUNG DES DOKTORGRADES
AM FACHBEREICH 03, SOZIAL- UND KULTURWISSENSCHAFTEN,
AM INSTITUT FÜR SOZIOLOGIE
DER JUSTUS-LIEBIG-UNIVERSITÄT GIESSEN.

EINGEREICHT IM OKTOBER 2017 VON
KATJA KIRSTEN, MA

Erstbetreuer: Prof. Dr. Jörn Ahrens
Zweitbetreuerin: Prof. Dr. Karoline Noack

Gießener Dissertation im Fachbereich Sozial- und Kulturwissenschaften

Autor: Katja Kirsten

Umschlagbild: pressmaster/bigstock.com

Verlag: Giessen University Library Publications

ISBN: 978-3-944682-37-2

Printed in Germany and other countries

Bibliografische Information der Deutschen Nationalbibliothek: Die Deutsche Nationalbibliothek verzeichnet diese Publikation in der Deutschen Nationalbibliografie; detaillierte bibliografische Daten sind im Internet über http://dnb.dnb.de abrufbar.

Danksagung

Den Abschluss dieser Arbeit verdanke ich vielen Unterstützer/innen, nicht nur auf fachlicher Ebene. Einigen von ihnen möchte ich hiermit meinen herzlichen Dank aussprechen.

Für die fachliche und konzeptuelle Unterstützung bei der Planung und Verschriftlichung dieser Dissertation danke ich Prof. Dr. Jörn Ahrens sowie Prof. Dr. Karoline Noack. Die investierte Zeit, die zahlreichen guten Hinweise und die wohlwollende Beratung waren für mich immer sehr hilfreich und wichtig.

Des Weiteren bedanke ich mich bei den beteiligten Museen und Museumspädagog/innen sowie bei den Schulklassen für die Möglichkeit, einen Einblick in die kulturelle Praxis der Vermittlung nicht-europäischer Kultur im Museum zu erhalten. Ohne diese Beobachtungen wäre diese Arbeit nicht möglich gewesen.

Ein besonderer Dank gilt dem gesamten International Graduate Center for the Study of Culture (GCSC), vor allem aber den Doktorand/innen der „Kohorte 9". Ohne die gemeinsamen Diskussionen, Infragestellungen, moralische Unterstützung, vielen guten Scherze und motivierenden Worte hätte ich die Arbeit sicher nicht fertigstellen können und wollen.

Zuletzt möchte ich mich für die Unterstützung aus meinem direkten privaten Umfeld, von Familie und Freunden, bedanken. Einzeln genannt werden sollen hier nur einige. Evi, du kennst mich so gut wie dich selbst und konntest daher Zweifel ausräumen, bevor ich sie überhaupt angesprochen habe. Anika, dein Glaube in mich ist meist stärker als mein Glaube in mich. Dafür danke ich dir sehr. Felix, geduldig und besonnen hast du mich die gesamte Bearbeitungszeit über begleitet und mit deiner pragmatischen Art manch eine emotionalisierte Sinnkrise ausgehebelt. Ohne dich wäre ich beim Verfassen der Dissertation wohl, wie beim Navigieren in unbekannten Städten, zwei Meter vor dem Ziel umgekehrt. Ich danke euch von Herzen.

List of Figures

Glossary

This glossary provides definitions of recurring terms specific to the field, such as types of ethnographic artefacts, terms from the realm of exhibition analysis, and terms from museum education. When these terms appear in the continuous text for the first time, a reference back to this glossary is included.
The glossary is ordered alphabetically.

Artefact · The term 'artefact' is used interchangeably with 'museum object' or 'object' to refer to the items displayed in the museums' <u>exhibition rooms</u>. Artefacts in this work usually refer to non-European objects, but they can be represented in different galleries as either art or ethnographic artefacts.

Adenla, ade · These terms describe types of headdresses, comparable to a crown, of the <u>oba</u> in Yorubaland in Nigeria and Benin.

Benin Bronzes · The Benin Bronzes, also referred to as 'Benin Plaques', are more than a thousand brass and bronze plaques that were forcefully taken by British soldiers during a punitive expedition in Benin (present day southern Nigeria) in 1897. Most of the bronzes have been acquired by different European museums; the biggest collections are to date located in the British Museum in London and the Ethnological Museum, Berlin. Since their forceful removal from Benin, there have been many public debates about whether the objects should be repatriated to Nigeria. Some private collectors have followed the demand of Nigeria's National Commission for Museums and Monuments to return the bronzes, but many European museums have been defending their right to keep them, for example by contrasting their agenda of reflecting the achievements of humanity at large with Nigeria's nationally oriented claims (cf. Coombes 1994, 223).

Call and Response	In this work, 'call and response' refers to a performative practice applied by some of the guides to interact with the students. The guides 'call' the students with a certain cue, upon which the students are supposed to respond with either the same cue or another corresponding cue. This sequence of call and response is performed various times in a row.
Death celebrations	This term appears in the context of the Africa gallery in Museum B. The guide speaks about a Cameroonian family celebration, which is celebrated months or years after someone has died. The celebration is performed to accompany the soul of the deceased into the ancestral realm. Many families are invited to these celebrations, even if they are not well acquainted with the deceased. According to the guide, this is to ensure a system of mutual insurance: By inviting many families, a network of connections is established that can be activated in case financial or other kinds of support are required in the future.
Dhoti	The dhoti is a traditional piece of clothing for men, which is wrapped around the lower part of the body. In this work, the term occurs in relation to Indian traditional clothes.
Exhibition room	Exhibition rooms are regarded in this work as the rooms in which the objects are displayed. The term is most often used in the analysis to refer to the concrete spatial structure or design of the specific rooms in which the guided tours take place. 'Exhibition rooms' need to be distinguished from 'galleries', which are defined as entire thematic sections museums that can consist of multiple exhibition rooms. The guided tours can move from one exhibition room to the next without leaving the gallery.
Gallery	Whereas 'exhibition room' is an analytical term that is used to describe the place in which the objects are

arranged, 'gallery' is a term taken from the material and is often used by the guides to speak about the different regional 'galleries' there are in the museum, such as the 'African gallery', the 'Islamic Middle East gallery', or the 'North America gallery'. The term is, therefore, used to refer to the regional sections in which the guided tours take place. These regional galleries can consist of different exhibition rooms. For instance, the Africa gallery of Museum C is divided into an exhibition room for masks, an exhibition room for musical instruments, and an exhibition room for figurative sculptures.

Gallery session

This term is taken from the material and is used interchangeably with the term 'guided tour'. It refers to the museum educational performance during which a gallery educator explains non-European cultural practices and artefacts to school groups. Some museums, particularly the British, prefer 'gallery session' as a description for these educational offers. This is because, in the British museums, gallery sessions do not necessarily involve a tour through the museum but can also be performed in a separate seminar room. In the German museums, in contrast, 'guided tour' is a more fitting term because there, the gallery educators guide the students through the galleries. However, both terms are used interchangeably in this work because the boundaries between what constitutes a 'session' and what constitutes a 'tour' are blurry.

Gallery educator

The terms 'gallery educator' and 'guide' are used throughout this work to refer to the person who explains and interprets objects and cultural practices to students on field trips to museums. The job titles differ greatly in the four museums as well as in the guide's own self-understandings of their roles. These self-understandings are discussed in the introductions of the guides in Chapter 2 as well as in Chapters 5 and

6. Other terms used by the guides include 'facilitator' or 'docent'. Yet, in order to prevent confusion, only 'gallery educator' and 'guide' are used throughout this work.

Glass display case	Glass display cases are regarded in this work as the glass cabinets in which the <u>artefacts</u> are often arranged, either in ensembles or as individual pieces. Another form of display could be freestanding objects (i.e., without a glass case surrounding them) or <u>in-situ displays</u> (i.e., more holistic, thematic displays that visitors can walk through and experience).
Guided tour	See '<u>gallery session</u>'.
Guide	See '<u>gallery educator</u>'.
In-context displays	Barbara Kirshenblatt-Gimblett distinguishes <u>in-situ displays</u> from in-context displays, both of which are diverse ways in which museums '[...] perform the knowledge they create' (1998, 3). In-context displays arrange <u>artefacts</u> according to frames of references, such as taxonomy or historical development (cf. ibid.). They thus prioritise logic and cognitive processes in the structure of information in the <u>exhibition rooms</u>.
In-situ displays	In-situ displays are, according to Kirshenblatt-Gimblett's definition, "mimetic re-creations of settings" (ibid.). They can take the form of dioramas and period rooms. In-situ displays are often designed as entire <u>exhibition rooms</u> or parts of exhibition rooms where non-European contexts are holistically recreated, as, for instance, in the form of reconstructed market places. In-situ displays prioritise experience and imagination and can immerse visitors in the represented non-European world.
Key Stage	The British school system is divided into various sets of forms or age groups, which are also used in

museum education to develop <u>session formats</u> for specific age groups. The relevant key stages in this work are Key Stage 1 (5-7 years) and Key Stage 2 (7-11 years).

Kiswa

The Kiswa is the black piece of cloth covering the Kaaba in Mecca. The Kiswa is replaced every year, and Muslim dignitaries and organisations receive small pieces of the removed cloth.

Label

An object label is used in museums to categorise and provide data on each <u>artefact</u>. Label information often include the designation of the objects, region and time of origin, materiality, and sometimes date of collection.

Learning department

This term is used as an umbrella term for the segments of the museums responsible for museum education. These divisions of the organisations are labelled differently in each museum, and comprise different responsibilities. In all of the observed museums, however, such learning departments were officially responsible for designing the <u>session formats</u> and organising the <u>guided tours</u> for school classes.

Learning department manager

In all of the museums, learning department managers, employed on a permanent basis, served as the coordinators of the educational offers. These managers were the first contact persons during the empirical research phase and arranged the observations of the <u>gallery sessions</u>.

Men's clubhouses

Men's clubhouses or men's meetinghouses were traditional assembly halls in Palau, used by unmarried men. Their exterior walls were often decorated with symbols signifying local legends or scenes. These clubhouses are today exhibited in museums or at local heritage sites in Palau.

Minbar	The minbar is the place in a mosque where the imam stands or sits while delivering sermons.
Nazar	The nazar amulet is a blue and white, eye-shaped amulet that is used to protect its owner from the so-called 'evil eye', i.e., a curse that is inflicted on someone through a malignant glare.
Nugluak game	This game is also called the 'whalehunt game'. A piece of wood with a hole in the middle is positioned vertically between four or more players. They need to push small rods or bars through the hole. As everyone tries this at the same time, the bars bounce off of each other. Those who manage to push all their bars through the hole first, win.
Njoya	Njoya is the name of a ruler of Kingdom of Bamum in today's Cameroon, who ruled from 1894 to 1933. From 1884 to 1919, Cameroon was a German colony. Njoya tried to establish good relations to the German colonisers in order to avoid the persecution of the Cameroonians by the colonisers.
Oba	The term 'oba' refers to a ruler at the top of the hierarchy in Western African regions. Some of the gallery educators translate it with the term 'king' in the observed guided tours.
Object	The term 'objects' is used synonymously with the term 'artefact'.
Obasinjom	In one of the observed gallery sessions, a guide uses this term to refer to a Cameroonian mask, which is used in the context of ritual healing. She also explains that this mask has its origin in the colonial period when Cameroonians tried to protect themselves from the violence of the German colonisers with the help of this ritual.

Okoso	Okoso is a game for children, played in Nigeria. Two children twist a coin. The winner is the child whose coin spins the longest.
Outrigger boats	An outrigger boat is a type of canoe that has one or more supporting crossbars reaching out over its edges. This construction technique was invented in the early 16th century in the islands of Southeast Asia.
Script	Scripts are comparable to session formats. Instead of providing a rough outline of the purpose and structure of the guided tours, scripts provide much more detailed information, and formulate almost all steps of the tours, including which objects to include in the sessions, what to say about them, and which interactive practices to use.
Session format	The session formats are more or less detailed outlines of the contents of the gallery sessions that are developed by the learning departments, and, sometimes, by the guides themselves. Session formats in the ethnographic museum usually revolve around a specific region or topic, and can be advertised on the museum's websites for the schools.
Text panel	In contrast to labels, text panels are more detailed descriptions of types of artefacts, non-European regions, or cultural practices. These extensive textual explanations are not provided for each artefact. Instead, they serve as context information or as introductory statements about certain regions or galleries.
Tippoe's Tiger	Tippoe's Tiger is an artefact from Mysore in South India made for Sultan Tippoe in 1782-1799. The statue symbolically represents an Indian tiger attacking a representative of the British East India Company. The artefact was taken to Britain by soldiers after Tippoe's defeat in Seringapatam in 1799.

1 Introduction: Constructing the Non-European

The guide[1] stands in front of the school class that has just arrived at the museum. The class has come to attend a gallery session[2] about Africa. Most of the students are six years old. They are sitting in the lunch room of the museum, waiting for the gallery session to begin. Two teachers and three accompanying adults are watching the students carefully, ready to intervene whenever they feel the children need assistance. The guide begins the gallery session by introducing herself and the plan for the session. She explains that she was born in an African country, and she concludes the introduction by stating: 'Now listen to me. Because I am going to change my accent now. I am from Africa, and I am going to speak like somebody who comes from a part of Africa' (GSG-MC, 35-36).

'And now', a colleague will reflect upon the situation months later, 'I am putting myself in a zoo'. Indeed, what makes this announcement (and its subsequent implementation) so disturbing, is the indication of a show; the idea that 'Africanness' must be conspicuous and audible for the purpose of the gallery session. The experience of the students is thought to be enhanced by the performance of distinct Africanness. It is not enough that the guide was actually born in Africa. Her British accent supposedly seems inauthentic. This conscious performance of a more typically African Africanness is the ultimate proof that representation enters, as Stuart Hall has phrased it, 'into the very constitution of things' and cannot be seen as 'a reflection of the world after the event' (1997, 5f.). The guide's performance of Africanness comes to be represented as more authentic than the fact that she was born in an African country. The session, therefore, contributes to the construction, imagination, and mediation of distinct non-European otherness.

---

[1] A definition is provided in the glossary.
[2] A definition is provided in the glossary.

In this work, such constructions of 'non-Europeanness' during gallery sessions are at the centre of attention. The focus is, thereby, placed not only on the bodily enactment of cultural otherness but also on ways of speaking and explaining non-European practices or communities. The work is thus concerned with the verbal and performative communication of non-Europeanness by museum guides in gallery sessions for school groups.

The hypothesis underlying this research interest is that certain patterns of communicating non-European otherness recur in different guided tours[3], and that these patterns point to the continued existence, dissemination, and even public acceptance of specific tropes and stereotypes about non-European regions and people. The aim of the following elaborations is to describe, analyse, and interpret these ways of speaking about non-Europeanness, and to explain why similar strategies and themes of communicating exist in these representations.

1.1　On the Relevance of this Work

As the analytical focus is placed on meanings offered in gallery sessions about non-European cultural contexts, the work is concerned with museums that own and display ethnographic artefacts[4]. These 'ethnographic' museums are understood here as European museums that display non-European cultural artefacts, partly acquired in the course of imperialist and colonial agendas,[5] in separate galleries categorised

---

[3] A definition is provided in the glossary.
[4] A definition is provided in the glossary.
[5] It is important to note that not all the objects represented in ethnographic museums have necessarily been obtained under circumstances of unequal power relations or by force. As Anja Laukötter has shown in the German context, there were mainly three ways to obtain artefacts from overseas: via private collectors working for the museum, from merchant houses that were specialised in the acquisition of non-European artefacts and, most importantly, by means of scientific expeditions that were either organised by the museums themselves or by cooperating institutions (cf. 2013, 240). Still, as it is often difficult to establish

according to broader cultural regions, such as 'Africa', 'South Asia', or 'Middle East'.[6]

In recent decades, ethnographic museums have been facing criticism in the wake of postcolonialism and increasingly international audiences who claim the right of interpretation, and, at times, even ownership, of the non-European artefacts in the museums' collections. Furthermore, discussions about appropriate ways of representing these objects and the regions associated with them, as well as about the ethnographic museum's history and its connection to colonial agendas, frequently resurface in the public and academic discourse. Only recently, for instance, a media debate arose about the plans for the new Humboldt Forum in Berlin (which will exhibit ethnographic artefacts), when the art historian Bénédikte Savoy resigned from the advisory board of the museum, criticising that too little emphasis was given to provenance research (qt. in Häntzschel 2017).

As a result of such discussions as well as due to the transformation of conceptions of 'culture' in the academic discourse, many European ethnographic museums have begun to reinvent themselves. Attention has shifted from an authoritative to a more inclusive production of meaning, for instance by inviting so-called 'source communities' to the museums and designing exhibitions together with them. In addition, many non-European galleries now feature contemporary works of art from the respective regions, and curators increasingly work with migrant communities to broaden understandings of the artefacts and traditions displayed in the museums. With the help of social media, museums further make their

---

the exact ways in which civil servants, soldiers, or merchants acquired the artefacts from previous owners, unlawful or immoral processes cannot be ruled out. Furthermore, as the elaborations in this work show, at least some of the artefacts that are addressed in the gallery sessions could be acquired due to conditions of unequal relations between European and non-European actors.
[6] This statement means that, in the context of this work, museums are also considered 'ethnographic' if they have a broader thematic focus, but additionally exhibit non-European artefacts in geographically ordered galleries.

4

research and conservation strategies more transparent, consequently becoming more accessible for wider audiences. Even the names of ethnographic museums are changing. For example, the German term 'Völkerkundemuseum' is increasingly replaced with the notion of 'world culture museums'.

Despite these democratising trends, some means of representation and communication in ethnographic museums are still questionable. Repatriation claims by non-European groups are often dismissed with reference to necessities of conservation, the objects' status as presents, or even with the argument that the artefacts must be made available to the entire world.[7] Furthermore, objects are still categorised according to their broad regional affiliations, regardless of the widespread academic conviction that this categorisation is reductive (cf. e.g. Kaufmann 2008, Sturge 2007). Moreover, many museums have still not incorporated galleries that make transparent collecting histories in their permanent exhibitions.

Because of these unresolved issues, ethnographic museums are subject to ongoing academic interest and criticism. Much research has, therefore, already been concerned with the functions of ethnographic displays (cf. Dicks 2004, O'Neill 2006, Lidchi 2006, Geurds 2013), either revealing larger structures of positioning the European museum as 'the brain of the Earth's body' (Preziosi 1996) or, with respect to Johannes

---

[7] Such claims have appeared, for example, when the British Museum in London has positioned itself as a museum for the whole world. As its former director, Neil MacGregor, noted in a contribution to ICOM News, the British Museum seeks to '[...] allow visitors to address through the filter of history, both ancient and more recent, key questions of contemporary politics and international relations, to assess and consider their place in the world and to see the different parts of that world as indissolubly linked. For good or ill, we are all interconnected' (MacGregor 2004, 6). This universal framing has subtly served to argue in favour of exhibiting all the museum's artefacts at the location in London, for the whole world to see, instead of repatriating some of them back to their previous locations.

Fabian's foundational criticism of ethnography (1983), demonstrating the smaller structures of rendering the objects, and the people who made them, in a different time or outside of time, for instance by means of an ambiguous use of tenses in text panels[8] (Sturge 2006). As these examples from the academic discourse on the construction of non-European otherness in museums show, the focus of this criticism has predominantly been placed on the curatorial arrangement and design of the exhibition spaces.

While the curatorial arrangement is a significant aspect of museum communication, this academic focus has neglected the realm of museum education as an important meaning-constituting process in ethnographic museums. Admittedly, there is an academic discourse on museum education; the subject has been discussed extensively, for instance, in terms of the demand to increasingly listen to visitors, to promote interactivity in the museum and to provide meaningful experiences for different types of learners (cf. Hooper-Greenhill 1994, Falk/Dierking 2000). In academia, museum education has, in this sense, been discussed as a *method* or strategy to engage audiences. In contrast, the *contents* of museum educational accounts and their implications with respect to constructing non-European otherness have not been investigated in detail. This exclusion is especially problematic because the contents of educational accounts are not merely a marginal addition to the museum experience but constitute and substantiate the messages of the exhibitions. The focus of the academic discussion about representations of culture on curatorial decisions, rather than educational measures, must therefore be seen as research gap. Especially because gallery educators[9] explain the visual narrative of ethnographic exhibitions to visitors, who

---

[8] A definition is provided in the glossary.
[9] A definition is provided in the glossary.

6

cannot be expected to have a sound prior knowledge of the represented history or culture, their explanations effectively *become* the exhibition. Taking the approach of the New Museology (Vergo 1989) seriously and thereby acknowledging the role of the museum as an educational institution hence also means taking seriously the interpretations and meanings constructed within museum educational accounts.

This work, therefore, directs academic attention to the contents, workings and implications of the explanations and performances offered by gallery educators during guided tours for school classes. The moment of mediation, when guides in their role as mouthpieces of the museum are required to make explicit what the exhibitions suggest, is the moment when understandings, and eventually constructions, of non-European otherness emerge. The analysis provides insights into the ways in which gallery educators explain non-European regions, and seeks to understand which pitfalls and problematic implications some of their statements can have with regard to the construction of non-European otherness. At the same time, the focus is on the several factors that affect the performances and utterances of the guides, and that may lead to essentialist and generalising representations of non-European regions.

1.2 Research Questions

From the aforementioned interests of this research project, three main research questions emerge. The first question is related to the content of the guides' accounts. What do gallery educators tell students on field trips about non-European regions? This question is concerned with the statements that the guides make during the gallery sessions. Special attention is paid to recurring themes and patterns of speaking about non-European regions. By investigating a variety of different guided tours with different thematic (and therefore regional) focuses, the analysis traces core patterns of communicating otherness, which may point to socially accepted ideas and imaginations of a generalised 'non-Europeanness'. By critically scrutinising these recurring ways of speaking about non-European regions, the work further presents implications of the guides' accounts with respect to the maintenance of power imbalances and condescending stereotypes.

The second question refers to the workings of the meaning-constituting processes of the guided tours. How are stories about non-European objects, and more importantly, about non-European people told? Which strategies of communication are applied? The analysis of the guides' accounts is thus not only interested in recurring characterisations of non-European regions and people, but also in recurring practices that the guides use to speak about and perform non-European culture. As in relation to the first question, the analysis of implications of these practices plays an important role.

The third question is closely linked to the two previous ones. Which external and internal factors influence the guides in their actions or the guided tours in their structure? If the communication of non-European otherness in different gallery sessions follows similar patterns, it is crucial to reflect on the actors and contexts that lead to these similarities. Although this work does not claim to give a full explanation of all of the guides' actions and statements, it does attempt to document the contexts in which the sessions emerge, and to thereby reconstruct possible explanations and influences of their actions and statements. These influencing factors are examined with regard to broader, continuously reproduced social understandings about non-European otherness.

1.3   Objectives and Theoretical Framing

While some of the objectives of this work have already been mentioned above, this section serves to articulate the self-understanding and intended contributions of this research to the academic discourse.

As previously mentioned, the main research interest of this dissertation revolves around the discourse on the construction of cultural otherness. By investigating ways in which non-European otherness is produced and articulated, or else negotiated, in guided tours in museums, specific practices, actors, and contexts by which people become marked as 'Other' are analysed in detail on a microscopic scale. By these means, local and small-scale meaning-making processes are related and compared to broader concepts of othering. Relevant concepts used in the analysis come from ethnology, such as Fabian's 'denial of coevalness of the Other' (1983), or James Clifford's 'ethnographic authority' (1988), from critical museum studies such as Barbara Kirshenblatt-Gimblett's 'destination culture' (1998) or Kate Sturge's 'translation' of Others in ethnographic museums (2007), but also from sociology and literary studies, such as Sara Ahmed's 'stranger fetishism' (2000) or Edward Said's 'orientalism' (1978).[10] The discussion presented in this work is situated within this cluster of different concepts instead of being tied to a specific theory or discipline because the subject matter at stake cannot be explained from one perspective or academic field only. The interdisciplinarity of the matter of representing non-European culture is evident, for instance, from the many foundational works related to this discourse, which have transgressed disciplinary boundaries, such as Said's 'Orientalism' (1978) or Homi Bhabha's 'The Location of Culture' (1994). It is, thus, one objective of this work to contribute to this interdisciplinary discussion by showing that these different concepts of the representation of culture can be used to comprehend not only literature, mass media, and visual narratives, but also the everyday practices of gallery educators who communicate non-European lifeworlds to school classes. Furthermore, the concepts' relevance in this work also points to the fact that the reproduction of

---

[10] These concepts are explained in more detail in Chapters 3 and 4.

essentialist and exclusionary ideas about non-European otherness is still ongoing in educational and public representations.

Despite this interdisciplinary positioning of this work, the arguments are still brought forward from the perspective of sociology and cultural studies. That means that the analysis is predominantly interested in social meaning-making processes while narrative, visual or educational discourses are only of secondary concern. Museum education is, due to this focus on the social production of meaning, mainly regarded as a signifying practice in reference to Stuart Hall's argument that '[t]he "taking of meaning" is as much a signifying practice as the "putting into meaning"' (Hall 1997, 10). This signifying practice is closely connected with the 'work of representation' (ibid, 13) which Hall defines as 'the production of meaning through language' (ibid, 16). Hall's conceptualisation of culture as the process by which meaning is produced and understood through representations that work on the basis of shared codes in a community is thus the theoretical foundation of this work. This focus on representations and signifying practices also points to the constructivist perspective on meaning-making that is applied throughout this work. The analysis follows Peter Berger's and Thomas Luckmann's argumentation in *The Social Construction of Reality*, where they postulate the social relativity of 'reality' or 'knowledge' (cf. 1966, 15). They further explain the human capability of reification, that is, of '[...] forgetting [human] authorship of the human world' (cf. ibid., 105). Although reality is socially constructed, it does not appear like a construct, but seems manifest as something outside of the human sphere of influence. The application of this sociological perspective on the construction of meaning affects the argumentation in so far as the main emphasis is placed on the deconstruction not only of seemingly obvious statements about non-European contexts, but also of the existence of cultural otherness as such.

In order to engage in this deconstruction of cultural otherness, this work argues from a transcultural perspective. Wolfgang Welsch's conception of transculturality as a '[...] multi-meshed and inclusive, not separatist and exclusive understanding of culture' (1999, 199) has been contested and further developed by a wide range of scholars. In this work's appropriation of the term, transculturality refers to the acknowledgment of the unstable nature of cultural and social identity, which is shaped by constant processes of negotiation, exchange, appropriation, rejection, and conflict. From a transcultural perspective, cultures cannot be homogeneous entities because people's identities are neither exclusively determined by geographical location, nor to be seen as static products. Transculturality thus discards categorisations and classifications of people and objects according to fixed labels of identity. This conception is especially fruitful in the context of art history, archaeology, and museum studies because these disciplines have long worked with geographically and temporally fixed categories, thereby obscuring processes of transculturation in the production and exchange of objects. In the context of gallery sessions in ethnographic museums, this transcultural perspective similarly facilitates the questioning of processes of ascribing unidimensional identities to objects and people from non-European regions.

By adopting a transcultural perspective, this work seeks to contribute to the academic discourse on transculturality in two ways. First, by critically scrutinising essentialist representations and explanations of homogenised 'culture', the study of transculturality is further developed as a lens or method through which ascriptions of identity, powerful means of 'othering', and unquestioned ideas about non-European regions are revealed. Thereby, transculturality becomes a tool to analyse constructions of otherness. Secondly, in the concluding suggestions of this work, transculturality is also recommended as an approach to negotiate cultural identity in guided tours in ethnographic museums. Although the development of such an approach is not the part of this research, and an educational methodology is not established, these transcultural suggestions serve as starting points to translate transculturality from an analytical lens to an approach, thereby further contributing to the discussion on how to prevent cultural ascriptions in education (cf. e.g. Takeda 2010, Lutz-Sterzenbach et al., 2013).

Besides this objective of contributing to the academic discourse on transculturality, another main aim is to provide further insight into processes of constructing otherness by identifying a range of patterns of speaking about non-European otherness. These patterns, that refer to recurring motifs and strategies in the guides' communication, are postulated as socially accepted ways of conceiving of non-Europeanness. Furthermore, because this work compares guided tours in German museums to guided tours in British museums, some of these patterns are regarded as broader conceptions of otherness which are not only determined by organisational or regional factors, but partially exist as 'European' stereotypes or myths. Although the sample of the empirical research is too narrow to speak of 'European' ways of communicating otherness, the intention of this work is to show that some understandings of non-European culture are shared across national borders.

In addition, this analysis also seeks to provide explanations for the prevalence of the recurring themes and practices of speaking about non-European otherness. The influencing factors developed from the analysis are meant not only to provide a deeper understanding of the ways in which essentialist representations of non-European regions emerge, but also to facilitate an understanding of how the organisation of the ethnographic museum and the different agents involved in the preparation of the guided tours affect the construction of otherness.

An understanding of the social and material processes that shape the communication of the guides in the sessions is further important in order to raise academic attention for the work of museum education as a signifying practice. As already mentioned, gallery sessions have been of marginal interest for academic discussions besides the development of educational approaches. Yet, as this work shows, the actions and statements of the guides are not less momentous and significant than the visual representations in the exhibitions. This research hopes to direct attention to this interesting practice of museum education, and to inspire further research that departs from museum educational methods, and instead focuses on the self-representation of the museums, the guides, and the ethnographic truth claims apparent in guided tours or other museum educational measures.

As a final contribution, although this work is mainly concerned with a sociological perspective, it partly uses narratological methods to analyse the guides' accounts. This adoption of narrative analysis can be explained by the often story-like framing of the explanations of the guides, as well as by previous works on exhibition analysis which have similarly adopted narrative analysis (cf. Bal 1992, Nitz 2012). In this sense, one of the aims of this work is to further broaden the scope of narrative analysis, and to show how narratological categories can be used to gain deeper insights into the composition and strategies of the accounts of gallery educators.

Finally, in light of the various objectives that have been mentioned, it may be helpful to briefly explain what this work does not do, in order to avoid misunderstandings. Most importantly, the analysis of the guides' accounts does not provide factual information on non-European regions. This means that the statements that the guides make about non-European objects and practices are not discussed in relation to their verisimilitude. Correcting the guides' accounts would be presumptuous in so far as it would involve contrasting their constructions of otherness with alternative constructions of otherness. For the purpose of analysing the constitution of reality, the translation of non-European contexts, and processes of othering in the guided tours, the truth value of the accounts is irrelevant. Secondly, this work does develop an educational method of how to speak about non-European otherness. This would be impossible to implement as the focus of this work is on the guides' practices and statements, and not on the learnings that the students gain from their visits. Although, as mentioned, the final reflections of the findings include suggestions for change, these cannot be regarded in terms of an educational methodology, but serve as an exploration of alternatives of communication non-European otherness.

1.4   The Structure of this Work

The following elaborations are distributed in six chapters, Chapters 2 to 7. To make transparent the research design and to reflect upon the experiences in the field, Chapter 2 introduces the methodological considerations part of this work. This chapter also includes an introduction of the four museums that were chosen as research sites, as well as brief introductory remarks about the gallery educators observed within these museums. Furthermore, the methods used to analyse the material are explained in more detail in this chapter.

Although Grounded Theory suggests developing findings from the material rather than premeditating findings through a prepared set of theories, Chapter 3 introduces various concepts that are important to clarify in order to limit the scope of the research interests but also to make clear how the very broad terms of 'communicating' and 'otherness' are used and connoted in the analysis. As is explained in the beginning of this third chapter, the boundaries between the results from the findings and the clarifications of concepts are sometimes blurry, which is a result of the entanglement of theoretical and empirical findings. However, the third chapter still aims at merely introducing the way in which certain concepts are defined in order to then facilitate their further development and elaboration in the discussion of the findings in Chapters 4 and 5.

Chapters 4 and 5 represent the main analytical chapters. While Chapter 4 provides a classification of recurring themes of communicating non-Europeanness in the guided tours, and interprets the strategies and practices that the guides use to communicate otherness (in accordance with the first and second research questions), Chapter 5 introduces the contexts of the gallery sessions, thereby offering a reflection of possible influencing factors and core principles affecting the guides' practices and utterances (corresponding to the third research question).

Chapter 6 synthesises the findings by reflecting upon differences and similarities in the British and German case studies and by pointing out overall core findings observable in all of the observed sessions, regardless of regional and organisational determinants. From these considerations, suggestions for alternative ways of negotiating non-European lifeworlds in guided tours are presented. At the end of Chapter 6, the limitations of this research and suggestions for further research are discussed.

Chapter 7 concludes this work with some summarising final remarks.

2 Methodological Considerations

Chapter 2 illustrates the methodological framework of the study. It includes an overview of the organisation of the empirical research, a description of the methods that have been used to analyse the material, a reflection on the positions and conditions in the field, an explanation of the use of language and references to the source material, as well as some brief remarks on the transcription system that has been used to transcribe the gallery sessions and the interviews.

As a general note, it is important to clarify that this work is a qualitative study which makes no claim to representativity, completeness or universality. The interpretation maintains a critical perspective on matters of comparability, reliability, and validity. Especially with respect to the constructivist theoretical presumptions featured in this study, an acknowledgment of a certain subjectivity and individuality of the research results is crucial. Although project plans were regularly discussed and revised with supervisors and colloquium members, the actual process of collecting and analysing data was determined by inadvertent situational factors, such as the perception of the research project by the focus group, the behaviour of the actors in the field, as well as the research conditions determined by the museums. While the analysis is, therefore, neither entirely objective nor representative for museum education in general, the presented results still provide interesting insights into the workings of the communication of non-European otherness during guided tours for school classes. The prerequisites for the utility of these insights is the provision of detailed and transparent information about all research decisions and conditions, which is why the following elaborations are presented as detailed as possible.

2.1 The Structure of the Empirical Research

Before explaining the methods of data collection and the structure of the empirical research, some introductory information about the set-up and coordination of the gallery sessions in the ethnographic museums part of this study need to be provided.

The museums selected for this study all present non-European artefacts in separate exhibition spaces which are structured according to regional categories, such as 'Africa', 'Orient', or 'China'. The learning departments[11] of the museums develop session formats[12] that pertain to specific regions, such as 'African masks' or 'North American Indians'. Depending on the individual museum, school teachers can either book these session formats or arrange more general guided tours. When they arrive at the museums, freelance gallery educators perform the sessions.

As a means of analysing such gallery sessions, participant observations of the guided tours as well as interviews with the respective gallery educators were conducted in four museums located in Germany and Great Britain. This relatively small number of research sites can be explained by the qualitative orientation of this work, which prefers a deeper investigation of a smaller number of museums instead of a more general comparison of many museums. By conducting several observations and interviews within each museum, individual museum backgrounds, working conditions, as well as various processes of conceptualising the sessions in each of the selected museums can acknowledged in the analysis. Furthermore, although this work does not claim to be representative, justifiable statements about the communication of otherness can only be made if several gallery sessions and guides are observed, interviewed, and thus compared *within* each of the museums.

---

[11] A definition is provided in the glossary.
[12] A definition is provided in the glossary.

To gain insight into the variety of guided tours in each museum, at least three different session formats were observed within each museum. Furthermore, these three sessions in each museum had to be conducted by three different guides. This rotation between different sessions and guides was often automatically the case because, as already explained, different sessions in different regional galleries were usually presented by different guides. To illustrate this design of the empirical research, Figure 2.1 shows an overview of the original plan for the organisation of the participant observations.

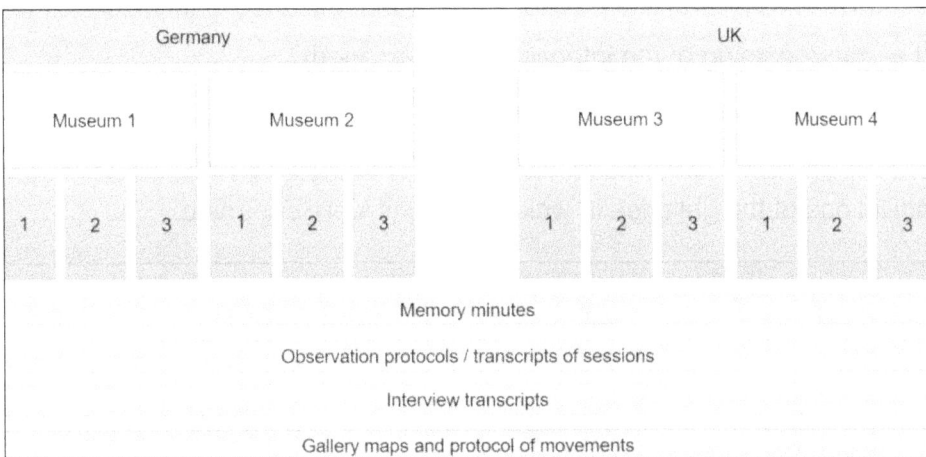

Fig. 2.1 Plan for the structure of the empirical research.

As is visible in Figure 2.1, each of the participant observations was accompanied by detailed memory minutes, observation protocols and, where allowed, recordings of the sessions and interviews with the guides. In addition, gallery maps of the exhibition rooms[13] and the movement of the school groups within them were prepared. These means of gathering information were complemented by conversations with the managers of the learning departments and with the school teachers as well as by the

---

[13] A definition is provided in the glossary.

collection of material describing the museums' organisational set-ups, i.e. annual reports and reviews, press releases, and mission statements.

In practice, due to issues of scheduling sessions and unforeseeable changes, more guided tours were observed than originally intended. Of the 17 gallery sessions that were observed, 14 are included in the analysis. The remaining three are excluded because they do not match the thematic focus of this dissertation (i.e., a guided tour on British clothing in the 17th and 18th century), because of repetitions of the same sessions (i.e., the same session by the same guide was observed twice because of a splitting of the school group), and because of technical issues (i.e., the recording of the interview was damaged).

Fig. 2.2 gives an overview of the final organisation and time frame of the empirical research. The illustration also shows the regional affiliations of the galleries in which sessions were observed.

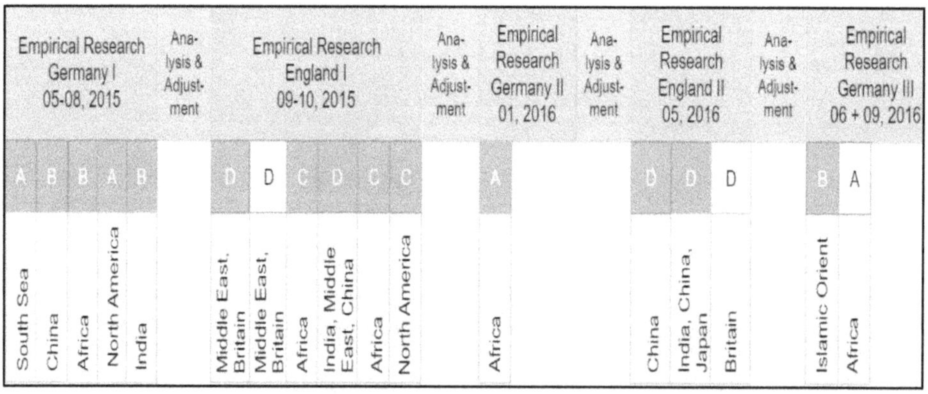

Fig. 2.2 Overview of research phases and galleries featured in the observations. Note that those sessions that have not been included in the analysis are marked with a white background colour.

The selection of the concrete sessions to be observed was usually made in correspondence with either the employees responsible for school bookings (German context) or the learning department managers[14] (British

---

[14] A definition is provided in the glossary.

context). The organisation of this selection process differed in both contexts.

In the German museums, teachers can book session formats or more general guided tours in different exhibitions all year round, and only few weeks in advance, which is why the organisation of the observations unfolded in a similarly spontaneous manner. The criteria for the selection of the sessions, including the difference between the thematic focuses of the three sessions, the observation of different gallery educators, and the age groups of the students (discussed in Chapter 2.1.2) were explained to the booking officers on the phone. They then browsed their interactive calendars for suitable sessions that teachers had booked. Observations were then arranged, and the booking officers asked the guides and, sometimes, the teachers for their permission of the observations.[15] While this process was relatively easy, there were not many guided tours in the interactive calendars (because of the spontaneous planning), which is why, in some cases, observations had to be arranged without knowing whether a more suitable age group would book a session later in the same month.

In the British museums, specific session formats and dates of gallery sessions are published on the museums' websites each autumn, and school classes must register for these advertised sessions in advance. In these cases, the planning of observations unfolded in a more structured way. The learning department managers provided a list of offered sessions in the upcoming weeks, upon which specific guided tours could be selected. However, the lists provided by the learning department managers were sometimes already curated by them, in so far as some sessions were not allowed for observations. After the selection had been made, the learning department managers asked the guides for their permission.

---

[15] In two cases, observations were cancelled due to teachers' objections.

Once consent had been obtained, the interviews and observations were prepared. This preparatory phase included studying the resources provided by the museums about the session formats, designing and updating the research instruments (described in Chapter 2.1.3), and preparing the electronic recording device and camera.

Fig. 2.3 shows a typical sequence of empirical research conducted at the museums. Upon first arriving at the museum and registering at the ticket office, the exhibition analysis was usually conducted at first, not only to get an impression of the space, but also to analyse the visual narrative before the interpretation by the guides would be added. Subsequently, the school groups arrived in the learning centres (British context) or the foyers of the museums (German context), where short conversations with the guides and the teachers were held in order to introduce the project and to learn about the educational contexts in which the teachers had placed the sessions. The guided tours usually took between one hour and one hour and a half. During the guided tours, observations were focused predominantly on the guides' statements and performance, but reactions of teachers and students were also documented.

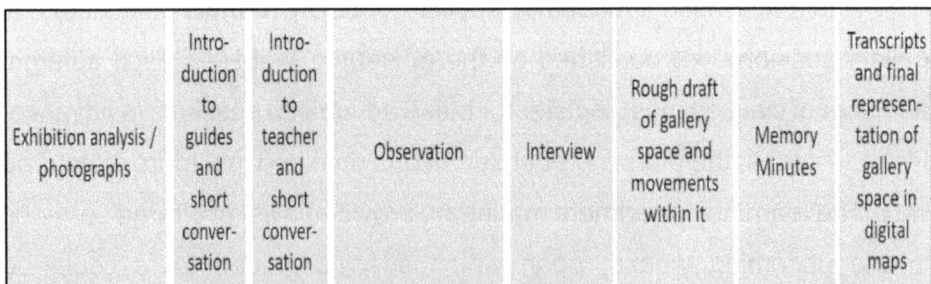

Exhibition analysis / photographs	Intro-duction to guides and short conver-sation	Intro-duction to teacher and short conver-sation	Observation	Interview	Rough draft of gallery space and movements within it	Memory Minutes	Transcripts and final represen-tation of gallery space in digital maps

Fig. 2.3 Illustration of a typical research process in Museums A, B, C and D.

Directly after the observations of the guided tours, the interviews with the guides followed. This structure was possible in almost all cases, but in some instances, gallery educators had to leave immediately after their sessions so as to commute to another freelance job. From these two cases, only one was relevant for the analysis. In this case, the guide asked to answer the interview questions in a written form. While this was not ideal in terms of comparability and the observation of her reactions to the questions, this method was agreed upon to retrieve at least some information. As the interviews were mainly understood as explorative conversations about the guides' motivations and actions, the answers from this interview questionnaire can still be considered and compared to the experiences of the other guides.

After the interviews had been conducted, another exhibition analysis was carried out, this time focusing more on the structure of the room and the position and framing of the objects emphasised and addressed in the respective sessions. A rough scheme was made to recapitulate the exact structure of the galleries and the movements of the groups in the spaces. Finally, meeting minutes were produced, recordings were transcribed, and the rough exhibition schemes were transformed into digital gallery maps.

2.1.1   Introduction of the Research Sites and the Guides

As noted above, the participant observations of the guided tours were conducted in four museums, of which two are located in Germany, and two in Great Britain. The comparison of guided tours in these two countries was envisaged so as to position the communication of non-European otherness in museum educational measures not as a specifically German, but as a wider European issue. Although the situations in the four selected museums cannot be understood as representative of the general situation of museum education in all European museums that hold non-European objects, the inclusion of British cases significantly diversifies the research outcomes and the analysis compared to a study conducted only in the German context. This diversification is due to several reasons.

First, the development of museum education and its institutional and political acknowledgement differ in both contexts. While in Great Britain, initiatives to improve and develop museum education are required by the state's financial support of National Museums (cf. Hooper-Greenhill 2007, 7), German museums do not have to explain themselves to their public investors specifically with respect to social and ethical responsibility (cf. Bystron/ Zessnik 2014, 327f.). Hence, whereas British museums have been rewarded for their expansion of museum educational activities, there are less incentives for German museums to specifically instigate new educational strategies. As Daniela Bystron and Monika Zessnik have stated, the perception and representation of museum education in German museums are therefore often outdated, as many curators and directors do not reflect upon current discourses, but reproduce clichés such as the idea that museum learning was a field of work separate from the development of exhibitions (2014, 324).

Secondly, differences in the appreciation and visitor-orientation of museum education in Germany and Great Britain are also connected to a less standardised training and practice of museum education in Germany. In this context, Markus Walz explains how different disciplines such as museum sociology or museum psychology have been established in Germany, that they have not had an effect on museum work (cf. 2016, 2). Furthermore, there seems to be a lack of common guidelines of museum educational practice. In Germany, the *Bundesverband Museumspädagogik* has developed criteria for museum education (2008), but these have been described as non-binding and loose (cf. Fromm 2010 and Wollesen 2012 qt. in Walz 2016, 2). In contrast, the Museum and Galleries Commission in Great Britain has published (optional) standards for museums in 1996 and the Labour government introduced specific guidance for museums in 1999 on how to improve access and decrease social exclusion in museums (cf. Lang et al. 2016, 22).[16] Additionally, in 1988, a new British national curriculum emphasised the role of artefacts

---

[16] Although these standards are not mandatory, they have affected change in terms of action plans for British museums willing to benefit from the financial incentives combined with them.

and museums in formal school education (cf. hereto Hooper-Greenhill 1994, 14ff.), making it easier for teachers to integrate school field trips into their learning agendas. This emphasis on museums in the national curriculum was sustained by subsequent governments. During the empirical research, this aspect was identified by one of the British learning department managers as a significant factor encouraging teachers to organise museum field trips. She lamented that the government had recently relaxed control of this connection in the curriculum, fearing that fewer schools would come to the museum in the future. Meanwhile, in Germany, there is no particular curriculum-encouraged incentive to visit museums. German museums, therefore, often need to specifically advertise their sessions to specific schools so that relevant competences or topics addressed in the guided tours become visible for the teachers.

Finally, there is a difference in the professionalisation of museum education in both countries. In the British context, most guides in the museums observed in this study had a background in museum studies or education. Most of the guides interviewed had completed a postgraduate degree in 'Museums and Galleries in Education' at the University of London. In the German context, in contrast, museum educators are still mainly recruited from subject disciplines (cf. Bystron/ Zessnik 2014, 323), as for instance ethnology or sinology.

These aspects show that a comparison between Germany and Great Britain is worthwhile not only because it makes it possible to include a wider spectrum of museum conditions in the study, but also because it is interesting to investigate the effects of a tendentially more visitor-oriented and learning-centred orientation of the British museums on the communication of non-European otherness during guided tours. Besides these conceptual differences, pragmatic reasons such as the relative proximity of the research sites as well as language skills also played a role in selecting Germany and Great Britain as field sites. Neither of the research sites required a translator to manage the collection and analysis of data, which avoided translational interpretations by a third party.

The museums selected for the empirical research were chosen based on their size, their non-European collection, and their educational programme. Prerequisites for the conduction of observations were subject to the research objectives outlined above and included the division of non-European artefacts in separate regional galleries and the offer of gallery sessions for school classes.

In this work, the four museums in which research was conducted are not disclosed. As this anonymisation is a relatively unusual decision for a work concerned with museology and museum education, the reasons for this practice are shortly discussed in the following.

The most important reason for avoiding to explicitly state which museums have been selected as research sites is the protection of the anonymity of the gallery educators who were interviewed and observed for this study. As there are only a few guides responsible for specific galleries in each of the museums, it would be easy for teachers, accompanying parents, as well as fellow members of staff to find out whose statements and performances are critically discussed in this work.

Furthermore, the managers of the learning departments know which guide was observed in which gallery[17] because of the scheduling process. If the analysis was connected to the specific museums, the examples of communications of otherness that are criticised in this work could easily be traced back to individual guides by the learning department managers.[18] Even though this work does not see itself as a critique of individual actors, but is rather interested in systems and patterns of

---

[17] A definition is provided in the glossary.
[18] Because of the descriptions of the museums apparent throughout this study and due to the examples given from the gallery sessions, it is clear that insiders may still realise which museums are referenced. This cannot be prevented entirely. However, the decision to refrain from disclosing the names of the museums is an attempt to complicate the identification of individual guides or sessions.

meaning, the analysis of the guides' accounts could reflect negatively on the gallery educators. Therefore, it is crucial to protect the anonymity of the guides so that they will not face individual consequences or reactions by their peers or heads of department. Rather, the intention of this work is to encourage more reflection on the value that is currently placed on museum education, and to motivate structural and conceptual change rather than change of personnel.

Finally, the disclosure of the names of the museums is not regarded necessary in this work because the objectives differ from those of research projects on representations of otherness in ethnographic exhibitions, and research projects on educational methods in specific museums. In the cases analysed here, the similarities and patterns within the different guided tours play a bigger role than the specificities of the different museums. This research is not written as a project report from the perspective of the museums, or as an individual critique of a specific gallery or museum educational programme. Instead, the analysis is interested in underlying and overarching strategies, practices, and themes, which recur in all of the museums. Therefore, it does not understand itself as a critique of a specific museum, but rather as an analysis of a social situation (i.e., the guided tour) that takes place in different museums. This point is also related to the relatively separate position that museum educational measures have in the museums. Often, the learning departments are considered as distinct from the curatorial work, which is why it is possible to regard gallery sessions in museums as a social and cultural practice in itself. This does not mean, of course, that the contexts and settings are disregarded or seen as irrelevant for the performance of the guides. However, these contexts and settings can be described without disclosing the names of the museums. This work can then be understood as comparable to sociological or anthropological research in offices, banks, or in classrooms. In these cases, the settings and situations are equally important, but can be described and analysed without revealing the name of the company, bank or school.

As the individual museum settings are still regarded as crucial for the analysis, they are outlined in detail in the following. Thereby, the museums are referred to in terms of the letters A, B, C, and D, wherein Museums A and B represent the German museums and C and D the British ones. These labels will be used throughout this work. Additionally, each description of the museums includes a short introduction of the guides observed and interviewed during the empirical research. These guides have been anonymised by means of name changes.

Museum A, Germany

Museum A is a typical ethnographic museum in Germany in that it categorises artefacts according to their 'original' locations. The collection includes artefacts from Africa, Asia, America, Australia and Oceania. The observed sessions took place in the 'Africa' gallery, the 'North America' gallery, and the 'Oceania' or 'South Sea' gallery. The objects in these galleries are predominantly arranged in glass display cases[19], but there are several freestanding large-scale objects as well. Text panels are generally written from a distanced, objective perspective, and the labels[20] provide information on the location that the artefacts have been 'found' in, the century of their production, and the materials they are made of. Some labels also provide a short description of the artefacts in terms of their composition, functionality, and original usage.

At the time of research, the museum's permanent exhibition did not include references to its own colonial history or the history of the collection in general. Neither was there a separate gallery dedicated to matters of cultural contact or transcultural entanglements. However, during the initial research phase, temporary exhibitions provided insight into alternative

---

[19] A definition is provided in the glossary.
[20] A definition is provided in the glossary.

approaches to exhibiting non-European objects. As these temporary exhibitions were not part of the permanent set-up of the museum, they were not included in the analysis.

The museum is funded by the German government as well as the federate state that it is located in. Additional income is generated through admission fees, commercial events as well as through the educational offers. Although the museum has been invested in some annual events and cultural activity to promote itself within the public, there has been a decline of visitors over the last decades. At the time of research, during weekdays, the museum was mostly visited by student and school groups, individual researchers, and a few senior citizens. At the weekends, however, more visitors come to the museum.

In terms of educational offers in the museum, there are so-called 'exhibition talks' (i.e., the gallery sessions) and workshops provided for school children, and different other events for families. The gallery educators who deliver the sessions are employed as freelancers and are called in on demand. The guided tours are organised by a central department for the conception of educational services that works on session formats and educational programmes for several museums in the same city. However, the situation in Museum A is more complex than that. While gallery session formats are officially developed by the overarching department, in the interviews conducted with the individual guides, the gallery educators explained that they had developed the formats of the sessions by themselves. Furthermore, although there are prepared session formats advertised on the museum website, the guides explained that teachers usually booked sessions with broader thematic wishes, such as 'masks in Africa' or 'project week Oceania'. The guides thus worked on a more spontaneous basis, developing the session contents themselves and often improvising during the guided tours. This aspect is described further in Chapter 5.

Antonia

Antonia is a freelance guide of middle age who describes herself as a researcher (cf. EIA, 113-114). She holds a PhD in Ethnology and performs gallery sessions in the 'South Sea' and in the 'North American Indians' galleries of Museum A. Her goals as a gallery educator revolve around the translation of cultures. Accordingly, she argues that her position has a translational function (cf. ibid., 21). Other goals she pursues in her work include the destruction of clichés and the evocation of tolerance (cf. ibid., 30-32). She also explains that it is important for her to create a dialogical learning situation and to avoid frontal learning (cf. ibid., 102). As she has already been in her position for a while, she reports that she can perform her sessions rather spontaneously, without having to read up on the facts (cf. ibid., 42-43.). She also states that she can and does provide sessions for a wide range of target groups, be it children or academics.

In general, Antonia seems tense and slightly irritated during the interview. However, during the session, she appears calm and competent. Her irritation might be related to a topic that we discuss during the interview, namely, her position in the museum and the contact to the curators. Antonia describes the museum as a hostile working environment, explains that the curators exclude the educators or have no contact to them (cf. ibid., 46ff.), arguing that they are afraid of competition (cf. ibid., 56). At several moments of the interview, Antonia relates to the problems she sees in the museum and to the lack of acknowledgement she feels she receives for her work.

Doreen

Doreen provides sessions in the 'North American Indians' section of the museum, but also in the 'South Sea' exhibition. She is slightly older than Antonia and has worked in Museum A since 1999, and as a museum educator since 1994 (cf. EID 18-19). Doreen has a degree in ethnology as well as in theatre studies (cf. ibid., 21-22) and works as a freelance gallery educator in different museums, and, in addition, as a storyteller. She regards her work as a calling (cf. ibid., 29), explaining that her aim is to provide access to the museum because it seems so abstract for many people (cf. ibid., 32-34). She also provides sessions for all kinds of groups, both adults and schools. With regard to schools, however, she mentions that the educational or disciplinary level is often important, giving some examples of how she reprimanded students during her sessions. Just like Antonia, Doreen also explains that her performance during the sessions is rather spontaneous, depending on the interests of the school groups (cf. ibid., 144-147).

Interestingly, Doreen equally describes the problematic position she feels she has within the museum. She compares her situation with that of a nurse (cf. ibid., 393-395), explaining that the guides do all the work, but receive little appreciation for it. However, despite this criticism, Doreen appears much more relaxed and accessible during the interview than Antonia. She is willing to discuss her work in detail and takes her time to describe the conditions of her work.

Johan

Johan is the only male guide in this study. From all the sessions observed and talks with the learning department staff, it seems that gallery education is a predominantly female line of work. Unfortunately, Johan does not have much time to talk, which is why the interview is not recorded or documented, but merely conducted before the guided tour in the form of a looser conversation.

In the gallery session, Johan explains that he is from Nigeria. He does not only work as a freelance gallery educator, but also as a performer and artist. Johan explains that he also provides theatre workshops for schools and wants to communicate Nigerian culture to children and thereby prevent racism. He is responsible only for sessions in the Africa section of the museum and explains that he has worked for the museum since the year 2000.

During the session and the conversation, Johan seems calm and optimistic. He enjoys the work with the children and uses various methods for them to be activated during the guided tour. He explains that he does not like students in his sessions to be passive, but that he wants them to dance, sing, and move. This, he argues, is easier with smaller children, but he still tries to get older students activated as well.

Museum B, Germany

Similar to Museum A, Museum B is also funded both by the city and the federate state in which it is located. Additional income is generated through the admission fees, the museum shop and the educational programme. The learning department offers workshops and guided tours for families and schools. Sessions are divided into age groups of 6-10, 10-16, to 16-19. The permanent staff of the learning department conceptualises session formats for teachers to book, which are advertised on the museum's website. The guides who facilitate the sessions work as freelancers upon request. However, comparable to the situation already described with respect to Museum A, most of the guides also work on their own session formats or further develop the formats of the learning departments. Furthermore, the prepared sessions are rarely explicitly booked by the teachers, and the tours more generally revolve around the regions addressed in the respective galleries. The guides thus also meet spontaneous demands of teachers who would like the session to focus more on a specific topic. Gallery educators in Museum A are normally trained in ethnology or area studies, and are therefore able to integrate their own knowledge and experience into the guided tours.

The objects are arranged in the galleries according to their geographic origin. However, due to limited space, not all regional categories represented in the collection, which comprises objects from Africa, South America, North America, the Middle East, East Asia, South Asia and Oceania, can be displayed in the museum. At the time of research, the museum's permanent exhibition covered galleries of North America, Africa, the 'Orient', Oceania, as well as South and East Asia. Visitor numbers depend largely on the themes of the popular temporary exhibitions that often combine contemporary culture in the respective regions with objects from the collection. The exhibitions visited for this study included the African-, the Islamic Orient-, as well as the East Asia- and the South Asia galleries.

The galleries feature both in-situ displays[21] such as reconstructed market places or traditional buildings, and in-context displays[22] that arrange objects in the form of glass display cases and freestanding artefacts together with text panels. The galleries thus address various visitor types by enabling an imaginative relocation to the respective regions or times in the in-situ displays as well as offering detailed insights into artistic practices, rituals and traditions, or religious dimensions in the in-context displays. Equally diverse communicatory means can also be observed in the museum texts. There are detailed and distanced object[23] labels that only state the materiality, location, and temporal categorisation of the artefact, but there are also extensive explanatory text panels. These can be divided into more academic, analytical descriptions of types of objects, craftsmanship, or specific production modes, and text panels that provide general background information on climatic, cultural, or religious aspects. These text panels are written in a more inclusive way, using

---

[21] A definition is provided in the glossary.
[22] A definition is provided in the glossary.
[23] A definition is provided in the glossary.

32

comparably easier language and sometimes even actively addressing the visitor.

Britta

Britta is a middle-aged gallery educator mainly responsible for the 'East Asia' gallery in the museum. However, she also mentions that she is increasingly asked to take over sessions in thematically diverse temporary exhibitions because the guides are expected to work their way into different topics. Still, she explains that she feels most comfortable in the section she is familiar with. Britta has a degree in sinology (cf. EIB, 20-21) and has worked as a gallery educator in Museum B for eight years (cf. ibid., 377). Besides her work in the museum, she also teaches Chinese to children. Her main goal in her sessions is to broaden the students' horizons in terms of intercultural understanding (cf. ibid., 88-95). However, for her, the aspect of education and discipline is also an important issue because she realises that it is a challenge to balance both the educational and the thematic work (cf. ibid., 91-93).

During the interview, Britta is very self-conscious and sometimes argues that she could have elaborated on one or another topic in more detail. However, it also becomes clear that she herself has some rather fixed ideas about Chinese culture, which she also weaves into her performance during the session. Britta is not critical towards her role in the museum or the museum structure.

Christine

Christine is slightly younger than Britta, but has already worked as a gallery educator for ten years (cf. EIC, 68). She is a freelancer and also works in various freelance jobs at the same time. She has a degree in ethnology and is mainly responsible for the 'Africa' section of Museum B. Her aim is to revive the objects (cf. ibid., 17) and to mirror anything that may appear exotic back to the students so that they become more open-minded (cf. ibid., 95ff.). Just like the other guides in the German museums, she explains that her sessions unfold rather spontaneously.

During the interview and the session, Christine appears calm and careful. She always takes time to think about how she reacts to the students' (and to the interview) questions. Especially during the interview, she seems more detached than the other guides in the same museum. She is less willing to describe her situation in the museum, but gives short and concrete answers. Additionally, she seems stressed because she needs to travel to her next job soon after the observed session.

Eva

Eva has a degree in German, History, and Art History (cf. EIE, 39-43) and reports that she has lived and worked in Asia for three years (cf. ibid., 46-47.). Besides her freelance job as a gallery educator in Museum B, which she has practised for ten years, she also works as a yoga teacher, which explains why she does yoga with the students during her session. Her main aim is to mediate the exhibitions and the knowledge therein in a target-group-appropriate way (cf. ibid., 19-22.). Similar to the other guides, she explains that she organises her sessions rather spontaneously, but always follows a basic structure (cf. ibid., 78-85).

Eva mainly criticises the problematic situation of museum education in Germany (cf. ibid., 321f.). She compares her experience in Germany with that in Asia and explains that museums in Germany are generally not appropriate for children and difficult for them to be accessed (cf. ibid., 341-349).

Maria

Maria is a slightly younger gallery educator in Museum B, describing herself as a cultural mediator (cf. EIM, 18). She has a degree in Islam studies (cf. ibid., 136-137). For her research, she visited Museum B and was asked later on to work as a mediator in the Orient gallery. She explains that she never thought about working as a gallery educator, but that there is almost no research in museums. However, she asks herself how long one can work in such a freelance position (cf. ibid., 50f.). She has worked as a freelance gallery educator for two years (cf. ibid., 126) and reports that she is engaged in a lot of different freelance jobs at the same time (cf. ibid., 129). She provides sessions for different age groups and reports that her aim is to show parallels of religious contexts (cf. ibid., 150).

Maria seems confident with her working conditions although she admits that she would like to receive more training in education (cf. ibid. 211-219). She realises that her position is rather located at the margins of the museum, but explains that she thinks she is paid well for her work and that her salary is appropriate for the effort she makes planning and conceptualising the sessions. During the interview and the session, Maria appears relaxed and confident. She is wearing harem pants and seems genuinely enthusiastic about the cultural region of the Middle East. To some extent, most of the guides in the German museums share a specific curiosity and enthusiasm for the 'culture' they communicate.

Museum C, Great Britain

Museum C is one of Great Britain's 14 national museums which are funded by the state through the Department of Culture, Media and Sport. Additional income is generated by means of charged activities, fundraising, commercial activities, and sponsoring. While admission to the permanent galleries is free, visits to special exhibitions are charged.

Museum C is not a pure ethnographic museum, but displays a collection of art and archaeological as well as anthropological artefacts from many eras and regions in the world. While the permanent galleries are structured both in terms of regional and in terms of historical criteria, the non-European galleries are mostly subdivided into broader geographical areas. Similarly, the individual departments for the research of the collection are equally structured according to cultures and regions. However, while this suggests that cultures are once again represented as closed-off entities, individual parts of the galleries reflect transcultural entanglements such as connections between Europe and the Middle East. Furthermore, in many of the galleries, representations of contemporary art or cultural practices can be found alongside the traditional focus on allegedly 'authentic' rituals and practices.

As in the German museums, there are different forms of representation observable in Museum C. In the galleries visited throughout the research phase, however, there were no in-situ displays or reconstructed environmental displays. Instead, there are a variety of freestanding objects and glass display cases that are accompanied by descriptive texts. When compared to the German examples, the gallery texts in Museum C are easier to comprehend as they require less prior knowledge about the regions' historical and political background, but explain these events or situations. In general, while many of the German museums' texts, with the exception of the background text panels in Museum B, seem to address an academic expert audience, Museum C's descriptive and explanatory text panels appear to be catered to a larger audience.

The learning department is a strong part of the museum. Large spaces within the museum are dedicated specifically to education, featuring lecture halls and seminar rooms. School classes visit the museum on either self-guided or facilitated sessions. In order to respond to a rapidly increasing demand of educational services over the last decades, teacher resources for self-guided visits have been issued to schools in order for them to guide their students through the museum by themselves. Additionally, because of the considerable number of school groups visiting the museum every day, many gallery sessions first take place in specifically provided learning spaces and then move into the galleries with specific discovery tasks. This structure prevents the individual galleries from overcrowding, but it is also problematic in terms of a more direct interaction with the displayed artefacts.

As in the German museums, the learning department provides session formats for teachers to book, which are later facilitated by the freelance guides. These gallery sessions are normally conceptualised extensively and booked specifically by the teachers. Therefore, the observed guided tours are less spontaneous and individual than those in the two German museums as the booked session formats are performed according to their conceptualisation as planned. Sessions are offered on fixed dates and are developed for different age groups, ranging from 3-6 years (Key Stage[24] 1), over 7-11 years (Key Stage 2) to 12-16 (Key Stage 3) and 16+. The sessions observed during the empirical research were catered to Key Stages 1 and 2, with age groups ranging from 6-11. The sessions took place in the lecture halls and seminar rooms as well as in the African and North American galleries.

Gladys

Gladys is a slightly older gallery educator responsible for only one specific session format in Museum C. She has worked in the museum for ten years and is in charge of a session related to the 'Africa' exhibition space. This session revolves around fictional stories and storytelling. Gladys explains about herself that she loves writing and storytelling (cf. EIG, 114-115), which is why she took over the session. As most of the other guides in the British museums, Gladys has a zero-hour contract, which is comparable to a freelance position, but grants employees more rights. Gladys explains that she came to her job through a process of recommendation and that

---

[24] A definition is provided in the glossary.

she helped create the session she performs in the museum (cf. ibid., 39-51.). In the gallery session, Gladys explains that she is originally from Ghana. During the interview, she expresses that it is important for her to achieve that the children embrace their identity and that she feels the session in general is largely about identity (cf. ibid., 191-200.). In contrast to the German sessions, the gallery educators in the British museums are usually not expected to perform sessions for all age groups, but only for specific ones. Therefore, Gladys's sessions only cater to children of three to seven years of age. She argues that she sees herself not only as a learning facilitator, but also as a performer (cf. 81-83).

During the interview, Gladys appears enthusiastic, talkative, and slightly restless. Her descriptions are often confusing, and it is difficult to follow her train of thought. Gladys reports that she has been advised not to include overly political issues in her sessions (this is addressed in detail later on in this work). She seems to find it important to embrace her own African heritage and wants to encourage others, particularly children, to embrace their heritage as well. In the session, this becomes apparent, for instance, when she changes her way of speaking into a more 'African' accent, or when she encourages the children to refer to their grandparents in their 'native' language, thereby ascribing otherness to the children on the basis of their appearance.

Hilda

Hilda is approximately the same age as Gladys. She has worked in Museum C for two years (cf. EIH, 25-27), but has been freelancing in museums for fifteen years (cf. ibid., 74-75). Hilda teaches school classes of Key Stage 2 (ages 7-11). She teaches various sessions, among them a guided tour about Greek mythology and another one about the Egyptians. The session observed in this work revolves around the kingdom of Benin. Like Gladys, Hilda describes herself as being of African heritage and feels proud to work as an educator in the museum and to be given the chance to represent 'her' culture as well as to diversify the demographic of the museum (cf. ibid., 209-211). She explains that she does not have a background in museum education but is interested in history and storytelling (cf. ibid., 103-104).

During the interview and the observed session, Hilda appears very organised and competent. In the interview, she speaks a lot about her role as a person of African heritage within the museum and argues that she can bring in different perspectives. She also criticises the session format of the observed tour, arguing that it is outdated. Therefore, she adds information and diversifies the context. This is also apparent in the observed session. At one point, Hilda explains that Africa is not simply about traditional housing and traditional markets, but that there is a considerable film industry as well. This aspect is addressed later on in this work.

Isabel

In comparison to the other guides, Isabel is a relatively young educator in Museum C. She is the only permanent member of staff as she is not only responsible for delivering the session she provides, but also for developing and improving it (cf. EII, 43-44). She has worked for the museum for 16 months and teaches students in early years (3-5), key stage 1 (5-7) and key stage 2 (7-11). Unfortunately, Isabel does not have much time after the session and requests to answer the questions in a form. In this form, she explains that she has a master's degree in Museums and Galleries in Education and an undergraduate degree in history (cf. ibid., 28). One of the things she hopes that the students gain from their visit to the museum is that they learn how to behave in and to respect the museum (cf. ibid., 98-99).

Museum D, Great Britain

Just like Museum C, Museum D is not a specifically ethnographic museum. Rather, it can be regarded as an art museum because it focuses on the materiality and aesthetics of the objects more than on cultural contexts.

For example, text panels often describe the importance of specific patterns, shapes, and materials at a certain time and region, and only secondarily mention cultural practices if they relate to these aspects. However, the non-European galleries are still ordered according to regional categories such as 'South Asia', 'Middle East', 'China' or 'Japan'. Furthermore, although the focus is not on rituals, traditions, or region-specific ways of life, information pertaining to these aspects still play a role. Because of these dimensions, the museum has been involved as a research site for the empirical study despite its status as an art museum.

The museum categorises its own collection in terms of objects types, geographical regions, as well as historical periods. The non-European collections are, however, framed in terms of regional categories and comprise China, the Middle East, Japan, South Asia, and Korea. Unlike the German museums, both Museum D and Museum C are not exclusively focused on non-European objects, but also comprise collections and exhibitions on European arts and artefacts.

Just like Museum C, Museum D is a non-departmental institution that receives funding from the Department of Culture, Media and Sport. Admission to the permanent exhibitions is free, but temporary exhibitions are charged. The broad spectrum of temporary exhibitions and festivals organised by Museum D have been considerably popular in the public and contributed to large visitor numbers. As a consequence of the museum's popularity, as in Museum C, the demand for gallery sessions for school classes has been high, which is why materials for self-guided visits are issued to schools.

The museum's learning department consists both of a division invested in explicitly educational tasks and a division focusing on interpretative measures in the gallery design. This inclusion of educational concerns in the galleries is significant because it means that both museum education and visitor needs play a role in the planning of exhibitions. The educational division offers workshops and gallery sessions. In contrast to all other museums part of this study, Museum D does not offer guided tours on specific cultural contexts but provides sessions on broader themes such as materiality and design. Guides work on zero-hour contracts, and the learning department develops extensive scripts for them to follow during the guided tours. Unlike in the other museums, guides are not responsible for specific galleries or topics, but need to be able to facilitate all session formats for students of a specific age group.

The scripts are not regarded as similarly binding by all gallery educators, and the guided tours still contain many spontaneous and individual moments, but the general structure of the session is relatively fix and often only changed due to time constraints or the lack of objects due to refurbishment or reconstruction work in the galleries. The galleries visited throughout this research included the Japan gallery, the South Asia gallery, the China gallery, and the Islamic Middle East gallery.

As already explained, the texts in the galleries predominantly revolve around material or aesthetic topics that proceed from these aspects to the contexts in which the objects were used. Both the label texts and the text panels are written in an academic, distanced, and analytical style. Information given on the labels include the type of object, its approximate location or region of origin, and its time of origin, provided, similar to the other museums, in the form of centuries rather than decades.

Feona

Feona is a relatively young gallery educator who teaches students in Key Stages 1 and 2 (cf. EIF, 20-23.). Feona occupies different positions within the museum, but in her function as a gallery educator, she has no contact to the curators and is not involved in the development of the session formats (cf. ibid., 26-30). She has an undergraduate degree in Art History and a master's degree in Museums and Galleries in Education (cf. ibid., 45-47). Feona describes herself as a learning arts facilitator and explains that she wants the children to enjoy their visit and to get active in the museum (cf. ibid., 115ff.). She frequently applies the methodology of talk partners in her sessions because she believes that the students learn much more if they do something on their own (cf. ibid., 291-297.).

During the observed sessions and the interview, Feona seems very optimistic and positive, as well as enthusiastic. Although she explains that it is a challenge for her to manage so many different gallery sessions for different age groups in one day and to get used to the different school groups, she is very positive about her position and role in the museum. She voices no criticism regarding the museum and is generally pleased to work with children in the museum.

Kate

Kate has worked in Museum D for two years (cf. EIK, 26-27) and teaches Key Stages 1 and 2. In contrast to Feona, she only works in the museum on one day of the week. Kate describes herself as somewhere in-between a teacher and a tour leader (cf. ibid., 138-144). Unlike the other guides in Museum D, she has no educational degree, but a bachelor's degree in Classical Studies and master's degree in Classical Art and Archaeology (cf. ibid., 30-31). She explains, however, that she needed to gather a lot of work experience before getting a job in the museum because it is easier to 'get in' with an educational training (cf. ibid., 46-47).

Kate appears very structured and organised in the sessions. Despite her lack of educational training, her sessions do not seem less participative or dialogical than Feona's or Lynn's sessions. Methods of letting the students discuss about objects and of concentrating on craftsmanship rather than on cultural contexts are used by all of the guides in Museum D. This methodological style can be explained by the museum's agenda of facilitating visitors to be creative and engage in handicraft by themselves.

Although, in the sessions, it does not appear to be a problem for Kate to balance information and coordination of the school groups, she argues in the interview that it can be a challenge to teach different school groups every day (cf. ibid., 187-191).

Lynn

Lynn works as a facilitator in Museum D and used to be a primary school teacher. She explains that she always loved museums (cf. EIL, 31) and, at some point, wanted to experience something else than working only in classrooms (cf. ibid., 33). Lynn reports that she had to complete the master's degree in Museums and Galleries in Education (cf. ibid., 76ff.) to be accepted as a gallery educator in the museum. Similar to the other guides in Museum D, she does not criticise the museum or her position in it. The only challenge she expresses is connected to the ways in which the exhibition rooms can be used and what the museum guards will allow her and the students to do in them.

Lynn's session turned out to be unsuitable for the thematic focus of this work as it exclusively took place in the European galleries of Museum D. Her interview has, however, still been included in the analysis because, in it, she adds valuable experiences and observations to the analysis of working conditions and working contexts.

2.1.2 The Focus Group: School Classes on Field Trips to Museums

Although the Museums A, B, C, and D offer guided tours for a variety of groups of visitors, such as adult groups, senior citizens, and even for the blind, the focus of this work is on school groups. This focus group has been selected for a number of reasons.

One important reason is the in-between position between formal and informal learning that guided tours for school classes occupy. Because the students listen to the guides' explanations of non-European objects and culture as part of their school education, it is important to examine the ways in which otherness is negotiated within the gallery sessions. Although learning outcomes are not measured in this study, as this would exceed the scope of the work,[25] it is important to note that the accounts of the guides may be considered particularly trustworthy by the students because they are embedded in a school context. As a result of this formalisation, essentialist representations of non-European otherness could be further normalised.

Another reason is the relatively young age of the school groups (6-13 years of age). The students can be expected to have only little prior knowledge of the regional contexts introduced to them, and may not have

---

[25] While many studies have addressed learning outcomes of museum education (Falk/Dierking 2000, Parmentier 2005, Pierroux 2010), these studies are usually dedicated to the effects of didactic measures on motivations, creativity, and competences of students. It would be interesting to further investigate the effects of specifically ethnographic educational accounts on students. In the context of this work, however, this focus was not feasible as it would have required to register with the supervisory school authorities as well as to obtain agreements from the students' parents (which is nearly impossible considering the fact that the school groups come from many different schools and would have additional work facilitating a more in-depth study of learning outcomes). Furthermore, in order to make statements about the effects of the sessions, it would be necessary to conduct long-term studies. Even if such a research design could be implemented, it would still be difficult to measure learning outcomes because a correlation between student understandings after the guided tour and the accounts they are confronted with would not necessarily point to causation.

44

developed the competence of critically reflecting the explanations of their teachers. Therefore, the impact of the guides' accounts in terms of a construction or reinforcement of stereotypes or perceptions of otherness on this particular group must be recognised. Even young students already come to the museum with certain understandings about the world. Although these prior ideas have not been recorded strategically, some of them become apparent in the reactions or questions of the students during the guided tours. By analysing conversations between the guides and the students, as well as by observing student reactions and actions, some statements can be made about the implications that the guided tours have in relation to the confirmation or negotiation of these world views.

The low age of the focus group is further interesting for this work because it may specifically evoke reductions of complexity when speaking about non-European regions. The question about the level of detail and critical questioning that can be applied in guided tours for young school groups subtly underlies the discussion in this work. While it is, to some extent, understandable that gallery educators decomplexify and simplify matters, the degree to which this simplification is appropriate needs to be discussed. Especially because the students may be introduced to these non-European contexts for the first time when they visit the museums, the interpretational authority and power of the guides to construct first impressions and perceptions must be taken seriously. A critical reflection of the implications of their reductions of complexity is therefore necessary. Furthermore, as the reflections in Chapter 6 show, some of the observed guides' accounts show that complexification and critical perspectives can be integrated in gallery sessions for young students. It is thus essential that the argument of age and prior knowledge does not serve as an excuse for the stabilisation and naturalisation of cultural stereotypes.

Finally, organisational reasons have also affected the choice of this focus group. The school class is a relatively homogenous group, not only in terms of age, but also in terms of experiencing the guided tours in the same context and with similar intentions. The similarities in the formal structures and the organisation of guided tours, hence, facilitated the comparability of the cases.

As a means of limiting the focus group, guided tours for school classes from the first to the sixth form (6-13 years old) were observed. Originally, a narrower age range was intended, but due to partly difficult conditions of scheduling observations with the museums, a broader focus group had to be chosen. This broadening of the age range did, however, not negatively affect the comparability of the sessions. Many of the session formats are offered by the museums for wider age groups. For example, Hilda's session is catered to students aged 7-11, and there is only one script[26] for the session, meaning that the sessions are not always catered to specific ages. Although the German guides did accommodate their sessions to the needs of younger or older students, the gap between the guides' ways of speaking and performing for seven-year-old and for thirteen-year-old students was not too wide.

Finally, what has to be noted is that the students in the observed sessions of the British museums were generally younger (ø 7,8) than in the German sessions (ø 10,6). One reason for this difference can be found in the different school systems. As British students start school earlier than in Germany, British first-graders are younger than first-graders in Germany. Figure 2.4 again shows the overview of the observed sessions that has already been presented in the beginning of Chapter 2.1, now with the age groups of the students that participated in the sessions.

---

[26] A definition is provided in the glossary.

Phase	Code	Gallery	Age range
Empirical Research Germany I, 05-08, 2015	A	South Sea	6-10
	B	China	11-12
	B	Africa	11-12
	A	North America	9-10
	B	India	9-10
Analysis & Adjustment			
Empirical Research England I, 09-10, 2015	D	Middle East, Britain	8-9
	D	Middle East, Britain	8-9
	C	Africa	6-7
	C	India, Middle East, China	7-8
	C	Africa	7-12
	C	North America	6-7
Analysis & Adjustment			
Empirical Research Germany II, 01, 2016	A	Africa	12-13
Analysis & Adjustment			
Empirical Research England II, 05, 2016	D	China	7-8
	D	India, China, Japan	7-8
	D	Britain	7-8
Analysis & Adjustment			
Empirical Research Germany III, 06 + 09, 2016	B	Islamic Orient	11-12
	A	Africa	12-13

Fig. 2.4 Overview of research phases, galleries, and age ranges of the students in the observed sessions.

2.1.3 Research Instruments

The observations of the guided tours and the interviews were structured according to a set of analytical criteria developed on the basis of the research questions. These criteria were arranged in separate documentation sheets which ensured that each visit to the museums focused on similar matters. Different documentation sheets were prepared for the documentation of the school context, the exhibition context (i.e., the visual and spatial arrangement), the proceedings of the guided tours, and the interviews with the guides. In the following, the analytical criteria developed for each of these dimensions are described in more detail.

School context

In all of the museums part of this study, the schools organised the date, time, and topic of the sessions with the museum administration. As the gallery educators reported in the interviews, not much information about the schools is available to them before the school groups' arrival in the museums. This also made it difficult to gain insight into the school contexts before the observation of the sessions. However, as has been shown by museum education scholars, as for instance by John Falk and Lynn

Dierking (2000), the context in which an educational experience in the museum takes place is crucial to better comprehend its implications and relevance for the students. In order to learn more about the context in which the sessions took place, the documentation sheet for the school context therefore included questions to be directed at the teachers. In almost all of the observations, the timeframe between the groups' arrival and the beginning of the guided tours allowed only brief conversations with the teachers. The questions on the documentation sheet referred to the type of school, the number of students, the project or subject the sessions were integrated with, further remarks on what the school classes had already learned or done in preparation of the session, plans of the teachers regarding how to utilise the sessions in their classrooms, as well as expectations and ideas regarding the sessions. Although these questions were asked in almost all cases, the teachers' answers were often very short due to the limited timeframe. Some teachers saw the school trip as an addition to their work at school rather than as a learning experience specifically integrated by means of preparation and follow-up tasks. Others had a more formal purpose of the sessions in mind, using worksheets for the students to fill in during the guided tours or interrupting the guides by explaining how some information could be used for their work at school. Due to the already-mentioned focus of this work an, the ways in which follow-up activities were used by the teachers to frame the sessions were not documented. Still, the contextual information retrieved from the short conversations with the teachers provided, at least, some insight into the framing of the students' museum experiences.

Exhibition context

The documentation of the exhibition context was necessary both in order to acknowledge the agency of museum objects and spaces in the construction of meaning and to compare the guides' verbal accounts to the visual representations in the exhibitions. Furthermore, the documentation of the exhibition facilitated a recapitulation of the groups' movements in the exhibition rooms.

One of the means by which the exhibition space was documented was by creating rough schemes or gallery maps of each of the exhibition rooms in which the sessions took place. These maps documented the general set-up of the spaces and provided an overview of the different stations in the exhibition rooms that the guides led the student to. In most cases, the students strictly followed the path of the guide and did not read text panels by themselves, which is why text panels have only been included in the maps if they are directly linked to the sessions. However, besides the gallery maps, photographs of the galleries and some of the text panels were made in order to document how the communication of otherness works on the visual dimension.

While these forms of documenting the exhibition contexts can clearly be seen as methods of collecting data, a less distinct separation between data collection and analysis underlies the second focus of the documentation of the exhibitions, namely, on their means of visual communication. Besides the maps, an observation protocol for each of the galleries featured in the guided tours was devised, which contained questions about the focalisation in the exhibitions, the kind of information provided about the objects, and the subjectivity or objectivity of the presented contents. These observation criteria were developed from a narrative approach to exhibition analysis, which means that this form of documenting the exhibitions can simultaneously be regarded as part of the analysis of the material. This conflation of description and analysis results from the fact that an analysis of exhibition rooms is better undertaken on site rather than on the basis of photographs. As this form of documentation thus already relates to the analysis of the material, the following explanations explain the relevance and application of narratological criteria to the exhibition analysis.

Narrative analysis is often applied in the context of museum studies because it bears many advantages, including the emphasis on an understanding of exhibitions as stories, the possibility to focus on the visitor-as-reader instead of only looking at the curator-as-author, and the awareness that meanings of exhibition spaces are both created and consumed subjectively. As Mieke Bal explains, '[...] interpretation is both subjective, and susceptible to cultural constraints [...], turn[ing] narrative analysis into an activity of "cultural analysis"' (1997, 11). Narrative analysis, hence, discusses which meanings texts imply through their application of different narrative perspectives, characterisations, or forms of emplotment, but thereby never claims completeness or insight in the reception of exhibitions by visitors. In this sense, narratology's function to reconstruct 'narrative ways of worldmaking' (Herman 2009) can be used to unravel the strategies with which visual narratives are embedded in exhibitions. Furthermore, this narrative approach was also deemed suitable for the exhibition analysis as the guides' accounts are similarly analysed, in part, by using narratological criteria. As this approach builds a bridge between the guides' and the exhibition's perspectives, by for instance looking at the focalisation in the visual narrative as opposed to the guides' verbal account, it helps to better understand the role and agency of the gallery educators as well as of the spaces.

The selection of criteria of observation for the exhibition analysis was based upon considerations of narrative analysis in museums by Laura Hourston Hanks (2012), Mieke Bal (1992), and Heike Buschmann (2010). In a later research phase, the focus of the observations shifted to situations of performativity, which is why this category was added to the exhibition analysis as well. This performative dimension of exhibitions has been discussed widely, for instance by Kirshenblatt-Gimblett, who has argued that exhibitions can be seen as theatrical spectacles (cf. 1998, 20f.). According to this idea, exhibitions can immerse visitors in a different time and space, for instance through in-situ displays (cf. 1998, 3f.). Particular attention was, therefore, paid to in-situ displays or other kinds of staging culture in the exhibition spaces.

Analytical criteria from narratology included for instance the focalisation and the narrative voice of the exhibitions. As Bal has stated, exhibitions can be regarded as addressing an implied focaliser, namely the visitor (cf. 1992, 561). Although the stories 'taken in and taken home' by individual visitors can vary significantly, it is still interesting to consider through whose eyes potential visitors are encouraged to perceive the exhibition narrative. This intended lens through exhibitions are perceived can be traced in terms of zero focalisation, internal focalisation, and external focalisation. As Heike Buschmann notes with reference to Genette's definitions of focalisation, zero focalisation in exhibitions is applied when causes for a certain cultural practice or historical event are explained in a gallery text in retrospect while not having been recognised as such by contemporary witnesses (cf. 2010, 153). Internal focalisation is evident when visitors perceive a certain event from the perspective of those experiencing it, i.e., without external analyses or other changes of perspective (cf. ibid., 154), and external focalisation is applied when, for instance, the work of historians or archaeologists, who do not have an insight into the characters' feelings, is presented (cf. ibid.). Although, in practice, these perspectives often overlap and cannot always be marked as clearly as in fictional narratives, they do help to trace the construction of reliability, empathy, and even entertainment and excitement in the exhibitions. Other analytical criteria borrowed from Buschmann and applied in the exhibition analysis included the temporal organisation of the exhibition (cf. ibid, 156), gaps in the visual narrative (cf. ibid, 160f.), as well as intertextuality within the exhibition (i.e., the use of different forms of text) (cf. ibid, 166ff.).

Another major point of interest in the investigation of the exhibitions is their structure. As Hourston Hanks has argued, '[j]ust as for novelists, the creation of a coherent grand narrative is important for exhibition designers [...]" (2012, 30-31). She uses various structuring principles from narratology to analyse the Imperial War Museum and the Imperial War Museum North in Great Britain. From the multiple criteria she applies, aspects of plot and pace (cf. ibid., 27), sequence (cf. ibid.) and characterisation (cf. ibid., 29) have been applied to the analysis of the exhibition spaces and have thus been integrated in the documentation sheets in the form of a focus on spatial and architectural designs, the structure of suggested routes, the number of exits and entry points, and metaphors used in the visual representations.

Finally, Buschmann's translations of E. M. Forster's narratological concepts to the analysis of exhibitions have been adopted as analytical criteria in this work. According to this approach, 'events' can be regarded as the museum objects, the 'story' can be seen as the sequence of the objects, and the 'plot' can be interpreted as the causal connections between objects (cf. 2010, 154f.) While the first two aspects are easily found in the exhibitions, causal relations or connections between objects often have to be inferred by the visitors (cf. ibid.). This is where the guides come in: In most cases, they explicate the causal links that are otherwise rarely articulated as clearly in the exhibitions.

Observation protocol

The observations of the gallery sessions represented the main part of the empirical research. Together with the recordings of the guides' accounts, which were not permitted by all of the guides, these observations provided the basis for the analysis of the ways of speaking and performance of the gallery educators.

The observations were conceptualised as overt and relatively unsystematic. As the guided tours often unfolded in different styles and contained unforeseen interventions and reactions to the students, the observation protocol had to be conceived in a way that allowed for the documentation of unplanned activities. Hence, the protocol consisted both of blank spaces for noting down specifically interesting conversations and activities, and of a more structured part through which specific aspects were considered. As both Manfred Lueger (2000) and Uwe Flick (2009) have suggested, observations should develop from primarily descriptive remarks of all observable aspects to increasingly selective criteria that focus on already identified structures of meaning (cf. Lueger 2000, 120f., Flick 2009, 227). Putting these suggestions into practice, the initial observations in the four museums were used to get an overview of the situation whereas the final observations concentrated on specific aspects. Hence, the structured section of the protocol was only introduced at a later stage of the empirical research.

As the accounts of the guides are the main interest of this research project, both the contents of these accounts (sequence of events, wording) and the guides' practices of presenting information (tools, communicative strategies, movement) have been documented as detailed as possible in the protocols. In some of the later observations, however, student and teacher interventions and activities were focused on more in order to find out in how far they altered or affected the process of the sessions.

The more detailed criteria that were integrated at a later stage of the empirical research included the type of introduction of the guides and the opening sequence of the sessions, their teaching styles (lecture and text, discovery, constructivist), their narrative styles (commenting, explaining, criticising, asking), types of interactions with the students, non-verbal articulations, student reactions and behaviour, as well as teacher reactions and actions. In correspondence with this work's focus on explanations and performances, moments of performativity were given additional attention.

Whether participant or non-participant observations were conducted is a matter of interpretation. On the one hand, the fact of observation was clear to the guides, students, and the teachers, so that the research position remained clearly external to the situation. If research had been conducted as embedded in the school contexts, a more participatory position would have unfolded, but as the position of an external researcher was maintained, this research practice could be defined as a non-participant observation. At the same time, however, the research activities did not actively interfere with the sessions, so that the guides' main attention was focused on the students. Therefore, the position of this research has to be located in-between observation and participation.

Finally, it must be made clear that observations are not sufficient to understand the workings and the reasons for the ways in which the guides communicate otherness. As observation 'reduces social experience to what is visually perceived' (Hallam 2000, 262) and because it 'relies upon the notion of distanced, disengaged vision which is brought to bear upon, and indeed contributes to the definition of "others" as though they were the objects of visual perception' (ibid.), interviews with the guides as well as conversations with the learning department managers were equally important parts of the empirical research.

Interview guideline

In order to understand their working conditions and motivations, interviews with the gallery educators were planned before the empirical research began. Initially, these interviews were conceptualised as episodic narrative interviews so that both semantic knowledge, such as the guides'

54

perceptions of their positions in the museums, as well as episodic knowledge could be recorded (Flick 2000, 77).[27] The episodic parts of the interviews were aimed at encouraging a reflection of the gallery educators on their specific practices in the guided tours. Constructed on the basis of Flick's suggestions (cf. ibid, 79ff.), the guideline of the episodic interview foresaw the following steps:

- Introductory remarks about the research project
- Questions about the guides' understandings of their position and role in the museum (semantic knowledge)
- Questions about the guides' past experiences with guiding student groups (episodic knowledge)
- Questions about the guides' experiences with student groups in their everyday life (episodic knowledge)
- Questions about the translation of objects and cultural practices, consisting of semantic knowledge (what does this mean to you) and episodic knowledge (how have you experienced this?)
- General questions on the guides' opinions about their working conditions and their agency in the museum
- Final remarks and evaluation of the interview with the guides, asking whether they would like to add something that has not been mentioned yet.

While this methodology seemed suitable for the interviews with the guides, especially because it combined specific questions with more open questions, and hence promised information about both the conditions and the procedures of their work, an evaluation of the first three interviews showed that the method had to be altered. While the semantic questions had worked very well to gain insights into the guides' aims, motivations, and working environments, the episodic questions had not functioned as

---

[27] As Flick notes, the distinction between episodic and semantic knowledge goes back to Tulving 1972.

planned. The challenges of these types of questions were twofold. In some cases, the guides were not able to remember or chronologically structure their activities and experiences of the week before. In other cases, they said that they could not summarise their practices in the form of a typical episodic structure because every session was different. They felt uncomfortable pinning down episodes of their working experience.

Several reasons can be given for these reactions. First, as freelance workers, most guides maintained different job positions on different days of the week, making it difficult for them to think of their work in the specific museums in terms of everyday life. Secondly, regardless of the different forms of development and organisation of the sessions in the four museums, many guides endorsed the independence and singularity of teaching, emphasising that they constantly had to accommodate to different situations, which they often regarded as a positive aspect. Finally, with changing age groups, school types, and backgrounds of the many students they led through the galleries (often in several museum), it is understandable that they could not properly remember the structure of their days in the weeks before. As an additional problem, as previously mentioned, some of the interviewees did not have much time for the interviews because they had another job.

Resulting from these considerations, and as a means of gaining the trust and honesty of the guides, the interview guideline was adapted to the situation. While the semantic questions were differentiated to get an even better impression of personal motivations and understandings, the episodic questions were reformulated in a more specific way. Instead of asking about experiences in the week before, specific questions about the observed sessions were asked. During the observations, interesting or difficult situations were marked in the observation protocol. During the interviews, the guides were subsequently asked to explain what had happened in these situations and whether their reactions or accounts were intended, planned, or spontaneous. Furthermore, questions about the everyday practices were specified to refer only to the preparation of the guided tours, to the agency of developing the formats, or to the study of teaching practices. Additionally, the strict phases suggested by Flick were dissolved for the sake of smoother transitions and less distanced conversation situations.

While this transformation of the originally conceived interviews led to a less structured and often more personal interview situation, which is discussed in Chapter 2.3, the interviews were increasingly meaningful for the project. Not only did the additional semantic questions spark longer explanations about the guides' interests, backgrounds, comfort zones, and discontents, but the questions about 'episodes' of the guided tours also provided additional insights into the reasons for specific actions and interventions. Finally, as the interview guideline was not always adhered to in the prepared sequence, more open and hence much longer and more natural conversations unfolded, which immensely increased the value of the interviews.

2.2. Methods of Analysing the Material

The analysis of the collected data consists[28] of three strands. The first strand pertains to the analysis of the guides' accounts, whereas the second strand focuses on the contexts and agents influencing the sessions, such as the set-up of the learning departments and the working conditions of the gallery educators. The third strand is concerned with the visual narratives of the arrangement of the objects and the gallery texts.

---

[28] As the descriptions in Chapter 2.1 refer to the preparation of the process of data collection, which unfolded prior to this work, these elaborations have been framed in the past tense. As the remarks in the following chapters, however, are more closely connected to the analysis and interpretation, the present tense is used throughout the remainder of this work. Chapter 2.3 is an exception because it, again, reflects upon the process of empirical research in the past tense.

The described sequence of the first, second, and third analytical strand does not imply a hierarchy between these areas of interests. Neither can a chronology of analytical steps be inferred from this subsequent description. Although the analysis of the guides' accounts was prioritised in the beginning of the analytical process, the exhibition and context analyses always played a role simultaneously due to the entanglement of these dimensions.

2.2.1   First Strand: Analysis of the Guides' Accounts

A significant part of the analysis consists of the investigation of the guides' accounts during the guided tours. The material used for this analysis includes the observation protocols and the transcripts of the recorded gallery sessions. The documentation of the exhibition is additionally consulted to recapitulate the spatial framework and the movements of the groups within the galleries.

Due to the interdisciplinary orientation of the project and its focus on social meaning making processes, the analysis is performed by applying two methods from different disciplines.

On the one hand, the analysis of the gallery sessions unfolds on the basis of Grounded Theory (GT), using initial coding, focused coding, and theoretical sampling, based on the concretisation of the method brought forward by Kathy Charmaz (2006). This step is especially important in order to find core categories of communicating non-European objects and cultural practices in the guides' accounts. In the context of this production of core categories, a particular deviation of Charmaz's constructivist reformulation from traditional approaches to GT is noteworthy. While GT is normally based upon the development of a specific theory by narrowing down different codes to one concept, such a narrow interpretation of the guides' accounts would not be suitable with respect to this work's research questions. As an alternative approach,

Charmaz has argued against a restriction of research to one core category. For one thing, she has suggested that initial and focused coding are sufficient methods to work with if ambiguity can be tolerated (cf. 2006, 61). For another thing, she has stated that working towards just one core category might limit research processes based on constructivist understandings (cf. 2006, 132). Due to the multifaceted and international scope of the observed gallery sessions, multiple simultaneously existing explanations for the phenomena observed must be allowed for. Hence, from the start, the discovery of one theory to encompass all actions and accounts of the gallery educators is not intended. Instead, the processes of initial and focused coding are geared towards a comprehension of various categories and their interpretation in terms of different perspectives and implications.

In relation to the process of the analysis, the initial and focused coding of the first sessions have suggested the emergence of various recurring motifs in the sessions. These results have been reintroduced into the later phases of empirical research by focusing especially on these aspects while still collecting new material. These new sessions have been coded again, and comparisons between codes and fist categories have emerged. The categories have then again been verified by means of more observations and recordings of sessions. This structure of the analysis has been maintained throughout the empirical research. In the final phase, the main analytical work has been invested in proving concepts and categories and condensing them wherever possible and adequate with respect to the research questions. Through this coding mechanisms, findings from different materials (exhibition analyses, interviews with guides, session transcripts) have been compared and condensed.

Besides this method of GT, the material is also subjected to a narrative analysis, drawing again on the work of Bal (1992) and Buschmann (2010), but also on insights of Hayden White (1980), Jerome

Bruner (1991), David Herman (2009), and Ansgar Nünning (2009). Narrative analysis is applied to the guides' accounts because their explanations of cultural contexts often appear in the form of stories or anecdotes.

As Nünning has argued, some disciplines have appropriated narrative analysis without referring to the analytical frameworks that have been developed in narratology (cf. 2009, 149f.). Due to the story-like nature of the gallery sessions, the analysis in this work, in contrast, benefits from a more thorough application of narratological categories, such as focalisation, framing, eventfulness. Furthermore, and perhaps most importantly, a narrative approach makes it possible to consider the functions and implications of the guides' accounts as forms of worldmaking (cf. ibid, 152) through their ability to 'actively create models of the world' (ibid, 169) that are so coherent that they appear to be true (cf. ibid, 171). Particular attention is, therefore, paid to the constitution of worlds in the gallery sessions. Other focuses of analysis entail ordering principles, such as sequence, place, time, relationship, and point of view (cf. Bal 1997, 8), plot and pace (cf. Hourston-Hanks 2012), as well as the relationship of the parts of an account to the whole (cf. Bruner 1981, 8). Finally, the dimension of a sense of morality that is conveyed through the guides' explanations is relevant for the analysis. This aspect is investigated further by drawing on Hayden White, who has discussed the connection between narratives and morality, explaining that events recorded in a narrative seem 'real' because they '[...] belong to an order of moral existence, just as they derive their meaning from their placement in this order' (1980, 22). This insight can be applied to the guided tour in so far as this means of communication also claim truth by establishing a moral order. These aspects of worldmaking and truth claims are described in more detail in Chapter 3 and 4.

2.2.2 Second Strand: Analysis of the Contexts and Actors Involved

Besides the analysis of the specific themes and practices evident in the guides' accounts, the social and situational context is another main interest of this research project. To comprehend not only what is being said about non-European objects and groups of people, but also how these accounts come about and what motivations underlie them, an in-depth analysis of the interviews with the gallery educators is necessary. In order to further acknowledge the agency of the museum objects and the students, some of the session transcripts and the documentation of the exhibition rooms are considered as well.

The interview transcripts are coded and analysed according to Charmaz's redevelopment of GT as explained above. Again, initial and focused coding are used to develop categories that point to underlying factors affecting the guides' work. These categories are specified and verified over the course of the empirical research by comparing them to newly collected data.

As already mentioned, the interview guideline has been changed during the process of research. In the course of this redevelopment, categories have been verified and concretised: first, by repeating similar questions (motivation and aims of the guides, preparation of the sessions, communication with curators) and increasingly concretising questions on the basis of first findings (actors involved in designing session formats, specificity of the session formats, independence of the guides, perceived identification and acknowledgement of the guides' work); and second, by including new questions inspired either by codes developed from the first interviews (guides' perceptions of teacher interventions, difficulties in performing the sessions) or by already developed focused categories (objects as stage, objects as starting points, cultural comparisons as moral education). Through a continuous interrelation between the empirical research and the coding procedure, a concretisation, combination, and confirmation of the influential factors shaping the guided tours is achieved.

Another method of analysis used in order to analyse influencing factors of the gallery sessions is Actor-Network-Theory (ANT, Latour 2005). This method is used to better comprehend and demonstrate the relations between the different actors involved in shaping the guided tours. The further the research project has tried to understand how the museums, the curators, the artefacts, the learning departments, the advertised session formats, and the guides are connected, and how individual interventions of teachers and students can be conceptualised and adequately represented in this work, the clearer it has become that it is necessary to apply an analytical approach that facilitates managing the complexity not only within each museum, but also between the different museums.

ANT is, further, applied in order to avoid prioritising human agents in a setting that clearly acts through and with material objects. Similar to what Latour has argued in the context of religious understandings, the people involved in the making of meaning in museums may equally be 'deeply attached, moved, affected by works of art which "make them" feel things' (2005, 236). ANT is thus applied to follow the objects and to understand how they connect different actors in the field. This method makes it possible to sufficiently acknowledge the effect that each actor in the system has on the final performance of the gallery sessions.

As the analysis shows, the 'circulating entities' (ibid, 237) that can be found in the case of the guided tour are not limited to objects and spaces, but also comprise understandings of learning or expectations surrounding the museum as institution. The application of ANT facilitates comprising all these actors and practices within one analytical system. It shows that 'all the actors do something and don't just sit there' (ibid, 128) and, hence, avoids a focus on either the guides' or the objects' actions only. While not all of the actors are equally relevant, an illustration of their mutual interdependence is possible, which simplifies the process of evaluating which associations and actors to focus on in more detail.

Finally, by means of coding and by applying ANT not only to the interviews, but also, in part, to the gallery sessions, the students' potential to change the guides' accounts, or to draw their own conclusions from these sessions, is considered. As Bal has stated, a narrative approach is simply a proposal of how the contents of the text could be interpreted (cf. 1997, 11). By linking sociological and narratological approaches and thus focusing both on the product and on the process of the sessions, a more comprehensive analysis is achieved.

2.2.3   Third Strand: Exhibition Analysis

The last strand concerns the analysis of the exhibitions. In order to compare visual, verbal and performative forms of communication, and to comprehend the path ways and the logic of the spaces in which the guided tours take place, a general analysis of the curatorial structure of the exhibitions is carried out. As discussed previously, this procedure has been performed at the sites of research, which is why the methodology of the analysis is explained in Chapter 2.1.3. Due to the scope of this research, full exhibition analyses have not been performed. However, as already explained, especially those aspects that can be related to the guides' accounts are emphasised.

2.3. Positions and Conditions in the Field

As in all empirical research processes, actions in the field as well as research results are subject to its contexts and people. Therefore, in the following, my own perceptions of the field sites and the focus group's reactions to my presence are reflected upon.[29] Naturally, these aspects are entangled and, therefore, often influence each other. My own positions in the field are a response to the conditions of the field just as these conditions may in turn be a response to my positions and actions. If, for instance, some of my comments are perceived as criticism by my respondents, they may change their behaviour towards me. However, to some extent, I may also (perhaps falsely) ascribe their changes of behaviour to my own actions, and in turn change my behaviour during observations or interviews. This interrelation shows that it is not always possible to objectively comprehend the social signs and subtle implications that emerge in the field. Just as Clifford Geertz's reference to anthropological writing as '[...] fictions, in the sense that they are "something made," "something fashioned"' (1973, 15) suggests, my accounts of the observed situations and the interpretations therein are closely interlinked with my positions and perceptions in the field. However, applying Geertz's concept of 'thick description', my analysis always aims at contextualising the findings and to thereby take us '[...] into the heart of that of which it is the interpretation' (ibid., 18). The following remarks, thus, not only describe the conditions of the field in a differentiated way, but also contextualise these conditions and consider them from various perspectives. Yet, I am aware that not all factors that affect the conditions and positions in the field can be discussed here (as they are all filtered through my perception) or explained and categorised entirely objectively. Such a completeness is impossible not least because objectivity in research is always only an approximation. As Michael D. Jackson has explained, the construction of complete order leads to a 'misplaced

---

[29] In this subchapter, a first-person-perspective is chosen to describe positions and conditions in the field in order to raise awareness for the subjectivity of these remarks. Here, my personal experience of the field and the respondents is reflected upon, and it would be misleading to suggest objectivity in this regard. For the remaining chapters, a third person perspective is chosen in order to gain a critical distance from the analysed material.

concreteness' (quoting Whitehead) and can only be seen as 'wishful thinking' (1996, 5).

2.3.1 The 'Elephant in the Room': How Expectations Shape the Field

Discourses surrounding ethnographic museums are often marked by critical questions about matters of representation, repatriation, or the legitimacy to distinguish between European and non-European 'cultures' (cf. ter Keurs 1999, 68). Such debates have not only shaped my own ideas about ethnographic museums or museums that display non-European art and artefacts, but they have also had an effect on the self-understandings of the museums themselves. Not only in their mission statements, but also in their own research activities, European museums holding non-European objects have reacted to postcolonial criticism by casting themselves as spaces of intercultural contact, places for all, or places of cultural diversity. For instance, the *Musée du Quai Branly* in Paris presents itself as a 'bridge between cultures'[30] and the *Weltmuseum* in Vienna explains its own function as a forum for the exchange of different voices[31]. Before entering the field, I was aware of this friction that exists between the external criticism of essentialist and exoticising tendencies of these museums and their own self-portrayal as open-minded, dialogical places. This aspect raised my interest in the topic and runs as a key theme through the entire analysis and interpretation.

My critical thoughts about ethnographic museums, as well as the organisations' presumed anticipation of my museum-critical approach, affected the conditions in the field. For example, as already explained, it

---

[30] 'The Musée du Quai Branly', in Website of the Musée du Quai Branly. Last accessed August 27, 2017. http://www.quaibranly.fr/en/missions-and-operations/the-musee-du-quai-branly/.
[31] 'Über uns', in Website of the Weltmuseum Wien. Last accessed August 27, 2017. https://www.weltmuseumwien.at/ueber-uns/.

was not easy to find museums in which to perform the empirical research. Official reasons for museums rejecting my request to observe gallery sessions included the current workload of the museums and the conviction that the project did not fit to their research interests. While these reasons seem plausible, it still appeared to me that some of the museums were not willing to allow deeper insights into their museum educational programmes and practices because they were suspicious of criticism regarding the representation of non-European regions. This impression of the museums' suspicion derived predominantly from the conversations led with the learning department managers to inquire about the observations of gallery sessions in different museums. Both in those museums that denied my request and in those that accepted it, these conversations were marked by an intimidating atmosphere. The learning department managers wanted to know exactly what would be the focus of the observations and interviews although it was too early to explain exactly which aspects would be in the centre of attention. While they never explicitly asked me about a museum critical focus of my research, their detailed questions appeared to me like attempts to figure out whether a critique of museum representations was part of my interest. Despite trying to communicate my openness and positive attitude with regard to the museums' educational measures, I always felt that it was necessary to circumvent questions about representation and otherness, at least when introducing my research interests to the museums. At the beginning of the empirical research, the focus was placed more on the translation of objects into words than on the communication of essentialist otherness. As this translational focus seemed to me as innocuous, I often emphasised this focus during the conversations with the learning department managers in order to avoid a rejection of my request to observe gallery sessions. Because of this initially presented emphasis, it is impossible to say whether these managers would have allowed my participation in the guided tours if I had expressed a more critical research perspective. I am aware that this atmosphere of suspicion may have been a projection of my own insecurities onto the situations, and that I myself may have reinforced or even constructed this atmosphere. I certainly did not want to jeopardise the opportunity to observe gallery sessions and was particularly careful not to appear critical or negative.

Especially in the British museums, this atmosphere of suspicion further translated to the organisation of my observations. Unlike in the German museums, where the dates for observations were organised with different members of staff, in the British museums, these organisational matters were again discussed with the learning department managers. This organisation of my visits was a protracted process, and it seemed that some of the learning department managers wanted to choose specifically which sessions I should observe. In Museum D, various newly developed sessions were not permitted as part of my observations. As an external observer and interviewer, the researcher is always initially perceived as a stranger to the system, of whom nobody knows what to expect (cf. Simmel 1908). But even in later conversations with the learning department managers of the participating museums, my impression of having to be particularly careful about what to say about the museum remained intact. This 'elephant in the room' affected the research process in so far as the questions that I posed to the learning department managers often remained cautious and affirming, rather than critical and forceful. Furthermore, in Museums C and D, it is possible that the learning department managers, at least to some extent, affected the selection of the observed gallery sessions.

2.3.2 Between Complicity and Suspicion: On the Relation to the Guides

The feelings of suspicion and distance described above were not experienced in most of the interviews with the gallery educators. After initially showing a distanced reaction towards me, the guides appeared to transition from museum representatives to individuals during the interviews. Especially in the first part of the conversations, the guides seemed careful about what they said regarding their work, the museum, and their practices of explaining non-European objects. Especially because the interviews were recorded, they did not want to say something wrong or negative about the museums. Only when the interviews were reconceptualised in a more personal and individual manner during a later research phase did the guides feel more comfortable to talk about their personal impressions rather than about general organisational aspects.

Despite these more informal and personal settings in the interviews, many of the guides were still generally cautious in their reflections of their practices as facilitators. This reservation was especially apparent in the episodic parts of the interviews. When asked to reflect upon their sessions and their ways of communicating the objects and regions, the guides usually did not adopt a self-critical perspective, but merely described the methods they had used in particular moments. One explanation for this lack of critical self-reflection could again be based on the guides' perception of myself as an outsider and critic in these moments. Accordingly, this behaviour could be explained by the guides' anticipation of my accusations of misrepresenting non-European regions. Another explanation could lie in the self-perception of the guides as educational or ethnographic experts. In this sense, their uncritical self-reflection could be part of their professional performance as gallery educators. Arguing with Goffman, it was sometimes not clear to me whether the guides believed in

68

their optimistic and non-critical performance or whether they consciously *played* that part (cf. 1965, 10), as if still standing in front of a school group.

As the guides were critical of organisational and museum-related matters, but not so much of their own practices, my research practice at the museums fluctuated between experiences of complicity and suspicion. At times, the guides considered me to be on their 'side' and specifically explained problematic aspects of their work and their position within the museums. In this context, the degree of the guides' openness varied from case to case. While two of the guides directly complained about the curators' attitude towards the gallery educators as well as about the organisational structures, another guide referred to issues that they saw in terms of cultural representations in the museums. Some of these remarks were made particularly to raise awareness for the problematic situation in these museums, and I was asked by some guides to address these issues in writing. In other situations, however, I again felt that I had to be careful not to affront the guides by asking critical questions about their statements or practices during the sessions. Furthermore, when the guides did not have sufficient time for a longer interview and were eager to complete what they perhaps perceived as yet another task on an already busy day, the interview situations remained formal and the guides answered my questions only very briefly.

While the previous remarks have addressed positions and conditions in the field with respect to the learning department and the guides, my research experience was also partly dependent on the school teachers, accompanying parents, and students. However, as these actors are not in the centre of attention in this work, they do not receive as much attention in this section. It must be made clear, however, that the observation situation implies that the reactions of the students might differ from reactions that they would have shown if research had not been conducted.

Yet, considering that the guided tours were observed not only by myself, but also by the teachers, parents, museum guards, and sometimes even newly employed guides, it is doubtful that the children were significantly affected by my presence. In most of the situations, the teachers or guides explained to the students that observations would be conducted, and the students did not seem to notice my presence or to reflect upon it significantly. In three cases, individual students asked what my name was during the session, or wanted to know what I had written down in the observation protocol. However, in almost all the situations, the students were much more interested in the guides' explanations than in any activities happening at the margins of the sessions. Nevertheless, there is a possibility that some students did not dare to make statements or ask questions during the sessions due to my presence.

Finally, while I tried to have short conversations with the teachers in almost all cases, these were predominantly factual (i.e., school context) because of the lack of time they had. In five cases, teachers commented on the sessions after they had ended or even during their course, some even asking me for my evaluation of the guided tours. In these instances, a neutral perspective was taken in order not to affect the teachers' reactions or impressions.

2.3.3   My Position as a White, Female, European Researcher

Finally, what has to be acknowledged is my own position not only in terms of the ways in which I was perceived by the actors in the field, but also in terms of my role as a white, female, European researcher.

First, my 'Europeanness' and 'whiteness' did play a role in the way in which I was perceived by the learning department managers, the guides, the teachers, and the students. In a way, considering that most of the guides and the learning department managers were white Europeans, my own whiteness may have lowered their suspicion towards me because I may have been identified as a cultural 'insider' to Europe, from whom criticism regarding either the reliability or the suitability of accounts about non-European regions may not have been expected. Postcolonial criticism was not inscribed in my appearance, which is why it was perhaps easier for me to direct the attention away from an immediately critical perspective in the conversations with the museum staff. However, at the same time, one of the guides who described herself as being of 'African heritage' explained that she felt it was important that she performed a session on Africa because '[...] doing something as a person of African heritage is different from doing something as a person of European heritage' (EIH, 196-198). In this case, as she was identifying herself with her 'African heritage' and tied her agenda as a gallery educator to it, it is possible that the 'heritage' she ascribed to me (European) did not encourage her to go much more into detail about this agenda. Perhaps, if she had identified me as also being 'of African heritage', she would have been more explicit with regard to this critical agenda. A similarly vague system of ascribed affiliations can be assumed in relation to my gender. Perhaps some of the, predominantly female, guides reacted more positively towards me due to the fact that they also identified me as female.

In general, then, in so far as the people I interacted with in the field all ascribed certain cultural affiliations, social roles, and behaviours to me, the ascription of femaleness, whiteness and 'Europeanness' can be seen as having different effects on the guides' feelings of complicity and suspicion towards me. Such influences are, however, difficult to measure or evaluate because, what I might have experienced as a positive reaction of my respondents towards me, may be a wrong impression and cannot be explained by only one of the above factors. In addition, as already explained, the long conversations I had with the guides and my affirmative attitude during the conversations helped me to build rapport with most of the guides, which I felt overshadowed first impressions or ascriptions of identity to a significant extent. It is, however, important to note that my appearance and the identity ascriptions resulting from it may have had certain effects on the conditions in the field.

Secondly, my position as a white, female, European researcher may have affected some of the interpretations I have made regarding the material. Throughout the analytical research phase, I have been reflecting upon this aspect extensively. Am I too lenient with the gallery educators for acknowledging their good intentions? Am I too harsh in the analysis because of my general discontent with ongoing stereotypes and discriminations of non-European groups in media and public discourses? While it was important to reflect upon these matters during the analysis in order to avoid a bias in the interpretations, I prefer to place my results in the context of my academic socialisation rather than in the context of my cultural background. This is because the perspective of transculturalism that is adopted as a lens in this work also extends to the way I see my own identity in the context of this research. I do not regard myself as any more fixed in my 'European culture' than I regard the people discussed in the gallery sessions as fixed in their 'non-European' contexts. As a transcultural person, I am affected by various entangled influences that are constantly transformed, which is why I do not regard myself as exclusively determined by a vague category of 'European' or 'white' identity. Besides being affected, more concretely, by my social background and personal values, the ways in which I analyse the data are, to a considerable extent, dependent on my academic socialisation. This is why the concepts I am using in this work are described in detail in Chapter 3.

Thirdly, and most importantly, with regard to the elaborations that follow in this work, my position as a European researcher may affect the ways in which I myself am reinforcing fixed notions of otherness. Despite the fact that I do not consider myself determined by a cultural context, I do accept that my socialisation in Europe may have affected certain 'ways of speaking about non-European regions' that I may not be able to entirely distance myself from. As this work deals with socially accepted ways of speaking about non-European regions, I may not be exempt from all of these 'ways of speaking'. This is why, in section 2.4 of this chapter, I thoroughly reflect upon my usage of language and essentialist phrasing. Once again drawing on Jackson, I do not aim to free the analysis from misjudgement, but I aim to free it from 'misjudgement and error *that has harmful human consequences*' (1995, 7, emphasis in original). Thus, in my writing, I seek to maintain a reflected distance to my own language use in order to deconstruct and prevent essentialist framings through wording.

Nevertheless, the question of reinforcing what I attempt to criticise in this work is not simply dissolved by means of reflecting upon language use. By claiming that museum educational accounts about the Middle East, China, India, and North America partly work along the same lines, and contain comparable motifs and communicative strategies, I may contribute to the same processes of generalisation and essentialism that I criticise by reducing the guides' accounts to their potential 'essences'. However, in order to avoid such a theoretical essentialism, Chapters 5 and 6 diversify the scope of the analysis by discussing the different, and sometimes museum-specific, factors that influence the work of the guides, and by acknowledging the differences between the individual sessions. Yet, in the course of the analysis of the guides' accounts, patterns or mechanisms of communication have become apparent. When considering the seven recurring themes that are introduced in Chapter 4, it is evident that these themes and practices are not related to small-scale contents of the sessions (i.e., whether the guides address climate, food, religion or craftsmanship), but that these are underlying notions through which different regions are negotiated. For instance, the celebration of diversity or the dressing up of the students in traditional clothes are practices that reappear very often in different sessions and must therefore be seen as patterns in the mediation of regional 'culture' in the museums. The described recurring themes and practices of communicating non-European regions are, thus, not essentialist reductions, but underlying frameworks methodologically developed from the material.

2.4. On the Use of Language in this Work

As this work is concerned with the construction and mediation of cultural otherness, it is important to reflect upon how the usage of language in the analysis and interpretation of the material may itself be complicit in reinforcing common notions of otherness, belonging, and 'culture'. This is especially important considering my own position as a white, European researcher, which has already been discussed in the previous section. Besides the relation between my socialisation and the questions that are posed in this project, my background also makes it impossible to exclude myself from the criticism that I offer with regard to ways of speaking about non-European regions and people. As one of the arguments in this work is that certain tropes of speaking about non-European contexts are socially accepted, subtle means of producing difference may unintentionally be reproduced in the analysis through the wording or phrasing in my writing. In order to avoid such a production of difference 'through the backdoor' of language, the following reflections explain how certain terms surrounding 'otherness' are used in this work, and further seek to critically contemplate how distancing mechanisms are integrated in certain words and phrases commonly used. Additionally, Chapter 3 introduces the sensitising concepts that the analysis is based upon, which provide further insights into the usage of language in this research.

First of all, this work avoids using the terms 'Other' and 'otherness' to refer to the non-European contexts that the guides point to in their accounts. 'Otherness' is considered as a category that the guides produce, not as an entity that actually exists outside of their accounts or the museums. However, this distinction between the 'Other' as a construction and 'the Other' as describing the non-European communities addressed in the guided tours can sometimes appear blurry in the analysis. For example, a difference in meaning is already implicated in the phrases 'communicating otherness' and 'communicating the Other'. While both phrases could be read as relating to the mediation of cultural difference, the former phrase can also be seen as referring to the construction of otherness as a status. It is in this sense that the phrase is used in this work. This aim to distance the analysis from a reinforcement of the construction of non-European otherness is, thus, the reason why 'communicating the Other' is avoided as a phrase in the analysis: This phrase could be misinterpreted to suggest that 'the Other' was an actual entity which is then mediated by the guides. Instead, this work seeks to show how ideas about cultural otherness are constructed or negotiated by means of the communication of the guides. By using language carefully, the work, hence, seeks to avoid conflating the actual regions represented in the museums with the status of otherness that is attached to them in some of the guides' accounts or in the exhibitions.

However, the above-mentioned reference to 'non-European contexts' as a means of referring to the actual regions (as against 'otherness' referring to the ascribed status by the guides) is problematic as well. After all, the term 'non-European' is a far too broad category for the various regions, areas, and settings presented in the respective museums. Furthermore, the term 'non-European' not only generalises and 'lumps together' these areas, but it also identifies them in terms of what they are not (i.e., Europe), which again reinforces the idea of Europe as the centre and everything else as its periphery. Despite these important drawbacks of the term 'non-European contexts', the phrase does appear frequently in this work. A main reason for this is the difficulty of finding an adequate term to efficiently refer to the areas that the guides describe.

While the respective regional categories (e.g. Palauan, North American, Afghan) are used whenever the analysis discusses an account about a specific aspect, these terms cannot be used in many parts of this work because the analysis looks specifically at patterns of constructing otherness that can be found *regardless* of a regional affiliation. Hence, in order to be able to criticise recurring practices and themes of speaking about these regions and thereby pointing to overarching and socially accepted ways of conceiving of and communicating them, a common term that comprises all these areas needs to be applied. That is because this production of a common, overarching, non-European otherness is exactly what is at stake in this work. 'Non-European' is, therefore, used because of its specific relation to the topic: Most of the guides make claims about these regions from a European perspective, explaining practices that are constructed as external to Europe. The phrase is most suitable to relate to these processes as the connection between the guides' accounts is exactly this non-European framing. This application of the term does not mean, however, that the term is considered unproblematic in this work.

The issue concerning the usage of the term 'non-European' is further related to the general issue of finding suitable terms to describe the areas that are in the focus of the guided tours. Even the names of the countries, areas or regions represent analytical categories that fail to grasp the internal heterogeneity if used in the context of explanations of cultural practices or beliefs. Language works on the basis of signs, and these signs are necessarily reductions and merely serve as templates for broader ideas and concepts. In this work, as a means to avoid generalising about entire countries or reinforcing ideas surrounding 'ethnic groups', the terms 'areas', 'groups', and 'regions' are used. These terms seem relatively adequate as they refer to locations without exact borders or delimitations. Additionally, they can be used to describe larger geographic spaces as well as smaller ones, and therefore make it possible to avoid reinforcing either universal culturalism or arguments surrounding ethnicity.

Finally, a focus on 'areas' or 'regions' represented in the museums also avoids referring to 'cultures' as bounded entities. As has been mentioned, this work is written from a transcultural perspective and hence avoids the reinforcement of ideas surrounding closed-off, homogeneous, clearly determined 'cultures'. Instead, 'cultural practices' or 'cultural contexts' are phrases used to refer to the contents of the guides' accounts. These notions are general enough, yet focussed on more concrete practices and contexts rather than on an allegedly all-encompassing 'culture'.

All these considerations about the usage of language with regard to the representations in the museums and the guides' accounts may not entirely eradicate a reinforcement of the binary distinction between allegedly European and non-European 'culture'. However, note that these critical pitfalls of language have been pondered throughout the research project. Generalising or Eurocentric wording are avoided wherever possible. At some points, the terms 'us', 'we', 'they' and 'them' are used in single quotation marks to illustrate the construction of otherness during the guided tour. In these cases, 'us' and 'we' are used to refer to Europe on a broader scale, and 'they' and 'them' apply to non-European areas. This conception is not self-explanatory, of course, but develops from the material as 'we' is used by the guides to refer to the children participating in the guided tours at European museums. Especially considering the framing of these sessions in non-European exhibitions, this interpretation of 'them' as non-European people suggested itself during the observations.

As a final note to this issue of using words such as 'otherness' or 'non-European', the problem of how to discuss constructions of otherness without reinforcing and cementing these constructions has been a central issue in the conception of this work. It is, therefore, crucial to keep in mind that the focus of this work is on the level of communication and representation. What is at stake, is the way in which certain regional contexts are spoken about. What is not at stake, is any reference to or comparison of the guides' statements with what these regions are 'really like'. As will be shown in Chapter 3, the concept of 'worldmaking' (Goodman 1978) is used to emphasise the fact that the guides present certain world *versions* in their accounts, which are not analysed in terms of their verisimilitude or justification. This analysis only addresses what is being constructed and represented as Chinese, African, Oriental, etc. tradition, history, and identity, as well as the similarities of these constructions and representations in different guided tours.

Another dimension that needs to be addressed with respect to language is the usage of tenses in this work. Over almost the entire analysis, the present tense is used to describe and discuss the guides' accounts. This decision for the present tense results from the work's analytical focus on the observed situations and on the guides' statements. These situations are first described in the present tense, and then analysed in the same tense. In so doing, the analysis is meant to appear more immediate: Readers can think their way into the situations, and are taken along for the analytical process. A more comprehensible and accountable analytical process is, thus, sought for by using the present tense.

Yet, this explanation for using the present tense is only applicable to the concrete analyses of situations from the guided tours. The present tense is, however, also used for discussing the factors that affect the guided tour, as well as for pointing to recurring patterns resulting from the analysis. In these cases, the present tense is used in order to point to the repetitive and partly generalisable aspects in the analysis. Thus, when patterns in the guides' ways of speaking about non-Europeanness become apparent, the present tense serves to show that these ways of speaking *were* not only singular cases at a specific point of time, but need to be seen as ongoing and common practices. In a similar vein, when the working conditions or the organisation of the guided tours are described, it should be clear that these do not only apply to a specific statement, but frame the guided tours in a more general sense. The present tense can, therefore, also be understood as a means to abstract from the smaller context to a broader framework.

This dimensions of abstraction and generalisability must be regarded critically, however. In Chapter 4.4, the analysis of the guides' accounts addresses the usage of the 'ethnographic present' in the guided tours. This anthropological method, by which experiences in the field are described by using a distanced, seemingly objective style of writing in the present tense, has been criticised for its denial of coevalness between research subjects and researchers. Johannes Fabian has explained the development of the ethnographic present by means of an objectifying tendency of early anthropology, which had to prove its scientific legitimacy: 'In the end, they [anthropologists] will organize their writing in terms of the categories of Physical or Typological Time, if only for fear that their reports might otherwise be disqualified as poetry, fiction, or political propaganda' (1983, 33). As the analysis in Chapter 4.4 shows, some of the observed guides also refer to non-European cultural practices in the present tense, thereby generalising, eternalising, and objectifying these descriptions. In the analytical chapters of this work, however, the present tense is also used to refer to situations experienced in the field. This initially appears to point to a double standard: Why are the guides' statements criticised for their application of the ethnographic present when a similar process of generalisation and objectification seems to be applied in this work?

In this case, it is important to carefully distinguish between an anthropological account about a 'culture' or 'ethnic group' and the analysis of concrete situations in a contemporary working environment. By having introduced all the guides that have been observed during the empirical research, and by relating the analytical argumentation to these specific guides and the observed situations, there is no ambiguity as to the reference point of the analytical statements in this work. The generalisation unfolds on the level of the *observed* gallery sessions, not on the level of all gallery educators in Europe. Alternatively, whenever more general statements about the situation of museum educators are made, these are either substantiated by previous research results or marked as subject to debate. Broad generalisations about museum educators as a professional group are rarely made.

Furthermore, there is a difference between speaking about non-European cultural practices and traditions in the present tense, and speaking about gallery educators' practices in the present tense. Not only are the statements in this work not referring to an entire 'culture' or 'ethnic group', but there is also no considerable temporal gap between the observations and the analysis. While in Chapter 4.4, the indefinite time that the described non-European practices are relegated to is criticised, this criticism cannot be applied to this work.

Still, the tendency of present tense statements to appear more objective must be acknowledged in the analysis as well. Although this objectification is not the intention, and is avoided by providing different interpretations and reflecting the situations from different perspectives, a certain effect of apparent factuality cannot entirely be prevented. Nevertheless, the present tense is used throughout this work, also to enhance the reading flow. Note, however, that it is not meant to serve as a tool for generalisation or authentication.

2.5. References to the Source Material

Finally, what needs to be explained briefly is the way in which references to the source material are made throughout this work.

As already explained, the analysis has mainly concentrated on the observation protocols together with the recordings (and corresponding transcriptions) of the guided tours (if approved by the guides) and on the transcripts of the interviews conducted with the guides. As the analyses in Chapters 4 and 5 are predominantly based on these data, the argumentation offered within these sections is substantiated through direct or paraphrased quotes from this material. Additionally, descriptions of situations or performances during the sessions are also referenced in the analysis by pointing to the transcripts or observation protocols. Quotes or situation descriptions in the analysis contain references to the respective parts of the transcripts. Transcripts or protocols of the guided tours are referenced according to the structure 'GSA-MA', which, in this case, stands for 'Gallery Session Antonia, Museum A'. Interview transcripts are referenced according to the structure 'EIA', which stands for 'Educator Interview Antonia'. In order to specify where the cited quotes can be found, line numbers are provided with each of the references (e.g. 'GSA-MA, 113ff.). Note that, in references to the empirical material, the numbers in brackets always refer to *line* numbers while, in references to secondary literature, numbers relate to *page* numbers.

As an additional note regarding the quotations of dialogues between students, teachers, and guides in the material, it is important to clarify that the guides are always abbreviated with the initial of their first names (A, B, C, D, etc.), the students are abbreviated as 'S', and the teachers are abbreviated with 'T'. If a question posed in the interview is cited, the interviewer is marked 'KW', and the guides are again marked with their initial letters.

Besides these explicit or paraphrased quotes that mostly refer to the transcripts, the analysis also contains explanations of the guides, teachers or learning department managers. These statements from more informal conversations were not recorded strategically but documented through field notes and reflections. References to such conversations are, however, very rare because the most important aspects of the analysis have been developed from the interviews and observations.

Finally, it is important to note that all the quotes and summaries of the source material in the text are provided in English, which means that the original statements from the German cases have been translated. These translations are produced with a particular focus on expressing the same messages as the originals rather than with the aim to produce literal translations. However, as language is especially important in some of these situations with respect to this work's focus on essentialist or culturalistic framings of non-European contexts, there are some instances in which a direct translation is deemed necessary to illustrate the subtler meanings inherent in the analysed statements. This leads to the impression that some of the sayings and idioms are translated 'wrongly', however, this is an intentional choice to explain the implications of specific wordings.

2.6. Transcription System

The transcripts of the observed gallery sessions have been created on the basis of Thorsten Dresing's and Thorsten Pehl's simplified transcription system (2013). They draw on Udo Kuckartz's transcription rules (2010) but have concretised these on the basis of feedback from researchers and interviews (cf. Dresing/ Pehl 2013, 20). The concretised transcription system and changes made to it for the purpose of this work are explained in the appendix (p. 448).

3 Sensitising Concepts: Conceptual Starting Points of this Work

In so far as ethnographic objects '[...] are what they are by virtue of the disciplines that "know" them' (Kirshenblatt-Gimblett 1998, 2), their interpretation by gallery educators may cater to various research interests. Special attention could be paid to the educational methods that are applied by the guides or to the historical accuracy of the information provided during the guided tours. However, these aspects do not play a leading role with respect to the research questions posed. To avoid exceeding the scope of this work, it is, thus, inevitable to limit the multitude of analytical angles from which the material can be perceived. According to the methodology applied, this limitation is achieved by means of 'sensitizing concepts [that] suggest directions along which to look' (cf. Blumer 1969, 148). These concepts serve to translate presuppositions implicit within the research questions into explicit conceptual starting points. The following presentation of the sensitising concepts used in this work serves as a means of making transparent initial analytical assumptions that are relevant for the analysis of the material.

The sensitising concepts presented in this chapter are structured into three main concept clusters: 'otherness', 'communication', and 'performance'.

The first sensitising concept cluster concerns the meaning of otherness in this work. The subchapter discusses the definition of 'communicating otherness' in relation to similar concepts, such as 'othering' or 'cultural translation'. It explores the roles that identification, culturalism, and multiculturalism play in the conception of this work, and explains to what extent the distinction between immediate and remote otherness is relevant for this study. Finally, this section introduces the underlying concept at the basis of this work, transculturality, and explains once again in how far this approach is significant for the analysis.

A second important cluster of sensitising concepts addresses the notion of communication. It explains what is meant by 'communicating' in the context of this work and which theory of communication is applied by distinguishing 'communication' from 'museum education', 'knowledge transfer', and 'interpretation'. A particularly important focus is placed on the notion of 'speaking for and about others'. Furthermore, the role of the concept of 'narrative' is addressed. As explained in Chapter 2, this work applies narrative analysis as a method to analyse both the exhibition narratives and the story-like parts of the guides' accounts. Besides this focus on narratology as a method, in some instances of this work, 'narrative' can also be used as a concept to describe the explanatory mode of the guides. The elaborations below, therefore, contain explanations of how the term 'narrative' is understood and applied throughout the analysis. An important concept connected to this aspect is the concept of (narrative) worldmaking (cf. Goodman 1978, Herman 2009, Nünning 2010). Its meaning and usage in this work are also elaborated in this chapter.

The third concept cluster addresses the performative aspect of communicating otherness in guided tours. While it is enriching to analyse the accounts of gallery educators by means of narrative analysis, the gallery sessions do not only consist of texts, but also contain performances. The subchapter, therefore, explains how the notions of performance and performativity can be applied to the analysis of the material. In this respect, both the conscious performative actions of the gallery educators (performance) and the unconscious embodiment and performative production of otherness during the guided tours (performativity) are acknowledged. Furthermore, the idea that spaces and visitors can both be actors in the performance of meanings, is introduced in this section. Finally, the analytical relevance of the notions of 'putting the Other on stage' and of the 'presentation of self in everyday life' (Goffman 1965) are briefly addressed.

As a concluding part of the conceptual framework, the discussion of the narrative and performative dimensions of the communicative format of the guided tour leads to a short reflection on the gallery session's position in-between product and process. Subchapter 3.4 discusses what implications this position has for the analysis, and justifies the focus of this work on the production side of the meaning-making process.

As an additional reflection, it is necessary to clarify how these three conceptual directions are reconcilable with the method of GT that seeks to keep the interpretational process open instead of determining its outcomes by looking for what one wishes to find in the material. First of all, sensitising concepts 'provide starting points for building analysis, not ending points for evading it' (Charmaz 2006, 259). In one way, the three main sensitising concepts, thus, represent the conceptual pillars upon which the collection of data and the main focuses of analysis have been established. For instance, the conception of the guides' communication, not in terms of museum education, but in terms of a type of 'museum representation', underlies the entire argumentation in this work. At the same time, however, the initial coding of the material has resulted in an extension of these sensitising concepts. For instance, the double meaning of performance in the material (i.e. in terms of performance and performativity) has been developed from the analysis. In this way, the sensitising concepts, while providing a framework for the analysis, are also entangled with and shaped by it. It may, therefore, sometimes be difficult to clearly distinguish the sensitising concepts from the theoretical concepts formulated and exposed throughout the analysis. Yet, in contrast to these resulting concepts, the way in which the terms 'otherness', 'communication', and 'performance' are used in this work is a matter of informed choice. While the sensitising concepts are, at times, shaped by the material, they have still been chosen as limitations at the beginning of the project, whereas the analytical findings have been deduced from the material. The sensitising concepts can, then, be seen as the tools with which the analytical results have been achieved.

3.1 'Otherness'

3.1.1   Communicating Otherness as against Othering

In this work, 'communicating otherness' refers to the ways in which non-European regions are represented in ethnographic displays and in their translations by professional gallery educators. In so far as the term suggests that these representations and explanations assign otherness to the regions and people addressed, 'communicating otherness' can be compared to the concept of 'othering' as originally introduced by Gayatri Spivak. However, there are several reasons for using 'communicating otherness' instead of Spivak's 'othering'. Whereas Spivak has introduced the term to explain how colonial discourse has functioned to actively produce the colonised as inferior Other (cf. 1985, 252ff.), 'communicating otherness', in this work, refers to a more general process of assigning, constructing, maintaining, but also negotiating worlds and myths of otherness. By avoiding the term 'othering', this work remains open for interpretations of the guides' accounts that do not construct non-European groups as inferior. Moreover, as the exhibition narratives and the gallery educators' statements not only include information on postcolonial (e.g. present-day India, Indonesia), but also on non-colonial Others (e.g. China), simply adopting the concept of 'othering' could be misleading.

Another reason for preferring 'communicating otherness' in the context of the analysis is its emphasis on communication. While 'othering' also suggests that someone 'others' someone else, the way in which this othering is done remains relatively vague and is, in Spivak's reference to it, used to describe the function of an entire discourse rather than a practice of individuals on a micro-level. 'Communicating otherness' is, therefore, better suited to the analysis of the specific recurring accounts, speech acts, and performative practices that appear in the gallery sessions.

Finally, the distinction of the terms is further meant to distance the communication of otherness by gallery educators from the imperialist and colonialist ideology in which 'othering' is implicated. Certainly, it is true that the objects represented in the four selected museums are in part colonial objects, and it is also true that some of the guides' accounts reinforce, justify, or even repeat colonial practices of 'othering'. Yet, it would be a misrepresentation to frame all of the guides' actions as powerful acts of 'othering' in Spivak's sense of producing inferiority. 'Communicating otherness', therefore, also points to the potential of engaging in the explanation of objects or cultural practices without making derogatory or depreciative statements. This perspective is important because, interestingly, the label or status of otherness is, at times, maintained in the guided tours due to an appraisal rather than a devaluation of non-European practices.

3.1.2 Otherness as against Cultural Difference

As a second means of distinction, the analysis gives preference to the term 'otherness' as against 'cultural difference'. According to Bhabha, cultural difference refers to the 'process of the enunciation of culture as "knowledge*able*", authoritative, adequate to the construction of systems of cultural identification [...]' (1994, 34 – italics in original). The communication of cultural difference is, hence, a necessary part of identification processes in which 'cultures' constantly redefine themselves through the enunciation of difference. The concept of 'cultural difference' is based upon a more neutral premise, referring to the active practice of recognising and claiming differences in processes of encounter. Cultural difference is, thus, part and parcel of all cultural negotiation processes.

'Otherness', in contrast, evokes the idea that someone who is part of a group assigns to someone (or something) else the generalised category of 'not-belonging'. In using the term 'otherness', the aspect of generalisation is, thus, important in so far as the Other is not perceived as a complex and multi-layered subject or object, but as a holistic entity defined only by its general otherness from the in-group. This holistic framing is not the case in relation to the term 'cultural difference'. Cultural differences can be analysed, compared, and negotiated on an individual and specific level because subjects and objects that enunciate their cultural differences can simultaneously maintain and present cultural similarities. Perhaps, this is best explained from a grammatical perspective: There can be various, individual cultural differences in the plural, but otherness always only exists as a singular entity. The term 'otherness' implies a more essential and universal distinction between 'us' and 'them'.

Such an assignment of a *status* of otherness can be expected in the context of guided tours in museums representing non-European objects. The arrangement of the galleries, in which holistically conceived cultures are displayed in separate rooms, and which often lack representations of Europe,[32] already suggests that a fundamental otherness of the respective regions and people permeates the representations provided. In consequence, these museums categorically presuppose and construct the gazing, identity-ascribing subject as the European self, while the non-European Other is rendered as its object. This binary distinction is necessarily translated into the guided tours. Even if the guides engage in translational and negotiating practices, the premise

---

[32] This is not only widespread practice in traditional ethnographic museums. The new Humboldt-Forum in Berlin will equally exclude representations of Europe, which Friedrich von Bose has recently argued is a continuation of a traditional ethnographic museum practice in which Europe functions as an unmarked reference subject (von Bose 2015, 29).

of otherness remains because of the spatial arrangement and the positionalities implied by the activity of explaining something 'other' to the students.

This work is, thus, based upon the idea that museum representations, visual or verbal, more often produce than merely represent their objects (cf. Kirshenblatt-Gimblett 1998, 3). The concept of 'communicating otherness' points to the fact that ethnographic museum narratives and the guides' accounts do not simply show a variety of cultural differences to the students, but often construct and normalise a generalised otherness of the respective regions and people as a self-explanatory status.

3.1.3 Others as Selves

As explained above, this work does not understand the guides' accounts in terms of discussions of cultural differences because their statements and actions are based upon an idea of holistic otherness which is prefabricated by the settings and positionalities in the museum. Yet, it is still important to address the relationship between the guides' communications of otherness and underlying processes of identification, which are usually discussed in connection to the notion of 'cultural difference'. Identifications with or against an 'other' are necessary practices of conceiving of, constructing, and asserting an image of the self. This connection between the ascription of otherness and the formation of the self has commonly been framed by means of the concept of 'alterity'. In the context of the analysis presented here, 'alterity' is understood in a similar vein as Johannes Fabian has defined it; as an umbrella term for otherness, othering and other in the social sciences (cf. 2006, 141). The acknowledgment of the connection between alterity and identity is self-evident by now. In ethnography, as Clifford has shown, there has been a shift from looking at '[...] clearly defined others, defined as primitive, or tribal, or non-Western, or pre-literate [...]', to encountering '[...] others in relation to [one]self, while seeing [one]self as other' (1986, 23).

While this connection between self and other is also important in this work, in so far as self-reflection is posited as a prerequisite for genuine cultural negotiation processes, it is important to distinguish the academic discourse on otherness as a part of selfhood from the academic discourse on the production of non-European Others. Philosophical or psychological elaborations have conceptualised selfhood and otherness as two sides of the same coin by framing what is 'other' as the deficiency (Freud 1930), mirror (Lacan 1988), or the ungraspable neighbour (Levinas 1981) of the self. Yet, in anthropological discourse, the Other is a concrete figure, namely the non-European, the colonised, or the native. For the discussion in this work, this anthropological and political dimension of 'communicating otherness' is emphasised, while the psychological or philosophical discourse is disregarded. This focus is placed because, when discussing processes of speaking about non-European Others, an interpretation of the communication of otherness as a mere matter of identity formation may fall into the trap of forfeiting a critical perspective. This point has equally been made by Fabian:

> [O]ne decisive element of difference between previous philosophical concerns with otherness and the introduction of the concept into social science [...] and so on has been the historicization-cum-politicization of the other (the colony, the Orient). That other is not opposed to a self. To assume that all talk about otherness is (ultimately) about identity would amount to re-philosophizing otherness. self-assertion through domination, exploitation, or even 'stylization' (the invented Orient), or what I called devices of temporal distantiation (the invented Primitive) – to call these practices and conceptualizations acts of identity-affirmation would be analogous to examples of insane social scientific positivity, such as declaring South Africa under apartheid a pluralist society, or proposing to analyze concentration camps as social systems. (2006, 146)

If the analysis interpreted all forms of representing, negotiating or constructing the Other solely as forms of identity formation, it would fall short of a necessary critical and political scrutiny required by the power

90

imbalance implicit in the specific situation of communicating non-European otherness. A similar criticism can also be found in Ahmed's response to Julia Kristeva's suggestion that one could only tolerate the stranger if one knew that one was a stranger to oneself (cf. Kristeva 1991, 182). Ahmed explains that this relation between strangerness and selfhood, which constructs everybody as strangers, avoids 'dealing with the political processes whereby some others are designated as stranger than other others' (2000, 6). Here, the same problem as in Fabian's statement becomes noticeable. Approaches to otherness that normalise experiences of 'being other' as fundamental human experiences, while certainly being true in a general sense, tend to trivialise and obscure powerful processes of producing and materialising the Other in situations of political imbalance and inequality.

While the relationship between self and other is thus acknowledged as an explanation for certain situations in the material, this thesis is interested predominantly in a critical investigation of still-existing myths and oft-repeated stereotypes about non-European regions, which reinforce the idea of an essential difference between 'us' and 'them'. Therefore, the mutual relationship between self and other is here only addressed in terms of collective categories, as in 'Europe seeks itself in the exotic' (Sontag 1970, 185), and not in relation to individual or internal processes.

3.1.4   Immediate or Remote Otherness

Another important aspect of otherness in this work is the distinction between 'immediate alterity' (Augé 2002, 14) or 'alterity within/inside' (Fabian 2006, 147) and 'remote alterity' (Augé 2002, 14) or 'alterity without/outside' (Fabian 2006, 147). Fabian defines this disparity as the distinction between alterity that is part of one lifeworld (i.e., alterity within) and alterity as the recognition of other lifeworlds (i.e. alterity without) (cf. ibid.).

Remote alterity is the predominant focus of this work. This is because representations of 'cultures' in ethnographic museums are distant or remote not only in a spatial sense (i.e., the concentration on non-European contexts), but also in a temporal sense (i.e., the representation of objects from an indeterminate past). When gallery educators explain objects and cultural practices from China, India, or Africa, the experience of the students is not one of immediate, but one of remote alterity; not one of otherness within their own lifeworld, but of otherness outside of it. This association between ethnographic museums and remote otherness has its origin in the 19th century and is informed by principles of spatialisation (cf. Hallam 2000, 265) and temporalisation (cf. Fabian 1983). In ethnographic galleries, these frameworks are often still prevalent as evident, for instance, from the separation of different sections of museums according to broader geographical areas (i.e., Islamic Orient, Africa, China, South Asia, etc.).

The question that results from this focus on remote alterity in the museums part of this study and the guided tours, is whether this remote alterity is relevant for or has an influence on understandings of immediate alterity. Especially with respect to the previous notion that students participating in the gallery sessions may be introduced to problematic stereotypes of non-European Others, it is interesting to dwell shortly on the extent to which the guides' accounts can be considered relevant for the students' experience of immediate otherness in their own lifeworlds. There are two important points to be made in this respect, which relate, on the one hand, to the museum's cultural authority, and on the other, to the discourse on museum education and the opening up of the museum.

First, as Ivan Karp and Fred Wilson have emphasised, '[t]he conventions by which we understand objects and otherness are conventions produced, at least in part, by museums' (1996, 262). Although representations in ethnographic museums that portray non-European cultures as holistic and distant entities are not consistent with the globalised, integrated information age encountered outside of the museum, the ethnographic museum still exerts cultural authority, as Karp and Corinne Kratz have elaborated in more detail:

> Claims to cultural authority are not simply claims about knowledge and the 'accuracy' of representations. In institutions, they take the form of more direct claims about who controls the distribution of knowledge (usually curators and museums), and about the ranking and relations of types of knowledge and types of society. These claims help define who will set the standards for what is worth knowing about world cultures. They make museums into the repositories of truth and error, able to sort things out and tell us which is the best, what to look at, and how to relate to people in other parts of the world. (2000, 208)

Karp and Kratz define the cultural authority of ethnographic museums in terms of their power to contribute both to what society considers relevant knowledge, and to what information is considered true or false. The museums in this work, likewise, can be seen to have the cultural authority to convince the students that the representations of remote alterity in the exhibitions are relevant and trustworthy, even though these representations may not match the students' more heterogeneous and multidimensional experiences of immediate alterity.

It is interesting, in this regard, that the reliability and guidance that the museum is associated with works not only despite, but also because of this mismatch between the outside world and the represented world. The disparity between experiences within the museum and outside of it may seem appealing rather than discouraging for its visitors. By constructing and presenting a more coherent and ordered otherness (i.e., ordered in time and space), museums provide, as Jay Rounds has argued, 'ontological security' (2006, 139). The cultural authority of ethnographic museums may, thus, be maintained partly because of this discrepancy between immediate and remote otherness.[33]

The second reason for the relevance of the ethnographic museum's representations, despite the apparent focus on remote otherness, concerns the process of an opening up of the museum. It would be unfair to frame all ethnographic museums as equally invested in the representation of a fixed and static otherness. Over the last decades, the ethnographic museum has generally engaged in a process of self-examination and developed strategies of becoming a more socially inclusive place (cf. Gail Anderson 2004, 1). New techniques such as metanarrative, multiple voices, and fragmentation (cf. Albano 2014, 3) are increasingly applied in ethnographic museums and displays. Furthermore, as a response to postcolonial claims and a transformed perception of non-European groups in anthropology at large, many museums are now actively promoting cultural dialogue, diversity, respect, and tolerance. As a consequence, many mission statements include aspects such as the equal value of 'all cultures', the representation of diversity, and the self-understanding of the 'museum as a contact zone', as Clifford has proposed (cf. Clifford 1997). Such statements show that ethnographic museums try to relate their agendas and representations to the changing dimensions of alterity in the 'outside world' by acknowledging their 'increasingly diverse publics and communities who seem to redefine the museum's "use-value"' (Rectanus 2006, 385).

As these reflections show, understandings of immediate alterity can be affected by and connected to the representations of a more remote otherness in the ethnographic museums. Therefore, while still focusing on the guides' ways of constructing remote otherness, these connections have to be considered. In relation to this immediate otherness, the figure

---

[33] This point is elaborated in detail as one of the expectations of the museum that affect the performance of the gallery sessions.

of the stranger needs to be briefly mentioned. In the context of this work, the concept of strangeness is positioned in close proximity to immediate alterity and will, thus, only play a role with regard to the implications and understandings of immediate alterity that are facilitated by the communication of remote alterity. In this sense, the relation between the two kinds of alterity is interesting in so far as Zygmunt Bauman notes that the stranger '[…] brings into the inner circle of proximity the kind of difference and otherness that are anticipated and tolerated only at a distance' (1991, 60). The analysis, thus, pays attention to such moments in which toleration is granted specifically with respect to remoteness.

3.1.5   Culturalism

When museums state that 'cultures' have equal value and that that 'cultures' can enter into dialogue, this suggests an understanding of cultures as separate, bounded entities. Such a '[…] fixation on "culture as product" instead of "culture as production"' (Bachmann-Medick 2012, 105) can be considered as a form of culturalism. In the context of the analysis, culturalism is both understood as this holistic conception of culture as product and as the 'culturalization of difference' (Dominguez 1994, 249) in which differences between people are mainly understood in terms of their culture. In a similar vein, Wolfgang Kaschuba has warned that explanatory approaches that only acknowledge culture as a factor influencing differences between people fall short of acknowledging social and economic aspects (cf. 1995, 15). Such reductive approaches are often problematic in so far as culture functions, in these cases, as an unmarked substitute for ethnicity or origin, which may lead to a latent racism because of its emphasis on unalterable, external characteristics (cf. Adick 2010, 125). Culturalism is, therefore, considered critically in this work.

This culturalism is often implied by the way in which objects and meanings are arranged in ethnographic museums. To be *of* a culture compares to the idea of 'having a culture', which Clifford has related to notions of possessing and collecting which are crucial processes in the formation of the Western subject (cf. 1985, 237). Having a culture, in his words, means 'selecting and cherishing an authentic collective property' (ibid.). This idea of a collective culture-as-property is reflected in the spatialisation and temporalisation evident in ethnographic museum representations. Origin (of an object, of a person) defines culture and culture defines identity, ergo origin defines identity. The fact that artefacts in ethnographic displays are arranged according to their places of collection (or cultures) leads to an equally static fixation (in time, in space) of the cultural practices (rituals, norms, behaviours, values) implicated in these objects. Thereby, as Arjun Appadurai has argued, spatial confinement is related to intellectual confinement by means of constructing cultures as wholes and by tying the intellectual operations of the 'natives' to these concrete wholes (cf. 1988, 38). While the culturalistic identification of regional identity in art and artefacts is being criticised by scholars such as Thomas Dacosta Kaufmann (cf. 2008, 176) and Monica Juneja (cf. 2011, 281), this approach is still not uncommon in museum practice.

3.1.6   Multiculturalism

The concept of culturalism described above is closely related to the concept of multiculturalism. In this work, the criticism of culturalism and the concept of multiculturalism are closely interlinked. While culturalism describes the reduction of identity to 'culture' and of heterogeneous groups to separate 'cultures', multiculturalism, as understood in this work, refers to the celebration of and claim to tolerate this coexistence of separate 'cultures' within a given society. Multiculturalism is, then, based upon and contains understandings of culturalism, but adds the dimension of the (happy) coexistence of different cultural entities.

As Perry Anderson has explained, multiculturalism was adopted in Europe as part of the discourse surrounding the establishment of the European Union. Anderson argues that multiculturalism 'fitted the bill' of the EU's search for a concept that would help member states to come to terms both with the diversity between one another and with the diversity within their own borders because it connoted 'variety without antagonism' (cf. 2011, 529.). This idea of a conflict-free cohabitation of people with different religious and cultural practices within predominantly secular countries, however, entailed problems of hierarchy and sincerity:

> [...] where the Enlightenment, not to speak of radical and socialist movements, had looked forward to the disappearance of supernatural beliefs, official and left-liberal opinion now celebrated their multiplication, as if the more religion there was, the better. Typically, of course, proponents of the doctrine did not themselves adhere to any faith, as they celebrated the underlying harmony of believers [...]. (ibid., 530)

This issue of a superficial celebration of an awaited harmony of diverse 'cultures' as opposed to a sincere analysis and involvement with cultural, religious and social negotiation processes has been a major criticism of multiculturalism (cf. e.g. Welsch 1999, Barry 2001).

This conception of multiculturalism must be regarded as only one of various models. In Charles Taylor's theory of recognition, for instance, multiculturalism denies a mere 'happy coexistence' of different religious or local communities and argues in favour of an examination of 'their' values and practices by 'us', and not in favour of a pre-empt all-encompassing tolerance (1994, 68ff.).[34] Furthermore, multiculturalism as a political

---

[34] Despite this focus on recognition, Taylor's model still entails ideas of 'cultures' as homogeneous entities and can thus be seen as mirroring some of the critical dimensions that have also been taken up in the public discourse: 'With the politics of equal dignity, what is established is meant to be universally the same, an identical basket of rights and immunities; with the politics of difference, what we are asked to recognize is the unique identity of this individual or group, their distinctness from everyone else. The idea is that it is precisely this distinctness that has been ignored, glossed over, assimilated to a dominant or majority identity.

practice or, as Will Kymlicka states, 'multiculturalism-as-citizenization' (2012, 8) needs to be distinguished from the above-mentioned celebratory model in so far as it is '[...] about constructing new civic and political relations to overcome the deeply entrenched inequalities that have persisted after the abolition of formal discrimination' (ibid.) instead of revolving around '[...] displaying and consuming difference in cuisine, clothing, and music, while neglecting issues of political and economic inequality' (cf. ibid.). Considering these various models, multiculturalism must be understood as a 'travelling debate' rather than a self-contained concept (cf. Bachmann-Medick 2014, 130 referencing Stern/ Shohat 2005).

As the explanations above show, however, the understanding of multiculturalism applied in this work is related to what Jan Nederveen Pieterse has called a 'static view of multiculturalism' which is based on 'essentialist and territorial understandings of culture' (2005, 167). To define multiculturalism like this reinforces common post-multiculturalist critiques of the concept through characterising it as '[...] a feel-good celebration of ethnocultural diversity, encouraging citizens to acknowledge and embrace the panoply of customs, traditions, music, and cuisine that exist in a multiethnic society' (Will Kymlicka 2012, 4). This meaning of multiculturalism is chosen because the communication of non-European otherness in gallery sessions for school classes may be much more connected to this celebratory model than to the political one. This focus of the gallery sessions is already apparent from the focus on 'cuisine, clothing, and music' (cf. ibid.) in the advertised session formats on ethnographic museums' websites. Furthermore, in order to describe social expectations and understandings of non-European identity and cultural

---

And this assimilation is the cardinal sin against the ideal of authenticity' (1994, 38).

encounter that underlie the guides' or the teachers' explanations during the sessions, it is useful to approach the material with two contrasting concepts of cultural negotiation. While multiculturalism, in its static or celebratory conception, describes understandings connected to the celebration of a separatist coexistent of homogeneous cultural identities, transculturality is used to describe cultural conceptions related to heterogeneity, continuous identification, negotiation and hybridity.

3.1.7   Transculturality

From the discussions of 'culturalism' and 'multiculturalism' above, it becomes apparent that this work takes a critical stance towards bounded concepts of 'cultures'. The work, instead, argues from the perspective of a specific understanding of culture, which needs to be explained in more detail in order to make transparent the premises upon which it is based.

Throughout this work, a transcultural understanding is applied to point to the meaning of culture in terms of the heterogeneity of communities. In his book on Latin American and Caribbean intellectual history, *Cuban Counterpoint*, Fernando Ortiz first coined the term 'transculturation', referring to the complex and simultaneous processes of disadjustment, readjustment, deculturation, and acculturation, which accompany cultural encounter (cf. 1995, 98). Ortiz explained,

> I am of the opinion that the word transculturation better expresses the different phases of the process of transition from one culture to another because this does not consist merely in acquiring another culture, which is what the English word acculturation really implies, but the process also necessarily involves the loss or uprooting of a previous culture, which could be defined as a deculturation. In addition, it carries the idea of the consequent creation of new cultural phenomena, which could be called neoculturation. (ibid., 102f.)

Thus, 'transculturation', in its first definition, was suggested as a counter concept to the idea of an assimilation of cultural forms in moments of cultural encounter and confrontation. This conceptualisation of cultural transformations in terms of losses and gains has further been taken up by Wolfgang Welsch, who has applied it to modern cultures in a more general sense. Welsch argues that culture in the globalised world must generally be conceived as transcultural, due to the 'inner differentiation and complexity of modern cultures' (1999, 197). He explains that processes of hybridisation, sparked by the increasing availability of information all over the world, have fractured traditional, separatist understandings of cultures (ibid., 198). As an alternative, he suggests a concept of culture that is based upon notions of linking and transition, rather than isolation and separation (cf. ibid., 200), arguing that instead of having to decide whether globalisation processes lead to particularisation or uniformisation, transcultural identities retain local affiliations while being at the same time cosmopolitan (cf. ibid., 205).

Welsch's adoption and development of 'transculturation' can be regarded as an important reorientation of the concept of 'culture' from a separate, homogeneous entity to a multi-layered, continuously transforming, indistinct sphere. Yet, his focus on 'modern cultures' and, more importantly, his idea of a world in which everyone has the same access to information (cf. ibid., 198) and in which '[p]eople can make their own choice with respect to their affiliation' (cf. ibid., 205) needs to be revised. Welsch's idea of transculturality is overly optimistic, promoting a utopia of intermixing and commonness, but ignoring relations of oppression, conflict, and power. It is true that global media-, ethno-, techno-, ideo-, and financescapes (cf. Appadurai 1996, 33) have contributed to the transculturation of areas all around the world. It is crucial, however, to consider *where* and to *whom* these scapes are actually accessible. Not all people have the same access to information, and not all people have the same freedom to pick and choose their cultural affiliations. Furthermore, although Welsch admits that transculturality has already been evident in history (cf. 1999, 198), his focus on the inner differentiation of exclusively *modern* cultures is contestable. That is because the idea of neat cultural entities derives from an objectivity- and categorisation-driven positivism of the late 18th and 19th centuries, and has, thus, always been just another cultural construction. Cultural groups have always been internally homogeneous, made up by people with different statuses, roles, characteristics, and skills. It would be misleading to portray transculturation and transculturality as results of the new information technology, global economic system, or tourism industries because firstly, entirely homogenous cultural entities have never existed, and secondly, trade relations and the sharing of stories and information date back to long before the 20th century.

Despite these discrepancies, this work is still based upon some of the conditions of culture that Welsch mentions, including their unbounded nature, their intricate entanglement, and their hybridisation. In general, the conception of 'transculturation' or 'transculturality' that is applied here draws on the definition of 'transculturalism' that has been developed at the Heidelberg Cluster 'Asia and Europe in a Global Context' and that Monica Juneja explains in an interview with Christian Kravagna in the book *Transcultural Modernisms:*

> Contact, interaction, and entanglement make the transcultural a field constituted relationally, so that asymmetry, as one attribute of relationships (together with categories such as difference, non-equivalence, dissonance), is an element that makes up this field. This attention to uncovering the dynamics of those formations both in the past and the present constituted through regimes of circulation and exchange distinguishes our understanding from that of Welsch [...]. In other words, our research aims to investigate the multiple ways in which difference is negotiated within contacts and encounters, through selective appropriation, mediation, translation, re-historicizing and rereading of signs, alternatively through non-communication, rejection or resistance-or through a succession/coexistence of any of these. Exploring the possible range of transactions built into these dynamics works as a safeguard against polar conceptions of identity and alterity, equally against dichotomies between complete absorption and resistance, which characterize certain kinds of postcolonial scholarship [...] (Juneja in Kravagna 2013, 25)

This rather long quotation shows that the Cluster's conception of transculturality adds a historical perspective to Welsch's idea of the inner differentiation of 'modern cultures'. Furthermore, this definition includes notions of dissonance and resistance, countering Welsch's all too optimistic take on cultural encounters. Finally, the approach also departs from Welsch's framing of transculturality as a condition or 'form of cultures today' and instead applies a processual perspective by considering appropriation, translation or rejection as active practices that people apply to negotiate encounters, thereby themselves 'transculturating' communities rather than being confronted or subjected to 'transculturality' as a condition.

In this processual, active, more critical conception of 'transculturalism', the concept is also applied in this work. The critical statements that are made about the guides' accounts and the exhibition narratives are based upon this understanding of cultures as heterogeneous, unbounded communities that are continuously in flux, transformed and shaped by people who perceive themselves part of or opposed to them. Juneja explains that transculturalism can be regarded both as an object of investigation and as an analytical method (cf. ibid., 24). In this work, the concept is, accordingly, predominantly used as an analytical lens, facilitating critical questions about taken-for-granted myths and stories about non-European culture without again falling back into dichotomies of the oppressed and the oppressors. In this sense, Homi Bhabha's notion of hybridity as a 'third space which enables other positions to emerge' (1990, 211) also plays a crucial role for this understanding of transculturality. In his conception, encounter constantly creates these third spaces that generate new identities and subject positions as negotiations of prior knowledge and new knowledge acquired during the encounter. This notion of cultural identity as an ongoing, complex process of appropriation and contestation in individual and social terms serves well to investigate and interpret representations of non-European Others in gallery sessions in ethnographic museums.

As becomes clear, the theory of culture that is applied in this work must be regarded as a conscious choice made in order to deconstruct and question the conceptions of culture fostered and promoted within the observed guided tours and exhibition narratives. However, at the same time, 'transculturalism' is not exclusively seen as a convenient lens through which to criticise long-held understandings of cultures as fixed, authentic entities. In addition, the concept also shows that there are alternatives to essentialist and stereotypical representations of Others. Hence, the perspective from which the material is perceived is not only meant to deconstruct the guides' statements, but also to refer to transcultural elements in their accounts that could be further emphasised in order to approach culture in terms of processes of 'selective appropriation, mediation, translation, re-historicizing and rereading of signs, […] non-communication, rejection or resistance' (Juneja in Kravagna 2013, 25) that Juneja has mentioned in her explication of the concept of transculturalism.

3.2 Communication

Besides 'otherness', a further sensitising concept that is important in this work is that of 'communication'. For the purpose of referring to the exchange of statements or information about non-European contexts, the term 'communication' has deliberately been chosen instead of 'explanation', 'mediation' or 'interpretation' due to its broad and all-encompassing nature. For instance, media scholar Louise Ravelli has pointed out the various forms of communication that can be observed within museums:

> Communication within a museum potentially encompasses all of the institution's practices which make meaning - from the pragmatic effect of whether or not there is an admission charge (which makes

meaning about what the institution is, and who may enter it) to the overall aesthetic impact of the building, to the organisational layout of the galleries, to the written texts pasted on walls or written in brochures, which support exhibitions. (2006, 1)

To her list, the verbal accounts of the guides could be added as additional means of communication.

Of course, not all of the dimensions that Ravelli mentions are significant for the analysis of the observed guided tours. When considering the kinds of texts and contexts that the students encounter during the gallery sessions, three main forms of communication are directly relevant and therefore discussed in more detail in the following. These comprise the visual exhibition narratives, the verbal accounts of the guides, and the performative practices of the gallery educators, teachers and their fellow students. To offer a short definition of these communicative dimensions, the exhibition narrative can be regarded as the product of the synthesis between the exhibited objects, the modalities of their display (e.g. lighting, wall colour) and their discursive interpretation, for example through leaflets or text panels (cf. Albano 2014, 2). The accounts of the guides are those verbal statements that are presented to the students by the gallery educators. Finally, performative practices refer predominantly, but not exclusively, to the guides', teachers', and students' bodily practices. The two latter forms of communication (the guides' accounts and performative practices) are not permanently installed in the exhibition space, nor are they as static and 're-readable' as the exhibition narratives. Nonetheless, they are still understood as part of museum communication in the context of this work because they form part of 'the language produced by the institution, in written and spoken form, for the consumption of visitors, which contributes to interpretative practices within the institution' (Ravelli 2006, 1).

This subchapter concentrates on the concepts related to verbal communication in the broadest sense, i.e. the accounts of the guides and the exhibition narratives. The conceptual definitions of performative practices are subsequently discussed in Chapter 3.3. While performances are regarded as forms of communication as well, this formal division is made because of the comparability of the exhibition narratives and the accounts of the guides. Both are visual and verbal by nature, both are structured and ordered in a relatively coherent manner, and both can be interpreted by means of narratological tools and concepts. Performative practices, in contrast, are less ordered, cannot be sufficiently analysed with the help of narratological concepts, and require a more specific discussion as to who performs what or whom.[35]

Among the exhibition narratives and the guides' accounts, the latter are at the centre of attention in this analysis. Yet, as has already been mentioned, in order to understand and contextualise how gallery educators communicate non-European objects and cultural practices, it is necessary to comparatively consider the arrangement of the objects and the texts presented in the exhibitions. After all, these forms of communication belong to the environment that the students encounter during their guided tours. Furthermore, the exhibition narratives can overlap or interfere with the gallery sessions. For example, elements in the exhibition may divert the attention of the students away from the guides' accounts, or label texts can be used by the students as means of identifying unknown artefacts. While the accounts of the guides are regarded as autonomous forms of communication in the museum, this interrelatedness between visual representations, written texts and the guides' statements is acknowledged.

---

[35] The conceptual boundary between performance and narrative is, however, extremely blurry. Perhaps the best proof of this are the works of Austin (1997 [1969]) and Searle (1976) that show how verbal forms of communication can be performative when they actively change a situation. Yet, the point of this distinction is not to suggest that they are in fact separate in practice, but that different theoretical frameworks are used in this work to analyse their functions and workings in the guided tours.

Finally, this acknowledgement of the visual and textual elements of the exhibition alongside the guides' accounts can offer insights into the more official meanings that are encouraged by the museums. Although it would be wrong to conceive of the museum as a coherent whole, exhibition narratives can be regarded as more authorised and formalised means of communication than the accounts of the guides, which are often more spontaneous and contain improvised parts. By analysing the exhibition narratives, it is, thus, possible to arrive at the meanings that are institutionally approved. Ravelli has pointed to this relation between exhibition narratives and the museum by distinguishing between texts in museums and the museum as text (cf. ibid., 1). She argues that it is '[…] of course the institution as a whole which is the ultimate source of meaning making' (ibid., 139) because the meanings made by the institution transcend the exhibition (cf. ibid.). Exhibition narratives can be designed to resonate with the macro-level self-representation and mission statements of the museums, whereas gallery educators may make oppositional or subversive statements on a micro-level.[36] A comparison between these approved narratives in the exhibitions and the guides' accounts, thus, allows for a reflection of the degree of criticism, subjectivity and individuality that the gallery educators contribute.

3.2.1   Museum Education, Mediation, and Knowledge Transfer

Throughout this work, the analytical focus is placed on 'communication' rather than 'museum education', 'knowledge transfer' or 'mediation' (in German: 'Vermittlung'). One reason for this focus has already been mentioned: 'Communication' is used because of its conceptual openness,

---

[36] The freedom that the guides have in their interpretations of the objects and cultural practices differ greatly in each museum. However, subversive or subjective elements can be traced in all accounts. The restrictions of the guides are explained in detail in Chapter 5.

which makes it possible to simultaneously refer to visual, textual, and performative practices of exchanging information or making statements. The same comprehensiveness would not necessarily be implied by the terms 'museum education' or 'knowledge transfer', as it may be difficult, for instance, to understand statements that the guides make about their own professional experience in terms of knowledge transfer or education. 'Communication' has been chosen to keep the possibilities for analysis open instead of prematurely limiting the material by directing attention only to those statements that produce or transfer knowledge.

Another reason for not using the term 'museum education' is the fact that it has been abandoned in many of the museums' official statements and replaced with notions of 'learning'. This development can also be found in a British study by museum scholar Juliette Fritsch, who has found that the term 'museum education' is often perceived negatively by museum professionals (cf. 2011, 241). Her findings suggest that professionals outside of the learning departments do not have clear professional understandings of the meanings of 'education' (cf. ibid.). This negative connotation of 'education' can be explained by a conceptual shift in museums away from passive 'teaching' and towards active and free-choice learning. For example, Eilean Hooper-Greenhill has argued that learner autonomy is more relevant in cultural institutions than in formal contexts because formal education involves clear learning outcomes and external standards that every agent of the communicative process is aware of (2007, 32). Different preconditions apply to learning in museums: Most visitors of museums

> [...] have their own agendas for learning (some of which are very unfocused and undeveloped) and they are not required to disclose these in advance. It is inappropriate for cultural organisations such as museums to measure their users against external standards. However, visitors and users themselves make their own judgments about the success or otherwise of their visit [...]. (ibid.)

This free-choice learning cannot entirely be applied to the gallery session which is normally much more structured and connected to learning outcomes than an unprepared visit to the museum. Nevertheless, due to this general shift in concepts of learning from the metaphor of acquisition to the metaphor of participation (cf. Sfard 1998), 'museum education' or 'mediation' are now less preferred in the museum context than the concept of 'learning in museums' which allows more agency on the part of the learner.

Still, even 'learning' is not used in this work as a reference to the guides' actions. This is because learning still suggests that the students gain any kind of 'knowledge' from their experience in the museum. This, however, is neither the focus of this work nor can it be measured by means of the methods of empirical research applied. To think of the meaning-making processes in the observed sessions in terms of communication rather than 'knowledge transfer', 'learning' or 'education', therefore, also disconnects the analysis from the idea that it is possible to adequately measure, evaluate, or judge the specific information and learnings that the students take from their museum experience. Communication indicates a focus on the *process* of meaning-making, as well as on the information that is offered by the guides, rather than on the learning outcomes or products of the gallery sessions.

Furthermore, the focus of this work is on representations of non-European regions rather than on educational methods of facilitating learning. Concepts of knowledge are often discussed in the context of museum educational discourse, with George Hein arguing that a theory of education requires a theory of knowledge, a theory of learning, and a theory of teaching (cf. 1998, 16). He explains that education in the museum is closely related to the theory of knowledge that it is based upon, drawing on the two well-known extremes of knowledge theories: realism (the world exists independent of human ideas) on the one hand and idealism (the world exists only in the human mind) on the other (cf. ibid.). In research projects that focus on methods of teaching and processes of learning, the examination of underlying theories of knowledge is undoubtedly important. However, the analysis in this work is only marginally interested in the educational strategies of the guides or the learning outcomes for the students. By specifically avoiding conceptualising the explanations and statements of the gallery educators, or the texts in the exhibitions, as forms of 'knowledge production', the work points to an analytical focus on cultural and social processes of meaning-making. While the understandings of knowledge and learning that the guides apply during their sessions will play a role as factors influencing their communicative actions (see Chapter 5), their statements and explanations are not by default regarded as means of knowledge transfer. This is because, from a cultural studies perspective, what the guides and the exhibition narratives facilitate is not only knowledge (as information about the world either constructed in the mind or external to it), but more precisely impressions and images, stories, and imaginations of 'other' regions and people.

Finally, as this work is interested in the ways in which otherness is communicated during gallery sessions, the question is not so much what knowledge the students gain, but what stories, statements, imaginary worlds, and characterisations the gallery educators offer, and which practices they use to communicate these aspects. This thesis, thus, understands its main material, the guided tours, as a part of museum communication that needs to be analysed in similarly critical, but culturally analytical (not necessarily educational or didactical) terms as the exhibition narratives that are regularly subjected to critical scrutiny by museum scholars and ethnologists (cf. Karp/ Lavine 1991, Riegel 1996, Sturge 2007, Lonetree 2012). Because the analysis positions itself in the tradition of postcolonial critique and critical ethnography, rather than museum education, it is not so much the alleged 'knowledge' that is produced about the non-European regions, but the myths, stories, ideas, and imaginations about otherness in general, that are at stake.

3.2.2   The Interpretation or Translation of Culture

In so far as the focus of the analysis is placed on the ways in which non-European otherness is framed and represented during the gallery sessions, it is closely connected to notions of 'interpreting cultures' or 'translating cultures'. While 'translation' is frequently used in relation to the guides' accounts in this work, 'interpretation' is not. The reasons for this disparity are explicated in the following.

The notion of the 'interpretation of culture' goes back to Clifford Geertz's work on the topic in 1973. He argues that anthropological interpretation is successful only when it is engaged in thick description, that is, when it 'takes us into the heart of that of which it is the interpretation' (1973, 18). If anthropologists manage to decode cultural signs and symbols in relation to their specific contexts and situations, he explains, they can interpret culture in a meaningful way (cf. ibid., 14). Still, he emphasises that the extrapolation of such miniature interpretations of specific observations to broader statements about entire cultural scapes can easily lead to generalisation (cf. ibid., 21). He maintains, therefore, that anthropological interpretation has to remain open for contestation, aiming at an increasingly defined debate rather than perfection (cf. ibid., 29). Considering this definition of interpreting culture, it becomes clear why the term is not applied as a general specification of the guides' actions during the gallery sessions. In their role as educators, the guides are not Geertz's anthropologists who provide second-order observations and interpretations of the first-order interpretations that a given community makes (cf. ibid., 15). In contrast, gallery educators have learned information about the respective regions from ethnographic writings, from materials issued to them by the museum, or from the curators. They are not, at large, expected to engage in interpretations themselves, but rather to repeat already existing ones.

As the interpretations that the guides offer in the gallery sessions are, hence, not anthropological interpretations in Geertz's sense, they can perhaps be understood in terms of 'hermeneutical interpretations' that Hooper-Greenhill has described as working 'dialogically between 'prejudices' or foreknowledge, and an openness to new information, experiences, and objects' (2000, 117f.). In her book *Museums and the Interpretation of Visual Culture*, she argues that museum interpretations are never fully complete and must remain subjective because they are dependent on personal experience (cf. ibid., 118). As she states, contemporary museum education is, however, often still stuck in forms of positivist object-teaching: 'The attraction of working with 'real things' rather than with textbooks can provoke a failure to acknowledge the constructed character of the real' (cf. ibid., 105). Gallery educators, similarly, rather occupy the role of interpreting objects (and cultural contexts) *for* the students by assigning to them meanings instead of facilitating interpretations *by* the students. The museum educational, hermeneutical conception of 'interpretation' is then equally misleading when applied this work.

As neither an anthropological definition of 'interpreting culture' nor a museum educational definition really describes the guides' activity, 'communication' seems to be the most suitable option in order to avoid misunderstanding. Yet, even though the guides' accounts may not match these concrete conceptions of 'interpretation', what has to be acknowledged is that the gallery session generally functions to render the represented cultural contexts more legible and accessible. In order to make this function transparent, the term 'translation' is used in this work.

As the 're-framing of meanings from one set of cultural categories to another' (Sturge 2007, 7), 'cultural translation' is applied to refer to the ways in which the guides transform the 'source text' of the non-European cultural settings into a form that is understandable for the target community, i.e. the students. The concept of 'translating culture' works relatively well in relation to the guides' statements, especially because the 'translation' metaphor is often understood in relation to a conception of 'culture as text' (cf. ibid.). This concept has been criticised for claiming 'a fixed textual meaning all too quickly' (Bachmann-Medick 2012, 104), thereby rendering cultural contexts in terms of homogeneous, text-like, and easily translatable entities. While such an approach is perceived critically in this work, the actions and statements of the guides can be described accordingly. This is because they seek to translate the non-European contexts and objects in understandable and familiar terms. The challenge hinted at in Doris Bachmann-Medick's criticism of 'translation', namely the concomitant construction of holistic source elements, is exactly what is of interest in this work.

Translation can be used as a suitable term to specify the direction of the communication of the guides when they explain or describe cultural practices. While 'communication' is therefore used as an umbrella term for all of the gallery educators' statements as well as the visual representations in the exhibition, translation is used to refer specifically to the guides' aims of making non-European contexts understood.

3.2.3 Speaking about Others

In this work, the practice of 'making non-European contexts understood' is not only described, but also subjected to criticism. This criticism derives from the powerful effect of framing anthropological analysis or experience in the form of a text. As Glenn Bowman has stated,

> It is not enough for the anthropologist to understand the logic of another culture; that logic must be elevated, through translation into a technical and universalising language, into something more authoritative and 'truthful' than anything an indigenous language

> could comprehend. [...] the anthropologist must dismember the world as experienced and reassemble it in accordance with a language that can [...] mark out the anthropologist as one who knows the truth behind phenomena. (2007, 43)

The ordering of information about non-European cultural practices or objects in a text establishes the anthropologist's 'ethnographic authority'. This concept refers to the function of ethnographic analysis to dissolve concrete situations or utterances in the field into 'an englobing context, a 'cultural' reality' (Clifford 1988, 131f.). Ethnographic texts not only document and, partly, construct otherness, but they also function to make a distinction between 'those who can think [...] and those who are thought for by their cultures' (Bowman 2007, 41). These implications of framing information about non-European contexts in the form of text can also be applied to the guides' accounts. In speaking about non-European cultural practices, the guides may establish an analytical distance between themselves and the described contexts. They, thereby, can turn the descriptions of non-European regions into 'cultural reality'.

This authority of the guides to construct cultural is especially important when considering that the ethnographic authority works in concert with other types of authority in the gallery sessions. Besides ethnographic authority, there is also the educational authority of the guides and the cultural authority of the museum. The cultural authority of the museum can be described as its public reliability and trustworthiness. Richard Caputo has defined 'cultural authority' as the 'construction of reality through definitions of fact and value' (1988, 13). The museum is still regarded by many as such an authority that endows knowledge and objects with value and trustworthiness.[37] Educational authority, in turn, is used in the context

---

[37] Despite the still-existing public trust in the museum as a reliable mediator of knowledge, the cultural authority of the ethnographic museum is uncontested. For example, Richard Sandell contemplates how museum displays that are less fixed in time and space (such as pop-up exhibitions or travelling exhibitions) may jeopardise their importance and thus their cultural authority (2005, 191). Similarly,

of this work to refer to the pedagogical and sometimes disciplinary roles that the guides take in order to manage the school groups in the galleries. This kind of authority can further be compared to what Caputo frames as 'social authority'. This concept describes 'control of action through the giving of commands' (cf. ibid.). Due to the combined effect of these three forms of authority, the reality-constituting functions of the communication process in the guided tours have to be acknowledged. As Chapter 3.2.5 shows, such aspects are analysed in this work by referring to the 'worldmaking functions' of the guides' accounts.

Finally, the authority of 'speaking about others' is also related to the process of 'speaking for others'. While these two dimensions cannot be clearly distinguished as 'when one is speaking about others [...], one may also be speaking in place of them' (Alcoff 1992, 9), it is still important to shortly reflect upon the effects that 'speaking for' others, and especially speaking for non-European Others, can have. In *The Problem of Speaking for Others,* Linda Alcoff presents a variety of functions of this practice, many of which are relevant for this work. For instance, she argues that speaking for others, even when practised with good intentions, contains notions of mastery (i.e., correctly understanding another's situation) (cf. ibid., 29), representation (cf. ibid., 9), and responsibility for the other (cf. ibid., 8). This work takes a closer look at the guides' ways of asserting mastery, and, if subconsciously, establish themselves as the ones 'who more correctly understand[s] the truth about another's situation' (cf. ibid., 29).

Tiffany Jenkins writes about the decline of the cultural authority of museums due to an increasing public scrutiny and criticism (2011, 389).

114

3.2.4   Communication as Narrative

The concept of narrative is important in this work not only because a narratological methodology is applied, but also because, as previously mentioned, this concept is commonly used to approach exhibition and museum meanings (cf. Bal 1992, Lidchi 1997, Hourston-Hanks 2012, Tricia Austin 2012, Albano 2014). As a general definition, this work applies Mieke Bal's explanation of narrative texts as texts in which 'an agent relates ('tells') a story in a particular medium […]. A story is a fabula that is presented in a certain manner. A fabula is a series of logically and chronologically related events […]' (1997, 5).

According to this definition, exhibitions can easily be interpreted as forms of narrative. The curator (or the museum perceived as a whole complex) tells a story through the medium of the exhibition. Furthermore, in galleries of non-European art and artefacts, the logically related events can be regarded as historical events, but also as temporally unspecific ritual practices or, as Heike Buschmann has argued, objects and object ensembles (cf. 2010, 154f.). This smooth application of definitions of narrative to exhibitions is the reason for the application of narrative analysis to the exhibition analysis in this work, as described in Chapter 2.

In contrast, the verbal accounts of the gallery educators cannot be perceived as 'narratives' in the same way as the exhibitions because they do not fulfil some important criteria of narrativity. If E.M. Forster's (1962) 'events' are translated into museum objects, as Buschmann suggests (cf. ibid.), one could argue that the guides connect the objects to one another in a sequential order. Yet, this assumption does not really represent what happens during guided tours. Chronological or causal links between individual objects and object ensembles are not always established by the guides. Instead, they lead the students to individual points of the exhibition that are then used, for instance, as starting points for anecdotes or references to materiality. The different elements of the guides' accounts do not necessarily form a coherent whole, as required, however, by Bruner's criterion for narrativity of hermeneutic composability (cf. 1991, 8). While there are moments in the observed guided tours when the gallery educators logically or chronologically link one object to another, storytelling in this strict sense of the term (i.e., with elements linked to each other, an evolving plot, or a development of one storyline from beginning to end) is not the defining or predominant feature of this form of communication.

Because of these differences between the accounts of the guides and the concept of 'narrative', the term is not applied in this work to refer to these particular forms of verbal communication. To impose the term on the material, or the material on the term, would not only do injustice to the aforementioned conceptualisations of 'narrative', but it would also cloud the sight of the broad range of statements that form part of the documented accounts. As already indicated, there are moments of 'storytelling' or 'narrative' embedded within the guides' accounts, but many more statements cannot fully be grasped in terms of narratives. In order to acknowledge both the story-like and the more descriptive forms of communication, the term that is applied throughout to refer to the guide's statements during the guided tours is that of an 'account', which the OED defines as 'a report or description of an event or experience' (OED 2008).

This conceptual distinction does not mean, however, that the insights of narratology are considered irrelevant for the analysis of the guides' accounts. In contrast, as has been explained in the methodology chapter, the analysis applies analytical criteria from narratology. Furthermore, besides the already presented analytical criteria, some conceptual or theoretical implications of the concept of narrative can equally be applied to the analysis of the gallery sessions. For instance, Bruner's criteria of narrative accrual (i.e., the development of stories from prior ones) and normativeness (cf. 1991, 15-20) can be applied to the analysis in order to provide insight into how the guides' accounts are developed and how they impart not only information, but also norms and principles. Ansgar Nünning's criteria of the eventfulness of events (cf. 2010, 199) could, similarly, be applied to understand which kind of objects or information are selected in the guided tours. By exploring whether the relevance, the unpredictability, the sequentiality, the irreversibility or the singularity (cf. ibid.) of information determines their emphasis in the sessions, it is possible to discuss preferences in the selection of specific pieces of information about the non-European regions.

3.2.5   Worldmaking and Narrative Worldmaking

An important benefit of applying conceptual approaches from narratology to the analysis in this work results from their reference to the relationship between storytelling and authority. As mentioned above, authority plays a crucial role in this work. Questions about the ways in which authority is established during gallery sessions and about the kinds of authority that emerge in these situations (cultural, ethnographic, educational) are important for various reasons. Not only is it crucial to generally reflect upon truth claims in museums because of the institution's public credibility, but it is especially important to subject authoritative truth claims about non-European contexts to critical scrutiny because of the problems of representation discussed in the section on 'otherness'. As Ravelli explains, exhibitions construct relevance of the content they show and thereby claim that it is worthwhile knowledge to learn (cf. 2006, 139). Such claims of relevance and trustworthiness can be deconstructed particularly fruitfully with the help of the concept of 'worldmaking', which is applied throughout the analysis.

The theory of 'worldmaking' has been introduced by Nelson Goodman (1978) and has been elaborated into narrative worldmaking by David Herman (2009) and Ansgar Nünning (2010). Starting out from Cassirer's thesis about the multiplicity of worlds that are created through symbols (Cassirer 1946 qtd. In Goodman 1978, 1), Goodman explains that this multiplicity is rather to be understood as a simultaneity of multiple perspectives and ways of describing the world (cf. 1978, 3). These perspectives are determined by frames of reference which cannot be overcome when speaking about the world (cf. ibid.). That means that, when there is a requirement to speak about the world, it is impossible to portray an 'undescribed' world independent of a frame of reference. Applied to the realm of museums, the representations communicated in exhibitions can only ever account for one (or some, depending on the acceptance of different perspectives) world versions, which, however, claim truth and rightness about the world as such (i.e., the real world).

Furthermore, Goodman clarifies that the worlds that are made in the process of describing them are made from other, prior worlds (cf. ibid., 6). According to him, ways of worldmaking are ways of 'building a world out of others' (ibid.). He introduces practices of composition, weighting, ordering, deletion, and deformation (cf. ibid., 6-17) which represent methods of reconstructing already existing worlds into new worlds.[38]

---

[38] As becomes clear from these elaborations, the concept of 'worldmaking' shares many aspects with 'mythology': Myths equally work on the basis of previously existing meanings. As Roland Barthes has explained, '[m]ythical speech is made of a material that has already been worked on so as to make it suitable for communication' (1957, 108). Barthes conceptualises myth as the process of transforming an already existing sign into the signifier of a new sign (cf. ibid., 113). In this process of re-using an old meaning (the sign) as a new form (the signifier), the older meaning loses its contingency (cf. ibid., 116). This system of meaning compares to Goodman's theory according to which the representation of 'a world' relies upon being perceived as the 'real world'. Despite these overlaps between mythology and worldmaking, worldmaking is used in this work to refer to the general process of staging cultural realities because it is not bound to structuralist semiotics, but can be applied more comprehensively to large-scale processes of constructing and naturalising compelling systems of meaning. While the term 'myth' can be used in the analysis to refer to specific stereotypes or ideas about otherness that the guides or exhibitions communicate, 'worldmaking' is regarded as a more overarching function of museum narratives and the guides' accounts about non-European Others. Worldmaking not only recognises a conceptual shift from one meaning to another (like mythology), but relates to the staging and

118

Such practices of producing new meanings or worlds from pre-existing ones are crucial in understanding the workings of museum communication. The arrangement of the objects, their descriptions in text panels, as well as the guides' accounts are marked by strategies of selection, arrangement and weighting of former meanings. Through these strategies, an imaginative new 'world' is constructed around the object, or else the object becomes integrated into the constructed world that is already in place in the museum. This process relates to what Kirshenblatt-Gimblett has explained with respect to ethnographic museums and the construction of the objects therein:

> Posited meaning derives not from the original context of the fragments but from their juxtaposition in a new context. As a space of abstraction, exhibitions do for the life world what the life world cannot do for itself. They bring together specimen and artefacts never found in the same place at the same time and show relationships that cannot otherwise be seen. (1998, 3)

The mere displacement of an object from its prior context, and its integration into an abstract situation in which its purpose is transformed from utilisation into either aesthetic appreciation or cultural signification, can be regarded as the creation of a world in which a new system of meaning is superimposed on prior meanings. This constellation further relates to what Svetlana Alpers has called the 'museum effect', the tendency of museums to '[...] isolate something from its world, to offer it up for attentive looking and thus to transform it into art like our own' (1991, 27). The new 'world' that is constructed around the object in the gallery is posited as the legitimate one. The artefacts may, thus, no longer be regarded as religiously powerful or ritualistic elements, but become posited primarily in terms of scientific interpretation and factual description. Further

---

naturalisation of entire realities and world versions complete with imaginative settings, characters, moral value systems, and practices. The specific myths or stereotypes of otherness that the guides communicate both reinforce and are perceived through the lens of these worlds that are suggested and naturalised in the exhibition.

processes of explication (by text panels, by gallery educators) can be understood as additional layers of meaning, which elaborate and verify the world version represented in the exhibition. Worldmaking is, hence, intrinsic to communication in the museum. The concept is perfectly suitable to describe meaning-making processes in the museum not only because of its emphasis on *active* practices, but also because it points to the normalisation of the created worlds: As Henrietta Lidchi has explained, the trust of visitors in the exhibition's reflection of reality is achieved by a process of normalising the visual narrative through the arrangement of objects and texts (i.e., photographs proof that artefacts were 'really' used like this; texts proof that the arrangement of the objects is authentic, etc.) (cf. 1997, 173). Through the self-affirming interplay of the arrangement of the exhibition space and the guides' accounts, the world that is presented in the museum becomes naturalised.

While Goodman's ways of worldmaking are already helpful in unravelling meaning-making strategies in the material, another concept in connection with worldmaking provides a deeper understanding of these processes, namely the concept of narrative worldmaking. As explained, this concept represents a development of Goodman's theory. David Herman, who has introduced 'narrative worldmaking', proposes that 'people use storytelling practices to build, update and modify narrative worlds' (2009, 71). While Herman argues that all of Goodman's practices of worldmaking could be applied to narratives as well (cf. ibid., 78), he adds concepts such as accommodation, which describes the imaginative relocation of readers to the storyworld (Lewis qt. in Herman 2009, 80) or minimal departure, which refers to readers filling in the gaps in the story with information from their own life world (Ryan qt. in Herman 2009, 81). Although Herman discusses these aspects in relation to fictional texts, it is not a far stretch to apply them to the communication in museums. During the guided tours, students are confronted with narrative worlds constructed and described by the gallery educators (on the basis of the worlds presented in the exhibition narrative). Students may imaginatively relocate to these worlds and they may fill in missing information by means of assumptions they draw from their own experience

Besides these analytical gains from the concept of narrative worldmaking, another function of narrative worlds plays a key role in the museum context: the construction of coherence through storytelling. Ansgar Nünning refers to this function in his reflections on narrative worldmaking when he writes about the crucial point of ordering narrative worlds (cf. 2010, 203) through emplotment (White 1973 qt. ibid., 203) and links this to Frederic Jameson's 'ideology of the form' (Jameson 1983 qt. ibid., 204). He argues that these concepts demonstrate how a sequence of events is transformed into a story (cf. ibid.). In relation to visual and verbal communication in the museum, narrative worldmaking can, therefore, equally be seen as a means of understanding how prior, often confusing information are arranged into seemingly coherent and ordered storyworlds. As has already been indicated in Chapter 3.1.4, this construction of coherence is an important appeal of the ethnographic museums. In the analysis of the guides accounts, attention is, therefore, similarly paid to the workings and implications of this coherence.

3.3   Performance and Performativity

As already mentioned at the beginning of this overview of sensitising concepts, the guided tour cannot only be regarded in terms of narratological concepts, but equally entails performative aspects. These aspects do not exhaust themselves in the gestures or movements of the guides, but are intrinsic to the entire practice of guiding meaning, speaking in front of others, and giving instructions.

There are many definitions of and approaches to performance and performativity, which, due to the scope of this research project, cannot all be accounted for here. The most basic premise that the following elaborations are all based upon, however, is that of the distinction between performance and performativity suggested by Judith Butler (1993):

> [...] performance as bounded 'act' is distinguished from performativity insofar as the latter consists in a reiteration of norms which precede, constrain, and exceed the performer and in that sense, cannot be taken as the fabrication of the performer's 'will' or 'choice'; further, what is 'performed' works to conceal, if not to disavow, what remains opaque, unconscious, un-performable. The reduction of performativity to performance would be a mistake. (Butler 1993, 24)

This distinction between performance as an act and performativity as the process of reiterating norms has also been framed by Eve Kosofsky Sedgwick as the theatrical dimension of performance, on the one hand, and its deconstructive or speech-act-related dimension on the other (cf. 2003, 7).

In this work, both of these perspectives are relevant. The guided tour can be regarded as an act; as something that the performer (i.e., the guide) presents to an audience (i.e., the students) who consciously perceive it as a performance. At the same time, the guided tour can contain instances that point to an unconscious reiteration of pre-existing norms. The example of the guides' change of accent described in the introduction would, for instance, reflect both the dimension of a conscious performance and the dimension of a reiteration of norms.

Having clarified this basic understanding of performance as both a theatrical act and as an unconscious reiteration of norms, the following pages further elaborate the concept of performance and its usage in this work by focusing on three dimensions of performative practices that are relevant for the analysis. The following elaborations help to limit the analytical focus because, with respect to performance, many different aspects could be looked at. Jenny Kidd has argued, for instance, that understandings of performance have become very nuanced, so that everyday activities like visiting a museum could be analysed as a performance (cf. 2012, 74). This and other interpretations of performance are, however, not further contemplated in this work. While it is true that a visit to the museum is a performance in itself, this notion is not of particular interest with reference to the research question posed here. The students do not predominantly want to express something to their peers by going to the museum – the visit is part of their mandatory school education. Hence, the dimensions of performance that are considered below have been chosen because they are related to the construction of cultural otherness in the specific situation of the guided tour.

3.3.1   Spaces and Visitors as Performers of Museum Narratives

As already explained in relation to museum communication, worlds are made not only through narratives, but also through performances. The agency of this 'performative worldmaking' is not limited to the practices of the museum, but 'worlds' can also be performed by the visitors. When Mieke Bal describes that the (implied) focaliser of an exhibition narrative is the visitor who perceives the order of the objects and constructs a story thereafter (cf. 1992, 561), this storying process also contains performative moments. In museum studies, this performative power of the visitor has been emphasised over the last decades, coinciding with the opening up of museums to participatory and interactive agendas. As Tricia Austin has made clear, '[t]he visitor can pause, touch, smell, listen and discuss exhibits with people who they came with. [...] They are immersed and entangled in the story-world through narrative, perception and embodiment' (2012, 112). Similarly, Albano speaks of a 'sensorial immersion' (2014, 4) of the body of the visitor in the museum. These practices also have an effect on the objects. Charles Garoian has put forward the idea that visitors, by means of the utterances they make about the objects on display, perform an action or do something *to* the objects: 'Thus, viewers' saying things about works of art [...] represents the act of doing [...]' (2001, 235). He draws on J.L. Austin (1997 [1969]) to suggest that such performative speech acts are more empowering for visitors than constative speech, which he understands as curators' academic assumptions such as 'Picasso was a cubist' (cf. ibid.).

Such optimistic suggestions (i.e., visitors can perform meanings in the museum by means of their utterances) can and should be relativised by questioning in how far the performative speech acts of visitors are in fact ways of expressing themselves or their own subjectivities. This question relates to Derrida's critique of Austin's speech act theory. Derrida doubts that the performative utterance really transforms a situation or constitutes its internal structure, as Austin suggests (cf. Derrida 1988, 13f.). He claims that, before an illocutory or perlocutory shaping of a statement unfolds, the locution itself already entails a system of predicates which 'blurs [...] all the oppositions that follow' (cf. ibid., 14). This assumption again refers to the iterability of statements and performances. The performative utterance does not transform a situation, but repeat a certain pattern or predicate that is captured within it. In relation to performing the museum and its authority, it, then, seems that Garoian's view that visitors can 'embody, signify, and re-present new museum narratives' (2001, 239) is a utopia that disregards determining factors in visitors' actions and utterances such as learned 'ways of speaking' in and about museums and objects, the social desirability of statements in the museum space, as well as the cultural authority of the museum.

This aspect of the predetermination of performative action in the museum space is an important part of the conceptualisation of this work. As the analysis aims at a critical reflection on communications of otherness in gallery sessions, the focus is particularly on the limitations and boundaries that the meaning-making practice of the guided tour causes. The work is, in part, concerned with degree to which the students are introduced to the predicates of speaking (about otherness, about the museum) in the museum during such guided tours. In this sense, the guides' performance could be regarded as a reiteration of norms that prescribe 'how to be' in the museum. Such questions directly refer to the third research question in that they address the issue of how communications of otherness in the guided tour are developed and by whom they are determined. This aspect of the performative agency or predetermination of the students in the museum is, thus, addressed in Chapter 5.

Another dimension of this predetermination of performative action is the design of the exhibition spaces. The ways in which museum spaces are designed can also lead visitors to certain actions, which is why these spaces can be regarded as 'performative' themselves. By walking through the galleries that guide visitors in a certain way, they (unconsciously) perform the exhibition narrative. While the matter of premeditated ways of speaking about objects and galleries does not appear in Garoian's paper, he does allude to the 'environmental conditions that evoke bodily responses in viewers' (2001, 246f.). Some of the elements of this environment that he mentions are the regulation of temperature and humidity, the choreographing of visitors through the architecture, as well as the lighting (cf. ibid.).

This predetermination through space can, however, again be perceived from a different perspective, namely in terms of the agency that visitors have in performing the spaces. For instance, in a study by Jenny Kidd, it becomes clear that visitors construct their own memories and autobiographies on the basis of the exhibition narratives (cf. 2012):

> The physicality of the museum thus played a pivotal role in contextualizing the performance, and the various rememberings that it elicited. The architecture is both a comforting reminder of the fixity of history and heritage (as we have come to understand it), and a guilty party in the narrative being portrayed. There is a peculiar aptness to its frame. In the best and worst senses, it appears as one respondent commented, 'you are surrounded by history in a museum'. Being immersed in such a space, for all of these reasons,

> enables the autobiographical narratives that we have seen above to
> emerge. (2012, 80)

Garoian similarly speaks of the performance or construction of one's own autobiography through the experiences one has in the museum (cf. 2001, 241f.). Even when, due to the aforementioned restrictions of utterances about museums and objects, the memories and autobiographies that visitors construct on the basis of exhibitions remain in their own thoughts, this construction needs to be acknowledged as an individual process of meaning making. Similarly, it is likely that students participating in the guided tour will connect what they see in the exhibition to their own experiences and memories.

Yet, as Kidd's statement equally shows, the museum site still provides a frame for such memories and autobiographies to emerge. This means that there can be counter-practices of visitors that oppose intended meanings in a way that is not foreseen by the museum, but that the relationship between visitors and spaces must rather be seen as in constant interaction and mutual determination.

3.3.2   Putting the Other on Stage

Besides in terms of spaces or visitors who 'perform' museum narratives, 'performance' is also understood in this work more concretely to refer to the staging of non-European practices or contexts in the gallery. 'Putting the Other on stage' can, then, refer to all processes of orchestrating otherness in the museum that play a role during the guided tour.

Once again, this putting on stage can be related to the agency of the space. For instance, as already mentioned, Kirshenblatt-Gimblett refers to the notion of the spectacle when she addresses in-situ displays. She argues that such displays bear the dangers of undermining scientific seriousness and of overwhelming both the ethnographic object and the curatorial intention (cf. 1998, 21). This issue can be applied to the guided tour in so far as the explanations and descriptions of gallery educators could also be undermined by the affective impression that in-situ displays evoke.

Apart from spatial means of putting the Other on stage, the guides' accounts about non-European contexts can equally be regarded as performances. With regard to Austin's speech act theory (1997 [1969]) and Searle's classification of illocutionary acts (1976), it is possible to interpret the guides' statements about the Other as means of performing the Other. According to Searle's classification, the guides' truth claims about otherness could be regarded as 'representatives' because the purpose of statements such as 'in culture x, people have large families' is to 'commit the speaker (in varying degrees) to something's being the case, to the truth of the expressed proposition (cf. Searle 1976, 10). This process again refers to what has already been stated with regard to speaking about the Other. The guide puts the Other on stage by speaking about or for them – the claims they make evoke the (absent) Other.

Another form of 'putting the Other on stage' can unfold by means of processes of speaking *as* the Other. As an interesting form of embodying the Other, gallery educators can also evoke otherness by becoming or 'playing' the non-European. This is, once again, the case in the situation of the guide who changes her accent. By performing her own 'Africanness', the guide puts otherness on stage. Such means of performance are regarded in this work in terms of the aforementioned concepts of performance and performativity. These practices of embodiment accordingly contain notions of performance, i.e. conscious enactment (the students know they are repeating the practice after the guide and that they only 'pretend' to greet each other) as well as notions of performativity, i.e., unconscious enactment (the students are not aware that they represent the Other, or that they perform the Other's otherness by repeating practices that seem particularly traditional to them).

3.3.3 The Presentation of Self in Everyday Life

Finally, another dimension of performance in the guided tour concerns the guides' self-representation, which can be related to Goffman's theory of *The Presentation of self in Everyday Life.* Drawing on Goffman, the guides' self-representations in the interviews are interactions (cf. 1965, 8) while their activities during the guided tours can be understood as the front of a performance, i.e. what the performer does while an audience (consisting of the students and the teachers) is watching (cf. ibid., 13). One could argue that even this performance transforms, at some points, into an interaction, given that the students and the guides do interact in some parts of the guided tour. Yet, the approach that is applied here regards the guided tour mainly as a performance (or, when its descriptive aspects are concerned, as an account). On the one hand, this perspective is taken because the interactive parts of the guided tour are often not genuinely interactive in that they are marked by the guides leading the students to a narrative or explanation that they already had in mind. On the other hand, especially when it comes to the guides' self-representation, what needs to be considered is the overall situation, which entails a person standing in front of a group of people, performing (translating, explaining, facilitating) the exhibition and the cultural context on display. It is, thus, important to understand how the guides position themselves and perform expertise in this overall performance that they deliver.

An important aspect, in this context, is the degree to which the guides believe in the role that they are playing (cf. ibid., 10). Goffman argues that one can be cynical (not believing in one's performance) or sincere (believing in one's performance) when performing the self. Although it may not be possible to achieve a full answer to the question of the sincerity of the guides (due to the guides' self-representation in the interest of social desirability during the interviews), the analysis points out divergences between their self-representations in the guided tour and in the interviews. Such divergences may also contribute to explaining the motivations and reasons for communicating otherness according to the themes and strategies resulting from the analysis.

Another dimension that can be applied to the guided tour is Goffman's distinction between appearance and manner (cf. ibid., 15). While appearance describes the 'temporary ritual state' of performers or their social status, manner is used to relate to their behaviour (cf. ibid.). In the guided tour, this distinction can be applied to the difference between the general position of the guides, which may be the same in all the observed cases, and the individual aspects of their behaviour during the sessions. This distinction between permanent and flexible traits is interesting with regard to a reflection on those means of performance that the guides can affect or alter, and those that they cannot change. For example, it is questionable in how far a guide can actually avoid being perceived as an expert or authority because this may be inscribed in their appearance rather than in their manner. However, the manner of the guides can still have an impact on how this expertise is interpreted when they, for instance, either point to diverse possible meanings of a given cultural practice or try to convince the students of one presented, single truth. One of the interests of the analysis is, therefore, in how far the guides try to dismantle the authority that is inherent in their position, and in how far they reinforce it.

3.4   The Guided Tour: Between Product and Process

As already indicated, this work understands the guides' accounts and performative practices as forms of museum communication. The focus of the analysis is, thus, on the production side of the communication process. The work reflects upon the ways in which the guides speak about otherness and puts these ways of speaking into the broader context of the exhibition narrative and the museum.

The disadvantage of this approach may be found in the fact that the perspective of the learners is only of marginal interest. Neither are the actual learning outcomes of the guided tours measured, nor are the students' perceptions of 'non-Europeanness' considered before and after the guided tours. How can this exclusion be justified, especially with regard to museum educational scholarship that emphasises the learner's internal meaning-making practices which transform museum narratives into personal stories that are connected to and determined by individual experiences and prior knowledge (cf. Hein 1994, Hooper-Greenhill 2007)?

The legitimacy of an analysis that focuses predominantly on the production of meaning within and through the museum, instead of studying the meanings that the students make and take home, derives from to main arguments.

The first point concerns the difference between institutional responsibility and student agency. Although the meanings that the guides offer may be interpreted differently by each individual student, the underlying cultural meanings that are suggested and woven into the gallery educators' accounts provide much insight into the ways in which accepted understandings of otherness are constructed, reinforced or negotiated. As the guides' performances and statements can already be seen as the result of social meaning-making processes, the representations implicit in these messages are at least as interesting for a reflection on the construction of non-European otherness as visitor interpretations would be. Yet, in this work, these signifying practices of the guides and the museums are considered even more interesting than the signifying practices of the visitors. This preference can be explained by the responsibility that results from the position of the guides' accounts as official 'knowledge' in a public institution. Due to the worldmaking function of the exhibitions and the guides' accounts, the notions of otherness articulated during guided tours must be acknowledged as powerful means

130

of the social construction of meaning. In a similar vein, Richard Sandell has rightly argued that

> [...] there are inherent dangers within this perspective. A celebration of audience over media agency should not be appropriated to deny the potential influence (and the concomitant social responsibility) of those who directly shape cultural spaces – curators, architects, designers and increasingly educators and other museum practitioners – determining what is displayed, how and with what purpose in mind. (2005, 186)

By adding gallery educators to the list of those who shape cultural spaces, this work, hence, pays special attention to the guides' 'media agency' as representatives of the museums. In so doing, the students' ability to draw their own conclusions is not denied or ignored. Yet, the analysis emphasises the responsibility of the museum as a public institution to be aware of the implications and suggestions implied in its representations.

The second argument is related to the alleged participatory nature of museum educational measures in museums today. If students are directly involved in the meaning-making process by means of a dialogical communication form and by including their own interpretations of objects and cultural practices in the guided tours, the question is whether it is still legitimate to think of the guided tour as a production by the museum. Yet, as already mentioned, only few guided tours are genuinely dialogical in nature. In many of the observed sessions, participation is encouraged on a methodological level, but not so much in terms of the content that the guides communicate to the students. For instance, while the students are often asked to guess at the original purpose of an object, 'wrong' guesses are rarely acknowledged or further discussed. Instead, the guides usually correct the students and explain what the 'proper' answer is. This constellation shows that the guides at least attempt to control the process of signification in the guided tours. Furthermore, as students and teachers come with the expectation to learn something about the regions on display, an entirely participative framing of the guided tour may even be difficult to put into practice.

While it, thus, makes sense to mainly conceive of the guided tour as a product of museum communication and to focus on the themes and practices evident within the accounts of the guides, this work still acknowledges that processual dimensions are important in the analysis. This processual dimension refers not only to the actual performance of the guided tour, which may be constantly interrupted by comments or actions of the students and teachers, but also to the development of the session formats, to the training of the gallery educators, as well as to their individual choices throughout the sessions. The guided tour must, therefore, be analysed both as a museum representation (i.e., product) and as a complex practice or conversation (i.e., process).

In the logic of the structure of this work, this in-between position is reflected in the separation of the analytical chapters. Chapter 4 documents the recurring patterns of speaking about and performing otherness during the guided tours. It, thus, focuses on the guided tour as a product or museum representation. Chapter 5 explains and contextualises the discovered themes and practices by reflecting upon the influence of different actors on the formation and performance of the sessions. Thereby, the processual practices that shape the guided tour are acknowledged by understanding it as a process.

4 Themes and Practices of Communicating Non-European Otherness in the Observed Guided Tours

The following analysis of gallery educators' accounts about non-European objects and cultural practices not only contributes to assessing and understanding the construction of cultural otherness in contemporary ethnographic museums, but it also provides insights into common, 'publicly acceptable' ways of speaking about non-European regions. As the chapter shows, the ways in which these regions are rendered legible by gallery educators are still often indicative of recurring patterns informed by an alleged internal homogeneity, authenticity, and remoteness of the regions displayed in the museums. While some of the guides' explanations challenge and destabilise oft-repeated myths and stereotypes about Africa or Asia, many of their statements are embedded in, and therefore reinforce, essentialist conceptions of non-European regions and associated cultural practices. Arguing from a transcultural perspective, this work considers such representations problematic not only because they are based upon an idea of culture that suggests insurmountable determination by origin and ethnicity and, hence, ignores processes of hybridity and cultural entanglement, but also because they fail to question modernist conceptions of the non-European Other as distinct and distant. In correspondence with the first and second research questions posed in the beginning of this work, the analysis of the guides' accounts seeks to explore in what ways and with what implications fix and internalised distinctions between 'us' and 'them' persist in educational measures of ethnographic museums.

Before the first recurring patterns in the communication of the guides are explained, the following introductory remarks serve to elucidate the structure of the work and the position of the chapter within it. After briefly clarifying the analytical distinction between Chapters 4 and 5, the logic and organisation of this fourth chapter is presented.

The main analytical findings of this work are presented in this chapter and the fifth chapter. These findings are developed by critically investigating both the ways in which the guides communicate and perform non-European otherness and the factors that influence their statements and communicative practices. For the purpose of clarity, these two analytical processes (i.e., analysing the contents of the guided tours and recapitulating the systems of meaning that affect them) are distributed among two chapters. While this chapter, as explained above, explores *what* the guides say about non-European regions, the subsequent chapter sheds light on *how* their accounts come about. Whereas Chapter 4, thus, critically scrutinises representations and imaginations of otherness in the guided tours and discusses their implications, Chapter 5 serves to put the accounts in a wider context. This separation of the message from its contexts and determining factors may appear artificial because it is not representative of the experienced reality. By making this distinction, the work pursues two main aims. First, it seeks to provide a clear analysis of both the contents and the contexts of the guided tour. Condensing these two dimensions into one would result in an oversized chapter that – for simple reasons of complexity and mass – would fail to give proper credit to the different dimensions of either the contents or the contexts.

Second, the explication of critical implications of the guides' ways of speaking about non-European regions is separated from the consideration of specific influencing factors in order to avoid a dilution of the critical angle. Regardless of the reasons for their emergence, many of the outlined accounts of the guides are problematic because they subtly construct the homogeneity, distance, and ultimate difference of the regions and people that they are concerned with. As these constructions of otherness occur in public, and even more so within an institution that is perceived as trustworthy, they need to be seen as cultural texts representing and reinforcing socially accepted ways of speaking about non-European regions. To critically discuss these common tropes and imaginations of non-Europeanness and to deconstruct them by taking a transcultural perspective is, therefore, a key concern of this work, which is separate from its second aim to explain and comprehend why these messages come into being, and which actors are involved in this process.

This chapter, therefore, presents seven recurring themes and practices of communicating non-European otherness, which have emerged from the analysis of the observed gallery sessions. The analysis is structured according to these seven common patterns: Each practice or theme is described and interpreted in detail and under consideration of the different forms it can take, as well as their implications. Examples from the material are used as much as possible, however, for reasons of conciseness, in some sections only one representative example is given to exemplify a pattern, while other similar situations are only mentioned briefly. Despite the structurally separate analysis of each theme or practice, the seven presented phenomena should not be regarded as entirely separate or fixed entities. In contrast, as becomes apparent in the analysis, many of these patterns are related to each other, and work by similar means. These connections are frequently highlighted through references within the individual subchapters. Furthermore, while these recurring themes and practices should not be interpreted as a typology of all the statements that the guides make during the gallery sessions, they give an overview of the similarities in the guides' ways of speaking about and performing non-European otherness.

The seven recurring patterns consist, as already mentioned, of *themes*, i.e. topics that are frequently addressed with respect to otherness, and recurring *practices*, i.e. strategies that are used consciously or unconsciously to speak about the objects and the cultural contexts on display. As some patterns could be regarded as both themes and practices, however, a distinct labelling of the observed phenomena as either one or the other is not applied in the analysis. Instead, the patterns observed in the guides' accounts are discussed both in terms of their recurring thematic patterns as well as in relation to the strategical or practical functions that they could have.

A critical point to additionally note with respect to the following remarks is that, in this chapter, the seven communicative patterns in the guides' accounts are regarded as relatively separate from the meanings provided in the exhibitions. This separate consideration of the statements of the guides is important because, during the sessions, the gallery educators do not extensively explain specific objects, but mainly provide additional information about cultural practices, rituals, and traditions. These 'additional' aspects are often not directly represented in the galleries themselves, but can be perceived as extensions of the exhibitions. While some links between the guides' explanations and the descriptions in the exhibition can be found, the presented ways of speaking and performing non-European otherness are often to be seen as the results of more personal or spontaneous comments and anecdotes that are not represented in the exhibitions. In Chapter 4, the guides' explanations are, therefore, considered as separate forms of communicating non-European otherness because the focus of the sessions is on their verbal explanations and performances. Chapter 5 subsequently acknowledges the relations between the guides' accounts and the exhibition narratives.

Finally, a particular focus during the analysis is placed on what is called the 'disimprovement effect' of museum education. This effect refers to a recurring pitfall in the observed guided tours: The gallery educators' often aim at raising the students' awareness for difference or at facilitating tolerance and respect, but in their attempts to do so, they unintendedly end up essentialising and stereotyping the Other. This 'disimprovement effect' can be observed in almost all of the described recurring themes and practices because the vast majority of the gallery educators' statements are guided by 'good intentions'. As the analysis shows, however, these good intentions are often implicated in notions of 'welcoming' the stranger, which Ahmed has rightly criticised as a subtle way of producing and manifesting 'the figure of the stranger' (2000, 4). In this chapter, this dilemma is pointed out wherever relevant as an implication of the guides' accounts. In Chapter 5, the 'disimprovement effect' is again taken up and put in context with the different factors that shape the gallery sessions.

4.1 Promoting Cultural Diversity

The first recurring theme of communicating otherness that is discussed in this chapter effectively illustrates the described contradiction of the 'disimprovement effect'. In many of the observed guided tours, the gallery educators emphasise the cultural diversity of the regions they address in their sessions, but, in doing so, they freeze and compartmentalise cultural identities. Their elaborations, intended to make the students aware of a diversification of meaning, carry messages that entail categorisations of people that confine meaning. For instance, the following two examples from Christine's session and Britta's session in Museum B, are indicative of this problem.

C: A short question to begin with: You have already dealt with Africa a little [at school]. What would you say is THE feature of Africa or of this part of the world? If you wanted to set Africa apart from all the other countries. What distinguishes Africa?
S: […].
S: Diversity?
C: Great. Exactly. That is what I wanted to hear. Diversity. In how far did you hear about this diversity?
S: In terms of the music, the peoples, and the religion, and also in terms of the languages.
C: Great. Then you already know the most important thing. Because this is what (-) if Europeans look at Africa, is sometimes forgotten. If, for example, one has a guest and then one says this is someone from Africa. And one does not speak about the country where he is from or the people that he is from. In many countries, there are more than a hundred peoples and languages. Und one has the feeling that in

Africa everything is somehow similar. And this is not the case at all. It's the continent with the most cultures and languages and peoples. And with the most differences.

(GSC-MB, 42-62)

B: We are now going to Asia. There are a lot of different countries there. And they are in part very different from each other. We sometimes merge them all into one. This is a problem because for us people in China, Japan Korea all look... (makes a pause for the students to fill in the gap)

S: Similar?

B: Similar. But when they come to us to Europe, then they think we are all / (again makes a pause for the answer, but there is no reaction from the students). Which swear word do they use for us? Do you know this? A word for foreigners? Look, (points at her nose) /

S: Pointed?

S: White?

S: Arrogant?

B: They do not say that we have a pointed nose. But a long nose. The Chinese at least. They like to call us long noses. Zhăng biz. Well, this is not so nice. Some people do not even have such long noses. [...] Therefore everyone always looks the same. Regardless of whether we come from France, the Netherlands or Switzerland. They cannot distinguish us either.

(GSB-MB, 81-98)

These two examples show the ambivalences that exist within the guides' statements. While claiming that there are many differences in relation to the languages, cultures and 'peoples' of the areas that they refer to, certain binary distinctions (Europe vs. Africa, Europe vs. Asia) and cultural stereotypes (Africa's cultural 'richness', 'Asians' all look the same to Europeans) are reinforced.

In the following, three critical implications of these statements are further explained to show the different dimensions of this recurring phenomenon. The first dimension concerns the guides' descriptive references to the diversity of the respective regions, which are embedded in traditional anthropological practices of cultural categorisation, and must be critically scrutinised from a transcultural standpoint. The second dimension moves from analysing the descriptive notions of these accounts to their prescriptive implications by addressing the multiculturalist ideals of

138

'our' behaviour towards 'them' that underlie the guides' promotion of cultural diversity. The third dimension combines the descriptive with the prescriptive level by showing how both the traditional anthropological and the multiculturalist framing of 'cultural diversity' subtly perpetuate power hierarchies and the dominant order.

4.1.1   Categorising Culture

In the two statements quoted above, the guides refer to diversity by initially positing negative examples of expected or common generalisations about 'Africa' and 'Asia' (e.g. 'one has the feeling that in Africa everything is somehow similar', '[w]e sometimes merge them all into one'). Subsequently, they counter these generalisations by alluding to the diversity of the respective regions. Yet, diversity, as it is framed in these statements, is a problematic counterargument because it counters broad generalisations with generalisations on a smaller level. For instance, the diversity promoted in Christine's account refers to the multiplicity of peoples[39] and is, thus, still predicated on the internal homogeneity of these peoples or cultures, even if these notions can be seen as smaller entities than entire countries or continents. Hence, Christine considers the ascriptions of African guests to 'Africa' inappropriate, but their ascription to specific cultures or ethnic groups legitimate. Similarly, in the second example, Britta's criticism is directed at making generalisations about Asia as a whole, but, if the individual countries in Asia are carefully distinguished from one another, there seems to be no problem. In her explanations, 'the Chinese' are still represented as a homogeneous entity.

The guides' references to diversity are, thus, connected to matters of categorising non-European regions rather than acknowledging social, educational, economic or individual differences among them. As Christine

---

[39] Christine uses 'peoples' in the sense of 'native peoples', as suggested by the German term 'Völker'.

and Britta initially criticise generalisations on a very broad level (Africa, Asia), the diversity that they then propose is connected to smaller (countries, 'ethnic groups' or 'peoples', languages, 'cultures'), yet similarly generalising, categories. Accordingly, Christine explains that 'in many countries, there are more than one hundred peoples and languages'. The underlying suggestion is that it is important to acknowledge diversity *between* these compartmentalised 'peoples' or 'cultures', but not within them. It appears from these statements, when 'one has the feeling that in Africa everything is somehow similar', one merely fails to apply the correct categorisation of people into smaller language-, ethnic-, or culture groups.

This understanding of diversity goes back to an idea of 'cultures' as homogeneous entities that has been self-explanatory in ethnology until quite recently. As Karl-Heinz Kohl writes in his introduction to ethnology, the discipline is concerned with small demographic groups that are marked by a 'homogeneity of language and culture' (2000, 29):

> [...] small peoples differ from bigger ones in that they are marked by a larger degree of coherence and homogeneity. Here we can neither find considerable cultural nor linguistic internal differentiation, such as dialectal deviations or class-specific ways of speaking. Even when stratified societies are concerned, lifestyles and value systems of the upper classes do not diverge much from those of the lower. Similarly, in the realms of economy, politics, law and religion areas, the degree of differentiation is definitely lower than over here. (ibid.)

This definition of ethnology as concerned with homogeneous, coherent, smaller 'peoples' can be connected to Britta's and Christine's statements. Although their categories are not that small, particularly in terms of their references to the level of the countries, they do refer to smaller entities that appear to be marked by internal homogeneity. Especially Christine's reference to 'cultures' and 'peoples' relates more closely to Kohl's definition.

From a transcultural perspective, this conception of 'cultures' as closed-off 'peoples' needs to be questioned. As explained above, exchange, interrelations, conflict, and assertions of identity are crucial categories through which to understand the process of cultural identification. Even if some African 'peoples' appeared homogeneous from the outside, a historical reflection on processes of community building through dispute and socialisation would counter the idea that these 'smaller peoples' can be generalised. Accordingly, Andreas Ackermann asks '[w]ith hybridity, one has to ask, which culture is not hybrid – and have 'original' cultures ever existed?' (2012, 5). From this angle, an interest of ethnology in 'homogeneous cultures' is problematic, not only because it denies the possibility of outside influences and individual differences, but also because it constructs cultures as clearly identifiable and representable entities. It is, thus, not legitimate to presuppose homogeneity for all the 'peoples' in Africa, especially if this homogeneity is, as in Kohl's definition, verified by means of a comparison with the situation 'over here': To measure the degree of inner differentiation 'in our terms' means to disregard local markers of differentiation and divergence. A view that unquestionably adopts the idea of remote, homogeneous 'cultures' justifies vague generalisations like those proposed in Christine's and Britta's statements and hence leads to representations of non-European regions in terms of neatly categorised language and culture groups, which must be seen, however, as rationalising myths rather than as forms of deeper engagement with actual intricacies of appropriation, transformation, and differentiation.

Similar forms of categorisation are evident in frequent references of the guides to the 'peoples', 'cultures', or 'ethnic groups' represented in the museum (cf. e.g. GSA-MA, 95; GSB-MB, 295). Although larger entities are always represented as diverse – this is something that most of the guides mention at some part of their sessions – diversity *within* is not acknowledged when speaking about 'the Polynesians' (Antonia), 'the Indians' (referring to Native Americans) (Doreen), and 'the Indians' (Eva). Of course, these are often unquestioned and handy categories to refer to, not merely because they relate to the separation of the galleries according to similarly generalised categories, but also because educational sessions that are expected to mediate non-European artefacts and culture may need to work with broader categories in order to even speak about the Other without getting lost in minor details and complexities. Yet, this argumentation does not change the implications of such statements and the systems of meaning they impose upon the absent non-European. Cultural diversity, in these framings, can be understood in the sense that cultural anthropologist Gisela Welz has proposed, namely, 'as a system of equivalent, mutually exclusive categories that allow for an exact allocation of each individual and every cultural form' (1996, 220). While many anthropologists are, thus, arguing against such systems of categorisation, they still seem to inform, at least to some extent, the work of the gallery educators in the observed sessions. Such framings of diversity as the *side by side* of clearly delineated and internally homogeneous 'cultures' in gallery sessions can produce and reproduce understandings of non-European life as essentially and unequivocally different from one's own life world. As Glenn Bowman has framed it, '[…] the 'native' as 'fixed' in a time and a place which renders his or her practices and beliefs representative of the entirety of those of a distinct and holistically conceived 'people'' (2007, 34).

Besides this understanding of diversity as the simultaneous presence of distinct 'peoples' or 'cultures', there is another dimension to the guides' paradoxical claims about the cultural diversity of the represented regions. The guides' compartmentalised understanding of culture is not only connected to mostly outdated anthropological conceptions of culture, but also to contemporary connotations of diversity in multicultural societies. This multicultural conception of cultural diversity and its relevance for the statements of the guides are further explained in the next section of this chapter.

4.1.2 Advertising Multicultural Diversity

The guides' statements are not only indicative of a tendency to categorise people according to ethnic groups or 'peoples'. They also point to an understanding of cultural diversity in terms of the described 'static view of multiculturalism'.

Consider, for example, the following situations: When a student explains to Britta that he thinks 'the bad thing about the Chinese is that they abuse their animals' (GSB-MB, 517-518), she responds by saying: 'You probably mean that the Chinese eat things that we would not eat and that they perhaps also kill their animals in a cruel way. Yes, you're right. This is a different culture to ours.' (ibid., 519-522). In Maria's session, a student tells a story that she had heard about a woman in India whose family believed she was accursed and whose curse would be devolved to whomever she would marry, which is why she had to marry a stray dog (cf. GSM-MB, 765-768). Maria answers by telling the student that there are many different beliefs in the world and that it can sometimes be difficult for the people who believe in them (cf. ibid., 725f.). Finally, the following extract from a conversation between Eva and the students in the India gallery of Museum B is equally telling in this regard:

E: [...] only half of all the people in India have access to toilets. And one needs to clean the bottom somehow. And you have the left hand. You have leaves (.) or cardboard and then...
S: Ugh! [students express disgust]
E: That's not 'ugh!'. Since when do we have toilets? Since the 19th century. Where did we go before that? So one has to (-). Other countries, other manners. The developments in the countries are very different. And your task is to be open-minded and to ask yourselves 'what is it like there?'

(GSE-MB, 273-282)

These examples show that many guides in the observed gallery sessions adhere to and promote a celebratory idea of cultural diversity in a multicultural society. Instead of reflecting upon and critically engaging with the statements of the students, they argue (explicitly or implicitly) along the lines of a universal tolerance for the diversity of all 'cultures' or 'beliefs'.

The guides' accounts can, thus, be connected to the predicates of culturalism, and, more specifically, multiculturalism as defined in Chapter 3. As explained there, the idea of multiculturalism promises 'variety without antagonism' (cf. Anderson 2011, 529) by celebrating 'other' cultural practices and tolerating different religions. A major criticism of this idea is based upon the issue of a resulting superficial celebration and an expected romanticised harmony of diverse 'cultures', which prevents a sincere analysis and involvement with cultural, religious and social negotiation processes (Welsch 1999, Barry 2001). The guides' celebratory approach to the critical comments of the students can be criticised with regard to this multiculturalist ideology. By celebrating difference on a superficial level, Britta, Maria, and Eva do not only prevent a differentiated engagement with notions of religion or cultural practices, but they also suggest that there are predetermined and insurmountable differences between 'cultures', which cannot be negotiated or discussed, but which simply need to be 'accepted' as they are.[40] This implication of the promotion of cultural diversity in the guided tours relates to Homi Bhabha's definition of cultural diversity as the 'recognition of pre-given cultural contents and customs' (Bhabha 1994, 34), but also as the 'separation of totalized cultures that live unsullied by the intertextuality of their historical locations, safe in the Utopianism of a mythic memory of a unique collective identity' (ibid.). The guides' celebration of multicultural diversity, aimed at evoking tolerance and acceptance, is complicit not only in the construction of 'cultures' as separate entities, but also, equally problematically, in the reduction of 'culture', as Barbara Kirshenblatt-Gimblett has phrased it, '[...] to style and

---

[40] In the examples from the material, this prevention of a deeper engagement is particularly problematic because the students' questions are predicated on cultural stereotypes or myths that would need to be deconstructed in a more intensive dialogue.

144

decoration, to spice of life. Cultural difference is then praised for the variety and color it adds to an otherwise bland scene' (1998, 65).

This framing of cultural diversity on the level of style leads to an apparent superficiality of the guides' answers to the students' statements. Their argumentation on the basis of a general acceptance of, and open-mindedness for, diverse cultures and beliefs works as a rhetorical commonplace. There seems to be no need to further explain or concretise what this diversity means. 'This is another culture', 'there are many different beliefs in the world', or 'other countries, other manners' appear as self-explanatory answers that promote a positive stance towards, yet safe distance from the Other. Cultural diversity, in these references, can mean nothing – or anything. Due to this hollowness, Anderson has argued, cultural diversity can be regarded as an empty signifier (cf. 2011, 528). The concept of the 'empty signifier' has been defined by Ernesto Laclau as a signifier whose 'signified' is determined as an 'absent totality' whose function is incarnated by different (political) positions at different periods of time (cf. 1996, 42). In the guides' accounts, this empty signifier of 'cultural diversity' correspondingly works as a general framework of explanation to manage challenging or culturally critical situations. Because of the concept's ability to signify whatever one wishes it to signify (e.g. a more extensive engagement with the Other or a mere acknowledgement of the Other's presence), cultural diversity works as a reassuring and unifying ideal that teachers and parents accompanying the students during their school trips will presumably appreciate.[41]

This multiculturalist framing further implies the 'disimprovement effect' that can be observed in all of the aforementioned extracts from the guided tours. While hoping to encourage students to recognise, tolerate and celebrate the diversity of cultural practices and religious beliefs, the

---

[41] This unifying and uncontroversial dimension of multiculturalism is further addressed in Chapter 5.

guides end up constructing bounded cultural entities ('This is a different culture'), sometimes relegated to different times ('[t]he developments of the countries are very different') and marked by exotic and strange practices framed as unnegotiable ('[t]here are many different beliefs in the world'). This contradiction between a recognition and simultaneous fixation of otherness is connected to what Ahmed has addressed by declaring that '[...] the matter of making strangers is not resolved by simply inviting them in – such gestures still take for granted the status of the stranger as a figure with both linguistic and bodily integrity' (2000, 4). The disimprovement effect can then be regarded as closely connected to this process of 'othering' implicit in the celebration and welcoming of the Other. This dilemma is, finally, also connected to multiculturalist framings, as Anne Phillips explains:

> Multiculturalism considers itself the route to a more tolerant and inclusive society because it recognises that there is a diversity of cultures, and rejects the assimilation of these into the cultural traditions of the dominant group. Much recent literature claims that this exaggerates the internal unity of cultures, solidifies differences that are currently more fluid, and makes people from other cultures seem more exotic and distinct than they really are. Multiculturalism then appears not as a cultural liberator but as a cultural straitjacket, forcing those described members of a minority cultural group into a regime of authenticity, denying them the chance to cross cultural borders, borrow cultural influences, define and redefine themselves. (2008, 14)

By celebrating difference, as multiculturalism demands, these differences are, thus, fixated and endlessly reconstructed, while aspects of cultural change, transformation, and hybridisation are disregarded.

4.1.3   The Non-Performance of Diversity

Besides the already explained homogenising and distancing functions of the guides' promotion of cultural diversity, what is further problematic about such accounts is that they potentially reinforce and perpetuate power structures by concealing them. This happens in two different ways that are shortly outlined in the following.

First, the aforementioned references of the guides to cultural diversity invite the students to tolerate unfamiliar practices. This respect for difference, however, does not appear very effective because it is predicated on the condition that these unfamiliar practices remain within the realm of the Other and do not need to be negotiated 'here', which statements such as '[o]ther countries, other manners' (GSE-MB, 280) or 'this is a different culture to ours' (GSB-MB, 521-522) indicate. In relation to this noncommittal implication of the demand for tolerance, Doris Feldmann has argued that an appeal to respect difference seems hypocritical if it concerns differences that are reconcilable with a dominant or hegemonic identity (cf. 2010, 66). In the guides' accounts, the promotion of respect for diversity is similarly predicated on a smooth reconcilability. To celebrate diversity *as long as* it does not question any existing power hierarchies, and to raise awareness for difference that does not pose a threat to the established order (because it is represented as 'far away'), eventually does not require any power of persuasion. If anything, students who learn that differences are culture-bound and unnegotiable will maintain cultural imaginations such as 'the Chinese torture their animals' (Britta's session) or 'in India, people marry stray dogs' (Maria's session). Whether or not they will accept or respect these presumed cultural practices, then, does not matter anymore: The moment in which these practices are believed to be true as general aspects of non-European culture, a form of othering takes place that subtly reinforces ideas about civilisation, normality and European progress.

When cultural studies and education scholar Carmen Mörsch, hence, postulates that 'a massive and hardly variable, hegemonically structured, institutionalised and in historically colonial and currently neo-colonial conditions reproduced power imbalance, is at the bottom of enterprises labelled as "intercultural dialogue"' (2011, 11), these power imbalances also need to be acknowledged when looking at the guides' celebratory adoption of the language of multiculturalism, tolerance, acceptance, and diversity. Drawing on Paul Gorski's questions surrounding intercultural education in the USA, it is important to consider whether cultural diversity is only advocated '[...] so long as it does not require us to problematize our own privilege' (2008, 3). In this sense, non-European otherness would be accepted and tolerated only as long as it could be imagined as having nothing to do with 'us'. At least in the guides' answers to the student questions quoted above, such a view seems to be implicit. In effect, the guides' statements can lead to the reinforcement of the prevalent system of value by suggesting that it is only the easily reconcilable aspects of a presumed otherness that need to be accepted and tolerated. Thereby, these sessions, by promoting cultural diversity, affirm an 'already sealed and written national story, with room at the most for a little non-threatening difference' (Littler 2005, 12), as Jo Littler has warned with respect to the implications of multicultural policies in organisations.

While this way in which references to cultural diversity can perpetuate and reinforce dominance and hierarchy is concerned with the guides' prescriptive calls for tolerance and acceptance of otherness, another means of perpetuating power imbalances is related to claims of diversity in the gallery educators' announcements of the cultural diversity of non-European regions. These announcements can be regarded as 'non-performative' statements which 'pretend' to act against power differences while actually obscuring them.

In an insightful essay, Ahmed has described how public speech acts targeted at the demonstration of diversity and racial equality actually work to *prevent* action and conceal inequality and racism (2006). In another essay on the same problem, she argues that '[w]e could describe diversity

148

as a politics of feeling good, which allows people to relax and feel less threatened, as if we have already "solved it", and there is nothing else to do' (2010, 44). The accusation in these writings is that the mere statement of diversity (as a speech act) suggests that action is taken and thereby blocks real action because the statement proposes that change is already on the way.

Although Ahmed's criticism is related to processes such as human resource management or corporate branding campaigns, a comparable non-performativity of diversity can be observed in the guides' statements about cultural diversity. The examples provided in the beginning of Chapter 4.1 are telling in this regard. The guides in these cases emphasise the diversity of the respected regions. Christine even argues that diversity was '*the* feature' of Africa. Similar statements appear in many of the observed guided tours. For instance, Antonia explains that the area of the 'South Sea' is twenty-three times larger than Europe and she concludes that there cannot be only one 'culture' or one 'people' in that region (cf. GSA-MA, 62-64). Similarly, Gladys speaks about the diversity of Africa in terms of 'lots of different countries' (GSG-MC, 135-136) and Maria speaks about the diversity of the 'Orient' that spreads over different continents and countries where many different languages are spoken (cf. GSM-MB, 87-90). Besides the already elaborated aspect of categorisation, what these statements have in common is that they are articulated rather early on in the guided tours and refer to diversity in a very explicit style. Here, the narrative mode is interesting: The guides do not necessary show diversity (mimesis), but explicitly tell the students about it (diegesis). This focus on an explicit announcement is interesting because it functions similarly to what Ahmed criticises with respect to diversity management. By initially clarifying that the regions are diverse (in terms of languages, 'cultures', etc.), it seems that the guides try to 'solve' issues of representation pre-emptively because many statements they subsequently make about the regions pertain again to what seem to be overarching and generalised entities. The following is a short overview of such statements.

A: The families there in the South Sea are very big still today. (GSA-MA, 96)
B: In China, eating is closely connected to God. (GSB-MB, 252-253)
C: If something happens that one cannot explain oneself, then often in Africa, one wants to find an explanation for it. (GSC-MB, 414-415)
D: When the Indians are hit by a raindrop, they don't start crying like we do. (GSD-MA, 177-178)
E: The Indians don't traditionally know pyjamas. (GSE-MB, 720)
G: In Africa, storytelling is very collective. (GSG-MC, 149)

All of these statements are made during sessions in which the cultural diversity of the respective regions has been emphasised at the beginning. After the guides have explained that there are many different 'cultures', 'languages', and 'peoples', they, thus, often go back to speaking about the entire region, country, or even continent.

In summary, there are many reasons why it is difficult for the guides to speak about the Other in a truly differentiated way (which are explained in Chapter 5). Yet, it is interesting that they announce diversity in such an explicit way only to then *show* the students that one can indeed make general statements about the entire regions. It seems that, in the guided tours, just as in multicultural policy papers, the introduction of diversity as a claim pre-emptively excuses practices that do not represent diversity at all. What has been observed about public or corporate institutions, in which change has only been introduced on the level of visible markers of identity instead of on the level of actual power structures (as in designing advertising material that depicts people with different skin colours) (cf. Dewdney et al. 2012, 116), can also be observed on a smaller scale in the way in which change is introduced to the museum. The guides explicitly claim diversity, but implicitly represent regions such as 'Africa', 'the Orient' or the 'South Sea' as generalised and bounded entities.

4.2   Evoking Respect for the Other

Closely connected to the guides' recurring references to the cultural diversity of the regions exhibited in the museums, the second recurring phenomenon revolves around the notion of respect. Attempts to raise respect for the represented practices and achievements of non-European societies can be found in many statements the guides, for instance in Antonia's claim that the 'Polynesians' were courageous and clever and therefore never went out on the sea with their boats alone, but always in groups (GSA-MA, 167-168).

How can such ways of evoking appreciation and respect for the non-European groups addressed in the exhibitions be understood? To again refer to multiculturalist discourse, the notion of 'respect' has been linked to the recognition of the identity of others, with Charles Taylor claiming, for instance, that misrecognition shows a lack of respect (cf. 1994, 26). The respect that is demanded in multiculturalism is predicated on a 'human potential' to shape one's identity (cf. ibid.), which is attributed to all individuals and groups. However, while the actual demand for respect is more complicated in Taylor's original conception of recognition, in the public discourse, the notion of respect for cultural Others has been adopted in a more general sense that is connected to an overall tolerance and admiration of different practices. This rather general and vague, public interpretation of a demand for respect has been criticised by those arguing against multiculturalism for its paralysing function. As Phillips summarises, '[a]sked to show respect for other people's culture but unsure of what this entails, they [social workers, police officers, judges] decide to do nothing' (2007, 73). This vagueness and non-performativity of the public conception of 'respect' is closely related to what has already been discussed in relation to 'diversity'. A similar appeal of the already described empty signifier of cultural diversity can, thus, also be observed in the guides' accounts of evoking respect for non-European cultural practices.

As the two concepts of respect and diversity share many aspects related to multiculturalism, they could be discussed within one subchapter. The guides' references to respect, however, not only have different implications, but are also articulated differently from references to diversity. In order to analyse these phenomena, diversity and respect are considered separately here Yet, despite the focus on these particular meanings implied by the evocation of respect, it is important to keep in mind its relation to multiculturalist agendas. As these have already been addressed in detail with respect to diversity, the concept's embeddedness in understandings of harmony, unity and cultures as separate entities is not again elaborated at this stage. Nevertheless, these conceptions considerably affect the ways in which respect for non-European groups is pursued by the guides.

4.2.1   Emphasising Non-European Achievements

As explained in the previous chapter, the guides promote diversity by explicitly stating it as a fact. In contrast, respect can be evoked both by *stating* the respectability of the groups on display, as the example of Antonia's statement about the foresightedness of Polynesians seafarers indicates, as well as by *showing* that they deserve acknowledgment. This application of a different *narrative mode* (mimesis) is possible because of the availability of 'material evidence' for the accomplishments of the groups on display. The exhibited artefacts are often used by the guides to visualise the creative and productive achievements of non-European groups. As James Clifford writes in *The Predicament of Culture* (1988), '[c]ollecting – at least in the West [...] – implies a rescue of phenomena from inevitable historical decay or loss. The collection contains what 'deserves' to be kept, remembered, and treasured' (231). By virtue of the artefacts being exhibited in the museum, they are bestowed with value. They are perceived as historical, material, cultural, or artistic achievements because of their selection and portrayal in the museums. This focus on achievements, which is already available in the exhibition, is further amplified by the guides' practices of pointing the students to these material accomplishments. By emphasising a particular mechanism of producing objects, or a specific skill that is needed in order to use these objects, the guides can show to the students that the groups represented in the museum *deserve* respect. Such demonstrations of respectability can be found in many of the observed guided tours and can have both positive and negative implications. The following elaborations first give credit to the positive aspects, before subsequently pointing to the critical dimensions.

Calling the students' attention to examples of cultural or material achievements of the exhibited groups can represent a successful means of cultural negotiation when it points the students to the ways in which people in different regions creatively develop objects or techniques to deal with local conditions. Furthermore, providing examples of expert knowledge or skills that are needed to make or use certain artefacts can serve as a productive means of translating the vague multiculturalist demand for respect into concrete acknowledgement. The students might be genuinely impressed by the material or artistic productions they encounter in the museum. This evocation of respect is especially fruitful if these achievements are not only relegated to the past, but represented under conditions of coevalness. This effect is evident, for instance, in the following account of Christine in the Africa section of Museum B:

C: [...] can you see what they are made of? [referring to vessels part of an in-situ display]
      [...]
S: Rubber?
C: Almost.
S: Tires?
C: Exactly. They are cut out of tires. This is why they have this round shape. And this is what you would call 'direct recycling'. And in principle this is a trend from the so-called developing countries. Not just Africa. And this has also come to us now. People make new things out of used ones. And you don't have the effort of firstly melting it down to rubber again. But you use it as it is and cut something out

> of it and make something new from it. This is a very intelligent thing,
> very environmentally friendly. And this is now also done here [...]
> (GSC-MB, 286-295)

In this instance, the guide evokes respect by drawing the students' attention to a specific practice, direct recycling, which is not only widespread in Africa, but has also 'arrived here'. By speaking about a contemporary practice, Christine actively unlocks the Other from a position in an unspecified past or passiveness and, thereby, facilitates a cultural encounter at eye level. Furthermore, by emphasising that direct recycling has been adopted in Europe, Christine also addresses processes of cultural borrowing and globalisation, thereby opening up the possibility that 'we' can learn something from 'them'.

This concentration on specific unfamiliar practices that may challenge or transform familiar practices is an important dimension to add to a vaguely multiculturalist notion of respect. Much criticism of multiculturalism is based upon the cultural relativism that references to the recognition of an 'equal worth' of all cultures imply.[42] On the one hand, this critique is brought forward because cultural relativism, as critics such as Kohl argue, '[...] results in the widespread ethnocentric perspective held by almost all cultures, which assesses other cultures solely on the basis of the codes and values of one's own culture' (2000, 149). On the other hand, the problem of positing the equal worth of all cultural practices is again connected to the concomitant construction of cultures as self-contained entities, which ignores processes of cultural exchange and mutual influences. This pitfall of cultural relativism has been summarised to the point by Satya Mohanty in a *PMLA* special issue on *Colonialism and the Postcolonial Condition*:

---

[42] Although Charles Taylor acknowledges that '[t]here must be something midway between the inauthentic and homogenising demand for recognition of equal worth [...] and the self-immurement within ethnocentric standards' (1994, 72), the notion of a general respectability of all cultures is still commonly associated with multiculturalism.

154

> If 'we' decide that 'they' are so different from us that we and they
> have no common 'criteria' (Lyotard's term) by which to evaluate (and,
> necessarily, even to interpret) each other, we may avoid making
> ethnocentric errors, but we also, by the same logic, ignore the
> possibility that they will ever have anything to teach us. (1995, 112)

The idea that all cultural forms have the same 'worth' can, thus, easily lead to an empty celebration of diversity without deeper understanding or engagement. If all cultural practices are by default equally 'good' or 'bad', there is no space for differentiation. Without differentiation, however, it is impossible to negotiate, appropriate or permeate unfamiliar practices – processes which are at the bottom of transcultural encounters (cf. Welsch 1999, 196f., Rogers 2006, 491, Juneja/ Kravagna 2013, 25). In contrast, the example from Christine's session can be read as a counter strategy to the communication of 'hollow' notions of cultural respectability. Christine documents a process of transcultural appropriation by explaining that direct recycling has been adopted in Europe for its environmental friendliness and practicability. The students are, thus, encouraged to respect this African 'invention', which may appear more impressive to them than the advice to show respect for a general 'human potential'.

Other examples from the material that can be read in similar terms include Antonia's reference to the cultural achievement of the catamaran invented by 'the Polynesians' that 'we' copied from them (cf. GSA-MA, 163) or Kate's reference to the 'very clever way of making metal' that the Japanese used to make swords for the Samurai and that only one other group in the world, the Vikings, was able to apply as well (cf. GSK2-MD, 717-719). In these examples, the innovative qualities of the displayed material productions are highlighted. Thereby, non-European groups are granted the role of engineers and inventors, which works against common perceptions of progressive Europeans and 'primitive' non-Europeans, or constructions of a '[...] cultural, technological, or moral superiority of the 'home team' through contrast with others' (Macdonald 2003, 3), as Sharon

Macdonald has explained with reference to the European possession and display of objects from 'other cultures' at the turn of the century.

Despite this potential of the guides' accounts to counter stereotypes and to evoke genuine respect in the form of acknowledgement or appreciation, not all of observed references to the cultural achievements from the represented regions are entirely unproblematic. Nonetheless, criticism has to be levelled carefully because subtle essentialist connotations that may be hidden within some of these statements can be sparked by a slight change of wording or emphasis that may neither be relevant for the overall message of the statement, nor noticeable to the same degree to different critics. Still, these more problematic dimensions of attempts to evoke respect need to be discussed, particularly because they are again often made unintentionally and thus illustrate the workings of the disimprovement effect. The following remarks thus centre around two key issues; the patronising function of the guides' claims of respectability and the inversion and reinforcement of systems of hierarchy.

4.2.2   Means of Patronisation

As indicated in Chapter 3, due to the authoritative and trustworthy position of the guides, their practices of speaking about and for the Other must be critically investigated. Alcoff has explained, correspondingly, that '[…] the practice of speaking for others is often born of a desire for mastery' (29), either to show that one knows more about the other's situation than they know themselves or that one is best suited to represent their interests (cf. ibid.). She acknowledges, however, that '[i]t is not always the case that when others unlike me speak for me I have ended up worse off' (ibid.). Yet, the ends do not always justify the means. Regardless of whether one is 'better' or 'worse off' when somebody has spoken in one's position, questions surrounding the mastery implicit in such speech acts still need to be posed. This is especially the case in the ethnographic museum because non-European groups that are spoken for are often not asked to speak themselves (Simpson 2001, 7ff.; O'Neill 2004, 197; Goncalves 2013, 28). Even if an interpreter identifies him- or herself as a representative of the non-European regions illustrated in the museum, the format of the guided tour still renders the question of 'mastery' pressing because there is only one single person representing an entire group, region, or country. This process itself – the representation of non-European interests by an 'expert' – is already an act of power as these interests are presumed for an entire group and represented from a position that suggests a necessity and capability to render 'them' legible. Therefore, when the guides evoke respect for the non-European groups displayed, implicit dynamics of mastery and patronisation need to be discussed.

To illustrate the subliminal nature of this problematic effect of evoking respect, it is helpful to compare the aforementioned example of Christine's statements about direct recycling with a similar, yet slightly more patronising statement of Gladys in Museum C:

G: I am trying to make the point that you have different things you like to play with. Children in Nigeria have all those toys as well. But you also have children who will pick up a tin and they will cut it up. And they will put a stick with it and they have made a toy. They can get wood and chop it up. Then they have a car. And they make games, out of shells out of coins. You don't have to spend a lot of money to entertain yourselves. These are some of the things that in this kind of countries we not always do. Games are not necessarily things that you have to buy. (---) But they have all the things that you have as well. (GSG-MC, 169-176)

Initially, Gladys's and Christine's remarks seem very similar. As in Christine's session, Gladys speaks about how new things are made out of old ones in Nigeria. Furthermore, as in the first example, it is possible to trace in Gladys's statement a suggestion of something that 'we' can learn from 'them' (i.e., '[g]ames are not necessarily things that you have to buy'). Additionally, presumably as an attempt to avoid stereotypes about poverty,

Gladys even emphasises that children in Nigeria have the same toys as children in Great Britain.

Despite all these efforts that Gladys makes to evoke respect for the Nigerian children's creativity ('they will put a stick with it and they have made a toy') and modesty ('you don't have to spend a lot of money to entertain yourselves'), her statement seems more stereotypical and patronising than Christine's. The reasons for this disparity become evident when approaching the text from a narrative perspective. Dynamics of patronisation can be found both on the level of the story, i.e. what information is provided, and on the level of discourse, i.e. how information is articulated. Accordingly, when perceived as processes of 'worldmaking', Christine's and Gladys's explanations construct two different African 'worlds' by 'weighting', ordering, and deleting information in their accounts (cf. Goodman 1978, 77f.).

For example, in Gladys's statement, the *distinctiveness* of the makeshift strategies of the children is given more weight than the similarity of children's practices in Great Britain and Nigeria. Whereas Christine highlights the adoption of the particular non-European strategy of direct recycling in European countries, Gladys more specifically points out the relation of provisional games to 'this kind of countries'. She does not try to relate or compare this practice to 'do-it-yourself' trends or creative arts and crafts productions of children in European countries but establishes makeshift toys as a distinct feature of non-European children (as 'non-European' is how 'this kind of countries' must be read). Because of this explicit confinement of the use of 'provisional' toys to 'this kind of countries', an implicit association with poverty might emerge depending on the students' prior knowledge and ideas surrounding 'Africa'.

This effect emerges despite, and arguably also because of the fact that Gladys actively tries to counter this connotation of poverty by referring to the children's ability to play with the same toys that British children have.

Closely connected to the aforementioned non-performative employment of 'diversity', Gladys's initial statement that '[…] children in Nigeria […] have all those toys as well' can be regarded as counterproductive because it functions as an empty statement considering what follows. In relation to this point, the aspect of ordering the represented 'world' is important. Gladys's description of makeshift strategies, which she confines to non-European countries, is framed by an introductory and a concluding statement of the equality between European and non-European children. Yet these short framing statements about equal opportunities are not further filled with meaning, while the intermediate explanations about distinctive makeshift practices are substantiated with examples and with a moral message ('you don't have to spend a lot of money to entertain yourselves'). The posited equal opportunities of the Nigerian children are, therefore, most likely not as noteworthy and memorable as their allegedly distinctive use of spare materials to make provisional toys.

Regardless, however, of whether this practice is associated with poverty, Gladys's account is marked by generalisation and differentiation despite her attempts to generate coevalness. Generalisation happens both on the dimension of 'Europe' and on the dimension of 'this kind of countries'. In case of the Nigerian children, no distinction is made between children living in urban centres and those living in villages; or between different socio-economic situations. Surely an attempt to counter the poverty stereotype, this simplification (i.e., all children in Nigeria have commercial as well as provisional toys) cannot complexify ideas surrounding Africa, but merely offers further vague and all-encompassing 'non-statements'. These statements are not intended to provide deeper insights into simultaneously possible cultural realities, but to communicate a vague sense of respect for the Other.

On the level of Europe, generalisation is evident from Gladys's suggestion that British children only play with commercially produced toys.

This assumption draws an essentialist line between Great Britain and Nigeria, or European and non-European countries: 'This kind of countries' are all about creativity, whereas Europe seems to be all about consumption. Yet, this is an unnecessarily sharp distinction: Gladys renders it a specifically non-European practice to make toys out of found material. Closely connected to the phenomenon of culturalism, in this case, an observation that pertains to socio-economic status is conflated with a cultural argumentation. Families that cannot or will not afford new toys and may therefore make toys from spare materials exist in Europe and Africa alike. There may be more such families in Africa because opportunities are, in fact, not equal, but this aspect is specifically not discussed by Gladys. Instead, she paints a picture of creativity and modesty that is represented as a distinctively *cultural* feature of 'this kind of countries' because she denies a relationship to economic factors (i.e., 'Children in Nigeria have all those toys as well. But you also have children who will pick up a tin and they will cut it up'). By representing the use of non-commercial toys solely in terms of 'culture', and by positing this 'culture' as admirable or superior to the idea that games are 'something you can buy', the allegedly European practice of buying toys is equally rendered solely in terms of a capitalist 'culture' of consumption. This is not to say that economic systems and situations cannot lead to different social and cultural practices. Yet, to generalise situations in entire regions and to separate the contextualising factors from these situations is to distinguish 'cultures' through notions of authenticity and seemingly natural differences. European people, it seems in Gladys's statement, are determined by a culture of consumption while Nigeria and 'this kind of countries' are determined by a culture of creativity and modesty. In this imagination of two different 'cultures' (consuming vs. making) a common nostalgia for an imagined morality and modesty of the Other reappears, which will further be discussed in Chapter 4.3.

In addition, Gladys's statement is again related to the disimprovement effect: While she tries to evoke respect for the non-European creativity and modesty, and intentionally highlights the similarities between African and European children (in that they own the same toys), Gladys falls into the trap of distinguishing or distancing two generalised entities, and of creating a nostalgic sense of African or Nigerian people in 'this kind of countries' as living a simpler and less consumption-oriented life. This form of patronisation in attempts to evoke respect is marked by nostalgia, generalisation, and the reinforcement of the stereotype of the 'poor, but happy' Other (cf. Bertram 1995, Crossley 2012) that has been observed in tourism research. This example shows how easily a well-intended narrative about the respectability of non-European groups can get attached to stereotypical and essentialist meanings.

Another, even less easily avoidable problem of evoking respect for non-European groups on the basis of the material and artistic achievements represented in the museum is the unidimensional focus of the guides' accounts on skills and knowledge. These skills are often confined to the situation or location that 'they' are ascribed to. This problem has been described by Appadurai as one of two traditional anthropologically constructed links between spatial and intellectual confinement:

> The links between intellectual and spatial confinement, as assumptions that underpin the idea of the native, are two. The first is the notion that cultures are 'wholes' […]. The second is the notion, embedded in studies of ecology, technology, and material culture over a century, that the intellectual operations of natives are somehow tied to their niches, to their situations. They are seen, in Levi-Strauss's evocative terms, as scientists of the concrete. (1988, 38)

As 'scientists of the concrete', non-European groups may be praised for their local skills, but not for any abilities or knowledge that go beyond that. The criticism inherent in this framing is that it suggests that abstract thinking does not come 'natural' to these groups, thereby reinforcing notions of primitivity.

Comparable to this criticism, in the guided tours, the achievements or skills of non-European people are explained almost exclusively with respect to concrete knowledge. 'The Indians' are presented as producing 'really good' fabric (GSK2-MD, 160-170), 'the North American Indians' as great horseman (GSD-MA, 549-553.), and 'the Polynesians' as skilful builders of catamarans (Antonia, GSA-MA, 138-164). The already mentioned examples from the two Africa galleries can also be read as ways of depicting non-Europeans as 'scientists of the concrete.' In many cases, the respect that is demanded for the respective groups is hence connected to the operations in their 'niches'. In most cases, these are skills or practices related to manual labour. Only in very few cases is abstract thinking or 'mental work' referred to. This is, to some extent, the case in the representation of concrete artistic skills such as Feona's reference to Islamic artists' meticulous planning of a repeating pattern for a decorative object of a Minbar[43] (cf. GSF-MD, 292-311) or in Britta's reference to the difficulty of learning the Chinese language (cf. GSB-MB, 346-349). In general, however, references to non-material achievements such as political, economic or scientific achievements do not occur in the observed sessions. Even when a student asks Eva in the India gallery whether the Indians invented the number zero (cf. GSE-MB, 740-742), this is not further elaborated by the guide. While this information could serve not only as an effective means of highlighting India's contribution to 'our' way of conceptualising mathematical problems, but also as a strategy to point to abstract knowledge, Eva only briefly states that 'they are quite good at this decimal system' (ibid., 743).

Certainly, what has to be considered is that the exhibition narratives that the guided tours are based upon specifically focus on the material and

---

[43] A definition is provided in the glossary.

artistic qualities of the regions and groups represented. It may not be regarded as the task of an ethnographic museum to provide information that goes beyond material achievements. Yet, the gallery sessions could still serve to fill such gaps by integrating stories about non-European innovations, inventions, and political decisions. Instead, however, most of the guides reinforce the narrative of the 'scientists of the concrete.' The outcome is, just as in the case of Gladys's reinforcement of the 'poor, but happy' stereotype, a process of patronisation that is especially noteworthy because of the guides' position as *speaking for* non-Europeans in these situations.

Finally, this positionality of speaking for others can become a problem if the guides perform their position of mastery while they speak about non-European achievements. One of the issues that Alcoff mentions with regard to speaking for others is that the identity of the speaker always has an effect on what he or she claims (cf. 1992, 6). In case of a European guide at an ethnographic museum who is speaking for non-European people represented in this museum, the power dynamics are particularly complicated. Consider, for instance, the following statement of Doreen in the North American Indians section of Museum A:

D: Listen, accidents also happened to the Indians. Even if we don't see this in the films. They also fell. They also drowned when they were sucked into whirlpools. Maybe they were eaten by bears if the bears needed food. [...] This happens and one does not see this in the films. But because they always practised every day, they were skilled in everything that they did. (GSD-MA, 618-625)

The problem with praising non-European practices in such a way, stating that 'they' are or were good at this or brilliant at that, is that it suggests the speaker was in a position to broadly evaluate its counterpart. In relation to this aspect, it is important to be careful not to confuse analysis with evaluation. As mentioned above, without being able to analyse unfamiliar or new practices and their potential to be appropriated, there is little room for genuine encounter. However, the difference between this kind of analysis and a broad evaluation of non-Europeans as courageous or brilliant can be found on the level of focalisation in the guides' accounts: Are practices or skills represented as valuable for a particular group or person or situation? Or are non-Europeans evaluated as generally clever, skilful, etc. as a fact, in terms of zero focalisation? In the aforementioned example about North American Indians, the statement appears patronising because it is general and normative rather than analytical and focussed.

This equally applies to statements in the observed guided tours that describe non-Europeans as generally intelligent and courageous (cf. e.g. Antonia, GSA-MA, 167), tough (cf. Doreen, GSD-MA, 177-178), or 'fantastic in using so many different materials' (Kate, GSK-MD, 98). The generality of these statements turns them into mere evaluations or labels, which again suggest superiority of those who locate themselves in an evaluating position, as Mark O'Neill has described in relation to universal museums and the appreciation on non-European art:

> While appreciation of a culture's achievement by outsiders is no doubt, A Good Thing, in a situation of unequal power, it can easily shade into an implication that the subjects of appreciation should be grateful that they are being appreciated. Their gratitude should be all the greater if it is not just anyone who is appreciating their work – if they are being judged meritorious by the people who decide the standards of what is to be appreciated, by Western scholars, and most flatteringly of all, by famous artists. (2004, 195)

In the cases mentioned above, the guides may acquire a position in which they become the 'people who decide the standards of what is to be appreciated.' This position is by default a patronising one because it claims a subtle authority of evaluating the 'worth' of non-European actions and skills. To simply posit the overall intelligence, courageousness, or skilfulness of the displayed people compares to demanding a general and unspecific respect or tolerance for 'them' which is not tied to precise situations or skills. As '[g]enuine respect depends on a judgment based on understanding, arrived at through difficult epistemic and ethical negotiations' (Mohanty 1995, 113), as Mohanty suggests, the aforementioned general ascriptions of respectability seem counterproductive to intentions of facilitating sincere acknowledgement.

4.2.3 Inversing the Hierarchy

Another recurring strategy connected to the evocation of respect is less concerned with the specific practices or skills that are represented, but with the relationship between the self and the Other that is insinuated in these statements.

In some of the observed sessions, the guides establish respect for non-European achievements by means of a comparison with the self. Consider the following two examples of Antonia's and Doreen's tours:

A: They [the Polynesians] were the biggest seafarers in world history. They discovered and settled an area twenty-three times as big as Europe approximately five thousand years ago. At that point, we here in Germany – which did not exist yet – still lived in caves draped in wolf skin. (GSA-MA, 77-80)

D: [...] The water is so cold there that they cannot practise swimming. [...] But what they do practise is to flip the boat around once it has been pushed upside down. And they are really good at that. This way they can get out of the water very quickly.
S: What happens if they don't manage to get out of the water?
D: Then they drown. And there are, from time to time, people that drown there. There, it's not all wrapped up in cotton wool as it is here. (GSD-MA, 772-786)

These examples demonstrate an interesting representation of the respectability of non-European groups on the grounds of a depiction of 'them' as more advanced or as tougher than 'we' are (or were). While the intention of such strategies is to destabilise notions of European superiority, they may in fact reinforce common binary distinctions and hierarchies. The reason for this reinforcement lies in the argumentative structure of the statements. What comparisons like those quoted above do, is to legitimise and substantiate the construction of scales of cultural comparison in terms of developmental status, power, or strength. Hence, instead of questioning ideas about cultural progress, Antonia's account authorises the premise that the value of different 'cultures' can be analysed in terms of a system in which it seems that the more production, construction and expansion can be observed at a given point of time, the more advanced or progressed is the respective 'culture'. Such statements not only create a sense of competition about which is considered the most developed country (or the tougher 'culture', in Doreen's account), but they also inverse common hierarchies between self and Other. In this respect, Mohanty has explained that such inversions do not work as a strategy of resistance: 'A simple inversion of the relationships of hierarchy is not enough, because the colonizer-colonized relationship is necessarily complicated and multiply determined' (1995, 110).

This problem can further be connected to the aspect of non-performativity described in Chapter 4.1. Just like means of welcoming the Other, these inversions of cultural hierarchies do not call into question the 'figurability' (Ahmed 2000, 4) of the Other ('stranger' in Ahmed's terms). Ahmed states that practices of embracing strangers are not effective means to counter their status as strangers. Similarly, in the two examples, the competition that is constructed further stabilises the Other as the opposite or counterpart of the self. Constantly asking how 'their status', 'their skills', 'their achievements' relate to 'ours' on an imagined, seemingly objective evaluative scale may ignore historical developments, socio-cultural contexts and local systems of value. Again, here it is important to carefully distinguish between an analysis and engagement with unfamiliar practices and a generalised judgment of these practices from a seemingly omniscient position. This disparity can be exemplified nicely by comparing Antonia's aforementioned evocation of respect for the Polynesian construction of the catamaran to her second statement about the advanced position of the Polynesians in comparison to 'us' Europeans. While the first case is specific and focuses on processes of appropriation, the second statement is general and predicated on the comparison of a hierarchical idea of developmental status. Cultural development and advancement, thereby, are framed as legitimate comparative dimensions on the grounds of which to distinguish between 'us' and 'them'.

4.3 Projecting Moral Values

A similar 'desire for mastery' as evident in the guides' evaluations of non-European achievements is at work in another recurring pattern of communicating otherness during guided tours. Only in this case, it is not accomplishments, but social or moral values that are at stake. This subchapter explains how gallery educators compare and project non-European social norms and moral values, and critically scrutinises associated connotations and implications.

In various of the observed gallery sessions, the guides make statements about shared ideals of behaviour and morality in the regions addressed in the exhibitions. These ideals pertain to either non-European social norms or moral values, and they are represented as constant, overarching features of 'their' social life. In brief, the guides claim generalised social or moral values as the grounds upon which the respective societies work. As already mentioned in the introduction, the following analysis is not interested in the extent to which these truth claims are correct or incorrect, but in their workings and in their implications for the construction and production of otherness as a status. Remarkably, for instance, the presented social and moral principles are often contrasted with equally generalised understandings of 'European' values.

Before going into detail about the specific variants and implications of this recurring aspect of communicating otherness, it is necessary to clarify shortly what is meant by 'moral values' and 'social or ethical norms' in the following elaborations. Yet, providing a definition is not as straightforward as it may seem. Considering that the guides do not explicitly refer to 'moral values' or 'social norms' in their statements, an ascription of the phenomena to either morality or ethics would imply a limitation of possible interpretations of their accounts. To avoid clouding the sight of possible meanings involved in their references to non-European behavioural ideals, the analysis works with conceptions of both social *and* moral values.

This conceptual openness means that, what is explained by the guides, is interpreted here to relate to both ethics and morality in that, as Douglas Kellner has distinguished, ethics is interested in the discourse about norms and models within a society (corresponding to Hegel's 'Sittlichkeit') whereas morality describes ideals about what is believed to be good (corresponding to Kant's 'Moralität') (cf. 2001, 146). While social or ethical values are perceived as norms of behaviour that are explicitly or implicitly demanded by the collective, moral values can be more individual and personal. Furthermore, the social norms represented by the guides may be compared to Durkheim's 'collective consciousness' (1984 [1893]) because they are represented as long-lasting (i.e. transcending multiple generations) and as independent from the individual's situation (cf. ibid.). However, while Durkheim notes that 'we form a part of several groups and there exist in us several collective consciousnesses' (ibid., 67 [footnote 44]), the guides often represent social values as unidimensional and homogeneous.[44] To avoid confusion, the following elaborations apply the term 'social norms' to refer to collective norms demanded by the social

---

[44] In a different context, this definition of morality would require a further critical reflection, especially with regard to understanding morality as a set of individual ideals of what is believed to be good (and bad). For instance, Nietzsche's argumentation in *The Genealogy of Morals* (1987 [1869]) which alludes to the development of moral values according to the interests of social groups (as opposed to individual perceptions of 'goodness') offers a more reflected notion of morality that entails rational choice and intentionality. However, for the purpose of the analysis, the distinction between individual and social values, or of what individuals regard as good and what is demanded by the community, is more fruitful because it covers the variety of functions of the guides' accounts.

group, and the term 'moral values' for references to individual moral principles about what is perceived as 'good' or 'bad'.

Often unrelated to the exhibitions, the guides' explanations about non-European social and moral values appear relatively spontaneously in the guided tours. These statements usually stand out of the overall text, without seeming 'necessary' for the structure and purpose of the sessions. They can, thus, be understood as supplements to the accounts – perhaps accessories – in that they add to the fascination or the 'reality effect' of what is explained. Alternatively, these accounts could also be regarded as side effects of the guides' presentation of information in the form of narrative. As previously mentioned, Hayden White has discussed this relationship between narrativity and morality. He argues that accounts about historical events do not seem real to their readers unless they relate to some kind of social order (cf. ibid.). This means that any rendering of history in the form of a story necessarily takes a certain system of norms and values as its starting point. White notes that narrative in general is connected to the topics of legality and legitimacy (cf. ibid., 13). This leads him to ask: 'Could we ever narrativize without moralizing?' Similarly, Bruner has argued that a story is only worth telling if it includes a breach of a script (cf. 1991, 11). Accordingly, moral and social values can be considered as shared scripts of the community. The guides' references to 'other' social norms and moral standards could, therefore, be regarded as breaches of 'our' scripts and could, thus, be seen as unavoidable consequences of the presentation of information about non-European regions in the form of anecdotal accounts.

Although these are certainly valuable starting points for comprehending the motivations of the guides to integrate these aspects into their accounts, there is more to this phenomenon than its narratological function. The ways in which these specific notions of otherness are communicated are interesting in many regards and contain implications that cannot be ignored. In the following, representative examples from the observed guided tours are presented to show and explain three divergent functions of the guides' statements about non-European values. These three functions comprise the disciplinary dimension of teaching moral values, the dimension of desire for non-European social values, and finally, the dimension of condescending veneration for values projected onto the non-European realm.

4.3.1   Value Comparison as a Pedagogical Measure

A common recurring feature in the guides' communication of non-European social norms and moral values is its educational or disciplinary function. In various of the observed guided tours, the gallery educators talk about norms of social conduct in the regions represented in the museums and then extrapolate from them conclusions or learnings for the German students' behaviour. Thereby, a generalised non-European social norm is projected onto the immediate situation of the guided tour.

This process is visible, for instance, in the following example. In a session about China in Museum B, the school group (aged 11-12) seems difficult to manage. Individual students run off, ignore the gallery educator's words or get distracted by other objects in the exhibition room. After the school teacher has intervened and reprimanded the students, Britta refers to Chinese social norms in order to make the students aware of their 'misbehaviour'.

> […] I just wanted to explain to you that in China when it comes to standing or sitting. Like when you got up from the bench before. It took a while but you did get up. And I just wanted to say that in China you would have completely different standards. That is to say it is like this. A teacher standing in front of you, and in our case, we have two teachers or tutors, I don't know, teachers. Then there is someone like me who can also teach you something, okay? I am a kind of teacher but in the museum. And such persons one would respect very much. That means that when a teacher says that we are stopping here to look at something then the children in China

170

> simply stop. And they would never sit down somewhere if the teachers did not allow them to sit down. So teaching is, coming from the old days, a very very important job. They do not earn so much today, the Chinese teachers. Sometimes they have to do different jobs next to teaching. But they are respected. And this is so because, and now we have a relation to what I wanted to tell you about the script, because the script in china is difficult to learn. That means someone who can read and write and has studied teaching has to be a very intelligent person or at least has done this very diligently. And therefore one, so to say, controls one's temper. Perhaps for information only that here it is perhaps very different by now. Just as a broad hint for you to keep up now because I would appreciate that. (GSB-MB, 331-352)

In this extract, Britta combines her informational account about Chinese society with a disciplinary message. This combination is explicitly announced as such. As she mentions herself, this short intervention is meant as a 'broad hint' for the students to keep up and actively participate in the guided tour.

Interestingly, this application of the Chinese situation to the German students' behaviour is at once particularistic and universalist. Not only do the students learn that Chinese pupils respect and listen to their elders because of their appreciation for the difficulty of teaching, but they are also told (implicitly) that the illustrated Chinese respect for teachers is a positive value in general. Respect for teachers is, hence, both represented as a specific social aspect in China and as a general moral value to be adopted everywhere. This framing is especially interesting in consideration of the aforementioned concepts of 'social norms' and 'moral values'. The situation includes a translation of what are represented as Chinese social norms (demanded by the collective) into moral values for the German students (immediate, individual, situational). Because students in China allegedly respect their teachers, the students participating in the guided tour (i.e., the school class in the museum) are requested to equally show respect for the guide in the immediate situation they are in. Thereby, the specific social contexts and reasons for the student-teacher relationship in

China are suspended for the sake of turning respect for one's teachers into a general, almost universal value.

When following this line of argumentation and criticism, it once again reverberates with the problem of the 'double-bind of culture' (Schöfthaler 1983, Adick 2010) which is caught in-between universalism and cultural relativism. As Adick explains, while universalism applies values derived from a European discourse (dignity, freedom of speech, freedom of religion) to non-European contexts and thus implies *eurocentrism*, cultural relativism considers 'cultures' only in terms of internal values and ideas, which denies the recognition of contact and thus implies *ethnocentrism* (cf. 2010, 123f.). Accordingly, Britta understands 'respect' as a universal value, which is evident from her 'broad hint' for the students to behave like the Chinese students she describes in her account. Respect, for Britta, is an unquestionably positive and desirable value anywhere in the world. By means of her statement, she suggests that a common idea of respect could be applied to all societies and thus disregards specific influencing factors that shape the social values in China. Yet, if criticism was levelled at this universalisation on the grounds that this particular type of respect could not be compared to the German situation, a cultural relativist and ethnocentric lens would be applied, which would imply that it was impossible to grasp or negotiate this 'respect' outside of specifically Chinese understandings.

Nevertheless, to consequently ask whether Britta should restrict her explanations about 'respect' solely to the Chinese situation without establishing links to her own society would mean to miss the point of what is critical about Britta's account; namely its essentialism and its disciplinary function. First of all, it must be clear that not all Chinese students do exactly what their teachers tell them to do, even though this is a common trope about China. Surely, teaching practices may be stricter than in most teaching situations in Germany and, thus, Chinese students may internalise a more hierarchical relationship with their teachers, but neither does this apply to all Chinese students nor can it solely be understood in terms of a simply existing 'culture' of respect. In this example, the detachment of cultural practices from their social contexts, but also from the factors and concrete influential aspects that bring them about, is not a matter of universalism or cultural relativism, but a question of culturalism and the reduction of complexity. Respect for one's elders, just like the example of using spare materials to produce makeshift toys in the previous section, is constructed as a deterministic, 'cultural' essence rather than as a practice emerging from social relationships and shaped by continuous processes of transformation. As a consequence, the impression emerges that Chinese children are essentially, 'culturally' different from German students, which denies identification or empathy.

Secondly, the disciplinary 'use' of this constructed ideal of well-behaved students in the context of the guided tour is interesting. While there seems to be no explicit connection between the provided cultural information and the situation in Germany (i.e., Britta herself explains that 'here it's perhaps very different by now'), Britta actively constructs a connection by identifying herself with the represented role of the teacher in China: 'Then there is someone like me who can also teach you something, okay? I am a kind of teacher, but in the museum.' She, thus, positions herself as a person to be respected. Although this is presented merely as 'a broad hint', it is evident that Britta constructs the Chinese 'ideal behaviour' as a moral compass for the German students. Regardless of the difference in socialisation, the German students *should* follow the Chinese example, at least for the duration of the guided tour. Britta uses an essentialised image of otherness as a method to claim respect for herself.

A very similar case can be found in a session about Africa in Museum C. In this case, Gladys explicitly refers to the respect that one ought to show to one's elders in general.

> Elders are people that are older than you. And in Africa and anywhere in the world they should command more respect. The older you are the more respect you have for the elder. [...] I am the storyteller. And the storyteller is like an elder because they pass down knowledge. (GSG-MC, 96-100)

Once again, Gladys's reference to non-European social norms is explicitly connected to her own authority as an elder in the immediate situation of the gallery session. Just as in the first example, by identifying herself as belonging to the group of people she categorises as persons commanding respect, Gladys establishes her own authority as a teacher or elder.

This appropriation of generalised non-European values for disciplinary purposes must be seen as problematic. As already mentioned, a crucial part of this analysis attends to the authority of the museum that the guides embody. Accordingly, Britta's and Gladys's accounts communicate a certain accepted 'habitus' in the museum. Helene Illeris has referred to similar disciplinary strategies in museums in terms of the 'disciplined eye', which she describes as visitor attempts to '[...] adopt the prevailing practice of looking' (2009, 19) conditioned by the museum. She argues that '[t]he unmarked other of the disciplined eye is the unreflected, uncontrolled chaos associated with visitors who do not know how to behave in museums' (ibid.). By insisting on the students' respectful behaviour in the museum (listening carefully, not wandering around, not interrupting), Britta and Gladys reinforce this 'disciplined eye' with which visitors perceive the exhibition. This disciplinary strategy also contributes to the cultural authority of the museum. The guides' self-representation as authorities to be respected and trusted contributes to the perceived expertise and infallibility of the museum. As White explains, historical narratives are always informed by the moral authority of the narrator (1990, 22f.). The self-authorising statements of the guides similarly establish and affirm the credibility and authority of the museum as well as of the gallery educators and thereby construct reliability of the represented reality. This construction is problematic not only because of the guides' generalising references to the respective regions (i.e., in China, all students stop when the teacher tells them to), but mainly because it may prevent a critical questioning by the students of the explanations they are confronted with during their visit.

This problem of the normativity of the guides' accounts relates to Ivan Karp's statement about the power of museums:

> '[m]useums and their exhibitions are morally neutral in principle, but in practice always make moral statements; [...] The alleged innate neutrality of museums [...] is the very quality that enables them to become instruments of power as well as instruments of education and experience' (1991, 14)

The expected neutrality of the museum comes into question in such moments of praising non-European social norms and establishing them as universal moral values. The specificity of the represented information becomes irrelevant and the guides inhabit a position in which they, with the authority that they have reinforced for themselves, establish what is right and what is wrong. The social contexts and their complexities are eradicated from view in these generalisations of moral values. The dictate to 'be more like them' becomes integrated with the more factual information about the non-European context. Thereby, an all-encompassing, generalising moral message is produced, not only about 'us' (we all should have more respect for our elders), but also about them (they all have respect for their elders). Yet, this moral message is predicated on a fantasy of 'them' as the projection surface for what 'we' are not (anymore), but want to become. This intrinsic veneration and adoration of such imagined and generalised values is further addressed in the following section.

4.3.2 Desiring Non-European Values

Shortly coming back to the examples mentioned above, what is striking about these guides' statements is the gallery educators' generally positive attitude towards non-European values. In fact, in all of the observed gallery sessions that feature statements about social norms and morality, non-European values are represented as either universally applicable or even superior to what are framed as 'European' values. For example, in another part of the aforementioned gallery session in the Africa gallery of Museum C, Gladys reads a fictional story about Africa to the students. Upon the story's ending, she summarises the story's moral and elaborates it into a more general comment about 'African' social life:

> If you don't have any money, it doesn't matter. Because if you give the people that care for you a big hug. that is the best present of all. In many parts of Africa, a typical household includes three generations. So, you have mother, father, auntie uncle, brothers and sisters, cousins, grandparents. And the door is always open. Here, you come, you ring the doorbell and they say (with a different, harsh voice) "I'm not home, go away, I don't want to see you!" But in Africa, the door is always open. (GSG-MC, 213-219)

In this example, the social norms of the non-European context are clearly marked as superior to the European ones. While the European social situation is described in terms of isolation and self-centredness, in an again generalised, imagined 'Africa', 'the door is always open'. This dimension of superiority of non-European social norms is obvious in this example, but it is implicitly inscribed in other cases as well. For example, in the situation in the China gallery of Museum B, the Britta's statement that 'here it's perhaps very different by now' may be read as a somewhat regretful observation. The implicit advice for the German students to behave like the Chinese ones is equally indicative of a wish to implement similar norms in the 'here and now'.

Whether the presented social or moral values are depicted as universally applicable or superior to one's own social norms, these positive evaluations show that there is a certain desire for non-European social norms evident in the guides' statements. This representation of the desirability of the elucidated norms mainly works on the basis of narratological cues. As Nelson Goodman describes in his theory of worldmaking, 'the making of one world out of another usually involves some extensive weeding out and filling' (1978, 14). This statement means that worldmaking works both by selecting aspects from a previous world that contribute to the worldmaker's agenda and by ignoring other aspects that may not be useful for this agenda. In relation to the guides' references to non-European social norms and moral values, what is being ignored or removed from their accounts, are those values that are not as easily commensurable with their own understandings or with those that they presume for their audiences, i.e., the students. As already mentioned, the accounts revolve around gratefulness, modesty, respect, and solidarity – values that can be expected to be accepted by the teachers and the parents accompanying the school groups. In this respect, the represented values do not indicate a full 'breach of the script' (Bruner 1981, 11), but can easily be translated to the immediate lifeworlds of the students.

This focus on commensurable values is related to the focus on tolerance and respect in the guides' accounts. These emphases can be explained by the guided tour's objectives – not only as a public educational measure, but also as a performance – to avoid controversy and instead achieve consensus, approval, and group formation (cf. Nünning 2013, 43). As Nünning has explained, narratives can serve as media of communitisation by contributing to social cohesion or to the formation of 'narrative communities' (ibid.). Similarly, Goffmann has compared performances as means of 'expressive rejuvenation and reaffirmation of the moral values of the community' (1965, 23). In this sense, the represented values in the guided tour can be understood as means of reaffirming and consolidating values that are already accepted and appreciated by the audience.

This reaffirmation is, however, not only achieved by avoiding possibly less consensus-building social norms in their accounts, but also by means of 'weighting', i.e. distinguishing perceived relevant from irrelevant information (cf. Goodman 1978, 10) and by means of 'deformation', i.e., reshaping information, which can be perceived as correction or distortion depending on one's point of view (cf. 1978, 16). As is evident from the presented examples, the guides do not only omit conceivably incommensurable social norms from their accounts, but they also structure their statements in a way that makes it easier to identify with the values addressed. For instance, Britta describes the value of respect as detached from its specific influencing factors and conditions in China. In Gladys's conviction that 'in Africa, the door is always open', there is no mention of historical or social factors that may have procured a strong solidarity or community cohesion. It is this superficiality and lack of specificity of the guides' accounts that renders the described situations and values suitable for a smooth appropriation and projection onto one's own context. This process relates to what Roland Barthes has explained in reference to the film 'The Lost Continent' in *Mythologies*:

> All told, exoticism here shows well its fundamental justification, which is to deny any identification by History. By appending to Eastern realities a few positive signs which mean 'native', one reliably immunizes them against any responsible content. A little 'situating', as superficial as possible, supplies the necessary alibi and exempts one from accounting for the situation in depth. Faced with anything foreign, the Established Order knows only two types of behaviour, which are both mutilating: either to acknowledge it as a Punch and Judy show, or to defuse it as a pure reflection of the West. In any case, the main thing is to deprive it of its history.' (1957, 96)

Barthes observations about the Italian documentary 'The Lost Continent' (1955), which represents the life of so-called 'native Indonesians', can equally be applied to the representation of social norms in the observed guided tours. The 'immunization' of the Other against genuine content and its superficial 'situating' in an unhistorical reality makes it possible to render 'their values' predominantly as reflections of 'ours'.

It is within this self-reflection implicit in the guides' accounts about non-European social norms and moral values that a desire for the represented non-European social conduct becomes most visible. The guides construct (not merely generalise) commensurable non-European values as a counter-image of perceived European values. Very much in the spirit of Said's *Orientalism*, the imagination of the Other is, hence, used as a projection surface for a confrontation with one's own ambiguous social norms and moral values (cf. 1978, 12). The perceived otherness of the Other remains, with reference to Julia Kristeva's *Strangers to Ourselves*, essentially a conflict within the self (cf. 1991, 191f.).

This simultaneity of self and Other, of information and projection, may best be illustrated by yet another example; this time from the North American gallery of Museum A. In a session about American Indians, a student asks whether it is true that 'the Indians' can remain silent for a long time. Doreen answers that this is often said about them because they were persecuted in the past and had to hide from their enemies. Then she goes on to explain that being silent is also useful for going hunting because one must not reveal one's hiding place by making a sound. Yet, subsequently she transitions from this rather specific account to a more general statement about the behaviour of American Indians:

> The Indians were raised differently. For example, if they had questions and wanted to ask the medicine man, you would simply go there and ask, right? The Indians wait until an adult allows them to ask a question. And then he answers your question and then he makes a sign. And all the questions that have not been answered so far, he will not answer. You learn from an early age to restrain yourself. And if there is food, it is shared. And it is shared in a way that some people get more than others, and children do not necessarily get the most. This is different here. [...] You learn to restrain yourself in every possible way, to look out for everyone else. [...] (GSD-MA, 592-604)

The change in tense at the beginning of the statement is noteworthy. This shift indicates a move from the articulation of specific information about cultural practices to the elaboration of social norms that have a disciplinary and moralising function. The solidarity that is referred to in this statement (i.e., looking out for others, sharing food, restraining oneself) represents another dimension of desirable values that are communicated in the observed sessions. This desire for solidarity also relates to what sociologist and tourism researcher Dean MacCannell has remarked about authenticity in tourism:

> In our society, intimacy and closeness are accorded much importance: they are seen as the core of social solidarity and they are also thought by some to be morally superior to rationality and distance in social relationships, and more 'real'. (1999, 94)

Similarly, in the presented cases of Doreen, Britta, and Gladys, the desired values are based upon ideals of intimacy, family cohesion, closeness, and reliability. They are contrasted (e.g. 'here it is perhaps very different by now', 'here, they answer "go away, I don't want to see you"', 'this is different here') with what seem to be dystopian understandings of European values; from the disrespect of the German students towards their elders, via the cold isolationist attitude of British residents towards unannounced guests, through to the selfishness of individuals in social interactions.

Kjell Olsen has argued that MacCannel's distinction between intimacy and closeness, on the one hand, and rationality and distance, on the other, presumes a previous stage at which social authenticity was still intact (2002, 166).[45] He argues that it is this previous stage that tourists often look for 'in the past or among the other' (ibid.). This desire for the past that is found in the presence of the Other can also be related to the

---

[45] In fact, MacCannel does refer to the nostalgia of 'modern societies' for their past 'Golden Epochs', however, he emphasises that the past always *appears* more orderly than the present (cf. 1999, 82), thus distancing his own analysis from this impression.

aforementioned examples. As the shift of tense in the example of the North American Indian gallery session indicates, the purportedly genuine or authentic values of social cohesion and solidarity are imagined in the realm of the Other, regardless of whether this Other refers to time, space, or both.

What is, hence, at stake in the representation of non-European social norms and moral values is a nostalgia for an imagined past, or, in Appadurai's words a 'nostalgia without memory' (1996, 29f.). The possibility to imagine these values to be still intact in another social context renders the desire to recover them in 'our' social context more realistic. As Appadurai notes, 'if your present is their future [...], and their future is your past [...], then your own past can be made to appear as simply a normalized modality of your present.' (ibid., 31) This statement alludes to the complex and problematic aspect of this desire for 'our' constructed past and 'their' constructed present: Not only are 'they' relegated to an unspecified time, but 'they' are also cast as a simple mirror that eventually only reflects 'us'. Thereby, just as Said's Orient, the Other in the guides' accounts is represented as '[...] silent, available to Europe for the realization of projects that [involve] but [are] never directly responsible to the native inhabitants, and unable to resist the projects, images or mere descriptions devised for it' (1978, 94). What appears as desire and veneration implies displacement (in time, in space), generalisation, and, at its worst, a condescending attitude towards the Other. This aspect is explained in more detail in the final section of this chapter.

4.3.3   Performing Condescending Veneration

As already explained, the comparison and projection of non-European social norms or moral values in the observed guided tours is marked by an emphasis on those values that can be anticipated as positively connoted among the audience (students, teachers, parents). This selection of commonly agreed upon values facilitates the representation of these non-

European social norms as desirable, which in turn makes the guides' statements even more effective as disciplinary or educational measures. This mechanism can be understood in terms of what Nünning has referred to as the 'social and cultural formation of coherence' (2013, 43) which functions in narratives by means of the narrator's identification with a social or ideological group as well as by the ability of the narrative to familiarise its readers with these values (cf. ibid.). When a narrator or, in this case, a guide, thus, represents and reinforces the values of the audience within a narrative, the story itself seems more convincing and trustworthy to this audience. Furthermore, connecting this idea with Stuart Hall's notion of 'signifying practice' (1997), it becomes clear that once narrators identify themselves with a group by means of such a reinforcement of shared values, they also begin to signify and shape the values of this group.

Likewise, in relation to the guided tours, the guides most often identify with groups like 'Europeans', 'Germans' or 'British people' and, thereby, not only represent, but also construct shared values within these groups.[46] Regardless of these specific identifications, however, in general, the distinction that all of the guides make is clearly between 'European' and 'non-European' culture and values. Yet, in identifying and thereby arguing from the perspective of one of these groups, the guides define what it means to 'be' *either*. This definition is inevitable because the comparison of values amounts to a contrasting not only of these values, but also of the groups that apparently represent them. This representation and signification of the two groups not only creates an artificial binary distinction between 'us' and 'them', but it also entails a basic

---

[46] While most of the observed guides speak from the perspective of 'the Germans', 'the British' or 'the Europeans', some guides also identify themselves as 'African'. This is the case when some of the guides identify themselves as being 'of African heritage' in the interviews (Gladys, Hilda). However, due to the migration backgrounds of these guides, their identification in these cases is ambiguous in some instances, with the guides speaking about 'us' both in reference to the German or British, and in reference to the African 'groups'.

anthropological problem that cultural anthropologist Sandra Wallman has referred to in an essay about appropriate anthropology. According to her, there is a two-fold challenge connected to representing Others. On the one hand, it is problematic to impose one's own views on 'them', but on the other, it is also wrong to 'freez[e] their views in our versions of their traditions' (2007, 262). This dilemma, which is closely connected to what has already been explained in terms of the 'double bind' of universalism versus cultural relativism, nicely illustrates what happens in the guided tours. When identifying with and arguing from one perspective, the guides may seek to refrain from imposing 'their' values on the non-European contexts by emphasising the benefits of non-European values. Yet, in so doing, they represent non-European groups as homogeneous and fixed entities, 'frozen in their views'. In some cases, even both fallacies can be at work, meaning that there is an imposition of values from one group to another, but at the same time a fixation of 'their' values. This is visible, for instance, in the temporal lag suggested in Britta's statement 'here it's perhaps very different by now'. The 'by now' suggests that Europe has progressed from these values, while they are still intact in China. There is, thus, an imposition of the view that these values do not adhere to contemporaneity. At the same time, this statement suggests that there has been no such progress in the Chinese social context, which freezes Chinese values in time.

A more illustrative example of these problems involved in comparing social norms and moral values can be found in the India gallery of Museum B. Eva asks the students how they think Indians greet each other. She then performs a so-called traditional Indian greeting habit in which a person slightly bows to another and says 'namaste'. Subsequently, she shows the students how to traditionally greet a teacher, parent or grandparent by making a much lower bow and touching the other's feet. While Eva describes the former practice as considerate and mindful, she defines the latter as 'a little submissive' and 'unmodern'.

E: Namaste. [...] That means the exceptional in me greets the exceptional in you. Everyone has something that distinguishes them from others. One might be a good a reader or a good calculator or a good writer. One might look good. Or another may be good at painting. Or at sports. So, everyone is special in some way. And the thing that is special in me greets the thing that is special in you. That is a very nice greeting. Very considerate and mindful. So now it is like this. We have greeted one another like this. And we have folded our hands and the thumb was here close to our breastbone. If I am now greeting my teacher this is something different. Or when I am greeting my parents or grandparents. Because I respect them very much. My teacher as well. He teaches me a lot. And my parents too. And I am grateful that they provide for me. That they give me clothes. And a roof over my head. So, among persons commanding respect one greets and says goodbye to each other like this. [points at a student] You stand over there. You are for the moment my grandfather. Now you watch what I am doing. [bows deeply for the student] Did you see it? So, I am bowing down a little and my fingers normally touch / it's warm in India so you must imagine you're not wearing shoes on your feet. This is my way of showing respect. And although you think 'well we are living in the twenty-first century. One doesn't do this anymore'. In India one still does that. How does this appear to you? Mhm (interrogative), would you also do that?

S: Unmodern.

E: Modern?

S: UNmodern.

E: Oh unmodern. Yes, unmodern is right. Something else? Would you do that like this or not so much?

S: No.

E: No. But this is / one debases oneself a little bit. It's a little submissive. But that is it. I am perhaps really below these persons commanding respect if they are my teachers or my grandparents or my parents. And I have to thank them for a lot of things. That is still the case in India.

(GSE-MB, 85-118)

In this situation, Eva constructs India as a homogeneous and bounded entity ('among persons commanding respect, one greets [...] each other like this', 'that is still the case in India'), but at the same time, she imposes 'our' views onto 'them' ('[y]es, unmodern is right'). When trying to relativise the perceived outdatedness and submissiveness of the represented greeting practice, Eva further stabilises and reinforces the stereotype ('[b]ut that is it. I am perhaps really below these persons [...] And I have to thank them for a lot of things. That is still the case in India').

Having already alluded to the disciplinary function and the desire for non-European values that is implicit in the phenomenon of projecting desirable moral values on the Other, these representations of boundedness, fixation in time, and homogeneity are at the centre of the critique offered here. All these functions are connected to each other: The generalisation and fixation of 'their' values provide a better argument for being more like 'them'. Equally, the nostalgia for the values of the Other is essentially based upon an understanding of 'their' maintained traditions and allegedly authentic values. Yet, the crucial aspect about the representation of the Other not only as 'unmodern', or 'submissive', but also as generous, modest, altruistic, respectful, etc. has connotations beyond mere nostalgia, romanticisation, or utopia.

This projection of positive values; this rendering of non-European values as ideals, connotes what Raymond Schwab has called 'condescending veneration' (Schwab 1986, 24). This term refers to Said's *Orientalism* and describes the move of the perception of the East by the West from 'incredulous bedazzlement to condescending veneration' (ibid.). Through this concept, the ambiguous relationship between veneration or desire and condescension, that can also be observed in the examples above, becomes clear. The position from which the Other is imagined, desired, and compared is not an innocent one. The articulation of the romantic ideal of respectful, modest non-European traditions powerfully renders non-European 'culture' not only as a generalised, unmoving entity, but also as the object of Europe's judgement. From the perspective of those who have ostensibly abandoned or progressed from these values, they are defined as appropriate, authentic, and positive. As social norms, however, they cannot be adopted in what is depicted as the progressive, modern world. They can only be appropriated as individual moral values, or as guidelines for one's individual behaviour. Non-European social norms are desirable (veneration), but they do not belong in the present (condescension). Thereby, render non-Europeans in these descriptions and comparisons as 'prisoners of their "mode of thought"' (Appadurai 1988, 37) hence implicitly represents the inferiority of the Other (in terms of emancipation, self-assurance, individuality) while explicitly referring to their moral superiority.

Finally, what needs to be addressed in this regard is the question of time and the denial of coevalness (Fabian 1983). As already mentioned, in the aforementioned sessions on China and India, there is an explicit relegation of the Other to a different time, which is evident from the statements 'here it is different by now' (Britta) and 'unmodern, yes, that's it' (Eva). In the session on North American Indians, there is a similarly implicit denial of coevalness in that the guide frequently shifts the tense of her narration.[47] This shows that the nostalgia for the Other is closely linked to an imagined 'time travel' to another country. What Fabian found within ethnographic and anthropological writings of the 19th and early 20th centuries, namely their function as 'time machines' (ibid., 39), is, thus, still observable in contemporary museum educational practices. While Appadurai has argued that 'postindustrial cultural productions have entered a postnostalgic phase' (1996, 30), grounding his argument in the fact that globalisation has led to a diversification of constructed cultural memories and a substitutability of historical periods, the examples discussed here raise doubts about this posited universality of nostalgic

---

[47] This temporal shift cannot be observed in the session in the African gallery of Museum C (both in relation to the guide's remarks about respect for elders and in relation to her statements on community support). While Gladys's account is clearly marked by an understanding of culture as a bounded, homogeneous entity, it does not include a temporal division between European and non-European affiliations. This may have something to do with the fact that the guide herself has a Ghanaian migration background and thus represents 'Africa' as part of her own present 'culture'.

practices. While it is possible that similar strategies of imagining otherness come into play in different areas of the world, and while non-European cultural representations may equally involve a projection onto European 'culture', the implicit power dynamics that are entrenched in this reinforcement and continuation of situating non-Europeans in an unspecified past cannot be ignored. Through such references to the past, non-Europeans, regardless of the specific regions or contexts they are connected to, are once more located outside of modernity.

Furthermore, these dynamics of representing non-European values as unmodern are even more problematic in so far as these representations refer to remote 'Others' rather than immediate 'Others' and can thus rarely be proven wrong. When Kristeva regards the acceptation of the other within 'ourselves', or the other as our unconscious, as means to deal with the Other without (1991, 183), this is impossible when the Other is depicted as remote and faraway, and not as an immediate 'stranger'. Correspondingly, the guides do not make a clear connection to any immediate, present person or figure. The social norms of the Other are, thus, illustrated as remote as their imagined space – a space where they must remain in order for these values to be successfully projected.

4.4   Authenticating the Other

The aforementioned emphasis of the guides on the moral superiority of non-European groups is, as already explained, connected to notions of nostalgia, traditional values, and authenticity. In the observed gallery sessions, these aspects are also part of a more general recurring theme in the guides' accounts. The construction of authenticity, in different facets of the term, permeates many of the guides' explanations and interpretations. Their statements often authenticate not only the represented objects, but also the people with whom they are associated. By such means, gallery educators tend to reinforce an idea of the 'pure', authentic Other, while they often construct notions of progress, modernity and change as inauthentic developments in non-European countries. The following analysis discusses the different dimensions of this authentication and explains how it works to distance the students from the groups of people represented in the galleries.

To begin this analysis, it is first important to concretise what is meant by 'authenticity' and 'authentication' in this specific context. A good basis for understanding authenticity in the museum is Goffman's distinction between front and back stages (cf. 1986, 69f.) of performances. Goffman notes that while '[…] accentuated facts make their appearance in what we have called a front region; it should be just as clear that there may be another region – a back region or backstage – where the suppressed facts make an appearance' (ibid.) Comparable to these two stages, the articulation of authenticity in the museum is usually connected to the idea that the 'front' that is exhibited in the gallery refers to a 'back' region that is normally out of purview for the average person. In this context, the 'front' represents the exhibition and the 'back' is what is constructed as traditional culture or authentic non-Europeanness. The ethnographic museum's offer is thus often connected to the claim that there is in fact a hidden and authentic 'back stage' of non-European culture and that the museum has the expertise to provide access to it. In the guided tours, these claims are reinforced by the guides, who attest the authenticity of the artefacts and thereby perform both their own and the museum's expertise.

This alleged provision of authentic experiences or access to cultural back stages in the museum needs to be regarded in light of its orchestrated character. In his application of Goffman's 'front' and 'back' to tourism studies, MacCannel has shown that what is framed as an experience of an authentic 'back' is often fabricated artificially, a phenomenon that he refers to as 'staged authenticity' (cf. 1999, 91). MacCannel then complicates Goffman's distinction between front and back. He does this by proposing a spectrum of six stages of authenticity, of which only the first and the sixth represent Goffman's pure 'front' and 'back' while all the stages between are hybrid forms.

The second stage, especially, at which tourist fronts are decorated with reminders of back regions, can be applied to the ethnographic museum. The museum experience is neither entirely a 'front' because it works on the basis of insinuating a 'back', nor is it a 'back stage' because the exhibition is a public and open space. Visitors know that they are inside a staged environment in so far as the objects and recreations have been selected and ordered by curators. Yet, many rely upon the fact that this staged environment gives them a glimpse into (rather than constructs) some form of authentic 'back'.[48] The staging of authenticity in the gallery is, thus, visible on the one hand, and invisible on the other. The performance is visible, but the constructedness of its content is not. The same is true for the students in the guided tours: While they know that both the museum and the guided tours are specifically orchestrated for them, the depictions of and accounts about non-European countries appear 'authentic' to them in so far as they believe that what they see and hear is a realistic and representative rendering of the non-European 'worlds'.

This brief definition of 'authenticity' indicates that in this work, the cultural 'back regions' evoked in the ethnographic museum are regarded as constructions. In this sense, the analysis departs from MacCannel's theory, which has been criticised for its inbuilt assumption that authenticity exists prior to the search for it by travellers or tourists (cf. Lozanski 2010,

---

[48] This is not to say that ethnographic exhibitions do not relate to real practices or circumstances. However, in many displays, it does not become clear to the lay visitor whether these practices belong to the past or to the present. Furthermore, despite the fact that museums represent practices that have been documented by researchers, these research results are usually not represented as theories or interpretations, but as facts. They are often depicted from a seemingly 'objective' point of view, which leads to their persuasiveness. The power that the museum, thus, occupies by articulating truth claims about the 'back regions' is questionable in itself, regardless of whether they are accurate or inaccurate interpretations.

744). While MacCannel's concept of 'staged authenticity' suggest that there is an 'unstaged' authenticity somewhere out there, the analysis in this work conceives of 'authenticity' in culture as a fabricated and nostalgic imagination. It thereby follows, for instance, the anthropologist Edward Bruner's perspective on authenticity. He has argued in favour of a constructivist take on the concept, which is practised by asking who has the power to authenticate (cf. 408f.). In this conception, authenticity is not a static product, but a continuous production of active agents. In the context of authentic non-Europeanness, these agents can be touristic companies, writers and journalists, as well as curators and gallery educators. Yet, in their authenticating practices, these agents never produce a final idea of authentic non-European lifeworlds. As Phillip Vannini and J. Patrick Williams have argued in their introduction to *Authenticity in Culture, Self, and Society*, '[a]s culture changes - and with it, tastes, beliefs, values, and practices - so too do definitions of what constitutes the authentic' (2016, 3).

Authenticity is thus understood here as a set of changing imaginations that become attached (and constantly reattached) to non-European cultural practices or regions in the museums and the guided tours, and that thereby facilitate the construction of imaginations about cultural 'back stages'. The assumption implicit in these imaginations is that there is a legitimate or essential 'world of non-European otherness' that is located either in the past or in a faraway land – two entities which are often conflated in authenticating processes, as Appadurai (cf. 1996, 31) and Fabian (cf. 1983, 15ff.) have shown.

In the guided tour, the communication of 'authenticity' can refer both to gallery educators' claims that the artefacts displayed in the galleries *originate* in what is constructed as the 'back' region, and to their statements about ways of life that are depicted as original and, therefore, more genuine These two dimensions of communicating authenticity in the observed gallery sessions are discussed in more detail in the following, both with respect to the ways in which they are communicated in the observed guided tours and with regard to their implications in terms of condescending representations of non-European people.

4.4.1 Authenticating Artefacts

In various instances during the guided tours, the gallery educators emphasise that the objects in the gallery are 'real'. For instance, Britta explains this as follows:

B: To maybe anticipate this immediately. Many students ask me whether they are real, the things that we have here. Everything is real. We did not recreate anything here. Maybe the pebbles we walk on are not really from Japan, but other than that the houses existed in Japan as they stand there. Someone has disassembled them there and brought them into the museum like many other things. (GSB-MB, 57-63)

In a similar vein, Antonia introduces the museum by saying that all the things are real: 'This is the great thing about museums' (GSA-MA, 42-44). Feona equally states that '[a]nything you see in this museum are objects that are really real' (GSF2-MD, 124). There are more examples that follow similar patterns. The 'realness' of the objects on display is an important aspect for the guides to include in their accounts.

In order to understand what this 'realness' implies, it is worthwhile to consider four different forms of authenticity that Edward Bruner has distinguished, which entail 'verisimilitude, genuineness, originality, authority' (cf. 1994, 401). Although his categorisation is related to heritage villages, it can be translated to the museum space. Verisimilitude, in Bruner's understanding, refers to the 'mimetic credibility' (ibid., 399) or resemblance of a representation to what it represents; genuineness means a historically accurate simulation (cf. ibid.); originality refers to the opposite of copy, to the aura of the real that cannot be achieved in recreations or reconstructions (cf. ibid., 400); and authority relates to the 'duly authorized, certified, or legally valid' (ibid.). Bruner explains that in his experience, the first and the second versions of authenticity are the ones predominantly used by museum professionals (cf. ibid., 399). As can be concluded from the examples above, however, originality seems to be the most frequent concern regarding authenticity in the observed guided tours. This difference to Bruner's conclusion can be explained by the fact that museums are cherished for their collections of objects from specific regions or times whereas heritage villages are often meant to resemble regions or times in a historically accurate way without claiming to use objects that originate in them. Verisimilitude, genuineness, and authority still play a role in the guides' accounts, but when the guides explain that the objects in the exhibition are 'really real', they reinforce the museum's value as a place where artefacts from other places and periods (not copies or reconstructions) can be seen.

There are two main implications that the guides' references to originality in the tours have. The first one is connected to the communication of the (cultural, historical, financial) value of the objects, whereas the second is related to the desire for the objects' 'aura of authenticity'. The two dimensions are interrelated but explained separately for the sake of clarity in the following.

The guides in the observed gallery sessions valorise museum objects by referring to their originality. Britta's statement that 'we did not recreate anything here', for instance, shows that the original location of the objects in the respective non-European region is considered valuable in itself. This is related to the common practice in museums of placing social and cultural value on objects by constructing them as original pieces. This valorisation works, for instance, by way of representing these artefacts as (historical) documents (cf. Kirshenblatt-Gimblett 1998, 25) or as 'pure', traditional specimen devoid of modernity and hybridity, thereby giving structure and continuity to the world (cf. Clifford 1988, 231). However, for

Britta, it is not necessary to explicitly emphasise the historical or traditional value of the objects because their posited originality is already a symbol for the access that the exhibition allows to the 'back region'. Additional value is achieved by combining this originality with the value of singularity or uniqueness of the retrieved objects. Antonia explains at the beginning of her session that the objects on display only exist once, and if they break, they cannot be replaced (GSA-MA, 47-49).[49] This focus on uniqueness in connection with the artefacts' originality facilitates a valorisation not only of the artefacts, but also of the museum as a place holding them. As Kirshenblatt-Gimblett has argued, the artefact's value is established through the ways in which ethnographers perform their expertise when speaking about it (cf. 1998, 33). Correspondingly, when the guides emphasise the objects' originality and uniqueness, they implicitly perform expertise. This is further connected to Bruner's fourth dimension of authenticity as authority (cf. 1994, 399). By attesting to the object's 'realness' and 'uniqueness', the guides implicitly demonstrate the authority of the museum to award this status. This can further be understood as a strategy to encourage the students to respect the museum and its objects, and to be careful around them. In this context, it is not only the evaluation of the objects as 'original' that is interesting, but also the representation of

---

[49] This is a questionable claim because many of the objects in museums are everyday items rather than singular masterpieces. To say that the objects cannot be replaced because they are originally from the 'cultures' represented in the gallery suggests that these 'cultures' have either vanished or are now incapable of producing items of similar quality, which is not usually the case. This pitfall of constructions of authenticity in the museum has been documented, for instance, by Laura van Broekhoven, who describes how an 'original' Guatemalan object stored in the National Museum of Ethnology in Leiden, the so-called 'Leiden Plate' was recreated by contemporary Maya artisans with the same materials for a Guatemalan museum. She asks: '[...] should we conclude that the Leiden Plate replicas will always be without auratic value? Or can a half manually and half mechanically produced replica, handmade by Maya artisans in Guatemala in the 21st century, with the same ancient Maya jade extracted from sources similar to those of the original, and proudly exhibited to a largely Guatemalan public, acquire a sense of aura all by itself?' (2013, 156).

the objects as the museum's property. An elusive example can be found in Christine's account. When a student asks what would happen if she dropped an object Christine has brought for the students to touch, Christine answers that in this case she would hope that the girl had a good liability protection (cf. GSC-MB, 556-557). Through such statements, authority and value is given both to the artefacts and, in effect, to their current owners, the museums.

In addition to this aspect of establishing value and authority, another implication of the guides' recurring emphasis on the originality of the artefacts is connected to the physical experience of objects that are perceived to transport an atmosphere of tradition and difference. The guides' concentration on originality can then be explained by the desire for the objects' 'aura of authenticity', or, as Walter Benjamin defines it, a desire for the uniqueness of the work of art and its embeddedness in tradition (cf. 1963, 16). This form of authenticating the objects in terms of their original embeddedness in exotic rituals and beliefs may be prevalent in the guided tours because ethnographic artefacts promise a kind of authenticity that is often regarded as lost in relation to mass-produced objects. In Benjamin's conception of the aura, the remoteness of objects (cf. 1963, 16) evokes the auratic impression. While mechanically reproduced objects are disconnected from these criteria and from their embeddedness in rituals (cf. ibid., 17), ethnographic artefacts are often regarded as retaining notions of distance and singularity. This has also been emphasised by Alexander Geurds in his book, *Authentication Processes in Ethnographic Museums* (2013):

> Ethnographic objects possess a force of empirische Einmaligkeit, identified by Walter Benjamin (1936) – the 'aura' of an original artwork. A certain tension exists in ethnological museums as a result of the mixed composition of the objects in their holdings, being part unique works of art, part mass-produced objects. Until quite recently, ethnology museums tended to disguise the latter as the former, seeking to present themselves as guardians of the 'temple of authenticity' (Handler 1986). (2013, 4)

When Geurds explains earlier museum techniques of granting visitors a '"true" view of the distant and exotic' (cf. ibid.), this promise still seems to be part, at least to some extent, of the appeal of ethnographic museums. This point will be further elaborated in Chapter 5, especially with respect to the exhibition contexts that evoke this 'aura of authenticity'. It suffices to mention here that the 'aura of authenticity' in the museum is increased by the guides' references to the original value of the objects on display.

Along with this main emphasis on the originality of the artefacts, the guides sometimes additionally interpret authenticity in terms of Bruner's verisimilitude and genuineness. Both means of authentication are used with respect to reproductions or recreations embedded in the museum displays. Verisimilitude is evident, for instance, when Maria explains what a market place from Afghanistan that has been recreated in the exhibition would have looked like originally, drawing the attention of the students to resemblances between the museum's reproduction and the original (cf. GSM-MB, 1094-1101). Genuineness is articulated, for example, when gallery educators try to authenticate objects that have not been retrieved from non-European regions, as in the case of Doreen, who shows the students a canoe that was purpose-built – historically and 'culturally' accurately – in the museum by a Native American: 'It's a real Indian canoe, but it has never been in water' (GSD-MA, 668-669). In this case, originality cannot be claimed because the object has neither been preserved from the past nor has it been found in a non-European region. Yet, in Doreen's logic, the fact that a 'real American Indian' made the canoe under circumstances that comply with what is known about traditional production processes makes the canoe 'real'. This is an interesting example because in the exhibition, the object is authenticated by means of a text panel documenting the (apparently traditional) rituals that have been practised during the canoe's production. Doreen similarly points to these rituals, thereby justifying the genuineness of the artefact in order to retain its value and appeal despite its lack of originality.

The aforementioned examples show that authenticity in museums is not only constructed by visual means, but also by means of the guides' ways of speaking about the artefacts in terms of their originality, their uniqueness, and their connection to rituals and beliefs. The guides rarely demonstrate these aspects, but state them explicitly. These statements are often articulated as objective facts by means of zero focalisation ('This tipi exists only once in the whole word' (Doreen, GSD-MA, 261). As a result, neither the idea of an original value nor the experience of an aura of authenticity emerge within a discussion between students and gallery educators. Instead, they are posited as irrefutable facets of the artefacts. The authenticity of the objects can then be seen as the basic presumption upon which every statement or story about otherness in the observed sessions is based, rather than a 'topic' of the guided tours. This point leads to the final part of this first section, which is concerned with the implications of this authentication of the museum objects, both in terms of the value that is constructed with respect to original objects and in terms of the aura of authenticity that is facilitated.

On the one hand, what has to be made clear from the start is that the integration of 'original' objects as opposed to recreations in exhibitions is not per se problematic. For example, museum education scholar Sally Duensing explains that the confrontation with such objects can spark imaginations of what it was like to be at a place at a certain point of time (cf. 2002, 356f.). This also applies to the guided tours. By pointing out the originality of the artefacts, the guides may facilitate the students' imagination of 'other' places or daily lives, which could contribute to broadening their horizons as well as to evoking empathy for unfamiliar practices. Such a facilitation of the students' imaginations about prior contexts of objects can then support the process of 'accommodation'

196

(Lewis qt. in Herman 2009, 80), i.e. the relocation of an audience to the presented story world. This process can contribute to the students' understanding of the represented world, and further induce affective reactions to the objects which might lead to changes in perspective or to the production of interest for these places and times.

On the other hand, as already mentioned, the 'realness' of the objects or their 'originality' is often posited as a self-explanatory fact. The guides convince the students of the basic argument that the objects are 'really real' (Feona). Such 'realness' is concerned with the place that an object comes from and how it has been used 'originally'. To define it 'real' by origin, however, disregards the complex circumstances of production and signification that the objects in the exhibition have experienced throughout their biographies. As Susan Crane asks in a paper on objects and memory, '[w]e can know an object's provenance, but does that really tell us the 'origin' of its significance?' (2006, 107). In contrast, the objects' value and aura that the guides communicate are predicated on ideas about identity and history that presuppose the existence of clear meanings and a specific context of usage. The problem of this framing has already been indicated with reference to Bruner's fourth meaning of authenticity as authority. Bruner claims that '[...] authenticity today is becoming a matter of the politics of connoisseurship [...] and of status discrimination; beyond that, I would claim, it is a matter of power, of who has the right to authenticate' (1994, 408). Rosemary Joyce's contribution to the book *Authentication Processes in Ethnographic Museums* also points to the processes by which objects are considered authentic. She explains that the

> 'moment of authenticity is not [...] when something originated. It is always a moment in the contemporary world of collectors and museums, when belief in the specific agents who conveyed the object to the next collection on its routes authorizes its use [...]' (2013, 54).

These self-reflective approaches to authenticity, that highlight the authenticating power of museums, are not addressed by the guides. By instead locating authenticity within the objects, the guides not only reinforce notions of bounded cultures, but also reinforce and naturalise the power of the museum to authenticate objects. Furthermore, because of the guides' declarative, seemingly objective language, a negotiation of authenticity and its meaning together with the students is prevented.

4.4.2   Authenticating 'Ways of Life'

As already indicated in the beginning of this chapter, in almost all of the observed gallery sessions, the guides do not speak predominantly about the objects on display, but instead use them as starting points for addressing broader cultural practices or 'ways of life' in the non-European regions. With respect to the communication of authenticity, however, this transition from descriptions of objects to descriptions of ways of life is especially interesting because it leads to a change of the meanings or implications that are attached to 'authenticity'. In order to explain this transition, consider the following example from Britta's session, which occupies a partway point between an account about the displayed objects and a description of 'authentic' cultural life in the respective region:

B: We have many things from ancient times. But if I show them to you and explain them, then you will see that many things from times past have some effects on today and we only understand some of the things in China today by looking back to ancient times. So it's not bad that there aren't so many modern things here. Because what would you see here If you went to China and bought modern things there. What would we show in our museum here? Think about it. What comes from China? And what material is it made from? [...]

S: Statues?

B: Statues. But think more practically. If you went to a supermarket now, what would you find there?

S: Tools? [...]

S: Chop sticks? [...]

S: Clothes?

B: Clothes. You haven't said what I actually thought you would, which would be all the toys. Everything that is 'made in China.' These are actually the things that we know from China today. Our clothes, our toys, games. When you turn those around you see they are made in China. China makes such things. We could also display this in the

> museum. Then we would have the everyday culture from today. But
> we have the everyday culture from the past.
>
> (GSB-MB, 190-224)

In the beginning of the statement, Britta speaks about the objects in the museum. Just like in the previous examples, she authenticates these objects on the basis of their origin, namely in China's 'ancient times'. Britta explains that although they do not seem exciting, the artefacts can reveal aspects of the past and the present. The value of the artefacts is, thus, established in relation to their historical significance as original specimen from 'old times'. This historical value of the museum objects is then contrasted with contemporary objects from China. The phrase '[s]o it's not bad that there aren't so many modern things here. Because what would you see here if [...] you went to China and bought modern things there?' suggests that historical objects are more valuable to the museum than contemporary objects. This placing of value on historical objects is common in ethnographic museums and collecting, as Clifford has found:

> This system finds intrinsic interest and beauty in objects from a past
> time, and it assumes that collecting everyday objects from ancient
> [...] civilizations will be more rewarding than collecting [...]
> customized T-shirts from Oceania. (1985, 241).

Although this hierarchical valuation is not explicit in Britta's statements, she nevertheless appeals to the antiquity of the objects as a source of their interest.

Perhaps more significantly, Britta's account not only refers to the exhibited objects, but also makes claims about China in general. When she asks the students what they think 'comes from China', they initially suggest statues or tools, but are subsequently corrected by Britta, for *toys* are 'actually the things that we know from China today'. The underlying assumption is that things like statues or tools are less common productions in contemporary China than toys, games or clothes. This claim helps the guide to make a distinction between valuable objects from the past represented in the museum and less valuable (because mass-produced, and plastic) objects from the present. Her statement, however, also contains subtle implications that present-day China has less to offer than China of the past. Associating contemporary Chinese products simply with toys, games and clothes suggests that objects such as statues or other handcrafted items are not part of China's everyday culture *anymore*.[50] While it may be true that China has a large manufacturing industry, it is clearly reductive to associate contemporary China simply with objects labelled 'made in China'. What becomes apparent here is reminiscent of what ter Keurs has described in terms of curators' worries about the threats of globalisation: 'An additional reason for worry is the conviction [...] that most of the new 'things' are badly made [...] and cannot be considered comparable to the 'good, expressive art' that was made in the past.' (1999, 74). Although Britta does not explicitly refer to a worse quality of contemporary objects, this dimension is insinuated by her statement that '[...] it's not bad that there aren't so many modern things here. *Because* what would you see here if [...] you went to China and bought modern things there [...] [a]nd what material would it be made from?'.

This example shows how subtle constructions of non-European everyday life can become intertwined with statements about the authenticity of museum objects. Implied in such statements may be an understanding that not only non-European objects, but also non-European 'cultures' in general reached their peak in the past. Although this assumption is not explicitly stated in the aforementioned example, the truth claims that are made by Britta about current Chinese products at least misrepresent contemporary China for the sake of 'old' China. This practice of trading off ostensibly authentic, ancient artefacts against contemporary

---

[50] Furthermore, this devaluation of 'toys, games, and clothes' also reinforces a hierarchy of cultural objects between arts and craft, which is also problematic in terms of authenticity and otherness.

objects in a guided tour can be particularly problematic because such statements can easily acquire condescending or evaluative connotations.

This evaluative component is especially problematic when the ascription of authentic value to objects from the past is connected to what Anja Laukötter has called the 'vision of extinction and rescue' (2007, 143). This was an agenda prevalent mainly in early 20th century anthropology, when museum anthropologists such as Felix von Luschan hoped to obtain and save as many artefacts as possible from what they perceived as rapidly extinguishing non-European cultures (cf. ibid.). While this perspective has long been overcome in ethnography, some of the guides' statements are still indicative of a perceived 'rescue' of authentic culture (i.e., the past) through the museum, as, for instance, Antonia:

> These clubhouses do not exist in Palau anymore. We once had a woman from Palau here as a visitor and she cried when she saw this house and she said: 'Oh it's here in Berlin, but we have no such houses anymore.' This is, well, in Palau everything looks like in America today, a little bit. So, there's McDonald's, and streets, okay? (GSA-MA, 301-305)

The similarity between Britta's account quoted above and Antonia's account in this example consists of the fact that both guides contrast past with present ways of life in the respective regions. In both contexts, the representation of the present is marked by references to consumption and capitalism ('made in China', McDonald's), which, especially in the second example, seem to have displaced cultural elements that are now only documented in the museum. This is where the 'vision of extinction and rescue' becomes evident. Cultural elements that have not been preserved in their countries of origin are allegedly safely installed in European museums. Such accounts not only elevate the significance of the ethnographic museum, but they also subtly justify its continuous and unquestioned ownership of these objects. The underlying message is: If European collectors had not taken these artefacts with them, they would be lost forever. This narrative is also evident, in a slightly different form, in

Maria's account about how the museum acquired a piece of an Afghan market place whose original was later destroyed in the war, leaving the only remaining original part of the market stored in the museum (cf. GSM-MB, 1103-1117).

In these examples, not only the artefacts, but also the 'ways of life' in the respective regions are authenticated. This is problematic for a variety of reasons. First of all, the present situations in these places are labelled according to generalised categories of 'Americanisation', 'consumption', or 'mass production'. In the example of Maria's session, the current situation in Afghanistan is described in terms of war and crisis. Secondly, these present situations are described as less authentic than what is represented as traditional culture in the museum. Authenticity in this case can neither be defined as originality nor verisimilitude nor genuineness, but appears in the form of an ostensibly appropriate, legitimate, or actual way of life of the non-European communities. The current situations in the respective regions are thereby posited as deviations from this authentic way of life. The fact that 'they' make mass-produced objects, have McDonald's stores and streets appears as something illegitimate or at least inauthentic in the statements of the guides. With respect to Maria's session, this is only slightly different: terrorism and war are equally depicted as forms of destruction of the authentic culture of the Other. She thus implies that the objects were rescued from times of war and therefore allegedly document a more authentic 'anteriority' of the displayed regions.

Such references to the alleged authenticity of non-European past 'way of life' can also be observed in other accounts, such as in Eva's contrasting of the traditional way of draping a sari with the new method 'influenced' by the British (cf. GSE-MB, 687-692), or in Britta's explanation that the Chinese and Japanese make chairs now, but that the did not originally have them (cf. GSB-MB, 141-144). While it is clear that the passage of time changes the realities of the regions represented in the museum, these accounts about change are often addressed as if they were particularly surprising or as if the 'actual' or 'original' way of life had to be set off from these changes. 'Change' is thereby communicated in terms of 'loss', which makes an enormous difference in terms of what is constructed as valuable and desirable.

These accounts not only portray a dimension of nostalgia for a perceived authentic way of life which has allegedly become tainted by change and modernity, but also distinctive perceptions of change in non-European and European regions. While it appears to be natural that European architecture has changed over the course of history, the 'loss' of original Palauan men's clubhouses[51] seems particularly noteworthy and regrettable in the guided tour. This imbalance between perspectives on European and non-European 'authenticity' can be explained by the awareness of the complexity of 'our own' history as and a lack thereof in relation to 'theirs'. This is closely related to what Appadurai has explained in reference to the term 'native':

> We have tended to use the word native for persons and groups who belong to those parts of the world that were, and are, distant from the metropolitan West. [...] We exempt ourselves from this sort of claim to authenticity because we are too enamored of the complexities of our history, the diversities of our societies, and the ambiguities of our collective conscience. When we find authenticity close to home, we are more likely to label it folk than native, the former being a term that suggests authenticity without being implicitly derogatory. The anthropologist thus rarely thinks of himself as a native of some place, even when he knows that he is from somewhere. (1988, 36f.)

A similar distinction is apparent in the authentication practices of the guides: European cultural realities are perceived as complex, diverse, and ambiguous, whereas non-European contexts are often framed in the light of a natural purity whose contamination by globalisation, capitalism or consumerism is undesirable. Problematically, modernity is, thereby, framed as inauthentic or illegitimate in non-European realms, whereas

---

[51] A definition is provided in the glossary.

Europe represents, in Dipesh Chakrabarty's words, 'the primary habitus of the modern' (2000, 43).

Another aspect that contributes to this problematic framing of 'change' and 'loss' is the equally problematic framing of 'time' in the guided tours. This is so because the 'past' that is addressed in most of the guides' statements about 'authentic' original practices or objects remains unspecific. Britta speaks about China's 'ancient times' (GSB-MB, 193-194), Antonia does not refer to any specific time frame, and many other guides speak about 'former times' (GSA-MA, 317-318). Yet this unspecified past tense, as Sturge has argued, excludes a sense of chronology from historical narratives in the museum (cf. 2006, 434). The fact that it does not seem to matter when exactly something happened, but that the simple label of 'former times' suffices to contextualise events, amplifies the impression that change, in the context of non-European culture, cannot be tied to specific historical or political circumstances, but is always merely interesting in so far as it represents a deviation from what is perceived as 'original'. Furthermore, by not articulating distinct stages of the past, but relegating non-European history to an unspecific anteriority, the people that are represented are denied a proper history, as Mieke Bal has stated: 'The nineteenth-century Siberian is conflated with thousands of years of the likes of him; the peoples in question do not have a history, not more than the 'nature' depicted in the dioramas' (1992, 575).

It is interesting that the same observations that Bal and Sturge, but also Henrietta Riegel have made with regard to the relegation of non-European groups to an unspecified past (cf. e.g. Riegel 1996, 88) can equally be observed in the guided tours. While the visual exhibition narrative may not facilitate insight into historically precise developments, the verbal accounts of the guides could function to put the information in context simply by introducing a rough time frame. They do not do so in most of the gallery sessions, however. Very rarely are precise dates or time frames mentioned. In most instances, historical contextualisation remains vague, which is especially surprising considering that the students come to the museum on school trips and could relate new information about non-European objects or practices to their already established knowledge about different historical epochs or global dates in history.

Even further adding to this issue of vague references to different times within the past is the guides' conflation of past and present, known in museum studies and anthropology as the 'ethnographic present'. Fabian has first conceptualised this way of communicating otherness:

> The ethnographic present represents a choice of expression which is determined by an epistemological position and cannot be derived from, or explained by, linguistic rules alone. [...] The use of the present tense in anthropological discourse not only marks a literary genre (ethnography) through the locutionary attitude of discourse/commentary; it also reveals a specific cognitive stance towards its object [...]. (1983, 86)

For a start, it is helpful to consider first the 'linguistic' dimension of this communication practice. In many of the observed guided tours, the guides use the present tense to refer to the non-European groups on display. For instance, Doreen says '[w]hen the Indians follow the animals that they hunt, they must take everything they have with them' (GSD-MA, 113-114) or '[t]he Indians believe that people who have died are not really gone, but that their life goes on. The souls of the deceased go up to heaven' (GSD-MA, 289-292). Eva explains that 'the Indians, the women sleep with their saris. And the men also sleep in their traditional clothes' (GSE-MB, 724-725). This means, the guides describe 'the Native Americans' and 'the Indians' (but also 'the Polynesians' (Antonia), 'the Muslims (Maria)) by using a subject in connection with the present tense. This linguistic construction is again indicative of the relegation of non-European groups to an unspecific time, and, importantly, to an unchanging reality. To these groups are ascribed certain practices, beliefs, rituals as a whole, without references to the past or a precise reference to the present. This way of addressing non-European 'ways of life' is therefore problematic already from a linguistic perspective because it locates people from these regions outside of time and presumes, as Bruner writes '[…] an original pure state, an authentic culture in the third sense, like the ethnographic present, before contact' (1994, 408).

Yet, in following this line of argumentation, the cognitive stance toward these groups, which Fabian refers to, needs to be considered as well. Fabian explains that the ethnographic present is used when ethnographers transform their thoughts into writing. In this manner, the time that the ethnographer and their subjects share during fieldwork is suddenly reframed in terms of a different understanding of time: Now, the ethnographer looks back at the time they once shared with the non-European subject, from the perspective of a different time. This is necessary because of the distance that the ethnographer needs to establish to turn observations into facts (cf. Fabian 1983, 87ff.) In a similar vein, when the guides speak about how 'the Indians believe' this or 'the Polynesians know' that, this is not only a claim to an authentic, vague timeless 'way of life', but also to an objective fact. This usage of the ethnographic present is also a means of articulating ethnographic authority: 'The anthropologist makes the peculiar claim that certain experiences or events in his past constitute facts, not fiction.' (ibid., 88).

The gallery educators in the observed guided tours likewise claim truth by making statements about non-European practices in an indeterminate present tense. Still, the communication situation in the gallery session is clearly different from Fabian's material of ethnographic accounts. The perceived scientific problem with these accounts, Fabian explains, is the fact that the ethnographer's information or knowledge about the contexts they study is autobiographical (cf. ibid., 89). Ethnography has long struggled with this necessarily subjective dimension of ethnographic accounts (cf. ibid., 87). The ethnographic present hence provides a 'way out' of subjectivity by making it possible to avoid relating to the ethnographer's own past when sharing observations about the investigated cultural contexts (cf. ibid., 88). The present offers an analytical view that moves beyond the ethnographer's experiences and turns ethnographies into seemingly objective descriptions (cf. ibid.). The guides themselves, however, rarely speak about their own experiences in the field when they communicate otherness. They either relate to the exhibition or repeat information they have learned from curators, books, or from their scripts.

While the guides do not communicate their own experiences, they still relate the descriptions of the non-European regions in terms of a factual language. This is connected to the museum's status – in contrast to tourism or heritage industries – as a repository of truth (cf. Karp/ Kratz 2000, 208). Although means of communication in the museum are becoming more diversified, 'facts' still seem to be its 'unique selling point'. Hence, instead of presenting information in a subjective way (i.e., along the lines of statements such as 'ethnographer x described the North American Indians as courageous'), the guides objectify and once again verify information ('The American Indians are courageous.'). This process needs to be seen as a subconscious adoption of a factual language that has been internalised by curators and other museum professionals. Still, it has the same effects that have been identified for the usage of the ethnographic present in gallery texts: It renders particular information as generally true (cf. Sturge 2006, 434) and represents the objects (and the people they are connected to) as 'stuck in time' (Yap 2014, 7). Furthermore, it continues to prevent the communication of other 'ways of life' under conditions of a shared temporality, which is, as Riegel rightly states, a political act (1996, 88). The people in the respective regions are cast as unchanging and as connected to an authentic or original 'way of life' that is firmly fixed in a land before 'our' time.

Finally, in addition to describing non-European 'ways of life' entirely in terms of the ethnographic present, the guides in the observed gallery sessions additionally often alternate between different unspecific times. They use the past and the present tense within one statement, making it entirely incomprehensible whether a practice is still evident in the respective regions today or whether this was the case in the past. This imbalance of using tense and referring to time can be again regarded in terms of the 'disimprovement' effect posited at the beginning. In some instances, the guides seek try to specify temporal frameworks, but in others they fall back into the trap of claiming ethnographic authority in terms of the ethnographic present. The result of this is, however, an even less clear and less specific reference to the displayed regions and people. In terms of authentication, this leads to the articulation of truth claims about traditional 'ways of life' that remain generalised and temporally imprecise. Furthermore, due to the temporal disassociation of the guides from the non-European communities, these truth claims contain assumptions about 'our' legitimacy to evaluate their authenticity: '[...] to be not yet what We are, is what makes Them the object of our 'explanations' and 'generalizations'" (Fabian 1991 [1985], 198).

4.5   Telling European Success Stories

As pointed out in the preceding section, the guides usually communicate the authenticity of the artefacts or 'ways of life' of the displayed non-European groups as a fact rather than explaining how certain objects and practices have been documented and interpreted by European ethnographers and researchers. This does not mean that European experiences are never addressed in the guided tours, however. Closely connected to practices of authentication, the next recurring phenomenon that is investigated concerns the guides' descriptions of the ways in which some of the artefacts have arrived in the museum. In such cases,

European actions do play a role, not with respect to ethnographic processes of observation and documentation, but in relation to the collection and acquisition of artefacts from non-European contexts.

To represent the history of the collection within exhibition narratives is often recommended in the realm of museum studies (cf. Shelton 1997, 53; Lidchi 2006, 97; Macdonald 2006, 92). As James Clifford has long argued, '[t]he history of collections [...] is central to an understanding of how those social groups that invented anthropology have appropriated exotic things, facts, and meanings' (1985, 240). The inclusion of these histories in the guided tour could, therefore, serve as a self-reflective and critical addition to the visual narratives of exhibitions, which otherwise often exclude the means by which the objects have come to be part of European collections. Yet, the ways in which these histories are told in the gallery sessions might lead not to a change in perspective with regard to European practices of appropriation, but instead to a reinforcement of notions of European superiority and legitimacy of ownership of the artefacts on display. This phenomenon is explored in the following sections, through analysis of different guides' accounts about European collectors' acquisition and appropriation practices.

4.5.1   Object Biographies or European Success Stories?

To illustrate this recurring theme, consider the following example from Antonia in Museum A. Her account revolves around the men's clubhouses from Palau that have already been addressed in the section on communicating authenticity. Of the three clubhouses represented in the museum, one of them allows visitors to enter and look at it from the inside. The students are equally guided inside during the tour, where they sit together on the floor of the house while Antonia tells them about the object's history:

> So there were German researchers in the South Sea, 100 years ago.
> And in 1907, one of them from Berlin was on the Palau islands. And
> there he saw this house. And he said: 'This is a great house, we
> would like to have this in Berlin in our museum. Could you please
> make one for me - but smaller so that it fits onto my boat?' And then
> the men on the island said: 'Yes, okay, we will do that.' And they built
> the same house in smaller dimensions. And this is this house. You
> just need to imagine it three times as big. (GSA-MA, 259-22)

This example depicts the basic structure of the recurring account that can also be found in other guided tours: The European researcher or collector arrives in a foreign context and decides to obtain an object for the collection in Europe. They are then confronted with a challenge, such as the German researcher's issue of transporting a big artefact back to Europe. The challenge is resolved in one way or another, and the object is successfully introduced to the European museum's collection. Such accounts further feature in guided tours about the Orient (Feona, Maria), India (Kate), North America (Doreen), and Africa (Hilda) and the main actors are European traders, scholars, soldiers, or even designers. The guides' representations can be more or less elaborate, but they share an emphasis on the success of the European endeavour to obtain the artefacts in question. While not all examples of this phenomenon can be described in more detail, the selected versions cover the most relevant aspects to be discussed in relation to this recurring phenomenon.

How can this method of communicating the object's trajectory into the museum be interpreted? Stories about the history of the objects in museums could be understood in terms of so-called 'object biographies' (Kopytoff 1986). Kopytoff argues that such biographies explain where the objects have come from, what their careers have been, and how their usage has changed over time (cf. ibid., 66f.). He maintains that this biographical approach can highlight the ways in which things adopted from another context get redefined in new contexts – a matter that he argues is more significant than the process of adoption itself (cf. ibid., 67). In the aforementioned example, by contrast, it is mainly this process of adopting a foreign artefact that is at the centre of attention. Similarly, in the accounts that are at stake in this subchapter, the focus is generally not on following the trajectories of the objects at various stages of their existence, but on the moments of the objects' removal from their non-European contexts and their arrival in European museum collections. This means that only the acquisition, and in some cases, the integration of the artefacts into the museum narrative, are considered relevant in the guides' accounts. In these cases, the history of the objects is told only from the perspective of the museum, not from the perspective of the objects. Aspects such as ideas or artists involved in the objects' creation, their redefinitions at different stages in their biographies or even the reasons for European interest in obtaining them are not explained. As the attainment of the objects is the primary focus, these accounts cannot be regarded as genuine object biographies.

Instead, they must be seen as adventure stories. A common principle in the accounts of the guides seems to be the challenge or problem that the collectors have to overcome or solve. Unless the attainment is challenging or otherwise remarkable, the acquisition process of the objects is not addressed in the guided tours. Hence, common forms of acquiring artefacts for museums such as regular purchases or bequests are not discussed in the gallery sessions. This indicates that the aim of the guides is not so much to illustrate how ethnographic artefacts have arrived in European museums in general, but to tell an interesting story about the difficult, but successful procurement of a specific artefact. In so far as the artefact's history is not represented as an interesting aspect in itself, but as relevant merely in connection with the object's appropriation by European collectors, these accounts are better to be seen as *stories about collecting* than as references to the history of the collections. In this way, a principle that has been observed with respect to culture collecting in the 19th and 20th centuries resurfaces in the guides' accounts; namely that '[…]

the practice of collecting itself was [...] more important than the collected objects' (Geurds 2013, 2). It is in this vein that the account about the men's clubhouse, which revolves around the researcher's achievement to obtain such an artefact for the collection of the museum, should be understood. The clubhouse, thus, features as an object of desire in the story of the guide, and, the researcher's ability to convince the Palauan men to purpose-build a similar house for the European collection becomes the happy ending of this success story.

As an effect of this focus on the success of acquiring the object, the role of the European is highlighted and applauded while the 'men of Palau' are merely represented as happily recreating a house for the museum. By claiming that the reaction of these men was 'Okay, we can do that', the actual processes of negotiation, or the motivations of the builders, not described, are made to seem irrelevant. For instance, not the Palauan craftsmanship involved in reconstructing the clubhouse in smaller dimensions, but the researcher's idea of downscaling the house for transport is applauded here. The Palauan men are , thus, signified as passive bystanders rather than as active agents; they are merely secondary characters in this story of collecting objects.

This focus on the collector's achievement is equally the case in a very similar account about the acquisition of a part of an Afghan market place, described by Maria in Museum B:

> This market comes directly from Afghanistan. This is because the man who made this exhibition about forty years ago had his research focus in Afghanistan. And one day he came to a village that was called Tashqurghan. And he saw this bazar. And he liked it so much that he said: I would like to have this as it is. I would like to buy sixteen meters of it and take it to Stuttgart. Said and done. He really did that. And then this was all reproduced here as close to the original as possible. Later, you can look at this large photograph to find out what it looked like in Afghanistan. (GSM-MB, 1088-1096)

Here again, the main interest is to demonstrate the collecting efforts of the researcher, whereas local perspectives are not included. How did the curator convince the vendors of removing this piece from the bazar? How did local people react when a European researcher wanted to 'cut out' a piece of their market for the purpose of display in a museum? None of this is addressed. The point of criticising the way in which the perspectives of the local residents are excluded from these accounts is not to suggest that they were always forced to provide Europeans with the artefacts or oppressed by them. Collecting processes were extremely complex (cf. Laukötter 2007, 142ff.), and it is often difficult to reconstruct exactly how power relations and negotiations played out in such situations. The problem in both accounts quoted above, however, is that local reactions or perceptions do not seem to matter at all. The 'said and done' narrative about the researcher's actions completely erases the relevance of a non-European approval or objection.

This framing of non-European groups as passive or irrelevant in the collecting process was a common trope in early anthropology. This was due to the general attitude towards these groups that was prevalent at the time of documenting information and artefacts from non-European contexts in 19th- and 20th century ethnography. As Clifford has argued, '[s]ince they were generally treated as passive specimens (or victims), their views seldom entered the historical record' (1997, 198). The effects of this process can still be seen in ethnological exhibitions today. As Sturge has shown, museum displays only very rarely provide information on translators or source authors (cf. 2006, 434). As apparent in the examples above, this also affects the guided tours. The disregard of non-European perspectives in these stories about collecting then not only is an unfortunate side effect of insufficient anthropological documenting practices, but also has become a relatively unquestioned way of conceiving of the histories of museum objects in museums today. Because it is taken for granted, this 'history of winners', which focuses on European success and excludes non-European contributions or resistances, may well appear self-evident to the guides. Regardless of the reasons for the exclusion of non-European perspectives on collecting histories, the guides' rendering of the respective regions as passive or irrelevant accentuates the European collectors' skills and success. In effect, such accounts can become means of reinforcing European superiority. This is further explained in the next section of this subchapter.

4.5.2 Communicating Superiority

Consider, for instance, the following example from a guided tour in Museum D. The students (aged 7-8) have just arrived at a vitrine featuring an artefact from India and have already learned about the arrival of the British in India in the 18th century as well as about their intention to acquire Indian goods and produce. The students have listed several things that the British may have wished to obtain from India, such as silver, gold, diamonds, tea, and fabric. The conversation, then, shifts to the ways in which the British were able to collect an artefact called 'Tippoe's tiger'[52].

K: What do you think the British did with India. They wanted all these things. So what did they start to do?
S: Killing them?
K: They didn't just walk up and start killing people. No.
S: They invaded all of the kingdoms?
K: Not quite. Not to begin with. What do you do if you want something?
S: You try and persuade them. [...]
K: To persuade them. How do you persuade them?
S: Have a debate?
S: You trade?
K: You trade with them. Fantastic. They bought them. They gave them money. Britain had a lot of money. So yeah. They started trading. They exchanged goods and money. And this meant that Britain started moving into India because they were looking after all of these interests that they had. And they started to trade more in some areas and get more and more influence over the Raj and the Sultans that ruled there. Okay. And yes. Eventually. They also did quite a bit of invading. Now. Some of these sultans and rajas did not like the fact that the British were there at all. And one in particular was called the Sultan Tippoe. And he really hated the British. So, what do you think

---

[52] A definition is provided in the glossary.

he did? If you've got all these people in your country. And you want them out. What do you do?

S: Kill them.

K: Yes. You have a fight. You have a war. You have battles. Okay. And they had four really big battles. And then in seventeen ninety-nine right at the end of the seventeen hundreds, what do you think happened in this last battle against the British?

S: The Indians got defeated.

K: He died. Yes. He died and all of the soldiers who had come the army was there as well to look after all the trading that was going on and the invasion. All of the soldiers went into his palace. And took all of his stuff. And brought it back to Britain. Actually, his stuff is all scattered around the country. In many different places. But everything in this case belonged to him. Okay?

(GSK2-MD, 202-234)

This account is at first structured in a comparable way to the examples above. The British enter India because they are interested in acquiring goods, which they achieve by means of successful trade and an unfolding stronger influence over some of the Indian areas. Yet the actual challenge and resulting success represented in the account revolve around the defeat of the Sultan and the attainment of the represented artefact (as well as all the other objects in his palace). As a result of this victory, the Sultan's 'stuff' can now be found all over Great Britain.

For a start, it is remarkable how this story initially represents the British as decent traders who used humane methods of persuasion instead of means of invasion or war, but then moves on to show that they did actually end up invading and, ultimately, 'killing them'. But the key point here is the idea of 'ending up'. The British are not represented as initiating struggle, but as reacting to it. The source of the fight is portrayed as the Sultan's hatred of the British: 'He really hated the British. So what do you think he did?' Interestingly, while Kate reacts with slight irritation upon the students' idea that the British may have got what they wanted by 'killing them' ('[t]hey didn't just walk up and start killing people.'), the same answer seems fine in connection to the Sultan's actions ('Yes. You have a fight.'). This disparity makes it seem as if methods of persuasion or negotiation were not applied by the Sultan, as if his first reaction to the British presence had been to fight them. His motivations, unlike those of the British, do not appear to be guided by diplomatic relations and logical considerations of his options, but by pure hatred. Furthermore, while the British act as a community (and for their interests as such), the Sultan seems to act as an individual, and hence, regardless of political interests.

Even though the guide-as-focaliser gives insight into both British thought processes ('they wanted all these things') and Indian perspectives ('they did not like the fact that the British were there'), and functions as a zero focaliser with seemingly omniscient knowledge about the course of events, the way in which information is provided still suggests that the account is told from a British perspective. If this were a fictional adventure story, it would be quite clear whom the reader should identify with: The British come with apparently legitimate economic interests, and yes, they start having an influence over many areas, but then they are attacked by the Sultan. Eventually, they defeat him and get to go back home with all his possessions (which they deserve because of their victory). Although the course of events is not explicitly framed in this way and Kate is careful not to express judgment, it is especially that which is *not* said that casts this account as a European success story. What methods did the British use to increase their influence over some of these areas? What did this 'invasion' mean for local residents? Why did it appear natural to the British to do 'quite a bit of invading'? None of these questions are addressed. The British are not represented as aggressors, colonisers, or invaders, but as soldiers who finally managed to defeat the Indians and recover the Sultan's belongings.

This representation of the object's procurement as the result of an ostensibly 'fair struggle' that the Indians lost serves to some extent as a means of legitimation for the British soldiers' retrieval of the Sultan's artefacts. Consequently, this account highlights the status of the object as a 'trophy of the conquest of a strange and faraway place' (Karp/Kratz 2000,

216

194/5). The legitimacy for owning the artefacts that used to belong to the Sultan is hereby represented as based upon the superiority of the British over the Indians, both in terms of diplomatic strategies (i.e., the gradual broadening of influence over the country) and in terms of military strength. By justifying British ownership of the artefact as based upon Britain's greater power, Kate's account fails to provide a critical reflexivity towards both the colonial history, and the museum's continued unquestioned possession of the object. The account does not allow any doubt about the rightful ownership of the Sultan's artefacts. Even though the students in this session are very young, the story could be told in a more critical style, addressing questions about why the British did not leave although the Sultan disapproved of their presence, and why the soldiers took the objects with them after the defeat. Instead, Kate's account reinforces the idea that the British 'deserved' the artefact because of their superiority.

Such a connection between legitimacy of ownership and superiority is a common feature in this type of account. The problems that are connected to such frames of reference become particularly evident in another example. In Museum B, Maria explains how a part of the Kiswa[53] has come to be displayed in the museum. She clarifies that it is forbidden for non-Muslims to visit the Kaaba in Mecca, but that in the nineteenth century, a Dutch researcher, who knew a lot about the Islamic Orient and spoke near-native Arabic, dressed up as a Muslim dignitary, went to Mecca and managed to get hold of a piece of the Kiswa on the day of its annual exchange. He later gave this piece to a friend who bequeathed it to the museum. Maria adds that today, the displayed Kiswa is something special for many Muslim visitors, particularly if they haven't yet travelled to Mecca (cf. GSM-MB, 489-492).

Just as in the first example, the representation of superiority is central to this story. While the previous narrative works with superiority in

---

[53] A definition is provided in the glossary.

the sense of military strength, superiority in the account about the Dutch researcher in Mecca is illustrated in terms of his ability to 'act like' a Muslim dignitary because of his knowledge (i.e. his studies of the Islamic Orient, his language skills), which eventually enabled him to succeed in deceiving the non-European previous 'owners' of the object. Here again, the retrieval of the artefact is portrayed as a success story. The main character is intelligent, knowledgeable, powerful enough to take the artefacts 'home' with him. In the Kiswa story, as in the story about the sultan, a celebratory tone underlies the explanation of the artefacts' acquisition.

In this way, these accounts continue the traditional effect of ethnographic museums of representing European superiority by displaying material culture recovered from non-European countries (cf. Coombes 1988, 61; Bal 1992, 594; O'Neill 2006, 102f.). As Macdonald explains,

> [t]he possession of artefacts from other cultures was itself important for such artefacts were, for colonialist nations, also signs of the capacity to gather and master beyond national boundaries. As such, they were claims of the capacity to know and to govern; signs too for the visitors that theirs was a nation, or a locality, that also played on the global stage. [...] This was often put to more specific work in highlighting the cultural, technological, or moral superiority of the 'home team' through contrast with others. (2003, 3)

Although Macdonald speaks about museums in the 19th century and many of today's ethnographic museums have changed their self-understandings by, for instance, conducting critical research on their own collection history (cf. Harris/ O'Hanlon 2013, 10), notions of knowing and governing on a global scale or of the superiority of one's 'home team' are still evident in the presented guides' accounts about the retrieval of foreign artefacts. In Maria's description, the process of obtaining a piece of the Kiswa appears as an adventure story, with the European main character successfully masquerading as the Other to effectively *steal* an object. Just like in the first example, his eventual success seems to legitimise the ownership of the artefact. Notions of deception and theft are not connected to this account, which functions, as in the case of the British in India, as a means of shutting down discussion about ethical und unethical collecting practices. This lack of discourse about the conditions of obtaining artefacts from non-European contexts may serve to relativise both the power that was exerted during the procurement of some of the artefacts and the museum's general historical legacy as practising 'comprehensive collecting as a form of domination' (Bal 1992, 560). Even if only some of the artefacts on display have been obtained by force, failing to address the dimension of superiority or domination in connection to the histories of objects (and particularly in relation to the objects in the guides' accounts) risks reinforcing the idea that 'we' really were superior.

This problematisation of power imbalances is particularly noteworthy with respect to Maria's account about the 'stolen' piece of the Kiswa. As she emphasises in her explanation, the Kiswa is an important object because it covers the holiest place in Islam. The importance that is attached to this object is even further highlighted when Maria states that only Muslims are allowed to see, let alone touch it, and that many Muslim visitors find it particularly thrilling to see this piece in the museum, especially if they have not managed to undertake a pilgrimage to Mecca yet. All these statements refer to the value that is connected to this object in its 'original' context. Maria thereby even increases the significance of the museum's possession of the object, because, as Deborah Root has argued, '[t]he point of owning a ceremonial object seems to be to display ownership or, more precisely, to display the ability to possess something of value to someone else' (1989, 81). In this instance, it becomes clear that subtle connotations of domination can be implicit in the guides' stories about the objects in the museums' collections. This is especially the case when the fascination with the object is neither encouraged on the basis of its artistic skill or beauty, which Greenblatt has called 'the mystique of the object' (1991, 52), nor in relation to its contexts and meanings, labelled 'resonance' (ibid., 42), but when wonder is constructed on the basis of the 'spectacle of proprietorship' (ibid., 52). If the guides relate to the objects simply in terms of how desirable it is to possess them, a dimension of overpowering the non-European counterparts, of being able to take what 'they' valued most, is difficult to avoid.

4.5.3   Framing Europe as the 'Brain of the Earth's Body'

Finally, and closely related to the representation of the 'spectacle of proprietorship', what needs to be addressed are connotations in the guides' accounts that non-European groups should on some level be grateful for the artefacts' 'safe' storage in European museums. This has already been addressed with respect to the apparent 'preservation' of authenticity in the museum (Chapter 4.4), reinforcing the 'vision of extinction and rescue' prevalent in early anthropological collecting (Laukötter 2007, 143). The claim of such accounts is that the objects stored in the museum would, if they had not been retrieved by European collectors, have vanished or been destroyed by now.

It is no surprise that such connotations are connected to two of the guides' accounts that have already been addressed in the previous discussion about authenticating non-European ways of life. As has been shown, the value of the objects, and the value of their acquisition, are closely related to their originality and uniqueness. Accordingly, in case of the Palauan clubhouse, as already explained, Antonia tells the students about a Palauan woman who once cried in the gallery because none of the clubhouses remain in Palau while the museum owns three of them. Furthermore, in relation to the market place in Afghanistan, Maria explains how the museum has received notice some time ago that the original market place was destroyed during fights against the Taliban. The fact that the originals have vanished or been destroyed raises their value as museum objects; yet it also seemingly justifies—in hindsight—their removal from their original locations. This representation of the acquisition of artefacts as a form of rescue has been framed by Ruth Adams as the "safe pair of hands argument" (2010, 72), which, as she argues "is a contention that is often based much more on assumptions about the 'superiority' of Western cultural guardianship rather than empirical evidence" (ibid., 72f.). She explains that with respect to Indian artefacts held Great Britain, about 95% of the holdings were kept for thirty years in a "less than waterproof warehouse" (cf. ibid.), which shows that the myth of Europe as the saviour of cultural heritage does not necessarily comply with reality. Still, as can be seen in the two examples of Antonia's and Maria's accounts, notions of rescuing non-European artefacts from extinction or loss can still reverberate within museum communication, especially if collecting efforts or the value of the objects on display are emphasised.

Such a rendering of European collectors not only as superior, but as benevolent guardians of non-European cultural heritage again represents Europe not only as the legitimate owner of these objects, but also as generally more reliable, safer, more stable, or more skilled in conserving and displaying objects than the groups who previously owned these objects. In the accounts about European collectors' efforts to retrieve non-European objects, it is never questioned why there was such a great desire to own these objects. The motivation is always described in terms of Europeans 'wanting to have something' – the guides do not seem to feel the need to elaborate the reasons for or the ideology implicit in this desire of European collectors to possess objects from non-European places. Yet, the systems of thought that led to this interest in collecting ethnographic artefacts in Europe is an important dimension of the 'success stories' that the guides advertise. As Donald Preziosi has argued, from the 19th century onwards, objects were regarded as means to organise the world: if they could be 'emplotted' 'into a configured story culminating in our presence' (cf. Preziosi 2003, 106), so too could the modern citizen be framed as an 'emplotted agent' with a meaningful life narrative (cf. ibid.). The aim to turn non-European material culture into scientific specimen was hence informed by a specific value system that was based upon ideas related to the Enlightenment, such as scientific objectivity and a focus on systematising knowledge. This system of value, which Clifford has similarly framed in terms of his 'art culture system' (cf. 1988, 224), functioned to classify some (especially exotic) objects as more valuable than others. Although the meticulous ordering of the world has come into question and has been shown to bear the essentialising dangers of strict categories and broad identity ascriptions by postmodern scholars, the guides' 'success stories' about the museums' efforts to save objects from extinction or of the collectors' success in obtaining non-European artefacts for research and preservation, value systems of European scientific superiority still seem to play a significant role, or at least go unquestioned.

By default, such categorical value systems that posit ownership of non-European objects as a fortunate turn in the objects' histories exclude and overwrite systems of seeing the objects that were applied in their prior contexts. When the guides speak about the retrieval of foreign artefacts without incorporating a critical perspective, this system of value is adopted without further reflection on it. It is a value system that, as Donald Preziosi has remarked, is posited on the perceived affordance of the objects to be ordered, to be classified, to be subjected to chronology. The artefacts are framed as 'in need' of European collectors, who analyse and preserve them. Thereby, Europe becomes represented as the 'Brain of the Earth's Body', or, as Preziosi defines this term, 'the point of seeing and speaking; the vitrine in which is recollected the rest of what has thus become a remaindered world' (2003, 38).

Finally, this process of constructing Europe as the 'brain of the Earth's body' again shows the 'disimprovement effect'. The guides may wish to explain how the objects have come to be displayed in the galleries,

222

thereby making it possible for the students to reconstruct how museums work. Because they exclude critical aspects such as the history of colonialism, problematic acquisition practices, or possible resistance from the original owners of the artefacts, however, these accounts fall into the trap of communicating a certain self-evidence of European collecting of artefacts from non-European regions. When James Clifford asks '[w]hy has it seemed obvious until recently that non-Western objects should be preserved in European museums, even when this means that no fine specimens are visible in their country of origin?' (1888, 221), this question could similarly be raised in connection to the guides' accounts.

4.6 Creating Immersive Storyworlds

An important means of communicating non-European otherness can be seen in terms of fictional or immersive practices of the guides. Such practices have already been identified in passing in some of the previous subchapters, as for example in references to the guides' communication of events that happened in the past in the form of narrative. This construction of historical storyworlds is closely related to Whites' argument that historical accounts are generally marked by a narrative structure, which results from an imposition of formal coherency on past events in the course of telling or writing history (cf. 1980, 19). This coherency is achieved not only by retrospectively establishing causal relations between consecutive historical events (emplotment, cf. ibid., 20), but also by providing some form of completeness or closure to these events (cf. ibid., 20) and by framing them in the context of a shared moral or social order (cf. ibid., 22). As a result of this process of historical emplotment and moralisation, historical narratives tend to appear real to their audiences (cf. ibid.). In the guides' accounts of European 'success' stories, historical events are presented in the form of narrative: The acquisition of the museum objects is portrayed as a coherent story (i.e., the collector wanted to acquire the artefact for the museum and hence pondered ways to transport it to Europe), with a moral message (i.e., the European museums deserve to 'own' the objects because of the troubles the collectors endured to obtain them), and a happy ending (i.e., the objects are now in the museum to be looked at by the students).

However, this kind of non-fictional storytelling is not the only way in which gallery educators immerse students in the storyworlds that the museums represent in their non-European galleries. In the observed sessions, the guides use various means related to imagination and fictionalisation that function to amplify the coherency and persuasiveness of the 'worlds' presented in the galleries. In this context, the guides' storyworlds can refer to fictional or non-fictional events, but must all be regarded as semi-fictional in so far as they follow White's patterns of emplotment and are, thus, fabricated as coherent, morally unambiguous worlds. This rendering of history or cultural descriptions in terms of semi-fictional *storyworlds* is also applied by the guides to raise the interest of the students for the objects on display. This is evident, for example, when Doreen explains in the interview that, although the students cannot touch anything in the gallery, the exhibition comes alive through storytelling (cf. EID, 255-257). Equally, Antonia states that she tries to find connecting factors to translate the exhibition by working with stories or personal anecdotes (cf. EIA, 24). Further, Gladys remarks that she uses storytelling practices not least to make the children in the gallery session interact with her and discuss the story (cf. EIG, 114-116). These statements show that the guides use storytelling consciously during their sessions in order to create immersive and experiential learning situations.[54] The immersive

---

[54] As this research is not as much interested in the museum educational methodology applied by the guides, but rather in the ways in which they communicate otherness throughout guided tours, the value of storytelling as an educational method is not further addressed in detail. It suffices to mention at this point that the deliberate usage of narratives in museum education is a popular

strategies that the guides use are important in this analysis because they are a major means by which otherness is communicated. The following elaborations serve to explain both the means of immersion in these 'worlds of otherness' and the implications of those immersive techniques.

The guides' immersive storyworlds appear in three different forms; namely as nonfictional or fictional stories, as imaginations of the guided tour as a journey, and as plays or performances of non-European situations and people. By applying these immersive methods, the guides intensify the previously explained 'fundamentally theatrical' nature of exhibitions (Kirshenblatt-Gimblett 1998, 3). They use performative and narrative methods which increase the 'reality effect' of the exhibitions (cf. ibid., 216), and imaginatively relocate the students to the represented non-European worlds. When such theatrical or performative measures are taken in the observed guided tours, the respective exhibition spaces merely serve as stage decorations. The performances take centre stage; they might overshadow the exhibition, and are simultaneously supported by it.

To show how this process works, the three ways of immersing the students in the museums' non-European worlds during the guided tours, i.e. storytelling, imagining going on a journey, and performing non-European practices, are elaborated below. Beforehand, it is important to address both the possibly negotiational as well as the essentialising implications of these measures. On the one hand, the guides' storyworlds can cause changes of perspectives, feelings of empathy with the represented people and contexts, or relativisations of difference to emerge as a result of the 'accommodation' of the students to the non-European world. As Jörn Ahrens has argued in his book *Wie aus Wildnis Gesellschaft wird*, the space of imagination is not primarily a topographical space, even

---

desideratum in museum education scholarship (Roberts 1997, Glover Frykman 2009, Pierroux 2010).

if topographical places can be referenced within it (cf. 2012, 277), but a reflection space in which society is able to step out of and thematise itself (cf. ibid., 295). Hence, the imaginative storyworlds of the guides may function as means of reflection to allow the students to change perspectives and negotiate difference in a playful 'what if'- game. On the other hand, due to their narrative cogency and 'reality effect', immersive storyworlds can reinforce essentialist explanatory approaches or superficial celebrations and resultant fixations of otherness. The subsequent remarks show that both processes are observable in the material, and point to what types of accounts may be seen as problematic in this respect.

4.6.1   Storytelling

In many of the analysed accounts, the guides recount short fictional or non-fictional stories as part of their explanations of the cultural regions on display. There are three kinds of such immersive story types that occur in the guided tours: the already-described presentation of historical events in the form of a story (e.g. the European success stories), the telling of local stories or myths that are popular in the respective regions and the repetition or citing of well-known fictional stories situated in non-European contexts (i.e., *Arabian Nights, The Jungle Book*). Before discussing the distinct features of these story types, it is important to point out the connecting factors that apply to all of them.

First, in contrast to the overall accounts of the guides that, as has been explained in the beginning of this work, are not regarded as 'narratives' despite the application of narratological tools to their analysis, the stories that are at stake in relation to this recurring phenomenon can be regarded as 'narratives' in the stricter sense of the term. Once more relating Bal's definition, stories are series of logically related events that are told in a certain way by a distinguishable agent or narrator, whereby events are defined as transitions from one condition to another (cf. 1997, 5). While the communication in the guided tour is predominantly descriptive or explanatory and often does not contain a definite sequence of events or overall structure with beginning, climactic scene, and ending, the short stories that are discussed in this subchapter do fulfil these criteria of narrativity.

Besides their status as complete, relatively independent stories, another connecting factor of the story types presented by the guides is the fact that they are recitations. As Bal explains, a story becomes a narrative by being told in a specific medium (cf. 1997, 8). In the particular cases discussed below, the stories that are told exist prior to their narration. The gallery sessions can then be seen as Bal's 'medium' in which pre-existing stories are transformed into signs (i.e. through the verbal recitations of the guides). Consequently, the guided tour adds a layer of signification to these pre-existing stories because the medium logically has an effect on the stories. This situation becomes even more complex if different guides tell the same stories with slight variations (e.g. if two different gallery educators work in the same gallery and refer to the same fictional story as part of their guided tour). In this case, due to its immediate and verbal nature, each recitation is its own narrative or its own way of telling a pre-existing story. This connection between the narrative of the guides and prior story versions is interesting with regard to perceptions of the authority of the narrators (i.e. the guides) as against the authority of the underlying stories. For example, if the students already know the story of *The Jungle Book*, the guides' recitation presumably has less authority than the 'original' version of the story. In the case of historical events presented in the form of a story, however, the students are less able to tell which elements the guides add to pre-existing stories because they may not be aware of any prior versions. This question of authority is again connected to different layers of worldmaking (Goodman 1978). Goodman explains that considering one world version to be true is usually a matter of utility, coherence and duration (cf. ibid., 122-125). Absolute, permanent credibility cannot be established, but strength and durability of credibility can (cf. ibid., 124). Therefore, the elaborations of the specific story types investigate how the guides establish their own credibility.

Departing from these general observations about this recurring phenomenon of working with fictional and non-fictional stories, the first story type, namely the representation of historical events in the form of a story, is most revealing with regard to the question of how and when the gallery educators in their role as narrators establish their own credibility. On the one hand, as these narratives feature historical events, the necessity of authorising these stories seems evident. On the other hand, as previously mentioned, it can be assumed that neither the students nor the teachers come with much background knowledge about historical details of non-European countries, which is why lengthy justifications of facts may not be required. An example is Britta's account about China:

> There are fifty-thousand [Chinese] signs that one could learn if you wanted to learn Chinese front to back. Probably nobody knows them all. There was once an emperor and he told all the people or servants who had nothing to do: You travel to all parts of the empire and collect on a paper roll all words that you can find there. All the signs. And in three years you come back and we meet in Beijing at the main palace. And you show me your words and we collect them together. And that is what they did. And then they created a dictionary out of it. And the dictionary is not just this big or that big. But it's approximately eight meters long. It has a name – it's called cí hai. and cí hai means sea of words. And this is like an infinite ocean. Quite a lot. (GSB-MB, 501-515)

Although Britta's account is a very short story, it fulfils the aforementioned criteria of logically related events, coherency, and completeness. While this is again connected to Hayden White's argument about the general rendering of history in terms of narrative (cf. 1986, 19), the story-like nature of the account is increased due to its timelessness ('there was once an emperor'), the usage of direct speech ('You travel to all parts of the empire'), and its simple or informal style. Yet, although it appears like a fictional story, its relation to historical events becomes clear.

The reliability of the story quoted above is established by means of its framing and by its relation to a manifest object as evidence, namely the described 'cihai'. The story is told as a means of illustrating how many signs there are in the Chinese language. As the initial statements about the language are presented as facts ('There are fifty-thousand signs'), the illustrating story also appears real. Of course, this is also due to the fact that the story is not introduced as a myth or a legend. Interestingly, in the space of the museum, the lack of a reference to fictionality serves as a marker of reliability. The space of the museum already promises reliability. Unlike the festival, the theatre, or the cinema, a reputation of integrity and authority precedes the museum, which also devolves upon the guides as representatives: innocent until proven guilty. As Crew and Sims write in their contribution to the anthology *Exhibiting Cultures*, "[a]uthenticity— authority—enforces the social contract between the audience and the museum, a socially agreed-upon reality that exists only as long as confidence in the voice of the exhibition holds' (1991, 163). This dimension of establishing reliability must not be underrated, even though it is not in the text itself, but instead evident in the absence of the need to clarify whether the story is fictional or nonfictional.

While these considerations remain on a structural level, they have important implications for the meanings that are constructed in these non-fictional narratives. These ramifications may best be exemplified by reference to the European success stories addressed in the previous chapter. In these success stories, the establishment of authority similarly works mainly on the basis of the self-evident style of the narration which does not leave much room for doubt or questions concerning either the recounted events or the underlying value system in which Europe is depicted as the 'brain of the Earth's body' (Preziosi 1996). Yet, this is exactly what needs to be considered in all non-fictional stories included in the guides' accounts. Due to these narratives' 'reality-constituting power' (Nünning 2009, 169), subtle instances of constructing otherness that are embedded in them can appear to be unshakeable facts. Just as the underlying value system of Europe's superiority may remain unquestioned in the stories about the acquisition of objects from India or Palau, other non-fictional narratives may equally render implicit judgments of non-European practices and contexts as objective facts. Julia Nitz has shown that this not only happens in guided tours, but also in exhibitions. With regard to an exhibition at the *Queen's Gallery* in London, she relates that

> [...] the exhibition sells and image of George III as an enlightened monarch, which is highly problematic since it is not based on thorough historical research and hard evidence but primarily on a very biased way of interpreting the king's actions. But, and this is the crux of the matter, in its paratextual outline, the exhibition claims to have a high (institutional) authority. (2012, 177)

Similarly, in the observed guided tours, the guides rarely represent themselves as subjective speakers, but usually express objectivity and thus authority either explicitly by referring to their academic background or implicitly by using objective language, zero focalisation, and the ethnographic present. Possible biases embedded in these stories are, therefore, represented not as interpretations, but as factual statements.

In contrast, the second story type addressed in this chapter, semi-fictional stories popular within the regions on display in the museum, does not rely heavily on notions of authenticity or reliability because here, no truth claim is embedded in the narratives. Still, these local stories are told to provide insights into shared ideas, beliefs, and folk heroes of the respective regions. Doreen, for instance, tells the students a story about a raven who brings back the sun and the moon after two giants have stolen them (cf. GSD-MA, 403-442). She states that every Native American child knows that the raven brought back the sun and the moon, which is why ravens are regarded as important animals (cf. ibid., 442-443). In many of the observed guided tours, similar local legends and myths are woven into the guides' accounts. In most cases, these stories are inscribed on the displayed objects and are therefore addressed in the gallery sessions. This is the case, for instance, in Britta's description of a Chinese partition screen that Chinese students once gave as a present to their teacher. This screen features paintings depicting a Chinese legend. Britta introduces the students to the story behind the paintings, which revolves around a group of people who are guests of a queen who lives in the mountains She gives them magical peaches to eat, which makes them immortal (cf. GSB-MB, 855-871). Britta tells this story in order to explain not only the depictions on the screen, but also to elaborate on the meaning of the artefact as a present: 'Those who eat these magical peaches are immortal. […] And the old Chinese wanted that very much. So, they [the students] thought: That fits because [the teacher] is sixty years old and will soon retire. […] They wished for him to live forever' (cf. GSB-MB, 871-876).

This story type is interesting with regard to the communication of otherness because it introduces the students to folk tales that are well-known in the respective regions. Britta remarks that peaches are a common symbol in China and that the legend is well-known in China (cf. GSB-MB, 877-884). Similarly, as already mentioned, Doreen explains that all Native American children know the story about the raven's retrieval of the sun and the moon (cf. GSD-MA, 404). The references to the prominence of these stories in these regions can facilitate a fruitful cultural negotiation process. As Nünning has noted, cultural narratology is concerned with the 'narrativity of cultures' as well as the 'culturality of narratives' (cf. 2009, 161). The former refers to the relation between narratives and cultural identity, memory, norms and values, or rituals (cf. ibid.). The latter describes the ways in which narratives and its structures are specific to culture or depend on culture (cf. ibid.). This interrelation between narratives and cultural phenomena is highlighted in the inclusion of folk tales in the guided tours. The students learn about local beliefs and values through stories that are well-known in these areas, which somewhat relativises the powerful position of the guide speaking for or about 'them'. Even though the guides function as narrators, the stories still provide an alternative 'way into' systems of beliefs and values shared in the regions on display, and also to the objects that are exhibited in the galleries.

There is, however, still the problem of binary distinctions that again emerges in relation to this story type. The focus on 'their' stories and 'their' distinctiveness suggests a distinction between 'ours' and 'their' storyworld, when, interestingly, it is exactly the universal narrativity of cultures that could serve as a connecting factor here. The stories that the guides tell are different in terms of the names of the characters, the settings, and perhaps also the specific values that are foregrounded. Yet they share a common structure, the empathy with the main character, or the inclusion of general moral messages. It is particularly this common structure that renders these stories legible in a different context. The methodological opportunity of these folk tales in guided tours thus consists in their potential to give insights into the specifics of cultural belief systems while at the same time pointing to the similarities of communicative strategies and moral values. To make both these aspects explicit while telling these stories would thus contribute to a more self-reflective communication of otherness.

What is interesting about the format of the folk tale or local legend is that there is neither a truth claim nor a specific reference to fictionality in most of the narrations. The guides who tell such stories leave open whether they are true or not. For example, Doreen does not specifically announce a fictional story, but rather an old story (cf. GSD-MA, 383-384). Similarly, Britta says at the end of her account that 'perhaps you will find a vendor at a market one day who sells these peaches. I haven't found him so far' (cf. GSB-MB, 881-883). This also applies to other examples. For instance, Eva explains the legend of the Indian goddess Durga or Kali, explaining that this is an important story that is repeated over and over and that this goddess is still being worshipped in Calcutta (cf. GSE-MB, 930-934). There is no mention as to the fictionality or truth of this narrative. Hilda also explains a short myth about the oba[55] from Benin who defeated the sea god Olokun and received coral beads in return (cf. GSH-MC, 204-208). Again, it is not clearly mentioned whether this is a fictional story. In only of the narrations of local myths in the guided tours, is there a definite reference to fiction: When Antonia tells the students a story that is depicted on one of the men's clubhouses from Palau, she refers to it as a 'fairy tale' (GSA-MA, 271). Even here, however, there is some indication of an 'open ending' because Antonia concludes the story by using the German equivalent for 'and they lived happily ever after', which literally translates to '[…] and if they didn't die, they still live today' (GSA-MA, 292). Although this is a typical ending of German fairy tales, it contains within it an option that these characters might have existed 'in reality' and thus draws a line from the storyworld to the world of the children.

Why are such strategies of open-endedness with regard to the fictitiousness of the stories used by the guides? On the one hand, as the narratives related to this story type often pertain to beliefs or folk legends, it would to some extent be disrespectful or even condescending to discount them as fictions. On the other hand, for the reasons stated above, it would be equally problematic to claim that they describe factual events. The guides' strategies here seem to be quite effective: By leaving the verisimilitude of the narrative open and not specifying it, they leave this aspect for the students to decide. This corresponds to what Daniel Spock has called 'the proper role of the museum' (2006, 178) with regard to museum education. He argues that this role '[…] may not be to close the window of knowledge by providing the authoritative last word, but to keep

---

[55] A definition is provided in the glossary.

the window open on a prospect of imaginative possibilities' (ibid.). This works very well in the case of the folk tales. By not declaring them as either fiction or non-fiction, the guides not only leave room for the students to decide this for themselves, but they also allow 'other' systems of belief to level with their own. In this sense, while Goodman explains that it is impossible to describe the world without a frame of reference (cf. Goodman 1978, 3), it may be possible to simultaneously accept multiple frames of reference, or even multiple 'worlds'.

The last story type will only be addressed briefly because it occurs in only four of the observed guided tours and the stories that are related to it do not derive from either the exhibition or the gallery session formats, but are widely known stories such as *The Jungle Book* (Eva), *Mulan* (B12), *The Arabian Nights* (Maria), and *Brother Bear* (Doreen), a 2003 Walt Disney Production set in North America at the end of the ice age. Interestingly, these references only occur in the German guided tours, which may be due to their more spontaneous nature (explained in Chapter 5.1.1).

On the one hand, these integrations of popular stories in the guided tours can be regarded as successful means of establishing a connection between the students' prior knowledge and their experiences in the museum. As John Falk and Lynn Dierking have shown, '[n]ew learning is always constructed from a base of prior knowledge' (2000, 33). They note that while individual experiences and prior knowledge have been acknowledged as important factors in school settings, their relevance for museum learning has not been investigated yet (cf. ibid., 187). The guides' efforts of reminding the students of books or films that they already know can thus be seen as movements in this direction. By asking the students, for example, about the kind of incense burners they know from fairy tales and stories (cf. GSM-MB, 1035-1040), or about the animals that live in the jungle (cf. GSE-MB, 421-424), the students are embedded into the guided tour by inferring from what they already know.

On the other hand, to suggest that the students have prior knowledge about the regions on display because they know these fictional stories can be problematic. *The Jungle Book*, *The Arabian Nights*, *Mulan*, and *Brother Bear* depict fictional worlds that, while being based upon settings that exist in reality, are marked by a high degree of romanticising, exaggeration, and nostalgia. *The Arabian Nights*, in particular, has been discussed in relation orientalism (Said 1978). An uncritical adoption of such depictions of non-European fictional worlds in the guided tour can thus lead to a projection of romantic, nostalgic and Orientalist imaginations on the nonfictional lifeworlds of Middle Eastern, Chinese, and Indian communities represented in the museum.

However, in their accounts, the guides manage to not simply draw a connection between these stories and the exhibitions, but to use the exhibitions to contextualise the stories. For example, Maria explains that the idea of the 'genie in a bottle' derives from the burning of incense that used to be practised commonly in the respective non-European regions due to its antibacterial effect (cf. GSM-MB, 1062-1068). Similarly, Doreen explains that the boy and the girl in the film *Brother Bear* can transform themselves into bears because in the earlier days, Native Americans believed that animals were dressed-up human beings (cf. GSD-MA, 713-733). Hence, in these cases, the guides actually provide a background to the prior experiences of the students. Thereby, they enable the students to combine what they already know with their experience in the museum, while at the same time keeping a distance from the fictional story by contrasting it with the explanations provided in the museum.

Finally, while in the cases of the other two story types, the students are not really involved in the process of storytelling, the last story type is more interactive. The students are constantly asked about what they know and are involved in discussions about additional information they receive. Such introductions of popular stories, therefore, if given in a relatively critical and contextualising style, can be fruitful tools not only to negotiate already prevalent ideas about the regions addressed, but also to actively involve the students in the course of the guided tour, inspiring them to ask questions that they find interesting. For example, a student in Maria's session asks why djinns are perceived as something positive, or as healing other people, because from her knowledge of the storyworld she thought they were considered evil (cf. GSM-MB, 1069). This question shows that the student tests her previous knowledge against newly acquired information in the guided tour, making it possible for her to renegotiate a previously established idea about the non-European context.

4.6.2   Communicating Being 'There'

Besides the telling of explicit stories, the guides also immerse the students in the non-European worlds constructed throughout the gallery sessions by employing games or means of pretending to travel to or 'be in' the countries represented in the museum. This story type is predominantly perceptible at the beginnings of the observed guided tours. Before they enter the galleries with the groups, some guides refer to the tours as journeys or time travels. The theme that hence frames their account is based upon the fictional notion that the students, teachers, and guides 'travel' to the countries represented in the museums. In some sessions, these initial references of the guides to an imaginary journey are repeatedly taken up as the group walks through different galleries. In other sessions, the notion of the journey is presented only once in the form of side notes during the tours or as means to smoothen the transition from one object to the other. Regardless of its intensity, this relatively simple idea of travelling to the places depicted in the galleries appears in the majority of the observed guided tours.

Of course, to conduct a guided tour in a museum that categorises its rooms according to geographic regions lends itself to projections of travelling, as Hooper-Greenhill has already suggested by comparing the exhibition to a map (2000, 18). The neatly separated areas in different galleries compare to the representation of the world on a globe. Just like the globe or the map, such location-based displays give visual order to the world, thereby rendering it more easily accessible. These notions are, for instance, mirrored by Antonia's statement that 'you will never accomplish a world cruise as quickly as today' (GSA-MA, 50-51) upon telling the students that they will have to cross some galleries to arrive at the part of the museum that is of interest to their visit. In a similar vein, the role of the guide compares to a tourist guide leading the way through foreign terrain. Likewise, Eva explains that 'I am your tourist guide today, so to say. And a tourist guide usually introduces herself by name [...]' (GSE-MB, 69-70). This frequent occurrence of this theme in the guides' accounts results at least to some extent from semantic intersections between travelling to remote countries and visiting ethnographic museums. In fact, as Kirshenblatt-Gimblett has argued, 'museums try to emulate the experience of travel' (1998, 7), while at the same time offering compact experiences in a short amount of time, which is often not possible in actual touristic journeys (cf. ibid.). Despite this higher 'density' of museum experiences, she argues that museums are increasingly facing problems in competing with the tourism industry, which allows more immediacy and adventure (cf. ibid.). The guides' encouragements to imagine 'being there' may, therefore, also be seen as endeavours to contribute to what the museum can offer by way of experience and adventure.[56]

As already mentioned, this 'adventure game' of pretending to travel to the countries rather than looking at objects collected in them, is often

---

[56] The influence of the immersive qualities of exhibition spaces on the practices of the guides is further elaborated in Chapter 5.3.2.

used as an initial framing of the guided tour in terms of an exciting voyage. For example, Feona announces at the beginning of the gallery session that

> [...] we will be travelling to a few different countries from around the world to see / it might be some paintings, it might be some objects and things, it might be some clothes, some pictures. To find out more about how people once dressed in different places. What they ate, what they did and (thought?). And to have a look at different materials [...]. (GSF2-MD, 63-67).

Similarly, Kate explains that 'we're going to go on a journey. We are going to be travelling to some different countries. and we are not only going to different countries. And we are also going to go back in time' (GSK2-MD, 64-65). Eva takes a lot of time at the beginning of her session to explain how the group would get to India by plane and asks them to imagine how 'we would be greeted there' (cf. GSE-MB, 56-74). These examples show that some of the guides cast the entire session in terms of a journey. Such initial framings are particularly interesting with regard to David Herman's focus on narrative openings. He asks, '[h]ow do these [...] evoke (a fragment of) a narrative world? What specific textual cues allow readers to draw inferences about the structure, inhabitants, and spatiotemporal situation of this world?' (2009, 80). In terms of the spatiotemporal situation, the reference to a journey signifies that the museum represents places and times that are somehow distant from when and where 'we' are. This again confirms that it is a 'remote otherness' that is represented in the museum. In terms of inhabitants, the journey metaphor does not inform much about the characters that are part of the represented 'world', apart from that they are 'somewhere else'. But this is already an implicit characterisation? Whatever and whomever the students encounter during this journey is bound to remain a part of the remoteness that can only be bridged by travelling or by visiting the museum. Here, a suggestion of spatial determination and fixation comes in: 'They' are there, 'we' are only on a visit.

238

In addition to these clues about the represented otherness that is embedded in these narrative openings, the immersive potential of the journey metaphor also becomes visible here. The students are invited to imaginatively relocate to the storyworld that is presented to them, which can be seen in terms of the process of 'accommodation' that Herman considers an important feature of narrative worldmaking (cf. 2009, 80). In these particular cases, this accommodation to the storyworld works on the one hand because all of the above statements are formulated in terms of the first-person plural: It is not only the students who 'travel', but the whole group pretends to travel together. By not distinguishing the imaginary experience of the students from an objective perspective of the teachers and the guides, the imaginary journey is made to seem more real. On the other hand, accommodation is also achieved because of the guides' self-evident way of speaking about 'travelling' in connection to visiting the museum's galleries. For instance, Feona asks the students 'what kind of country have we travelled to?' (GSF2-MD, 533) when they arrive in a new gallery, or Kate similarly asks, '[d]id anyone see which gallery we are in? What country are we in?' (GSK-MD, 60). Both questions demonstrate that the two concepts of 'gallery' and 'country' are used interchangeably. As if it was taken for granted that exhibitions could be conflated with the 'real' world, the guides do not introduce the *imaginary* aspect of the journeys as such, but simply work with the metaphor from the first moment on. These strategies support the accommodation of the students to the storyworld that encompasses travelling to different countries as they move through the museum. It is through this form of 'naturalising' the relationship between the representations to be experienced in the museum and the 'real world' outside of the museum that a truth claim about the trustworthiness of the same representations is constructed.

This imagination of the 'exhibition-as-world'[57] (Rodman 1993, 256) is, however, disturbed at some points by a relativisation or 'taking back' of the immersive qualities. This happens, for instance, when Antonia explains to the students that the Palauan men's clubhouse is only a replica and would be three times as big in 'real life' (cf. GSA-MA, 298-299) or when Feona explains that a valuable carpet is conserved through dim lighting (cf. GSF-MD, 383-393). This interesting 'reality check' can be explained by a still important focus on learning and factual information in the guided tours. As the sessions are not only about experience and entertainment, but also about education, it is difficult for the guides to continuously sustain the imagination of travelling to the countries displayed in the museum, especially when the exhibitions contain clear cues about the staging and arrangement of information. This clash between the imaginative immersion in the proposed storyworld and a visual experience that includes features that are visibly 'staged' could provide an opportunity for debate and discourse. While Yap has argued that an imaginative immersion in the world of the exhibition can on some level work to convey how a place or cultural setting would feel like (cf. Yap 2014, 10), experience-centred displays have been criticised for undermining understanding and critical dialogue (cf. Dicks 2004, 166; Bal 2010, 16). The deliberate breaking of such imaginary journeys during guided tours could, therefore, be a way of demonstrating to the students both some aspects of a non-European context and the fact that these features only constitute one version of many possible alternatives. However, in the observed gallery sessions, these breaks of imagination are not used by the guides as a basis for reflection and deconstruction.

---

[57] Rodman has suggested this inversion of the logics of Timothy Mitchell's term of the 'world as exhibition' (1989), arguing that some museums today not only bring the 'world' into the museum, but offer '[...] a place you can travel to without leaving home' (1993, 256).

4.6.3 Performing and Embodying Otherness

In most of the observed gallery sessions, the immersion of the students in the represented worlds is not only encouraged by their imaginative relocation to the respective countries or by means of storytelling, but also by bodily practices of enactment and performance. The students may be encouraged to dress up in a 'typical' non-European dress or to imitate non-European cultural practices. This form of immersion does not work on a cognitive level like the aforementioned cases, but is achieved through bodily experiences. Whereas with the first two dimensions discussed above, the students are merely encouraged to think about the guided tour as a voyage, or to listen to (and remember) stories, this last dimension requires them to actively perform these imagined worlds. They do not merely stand by, looking onto the represented worlds, but they themselves embody and represent them.

As already explained, this work distinguishes between performance as a conscious, 'bounded 'act'' (Butler 1993, 24) and performativity as the relatively unconscious 'reiteration of norms' (ibid.) or systems of meaning. With regard to performative practices of immersion in the guided tour, the definition of performance as a bounded act prevails. The students are aware of the fact that they imitate the non-European contexts and people; their actions are comparable to rehearsing a play. At the same time, the fact that these 'plays' are enacted in the public place of the museum and the students thus put an essentialised otherness on stage in front of other visitors – often in a stereotypical manner – suggests that performativity also plays a role here. After all, the students hereby unconsciously reiterate ideas about otherness in terms of appearance and rituals. If other visitors are present, one could even argue that the students occupy a comparable position to the 'life actors' that Kirshenblatt-Gimblett mentions as sometimes being part of in-situ displays, intended to increase their realistic representation (cf. Kirshenblatt-Gimblett 1998, 21).

The integration of forms of performance and play in the gallery session has generally been promoted as a more interactive and engaging method of learning in the museum. For example, Bernd Wagner has argued that performative play encourages children to experiment with different movements, spaces, objects, or sounds (cf. 2010, 197) and, in so doing, objects are embedded in new meanings that may deviate from common explanatory approaches, causing an unconscious questioning of European projections on the artefacts (cf. ibid.). While it is true that the appropriation implicit in 'playing' the Other can deconstruct common images of otherness, this is an overly optimistic take on the matter. As the following examples show, it is much more likely for the children to reproduce the characteristics of a premeditated European imagination of non-European otherness than for them to be able to use the objects and spaces as they please to create new ways of imagining non-European places.

As already mentioned, the performances of otherness in the observed sessions can take two main forms: dressing-up and imitating cultural practices. While these are closely connected, the former practice is often less active than the latter. In most of the cases in which the guides let the students dress up in a 'traditional' costume, there is no actual play or performance on the part of the students. For example, Eva chooses a girl and a boy to wear an Indian sari and a dhoti[58] respectively. The two students who volunteer to dress up in these clothes are positioned in front of the school group, simply presenting the garments while the guide explains how they are wrapped around the body and how they are typical in India (cf. GSE-MB, 626-697). Similarly, Kate dresses a student in a kimono in the Japan gallery, asking her to serve as a 'model' for the garment (cf. GSK2-MD, 608ff.). In these instances, the notion of the 'model' seems fitting: The students do not really engage with the clothes,

---

[58] A definition is provided in the glossary.

nor do they 'play' with them. Their bodies merely serve as visual templates illustrating the allegedly 'typical' appearance of the respective non-European people.

Even if the intention of such forms of playing dress-up may be to facilitate the students' experience of the fabric and materiality of unfamiliar garments, and for them to get an idea of what it is (or was) like to wear them, this is less related to the kind of performative role-playing that Wagner refers to when he points out the potentials of performance as an educational measure. This is so largely because the change of clothes that can be observed in the gallery sessions does not involve the taking on of other roles. With respect to Ralph Turner's definition of role-taking and role-making (cf. 1962, 21ff.), the students neither put themselves in another's perspective (role-taking), nor do they shape these perceived roles by performing them (role-making). Another example for this sort of performance that lacks the dimension of role-taking and role-making can be found in Maria's guided tour: In this session, the guide provides 'oriental costumes' for all students. Upon distributing them among the children, they start getting dressed in different pieces, laughing at each other and wondering how to wear some of the clothes. Maria only explains one piece of clothing – a burka – in more detail, while all the others remain uncontextualised. Furthermore, there is no continuation of this game of dress-up that links this practice with the remaining tour, which is why the experience remains on a superficial level. While Gadamer explains that when children play dress-up, they want '[...] at any cost to avoid being discovered behind [their] disguise' (cf. 1975, 113), these methods of trying on non-European clothes in the guided tour do not allow for a genuine imaginative immersion in the 'disguise'. As the performance is not embedded in a broader task that could point to the relationship between the clothes and multiple meanings, the act of literally putting the students in non-European 'shoes' does not correspond with its metaphorical connotation of taking another's perspective.

The emptiness of such performances is even more problematic because of the image that is represented through the selection of garments used for such occasions. In all of the mentioned cases, the students wear traditional outfits that seem 'typical' for the respective regions. But this typicality is problematic because it is based upon visual stereotypes of non-European settings and people. India becomes represented through the colourful sari and the dhoti, Japan through the kimono, the Middle East through the burka or the niqab. The fact that in most of the corresponding regions, these traditional costumes are – if at all - worn only by some people, gets lost in the visually impressive experience of these garments. This deficit is again related to issues of authenticity. The guides reinforce a construction of authentic traditional garments by specifically associating these countries with these clothes, and by not distinguishing between the past and the present. Eva, for instance, mentions that most people wear these clothes in the countryside, but that even in New Delhi people with simple occupations may be wearing dhotis (cf. GSE-MB, 605-641). As she does not then explain what other clothes may be equally typical in India (such as jeans and shirts), the association that remains is the one between India and saris or dhotis.

In general, what is important to note is that this form of dressing up seems to be a 'fun entertainment' part of the guided tours rather than a meaningful learning experience. The children are supposed to enjoy their visit and dressing-up may simply be a way of involving them or activating them. In a similar vein, Baz Kershow has explained that performances that involve retrodressing are increasingly important for the heritage and tourist industry, and are part of the construction of a spectacle that the industries consider ever more necessary (1994, 166). The guides in the observed tours likewise seek to create such spectacles during the guided tours by having the children visually stage a colourful otherness. In most of these instances, changes of perspective are impossible, not only because there are no reflexive questions or relativisations motivated by the guides, but also because the students' transformations only unfold on a superficial level, without facilitating corresponding imaginations and role-playing sequences. This lack of contextualisation, role-taking and role-making, as well as of empathy also leads to reactions on the part of the students such as laughing at their dressed-up classmates. The missing link to explanations of clothing types or to a relativisation in terms of the internal diversity of different attire *within* the respective countries can cause superficial stereotypes and condescending attitudes towards visual difference to emerge or to be normalised. Examples that prove that it is easily possible to achieve a more meaningful engagement with non-European 'garments' can be found in Maria's explanations of the different meanings of the burka within different contexts, as well as in Feona's session, in which she asks the dressed-up students how they feel when wearing the clothes (cf. GSF2-MD, 410). Still, a more explicit distinction of traditional from contemporary clothes and a more specific contextualisation of the garments in the sessions would be desirable to overcome the reinforcement of visual stereotypes.

In conclusion, the observations of performances of dress-up in this study contest what Julia Petrov has argued with respect to the material and imaginative potential of historical clothing in museum representations. She states that '[b]y inserting one's body in place of the missing historical body to whom the historical objects exhibited in the museum belonged, the visitor can gain a valuable understanding of the absent person's experience' (2012, 238). Although Petrov refers to the visitors' 'intuitive act of *mentally* 'trying on the garment for size' (ibid., 237), her argument suggests that mere act of wearing someone else's clothes evokes empathy (cf. ibid.). Yet owing to the lack of contextualisation by the guides in the observed guided tours, this automatic empathising seems improbable. The visual (and material) difference of the presented garments, and their reiteration of stereotypical signs of otherness (a turban for the Orient, a sari for India, a kimono for Japan), cannot help but be stronger than the potential to feel what it is or was like to wear them because the entire performative situation (i.e., the staging of the students in the ethnographic gallery, the 'model' function of the students, the lack of role-playing activity) is marked by differentiation and categorisation rather than empathy. This problem is also implicit in the entire act of dressing up as the cultural Other, as Raney Bench has argued:

> Playing dress up is often popular in children's areas in museums, but it is not appropriate to encourage children to dress up and pretend to be Native. Native American is not a profession, like other dress-up activities. Although dressing up in period costume from the frontier or settlement time is often understood as pretending to be part of the past, this is not true for dressing as a Native person from the same period. Because representations of Native people so often take place in the past, this activity becomes an extension of colonization and stereotypes, rather than one that promotes understanding. (2014, 84)

Along the lines of this statement, the elaborations above similarly point to the imbalance of power that can be implied in such performative practices. Especially because of the non-specific temporal situation of the non-European costumes, the students in the gallery sessions do not pretend to be 'part' of the past but perform a visual association of generalised culture.

This problematic aspect of performative practices in the gallery sessions can also be seen in the other dimension of performance; the imitation of non-European cultural practices. While this method is more interactive and actually enables the students to engage, to some extent, in role-taking and role-making, the observed examples are still marked by generalisation and temporal vagueness. Consider, for example, Eva's explanations of Indian greeting practices that have already been described in relation to the communication of moral superiority. Here, Eva does not only explain the alleged typically Indian greetings, but makes the students perform them. While the students thus imagine what it would be like to meet someone from India, this imagination is problematic for the same reasons that Bench remarks with respect to playing dress-up: The performed greeting practices are explicitly marked as 'submissive' and 'unmodern' in the guides' account. At the same time, other common greeting practices in India, such as handshakes, are not addressed. The role that the students take in this situation is not one that raises understandings for cultural difference, but that reproduces a desired version of authentic and distinct 'Indianness' or otherness. The same performance of generalised otherness is observable in Eva's later task for the students to demonstrate 'how people sit in India' (cf. GSE-MB, 229), Britta's equal request for the students to 'sit down like you think the Chinese sit' (cf. GSB-MB, 781-782), or Christine's (cf. GSC-MB, 247-255), Gladys's (cf. GSG-MC, 182-183), and Eva's (cf. GSE-MB, 754-764) tasks for a couple of students to carry objects on their heads in the Africa galleries of Museums B and C as well as in the India gallery of Museum B.

These examples show that the guides tend to make the students enact ideas about cultural practices in non-European regions that are based upon notions of tradition, and constructed authenticity as well as prevailing visual demarcations of otherness. This is not to say that these cultural practices are only European imaginations or constructions; they *are* part of the everyday-practices in some of the regions and of some of the people in the represented areas. Yet, they are only *part* of everyday life, only prevalent in *specific* situations or locations, *coexisting* with other practices that might seem more similar to the students' everyday practices. The fact that what is actively and bodily rehearsed by the students are specifically and exclusively the unfamiliar and exotic practices not only paints a problematic picture of non-European people as confined to traditional and 'unmodern' behaviour, but also encourages the students to internalise this augmented difference through their embodiment of these practices. In effect, the students may respond to non-Europeanness on the basis of learned stereotypes, which denies non-European regions and people individual preference or casts 'them' only in terms of deviations from the imagined norm.

In the observed guided tours, however, there are also some instances in which the imitation of cultural practices does not reinforce common stereotypes or generalisations. For example, Doreen shows the students a common game played in the Arctic, called the Nugluak game[59]. After they watch a film about the game, the students put together teams and play the game against each other (cf. GSD-MA, 926-961). Similarly, in Gladys's session, the students play 'Okoso'[60], a game common in Nigeria (cf. GSG-MC, 160-161). They also rehearse a 'call and response'[61] that the guide explains is usually performed before the storyteller in Nigeria begins to speak (cf. ibid., 80-88). In these moments, the performative acts of the students are based upon specific practices instead of on generalised ideas about 'authentic' ways of greeting or sitting. The three situations are not stereotypical but provide insight into concrete cultural practices. Especially the two games can serve as productive means of actively engaging the students in the course of the guided tour: Not only do they relate to the interests and lifeworlds of the children, but they also leave enough room for the students to try them out for themselves. In this sense, these forms of performance may even compare to Wagner's ideal of the performative play as a form of experimentation with different forms of movement, with different spaces or different objects (cf. 2010, 197). Playing games that are common in another region can thus become a successful tool of facilitating encounters between equals: They work according to familiar principles, they are easy enough to be imitated or

[59] A definition is provided in the glossary.
[60] A definition is provided in the glossary.
[61] A definition is provided in the glossary.

copied, and they allow for an uncontroversial appropriation of rules. Furthermore, as Helene Illeris has stated, if applied more elaborately as a method in the guided tour, games can open '[…] the way to much freer and less ritualized ideas of how an educational setting should be' (2006, 23) and thus even question the omniscient position of the guide (cf. ibid.).

Nevertheless, even in these forms of performance, it is questionable whether an identification with the represented practices can be achieved. After all, regardless of whether the students dress up in non-European clothes, whether they 'sit like an Indian' or whether they play a game that is common in the region of interest, the students know that the performance is only temporary and that they can go back to their 'real' practices at any time. Jay Rounds has explained this phenomenon with respect to the museum visit in general:

> Viewing an exhibition of an earlier time, or a different cultural setting, the visitor wonders, 'What would I have been like if I had lived there and/or then?' Like dressing up in old clothes, we play at being someone else, and test how we feel about it; but because it is 'only play,' it does not have to be taken seriously, and so does not threaten current identity. The museum offers a low risk environment in which to have these encounters. (2006, 146)

Thus, as these games are 'only play', it is unclear in how far an identification with otherness can take place. Especially because the guided tours are usually not centred on questioning one's own world views and practices, but on learning about the 'world of the Other', the students are not encouraged by the guides to reflect upon their own ways of sitting or dressing. Rather, the distinctions are posited and then performed by the students. Their performances of otherness are then comparable to a Bhabha's concept of mimicry: The students imitate Others, but they don't identify with them (cf. 1994, 61). In this sense, it is also a form of mastery to 'play' somebody else 'on the outside' while maintaining one's own practices and ideals on the inside.

Hence, while these practices of performing otherness are intended as means of putting the students in 'their' perspective, a counterbalanced process of cultural negotiation can only be achieved if some form of self-reflection is evoked by such performative acts. This self-reflection could be achieved, for instance, by means of improvised role-playing whereby students are asked to deploy cultural objects in all possible ways that they can imagine. Such practices would facilitate a discussion about the students' internalised scripts of behaviour and their similarities or differences to object-related practices in the respective non-European regions. Such reflective play might turn the imaginative space into the already-mentioned reflection space that Ahrens indicates in his book. By actually taking on the role of someone else, the students would be able to step out of themselves, and to critically reflect upon their own taken-for-granted practices and beliefs. Yet, when, as in the observed tours, the performance remains on a superficial level, it falls short of such a reflection.

As has been shown in the preceding comments on practices of immersing the students in the non-European worlds constructed in the guided tours, these imaginative strategies can contribute to processes of cultural negotiation, but they can also reinforce cultural stereotypes. This double function of immersion can be seen in connection with the domesticating function of cultural narratives. As Bruner and Nünning have argued, the constructed coherence in stories accustoms readers to new or unfamiliar experiences (cf. Bruner 1991, 90; Nünning 2013, 43). The same can be said about the children's engagement in dressing up: New materials, fabrics, colours, patterns, and styles of clothing are domesticated by means of wearing unfamiliar clothes. Yet, both in fiction and in the described forms of embodiment, the question is what becomes represented as 'new' or as 'outside' the (narrative) community in the first place. In this interpretative space, processes of stereotyping can become interwoven with attempts to domesticate difference.

4.7 Translating the Other

In Chapter 3, 'cultural translation' has been introduced as a concept referring to both the guides' translations of objects or spaces into words, and their strategies of explaining non-European 'worlds' in general. While these more wide-ranging conceptions can be applied to all of the already discussed themes and practices of communicating otherness because they all represent means of metaphorically translating unfamiliar cultural practices and artefacts, this subchapter is concerned with a more concrete dimension of 'cultural translation'. What is meant by 'translation' in this case is not only the general kind of 'ethnographic translation and the translation of cultures in museum displays' (Sturge 2007, 2) that Sturge discusses in her insightful book on *Representing Others*, but also the specific strategies that the guides use to connect the represented non-European 'worlds' to the lifeworlds of the students. This concrete conception of translation as the establishment of connections between the familiar and the unfamiliar is intricately linked to the more general notion of cultural translation noted above. To make the distinction clearer, it is useful to look more closely at the types of translations that Sturge investigates with respect to museums. In a chapter on museum representations, she applies the concept of translation both to the representation of cultures through museum objects and to the museum's written discourse and 'how it handles the worlds once surrounding the objects displayed' (cf. ibid., 131). Comparable to the latter of these two varieties of translation, this subchapter is interested in the ways in which the guides in the observed gallery sessions handle unfamiliar concepts (related to objects or practices) from the 'source regions' by connecting or *translating* them to the 'target region'. This recurring translational practice of the guides can be seen as a concrete means to the ends of the translation of culture generally pursued in the ethnographic museum.

Just like the previously discussed strategies of imaginative or fictional immersion in non-European worlds, 'cultural translation' can become a successful tool in cultural negotiation processes, but it can also result in a problematic construction or appropriation of these worlds. With regard to the situations discussed in this section, these two 'sides of the coin' of translation are noticeable in the observed sessions in the form of relational strategies of the guides, on the one hand, and ascriptive forms of translation on the other. For the sake of clarity, the former types are labelled 'comparisons' in this analysis, while the latter are termed 'equations'. This is a telling distinction as it already indicates which means of establishing links between the non-European and the students' concepts or ideas are applied in each case. As will become clear in the following detailed analysis of both forms, however, it is not just the general communicative act of comparing or equating that determines the negotiating potential of these accounts, but also their specific realisation in the individual situations.

4.7.1   Drawing Comparisons

The use of translational connection- or reference points, established by means of comparison, can be found in many of the observed guided tours. By configuring a shared ground of self and Other, the method of comparison can serve as the 'bridgehead of understanding' that, as Sturge has argued, is necessary for any intercultural communication (cf. ibid., 21). Furthermore, this shared ground helps, as George Hein has explained, to make meaning of the museum experience by connecting it to what the students already know (cf. 1994, 77).

In a few of these situations in which the communication of otherness works through comparison and, thus, through the communication of reference points between familiar and unfamiliar practices, the students are encouraged to establish these associations on

252

their own. This is, for instance, evident in Antonia's session when she asks the students to compare the form of Polynesian outrigger boats[62] with things they already know. A student suggests seaplanes, upon which Antonia confirms his suggestion and introduces the word 'catamaran', explaining that this term is originally Polynesian and is still used today (cf. GSA-MA, 161-163). In this situation, it is unclear whether Antonia expects the students to associate the outrigger boats with seaplanes in order to lead over to the term 'catamaran', but the students' association works well for her session. Without already premeditating what the boats could be compared with, Antonia simply points the school group to the fact that they know comparable objects, letting them brainstorm possibilities. In so far as the students are thus facilitated to use their individual prior knowledge to understand the artefact on display, the situation acknowledges their role as 'partners in the process of creating meaning, which results when they engage with museum objects in light of their prior experience, not simply when they memorize museum facts' (Silverman paraphrased in O'Neill 2006, 106).

It may seem that this is only a very basic example for such a co-creation of knowledge in learning processes in museums. By now, such inquiry-based means of learning, by which visitors are motivated to arrive at meanings themselves, are promoted widely in museum education (cf. Hein 1994, Black 2005, Allen et al. 2014). Yet, as already indicated, these more open methods are only rarely used in the guided tours, and the guides often position themselves as the experts who explain cultural contexts to the students. Comparisons or reference points *autonomously* established by the students, as in Antonia's session, are, therefore, very rare in the analysed guided tours. This may also be the case because it is not easy to create situations in which the students can identify reference points by themselves because, as Hooper-Greenhill has argued,

---

[62] A definition is provided in the glossary.

'observation depends on already knowing that for which one is searching' (2000, 15). Hence, the students initially need to be able to identify at least an aspect of the foreign artefact in order to compare it to something they know. Without a hands-on experience of the displayed artefacts, this is difficult to achieve.

Other cases in the material, in which the students are encouraged to connect the represented objects in the exhibition to something they already know, can predominantly be found in the guided tours observed in Museum D, which, as already mentioned, is focused on art and design. Here, comparisons are used widely to facilitate the students to draw inferences from the familiar to the unfamiliar, and to thereby slowly unravel the meaning of the artefacts. For instance, in order to explain Islamic tiles displayed in the exhibition, Feona tells the students to put the back of their hands on the gallery floor to comprehend what the material of the tiles would feel like (cf. GSF-MD, 188-190). She then asks them how they feel and what they notice about the tiles, letting the students make associations and describe their experience to her (cf. ibid., 165-175). They deduce from the materiality and the theme of the gallery that the tiles could be used to keep houses cool from the inside in warmer regions (cf. ibid. 175ff.). Such a comparison based upon experience and deduction gives the students the feeling that they have arrived at the explanation of the objects themselves, rendering the museum experience more meaningful to them personally. As Annabel Fraser and Hannah Coulson have argued in a chapter on 'incomplete stories' in museums, open-ended stories can provide 'a great sense of achievement when we have got to grips with something we could not comprehend at first' (2012, 230).

While independently made comparisons and their unfolding conclusions about the nature of the displayed artefacts can contribute not only to a relativisation of difference, but also to the sense of achievement in learning processes, such comparisons are, as already mentioned, rare in the observed sessions. A more usual form of cultural translation through comparison consists in the guides' explicit reference to the comparable aspect or practice in the students' lifeworlds. In most of the observed sessions, such hints to cultural analogies are given at various moments in the guided tours in order to establish a 'way into' the unfamiliar ritual, object, or situation. For example, in Kate's session, Japanese samurai are compared to European knights:

K: Now, we're right back at the end of the fifteen-hundreds. And what we can compare the samurai to is kind of to knights on horseback, in Europe at this time. So in Europe, what did knights look like?

S: They were wearing a lot of metal.

K: They wore lots and lots of metal armour. All over their bodies, didn't they? Big plates on their chests, all down the legs and arms. They got helmets on. […] And how could they can get around?

S: Horse.

K: On a horse, fantastic. So these soldiers were getting around on horses. Their armour is a little bit different, isn't it, than the knights' in Europe? To be a knight in Europe you had to be rich. Really rich. You had to be really rich so you could afford all your armour, to get your horse, to get your weapons. […] And it's exactly the same with the samurai. You had to be quite rich, and quite high up in society to be a samurai.

(GSK2-MD, 642-658)

In this situation, Kate provides the comparison herself (i.e. knights as reference points to compare the samurai to) instead of asking the students what the samurai uniforms exhibited in the gallery remind them of. Still, there is a lot of deduction in this dialogue as the students subsequently use their knowledge about European knights to better understand the samurai. Representative of many similar comparisons that the guides provide in the gallery sessions, such reference points introduced by the gallery educators serve as means of reducing the strangeness of the non-European objects and phenomena discussed in the gallery sessions and to thereby simplify the communication or explanation of unfamiliar aspects. As Wallman has argued, such reference points are especially necessary when communicating otherness: 'Especially where the idea to be conveyed is strange […] it behoves an intending communicator to start the negotiation with an image that her intended audience already knows' (2007, 244).

In Kate's 'translation' of Japanese samurai, what is notable is that the comparison to the 'target concept' of the European knights remains on the same temporal level as the 'source' concept. Both entities are situated explicitly in the 16th century. A denial of coevalness is, therefore, avoided not only because the non-European phenomenon is located in a specific time, but also because the comparison to a European phenomenon is situated in the same temporal framework. Unlike, for instance, Antonia's already discussed account of the Polynesians building catamarans while the Europeans were still living in caves, Kate's comparison between knights and samurai does not fall into the trap of insinuating a hierarchy of progress or cultural development. Furthermore, such a comparison on the same temporal level also prevents the framing of unfamiliar rituals and beliefs outside of modernity, which is often implicit in accounts that compare 'their' current practices to 'our' past. For example, it is problematic to explain the nazar amulet[63] and its function of protecting oneself from the 'evil eye', as Maria does, by stating that this is not only a belief in the Middle East, but that it also existed 'in our country' in former times (cf. GSM-MB, 657-660). This comparison suggests that 'we' have overcome something that is still prevalent in non-European countries. In contrast, comparisons in the same conversation that relate to the children's prior knowledge about nazar amulets from tourist markets or kiosks produce an association between the object and the students without locating the practices and beliefs related to it to a place outside of modernity.

Although the comparison between European knights and Japanese samurai thus avoids a denial of coevalness and contributes to the students' familiarisation with the role of the samurai, it can still be argued

---

[63] A definition is provided in the glossary.

that comparisons that are situated in the past are less easily comprehensible for the students than comparisons that relate to their immediate lifeworlds. After all, in case of the samurai example, the students have to accomplish two processes of translation at once. Initially, they need to imaginatively relocate to 16th-century Europe and visualise what they know about knights, before subsequently translating this image back to their present encounter of samurai uniforms in the gallery. As George Steiner has argued, '[w]hen we read or hear any language-statement from the past [...] we translate' (Steiner 1998, 29). He refers to translation as a process in which a distance or barrier must be crossed from source to receptor, no matter if the barrier is language or time (cf. ibid). Thus, in the example at hand, the students are asked not only to translate one cultural context to another, but also to translate between the past and the present. The translation process is, then, based upon the expectation that the students have sufficient knowledge about European knights, which may, however, not be available to all members of the school group. When trying to establish reference points between the children's world and the world of the object, the question is therefore what counts as the children's world, or what is presupposed and therefore constructed as 'familiar'. This issue demonstrates that autonomously made comparisons by the students based on their individual prior knowledge can be more effective than comparisons suggested by the guides because the latter strategy always requires assumptions about familiarity and, in effect, about identity and belonging.

Comparisons suggested by the guides can be especially problematic when presumptions about common reference points of comparison are imposed upon the non-European world. For example, Gladys tries to interact with the students by connecting the storyworld she presents to them about a Nigerian boy (looking for presents for his grandma) to the world of the students. She explains the word for 'grandma' in Nigerian and then asks the students what they would call their grandmas. When they all answer 'grandma' or 'grandmother', Gladys asks specifically for the words for 'grandmas and grandpas from cultures where we use that language like basbushka, amma' (GSG-MC, 113-114). When the children still say 'grandpa' or 'grannie', she says 'I am sure some of you have a name in your own culture' (ibid., 116-117), and the discussion goes on until finally someone mentions a 'foreign' word for 'grandmother'. In this situation, the problem of presupposing common ground becomes clear. Because of the children's appearance, Gladys assumes that they must call their grandparents different names in different languages. The reference point she tries to establish actually constructs difference rather than negotiating it: While they all use the word 'grandma' (which is also mentioned in the story about the Nigerian boy), Gladys tries to establish a connection to what she perceives as their 'authentic' identity. This reference point is based upon assumed ethnicity and therefore 'others' the children instead of connecting them to the represented world.

Such situations are very rare in the observed guided tours. Most of the comparisons by the guides refer to the present or immediate experiences of the students and are often based upon very general information that can be assumed as familiar to them. For example, Christine compares the wearing and performance of masks in Africa with 'a kind of job' (cf. GSC-MB, 574), Hilda compares African markets to markets in London (cf. GSH-MC, 108-114), and Feona explains the necessity of conservation strategies in museums by comparing the bleaching out of the displayed objects to the situation when one leaves a picture on the windowsill and the sunlight causes its colours to fade out (cf. GSF-MD, 386-390). All these points of comparison can be assumed to be familiar to the students, which is why these comparisons lend themselves as means of translating unknown concepts to their own lifeworlds.

258

Christine makes a particularly effective connection for the students between the unfamiliar and their own experience by describing an obasinjom[64] mask from Cameroon and explaining its newly acquired function in the football stadium:

> In Africa there are also often accusations with regard to football games that accuse someone of having done something illegitimate, this can also be something related to magic. Someone has, for instance, nailed up the goal, clouded the sight of the referee, or manipulated the ball. Here, people also believe sometimes that such things happened. And in these contexts, obasinjom can help as well. (GSC-MB, 454-460)

This comparison of obasinjom to 'a kind of mascot' for football games (ibid., 449) is especially interesting because it not only connects the unfamiliar object to a cultural practice that the students know (i.e., football), but also because thereby, common representations of African masks and rituals as firmly embedded in and determined by tradition are questioned. As Jonathan Friedman has explained, 'identity strategies that are local [...] emerge in interaction with each other in the global arena' (1990, 327). This interrelation between local and global spheres becomes apparent in the account about obasinjom's function in the football stadium. Besides thus translating the concept of obasinjom to the 'target' context, such comparisons, that relate to global phenomena or practices, also shift an often-reinforced focus of the ethnographic museum on 'monographic presentations of particular cultures or limited comparisons within regions' (Durrans 1988, 156) to a more transcultural translation of culture. Christine refers to the specific local aspects of the phenomenon while still embedding it in a broader, global context of football games. Here, the communication of otherness unfolds in a way that renders both differences and similarities comprehensible. Similar cases can be found in Hilda's session, when she explains that the kingdom of Benin was built close to a river '[...] [b]ecause what we do as humans, we will put our towns and our

---

[64] A definition is provided in the glossary.

cities or villages where there is water because we need water for life' (GSH-MC, 136-137) or in Antonia's session, when she shows combat uniforms from in the South Sea gallery to the students and explains that one can observe the will to make oneself seem taller in many different places in the world, comparing the helmets of the uniforms to crowns or big hats (cf. GSA-MA, 385-390). By alluding to a broader similarity of concepts and individualisation of local implementations of these concepts, the guides in these cases facilitate processes of transcultural negotiation, in that they show that non-European regions are not essentially different from European regions and that practices can be subject to change and appropriation.

Finally, comparisons between self and Other can also help to negotiate initially pejorative reactions of the students to unfamiliar or strange ideas and concepts. For example, Doreen explains that the Inuit use seal intestines to make waterproof clothing. The students are appalled by this information, upon which the guide explains: 'No, that's not disgusting. Listen, here [in Germany], every sausage is wrapped in intestines and we eat this. They only wear it. That's not disgusting.' (GSD-MA, 855-856). In this situation, Doreen contributes to what Kirshenblatt-Gimblett has called the 'reciprocity of the museum effect' by splitting the viewer's gaze to compare the exotic display to one's own everyday world (1998, 50). The guided tour can thus enhance this experience of reciprocity by causing such moments of self-reflection. The students are questioned as to their own practices in relation to those of the Other – and must finally realise that what they perceive as exotic strangeness is comparable to their own life in only a slightly altered way. These moments in the guided tour have the most potential to facilitate cultural negotiation because they deny a simple satisfaction with tolerance or indifference towards cultural otherness, and instead relativise a perceived cultural distance.

In so far as all of the comparisons can be regarded as means of self-reflection to some extent, this negotiating effect can be observed in most of the examples that are based upon a comparison between the represented cultural contexts and the lifeworlds of the students. However, the second form in which an establishment of connections between 'their' world and 'ours' can unfold in the gallery sessions is more problematic. Although 'equations' similarly translate the unfamiliar to the familiar, the self-reflections that occur in relation to them can be misleading and even essentialising.

4.7.2   Equating non-European Concepts

Unlike the examples above, which are admittedly the most common way of establishing reference points between the non-European concepts or practices and the lifeworlds of the students in the observed sessions, equations do not only bring the foreign concept closer to the 'target' context by means of approximation, but they can be compared to literal translations which claim an equivalence between non-European and European concepts. Sturge provides an example in reference to the African gallery in the Ethnographic Museum of Berlin:

> There, a theme panel on African religion uses unabashedly Christian language to describe what are for a line or two 'gods', but then become just 'God' with 'commandments' and a 'will' being done. This translation strategy generates a unified source text – all African cultures – which is simultaneously posited as fully commensurate with the target culture's own rituals and ritual language. (2006, 437)

What is thus missing in strategies of equating the unfamiliar with the familiar in the written discourse of exhibitions is a noticeable acknowledgment of the translatedness of the source text (cf. ibid.).

In the guided tour, similar equations are made through a variety of communicative acts, although in most of the situations, there is a very thin line between comparing and equating one concept with another. For example, Hilda explains the function of an 'oba' by stating that 'the oba is like the king' (GSH-MC, 154), the term 'like' referring more to a similarity and thus comparison, not to an equation of the concepts 'king' and 'oba'. Later, however, she describes the oba as wearing a crown (cf. ibid., 201) instead of comparing the local concept of the 'ade' or 'adenla'[65] to what 'we' call a crown. In this instance, the headdress of the oba is equated with the headdress commonly worn by kings and queen in European countries. Just as Sturge's example, this equation suggests the two concepts were fully commensurate. However, the 'ade' of the oba is very different from the idea of a 'crown' because it is made of coral beads and also differs in its form (cf. ibid., 201-203). Similarly, Doreen explains that the North American medicine man has his own tepee, which she describes as the 'work room of the medicine man' (GSD-MA, 142-143). While it may be clear to the students that 'work room' is merely a corresponding term, the concept may still evoke a variety of associations that define the way in which the position of the medicine man is perceived. This is not necessarily problematic because it does, in fact, contribute to the translation of his function into the lifeworld of the student, but as the 'translatedness' or comparative status of the reference point is not explicitly noticeable, it seems that the two concepts are entirely commensurate, with no difference between them.

Such equations can be regarded as domestications of difference that work by means of appropriation rather than negotiation. The foreign is perceived entirely in terms of, and integrated with, understandings related to the familiar. There seems to be no gap left between the two understandings; no reference to the local particularity of the 'source' concept. Instead, European conceptions of the idea of the 'crown' or 'work room' are conflated with non-European comparable concepts, while the work of comparison is not noticeable any longer. This kind of domestication of difference then relates to the naturalisation of representations of cultural

---

[65] A definition is provided in the glossary.

life in ethnographic exhibition. The fact that the rendering of cultural life is only a representation is obscured – the cultural phenomenon is 'domesticated and transformed – it is naturalized' (Lidchi 1997, 182).

It is possible to question whether this naturalisation of the translated non-European concepts is problematic. After all, the equations of the guides still contribute to the better understanding of the functions of the oba's headdress and the medicine man's tepee. Yet, what happens through this naturalisation of the terms 'crown' and 'work room' for the respective concepts is that these 'rough translations' (Chakrabarty 2000, 17) produce translucence (cf. ibid.) while they, however, *suggest* that they do indeed provide transparency. The distortion that necessarily happens in the process of translation is obscured, which does not lead to a negotiation of meaning, but to a simple assimilation of the unfamiliar meaning to the realm of the familiar. This suggested commensurability or literal translatability of non-European 'worlds' again relates to Alcoff's argument about the process of speaking for others and its implication in the desire for mastery over the other (cf. 1992, 29). There is an underlying claim of 'knowing' the Other in these naturalised equations – there is no remaining doubt about 'our' interpretations of 'their' concepts being appropriate, fitting, or sufficient.

The problem that thus presents itself with regard to reference points that equate the familiar and the unfamiliar relates to the question of translatability that plays an important role in the discourse on translating culture. For instance, Chakrabarty has shown that European concepts such as democracy or equality are used uncritically as universal analytical concepts in the scholarly work on non-European countries, whereas local traditions of political thinking are ignored (cf. 2000, 5f.). On the basis of this constellation, he argues that translation should be cross-categorical, which would work on the basis of contextualising and historicising allegedly universal categories of analysis (cf. ibid, 83). This broader critical view on the translatability of European concepts can also be applied to the translation processes in the gallery sessions. It is, in this sense, necessary to critically reflect why it seems natural to the guides to conceive of certain non-European practices or objects solely in terms of European analytical concepts. In order to avoid a traditional Eurocentric construction of mastery over the Other by grasping 'their' world through 'our' categories, questions about mistranslations or losses in translation would need to be embedded in their statements. Equally, Peter Burke has argued that more attention should be paid to '[…] what in a given culture most resists translation, and to what is lost in the process of translation' (2009, 60).

Furthermore, the aforementioned contextualisation of the process of translation may be key to familiarising the students with the difficult relation between particularity and comparability of meaning. For example, Hilda notes that while the oba is *like* a king, 'he was almost more than a king' and explains which facets distinguish the concept of the king from the function of the oba (GSH-MC, 154). In this context, what Kwame Anthony Appiah has called 'thick translation' (1993) is applicable to gallery education. Appiah notes that translation processes need to be embedded in their linguistic and cultural contexts (cf. ibid., 817), which is why, comparable to Geertz's 'thick description' (1973), whenever a translation unfolds, it is the underlying reasons and functions for the concept in the 'source' context that should be analysed and identified carefully.

This contextualisation or 'thick translation' could also help to prevent a too narrow fixation or definition of the phenomenon to be translated. As Derrida notes, the problem of translation is not only the distortion of translated meanings that happens in the process, but also the construction of a stable meaning in the source context (cf. 2005, 264f.). Hence, the equation of a term with a seemingly well-suited corresponding term from the 'target' context does not only suggest the full commensurability of two concepts, but also their coherent and unambiguous meaning. This is what Sturge criticises about the labels in the Ethnographic Museum in Berlin that not only equate, but thereby also construct 'all African cultures' as 'unified source text.' In a similar vein, the equation of the 'adenla' of the oba with a king's crown in the aforementioned example reduces a possible heterogeneity of the meaning of the oba's headdress. In Hilda's explanation, the object can only be interpreted as a crown – alternative associations are not acknowledged.

While this example of the fixation of meaning through translation remains on a rather indistinct and basic level, there are other examples in the guided tours that are more revealing with regard to the problematic relations that can unfold through the naturalisation of equations. For example, in her session about the African gallery in Museum B, Christine describes the ritual of Death Celebrations[66] in Cameroon, explaining that all of the relatives and acquaintances of the deceased are invited to these events even though this can get very expensive (cf. GSC-MB, 634-643). She then explains that the reasons for inviting all these people is 'typically African' (ibid., 599), namely that this is a kind of insurance: 'If you are generous to these people, they will also try to help you when you need something. [...] And the people also say that to be rich is to know people' (ibid., 654-655). Upon this explanation, the teacher of the school group intervenes by saying that she has an example that illustrates this situation for them:

> In the football team of my son there is a boy (.) with a tradition like this. And the family has a lot of children and meanwhile, they rely upon the parents of the friends of their son to take care of him. So after school he does his homework at the place of the other parents and these parents also took care of signing him up for a football team. And the family said that this entirely normal for his parents because in Africa, everyone takes care of each other. For them, this is not embarrassing or anything that another family thinks they need to support their son. (the teacher in GSC-MB, 658-668)

---

[66] A definition is provided in the glossary.

In this example, the equation unfolds through the statement of the teacher. The teacher translates the phenomenon that Christine has explained into her own life world, and thus tries to make sense of her own experience through the explanations of the guide. On the one hand, this represents an attempt to negotiate between the unfamiliar and the familiar, or the remote alterity depicted in the museum and the immediate alterity experienced in her everyday life. The teacher uses, as Charles Garoian has framed it in an article on the dialogic relationship between visitors and museums, '[…] museum culture as a source through which to imagine, create, and perform new cultural myths that are relevant to their personal identities' (2001, 235). On the other hand, however, her equation of the situation described by Christine with the situation described by herself is problematic because the two cases are not the same. First of all, Christine's account revolves around a specific ritual in Cameroon whereas the teacher's situation is applied to a vague concept of 'African culture'. Furthermore, while Christine's situation involves mutual relationships of insurance, the teacher's situation simply describes how the, supposedly German, family takes care of an 'African' child for his parents. Regardless of the many other problematic implications that come with this statement (i.e., the African family has a lot of children so maybe they cannot take care of all of them; they should feel embarrassed but they don't), it is the distortion of the initial description of the ritual that is enacted by means of its equation with a very different example. The only reference point between the two situations seems to be the generosity and solidarity of African families, which is, of course, an already existing stereotype that is only reinforced through this form of equation.

This example illustrates how equations can function as means of undermining complexity by forcing fixed conceptions on unfamiliar phenomena. This is particularly problematic with respect to the authority of translation. As Sturge explains, 'the translator makes the source text, not only the target text' (2007, 8), which is why the teacher's example may actually change how the initial situation is perceived. As a response, Christine could insist on 'thick translation' by explaining that this situation is not similar to the ritual she describes. To the contrary, however, Christine herself already insinuates a form of stereotypisation by saying that this practice is 'typically African.'

In conclusion, what becomes clear from the examples of equating the unfamiliar with the familiar is that they aim at coherence and easy comprehension. But while it may 'connect educational work back to life' (Hein 2006, 350), this coherent and literal translation or domestication of difference reinforces cultural myths that work against the negotiation that is the goal of the process of translation. Especially in a multicultural and globalised world, the myth that a cultural translation 'can be a coherent and accurate synthesis of a coherent and synthesizable whole' (Sturge 2007, 10) needs to be discarded not only in ethnographic research, but also, and even more so, in its communication in the museum. In this sense, students in gallery sessions need to be encouraged to 'ask what the translator's perspective was, which native points of view he or she was privy to and decided to translate, how those points of view entangle with other, contradictory ones, and so on' (ibid., 10). Thus, while the guides are better off applying comparative approaches to translation, because these make explicit the insecurity, ambiguity, and loss involved in the translation process, it would also be necessary to teach the students how to 'read' cultural translations.

4.8 Synthesis: Underlying Ideas of Speaking about Non-European Regions

The preceding seven subchapters have documented and explained recurring themes and practices of communicating cultural otherness during the observed gallery sessions in two German and two British museums. While specific situations differ in terms of their contextual details, common communicative acts such as celebrating cultural diversity *between* – not among – cultural groups, depicting non-Europeans as 'scientists of the concrete', or representing modernity and change as inauthentic aspects of non-European life can be found in various of the sessions. Certainly, there are practices that bear potential for a more meaningful engagement with cultural differences, such as the telling of local legends or the reference to connections between local practices and global phenomena. However, as has been shown, from a transcultural perspective many of the guides' explanations and performances still need to be criticised for their essentialising and distinguishing potential. The question that offers itself is why representations of non-European regions in guided tours of museums holding ethnographic objects are *still* often embedded in notions of stereotypical cultures as entities and 'condescending veneration'. Why do the accounts of the guides emphasise categorical difference between 'us' and 'them' while their declared aim is to generate understanding? How to make sense of this frequency of communicative strategies entailing cultural essentialism, generalisation, denial of coevalness, construction of authenticity, and reinforcement of stereotypical otherness?

To answer this question, the preceding analysis of recurring themes in the guides accounts and their implications points to three 'core factors' of the communication of non-European otherness that underlie most of the discussed phenomena. These factors can be seen as a synthesis of the preceding discussion, thereby aiming at condensing the multi-layered and situational analysis of individual cultural representations and their consequences into comprehensive concepts that serve as lenses through which most of the aforementioned problematic depictions of non-European regions and groups can be seen and understood. The entirety of the previously elucidated seven communicative patterns can, certainly, not be broken down into these three factors. However, the influence of these factors can be traced in almost all of the described patterns of communicating otherness, which is why an overview of these factors serves as a helpful framework to not only summarise previous findings, but also to transition towards the next chapter. As already announced in the beginning of Chapter 4, the fifth chapter is focused on explaining the actions of the guides by looking at various actors, such as the environment of the exhibition, the working conditions of the guides, or expectations surrounding the museum. These dimensions will be considered for each of the three core factors in order to facilitate a comprehensive consideration of explanatory approaches. In the last sections of this chapter, these three factors are, therefore, briefly listed and explained as a synthesis of the previous findings, before they are subsequently taken up as a basis for the explanatory approaches presented in Chapter 5.

4.8.1   The Performance of Authority

The demonstration and performance of authority can be traced as a factor underlying many of the analysed phenomena. As already explained in Chapter 3, in this work, 'authority' can appear in the form of the cultural authority of the museum, the educational authority of the guides, and ethnographic authority of both the curatorial arrangement and the guides' accounts. In relation to the recurring patterns in the guides' accounts, the two latter forms of authority are particularly relevant. Hence, the two overarching problems that affect the emergence of essentialist or generalising representations of otherness in the guides' accounts are their disciplinary practices (educational authority) and their unambiguous and seemingly indisputable truth claims about non-European practices (ethnographic authority). For example, educational authority is key in understanding the guides' generalising accounts about the moral superiority of Chinese or Indian children (see 4.3). Especially Britta's,

Gladys's and Eva's accounts about the respectability of teachers or elders in the non-European contexts can be explained by the guides' aims to represent themselves as 'elders' to be respected. Ethnographic authority, on the other hand, helps to elucidate the guides' practices of authenticating the Other by using the 'ethnographic present' (see pp. 205ff.). When the guides make statements such as 'The North American Indians believe that [...]' (Doreen, GSD-MA, 289, 309), they construct timeless, all-encompassing, general 'facts'.

In order to make the relation between the performance of authority and problematic communications of otherness even clearer, it is worthwhile to consider some additional examples. For instance, the guides' recurring references to the originality and value of the objects on display and their related instructions for the students to be careful around them can be understood in terms of educational authority because the guides make the students 'obey' their orders and restrictions by warning them that the objects are expensive and irreplaceable (see pp. 190ff.). Ethnographic authority, in turn, explains the guides' references to non-European regions as internally homogenous (see p. 137). As already mentioned, this kind of authority constructs the language of the ethnographer as technical and universalising, authoritative, and truthful (cf. Bowman 2007, 43). Furthermore, the guides' representation of real events in the form of stories can equally be understood in terms of ethnographic authority because this format suggests a certain completeness that makes these events seem more real (see pp. 207ff.). Finally, recurring references to the Other in terms of zero focalisation, suggesting omniscience about the events as well as insights into the thoughts of the Other, are equally comprehensible in light of this same authority. For instance, when Doreen explains that '[...] when the American Indians first saw the Spanish on horses, they thought this was one creature' (GSD-MA, 541-543), this statement suggests complete historical insight from the perspective of the

Other, without reference to the source or reliability of the information. As in the other cases, there is no opportunity to challenge the information, or to represent ambiguity or incompleteness.

Thus, the connection between these two forms of authority and the guides' problematic representations of otherness consists in the fact that authoritative strategies tend to construct reliability and truth, which can lead to a limitation of the critical scrutiny with which facts or rules are confronted as well as to an obscuration of the ambiguity and internal diversity that marks cultural contexts. As already mentioned, claims to the guides' own authority (as deserving respect and trust from the students) are closely connected to problems of speaking for or about others that Alcoff has presented (1992). This is because '[...] how what is said gets heard depends on who says it, and who says it will affect the style and language in which it is stated, which will in turn affect its perceived significance' (1992, 13). The guides' establishment of their own role as authority figures thus creates an atmosphere in which it becomes difficult to mistrust or question their statements. Similarly, by presenting information or descriptions about the Other as objective facts, opportunities for differentiation become limited. Hence, the statements of the guides are 'heard' in a way that leaves not much room for doubt, criticism or diversification. In the following chapters, these effects of the guides' ethnographic and educational authority are further associated with the workings of the ethnographic museum's cultural authority. In many ways, the authority that the guides perform is connected to the public expectation of the museum as a reliable disseminator of knowledge about non-European lifeworlds.

This finite nature of the guides' accounts, which prevents a relativisation of the trustworthiness of their statements and explanations, is not merely an accidental side effect of the tours but can be regarded as a conscious strategy: By presenting themselves as authority figures and representing information as facts, the guides represent themselves as seemingly 'incontestable'. The perceived necessity of such a 'secure' position in the eyes of the guides is an important aspect of this common problem of authority: Why do the guides want to be 'incontestable'? Why is it difficult to create participative, open learning environments and to communicate explanations about non-European as theories instead of facts? Why are aspects like definite facts, declarative language, truth and authenticity such common features in the observed sessions? Chapter 5 explores key factors that lead to this assertion of authority, thereby acknowledging both external factors that confer authority onto the gallery educators, as well as intrinsic factors that explain why the guides then reinforce and embody this authority.

4.8.2   The Reduction of Complexity

A second basic challenge that underlies many of the recurring themes of communicating otherness is the reduction of the complexity of cultural phenomena during the guided tour. As Bella Dicks has explained, cultural complexity is a problem for the ethnographic museum in general, which becomes apparent, for instance, in post-colonial accusations of cultural essentialism (cf. 2004, 168). She sees the challenge in representing the 'complexities that may not be obviously amenable to the tourist gaze' (ibid.) Hence, the fact that the guides consider it necessary to simplify what they want to explain to the students is not a surprise: Gallery educators are confronted with the challenging task of communicating multidimensional practices, objects, and historical events to a group of visitors who cannot be expected to possess a significant amount of prior knowledge. Furthermore, this task is to be accomplished in an average time period of only one hour. Reducing the complexity of the cultural phenomena they communicate hence seems unavoidable.

Therefore, strategies to reduce complexity are omnipresent in the observed gallery sessions, and they can account for many of the problematic communications of otherness analysed in the preceding chapters. However, the crucial point that leads to these problematic depictions of non-European regions does not consist in the fact that gallery sessions can only represent some of the dimensions and perspectives of cultural situations. Instead, it is the way in which the guides deal with this issue that causes essentialist depictions. This is because the guides' strategies of reducing complexity often appear in the form of a *denial* of complexity altogether: Instead of explaining that a situation or practice is difficult to explain or entails dimensions that cannot be discussed in the short amount of time, the guides suggest the existence of easily-comprehensible cultural systems by means of three main strategies: generalisation, trivialisation, and ordering.

Generalisation occurs when the guides reduce the complexity of a situation by representing one version or facet of reality as the entire story. This compares to what Geertz has called the Jamestown-is-the-US fallacy, in which little spaces are regarded as speaking for bigger areas (cf. 1973, 22). Such a conflation of a part with the whole explains, for instance, the guides' employment of ethnic or national categories to summarise the cultural practices of an entire region (see pp. 138ff.) as well as the broad generalisations and labelling of non-Europeans in statements such as 'China is fantastic in using so many different materials' (GSK-MD, 98) when trying to evoke respect for non-European practices (see pp. 150ff.).

Trivialisation is the case when the guides 'play down' the relevance or difficulty of a certain topic. For example, when students in Maria's session ask about the relation between Islam and terrorism, she clearly struggles, not knowing how to negotiate a complex topic like this in the short amount of time she has at her disposal. She tells the children not to worry about terrorism too much because '[...] you are children. You just have to live your lives [...] and it is natural that you have a lot of questions, but that does not mean that it will concern you at some point' (GSM-MB, 840-843). This form of reducing complexity by means of trivialisation can also account for the way in which European success stories are told without reference to illegal or immoral acquisition practices as in Kate's account of the British soldiers' retrieval of Tippoe's Tiger (see pp. 213ff.). Similarly, it explains how a trivialised and vague notion of cultural diversity is used as a means of 'negotiating' problematic questions, such as in case of Britta's answer to a student who claims that the Chinese torture their animals, which amounts to 'this is a different culture to ours' (GSB-MB, 521-522).

Finally, the strategy of 'ordering' is used when a certain coherence is imposed upon the situation to be described. Although Geertz has argued that coherence should not play such a significant role in anthropology for cultural systems do not have to be 'impeccable' (cf. 1973, 18), many of the described accounts of the guides are marked by coherency-establishing strategies of worldmaking and historical emplotment. As White argues, historical narratives provide a 'completeness and fullness of which we can only imagine, never experience' (1980, 20). Thus, the narrative structure of many parts of the guides' accounts constructs coherence seemingly automatically. This strategy of reducing complexity by means of ordering reality into the form of a story explains, for instance, the suggestion of the guides that visiting the museum compares to travelling to the respective countries, thus ordering the world of the Other according to the order of the galleries (see pp. 235ff.).

All these means of reducing or eliminating complexity are interrelated. For example, the framing of European collectors' acquisition practices in terms of European superiority and a willing cooperation of non-European actors (see pp. 207ff.) can be explained both by means of trivialisation (i.e., the power indifference is played down) and ordering a complex reality in terms of linear and coherent stories (i.e., the acquisition process is framed as a linear and logical narrative). Similarly, the authentication of the objects on the basis of their 'origin', which ignores the complex relationships that have led to their production, can be understood in terms of generalisation (i.e., a part of the object's history is represented as its complete history) as well as ordering (i.e., a logical and easily comprehensible narrative is imposed on the difficult production process). As already indicated, these three practices function as means of avoiding longer explanations, critical discussions or political issues. However, by replacing the complexity of cultural situations with the construction of less chaotic, less incoherent, less multidimensional worlds, the guides reinforce ideas about generalisable and primitive Others. The use of such strategies of reduction is not inevitable in the guided tours. Maria, for example, asks the teacher to further discuss the complex topic of terrorism at school (ibid., 837ff.) because the students are noticeably concerned with the issue. Such an honest admission that it may not be possible to sufficiently discuss this topic during the gallery session can be more fruitful than to deny that it is relevant for the students. Similarly, explicit references to cultural complexity would help to de-essentialise the aforementioned representations: Once it is made clear to the students that the represented realities are only part of a larger whole, or account only for one perspective out of many, the portrayal of partial realities is not as problematic.

However, the guides' accounts are clearly focused on the representation of seemingly complete, yet dangerously generalised and ordered realities. The reasons for their 'eliminations' of complexity, and factors that determine this practice, are further discussed in Chapter 5 by investigating both individual motivations of the guides and external determinants such as the expectations of the teachers or the self-conception of the museum.

4.8.3   The Amplification of Otherness

The last one of the three core factors that can be seen as internal explanations for the frequency and persistence of essentialist or stereotypical depictions of otherness in the observed guided tours is a far-reaching phenomenon that is labelled here – for lack of a better term – the 'amplification of otherness'. Many of the described problematic representations can be explained by, or are indicative of a general pleasure of speaking about otherness, of highlighting differences, and presenting the unfamiliar. This pleasure may be understood in terms of exoticism because it works through the production of spectacles and the elimination of historical specificity, as Barthes has defined it (1957, 94ff.). It can also be seen as a form of Ahmed's notion of 'stranger fetishism' because the accounts of the guides that are marked by this 'pleasure of otherness' may result in an unquestioned figuration of the Other as a 'stranger', no matter if these accounts are distancing or welcoming (2000, 4ff.). Finally, the phenomenon can be compared to the Orientalist '[...] will or intention to understand, in some cases to control, manipulate, even to incorporate, what is a manifestly different (or alternative and novel) world' (Said 1978, 12). Yet, these approaches only partially describe the function of this omnipresent 'desire for otherness' in the guided tours. Even the notion of 'desire' does not fully account for the connotations at stake because this 'longing' may rather be seen as a reason for this 'pleasure of otherness' to emerge.

What is at the basis of this last underlying factor is a special interest in and resulting promotion of otherness on the part of the gallery educators. Certainly, as Korff has rightly stated, the museum '[...] deals in and of itself with strangeness, with the experience of the other, or of 'alterity'' (2002, 29), which is why the increased concentration and celebration of cultural difference during the guided tours is not a surprise, but could be regarded as a necessary effect of the museum type and the design of the galleries in terms of representations of non-European cultural contexts. However, there is something more to this 'interest' than a focus on the gallery themes and the translation of non-European objects. In most cases, the accounts of the guides are not focused on the explanation of artefact, but their attention quickly shifts to the figure of 'the Other' in general, and then to cultural peculiarities and distinguishing features (– in short – to fundamental, timeless difference. The emphasis of the guided tours is then predominantly placed on the presentation of non-European otherness, and not on the history or specific qualities of the objects, or on negotiating cultural difference. This is why 'exoticism' and 'stranger fetishism' at least to some extent explain what is meant here: the guides seem to enjoy the otherness they represent (and construct).

Yet, what is important to note is that the otherness that the guides emphasise is 'enjoyable' mainly because it is depicted as easily comprehensible, commensurable, and mainly decorative: It's an otherness that does not challenge a sense of the self, that does not evoke critical questions or demonstrate the complicated system of meaning that is connected to cultural practices. This 'happy otherness' is based on stereotypes, pointing to a 'desire for an originality threatened by differences of race, colour and culture' (Bhabha 1994, 75). It is possible to celebrate, to enjoy, to promote this kind of otherness because it makes the world seem ordered, equilibrated, intelligible, and balanced. Perhaps it is a fear of a more complex engagement with non-European cultural realities that motivates this promotion of 'happy otherness' in the guided tours because, as Kristeva has explained, '[c]onfronting the foreigner whom I reject and with whom at the same time I identify, I lose my boundaries, I no longer have a container [...]' (1991, 187). Perhaps it is also the 'subject's desire for a pure origin' (Bhabha 1983, 27) that is connected to this phenomenon. Yet, while the reasons for the guides' pleasure of and desire for this 'happy otherness' are discussed in Chapter 5, the prevalence of this underlying problem becomes apparent when considering the examples of the preceding chapters that can be explained in terms of it.

For instance, the celebration of multicultural diversity and the ensuing representations of cultures as closed-off and decorative entities can be understood in terms of this 'amplification of otherness'. When Eva uses the 'other countries, other manners' explanation to answer to a students' appalled reaction to her statement that half the people in India do not use toilet paper (see p. 142), this is a good example for a case in which a guide emphasises superficial differences and frames them within notions of celebratory otherness. As already explained in this context, the promotion of cultural diversity *as long as* it does not confront 'us' is dangerous because it promotes a world view in which alternative views and practices need not genuinely concern 'us'. Similarly, the practice of dressing the students up in non-European traditional costumes is a case in point: Here, stereotypical, ostensibly pure otherness is performed and promoted, making it seem as if non-European cultural contexts were as straightforward as the colourful dresses and gowns that the students are supposed to wear (see pp. 222ff.).

It is not just the celebratory moments of the guided tours that can be understood in terms of 'the amplification of (happy) otherness'. When the gallery educators overly emphasise differences, as in the case of labelling 'their' social values as unmodern or submissive (see pp. 181ff.) or in the case of emphasising 'their' skills of 'using everything they have' in Gladys's reference to Africa, thereby reinforcing the common 'poor, but happy' stereotype (see pp. 156ff.), this is similarly representative of pleasure to distinguish 'us' from 'them'. Finally, the representation of an easy commensurability of non-European concepts through the equation of local concepts with European ones (see pp. 260ff.) can also be regarded as a result of an emphasis on 'happy otherness' with which it is not necessary to engage on a deeper level. Such emphases on a universally agreeable and easily domesticated difference are frequently observable in the guides' accounts and they demonstrate the widespread distribution of this 'desire for otherness' in the gallery sessions. It seems that this is a popular way of speaking about non-European regions, which is not surprising given the optimistic and conciliatory nature of these statements. However, as becomes clear in the examples, this underlying principle can only explain most of the accounts in connection with the other two core challenges, authority and reduction of complexity. In concert, they function to produce guided tours about a happy, visible, uncomplex, and appeasing world of otherness that is, however represented in the form of truth and definiteness.

In this sense, these three principles can be regarded as explanations for the 'disimprovement effect' that has been posited at the beginning of this chapter: The good intentions of the guides to undermine stereotypes and raise awareness for different ways of life in the world are often realised in terms of authoritative statements, reduced complexity, and the amplification of otherness. The guides show an otherness that they expect the students to admire and to understand, hoping to raise their interests for the Other, but through the reduction of complexity, the suggestion of 'happy' otherness, and the authority that they embody, the accounts eventually end up essentialising otherness and therefore reinforcing stereotypes.

The following takes these considerations as a starting point for a more comprehensive analysis of explanatory approaches to the dominance of these three factors in the communication of otherness. It moves from the descriptive and interpretational work of critically scrutinising *what* meanings the guided tours offer to a more contextualising and explanatory endeavour: *Why* do these meanings emerge in the observed guided tours?

5 Contextualising the Guides' Communication: Factors contributing to the Significance of Authority, Complexity, and Otherness

While the previous chapter has focused on the interpretation of recurring patterns of communicating non-European otherness in the observed gallery sessions, this chapter is concerned with the external and internal influences that contribute to the emergence of these patterns in the guided tours. In particular, the previously mentioned three underlying principles in the observed guided tours, including the performance of authority, the reduction of complexity, and the amplification of otherness, are at the centre of this chapter's attention. Whereas Chapter 4 has provided a classification and transcultural criticism of the guides' ways of constructing or negotiating non-European otherness, Chapter 5, thus, introduces the contexts that these ways of communicating are determined by.

As already explained, this separation of a critical reflection of *what* the guides say and do in the observed sessions from the contexts and factors that explain *why* they act accordingly results from a twofold interest in a poststructuralist and a contextualist analysis. The previous chapter has regarded the guides' accounts in a poststructuralist way, that is, as separated from the intentions and contexts of their authors[67] (cf. Barthes 1977, 147). This step has been crucial because the various possible implications and meanings of these accounts are not restricted to their immediate contexts or the guides' intentions. As a type of museum representation, the guided tour carries meanings and implications that assume a life of their own. The present chapter now complements this poststructuralist analysis by taking a more contextualist approach. It acknowledges both the actors in the field and the intentions of the guides that determine the performance of the gallery sessions. This analysis of

---

[67] In this case, the text's authors can be seen as the guides and the learning departments, but also as the spaces, the students, and the teachers because they all may contribute to the contents of the accounts.

the guided tour's embeddedness in a broader system of interrelations and influences shows that it is not only the individual gallery educator who is responsible for what is communicated. Instead, various social and non-social actors, which lie outside of the guides' personal sphere of influence, also shape the communication of non-European otherness in the sessions. In this sense, this chapter is further insightful with respect to the disimprovement effect because it can explain why the guides' intentions of broadening horizons and evoking mutual understanding are sometimes inconsistent with the messages they eventually convey.

In the following, each of the already-mentioned three underlying principles is investigated in detail with respect to the influences that, at least in part, affect the prevalence of these aspects in the observed sessions. The analysis does not restrain itself to a discussion of how the guides are influenced by other human actors in their vicinity, which have already been introduced in Chapter 2 (i.e., students, teachers, representatives of learning departments, security personnel). Instead, by applying Bruno Latour's perspective of social analysis manifested in *Actor-Network-Theory* (ANT), the focus is shifted from human actors to 'that which makes them act, namely the circulating entities' (Latour 2005, 238). These non-social 'circulating entities', which can be understood as determining the process or the 'flow' of a continuous establishment and reestablishment of associations and interrelations rather than indicating a final or stable set of relations,[68] help to consider not only that relations between actors in a field are in a constant state of flux, but also what it is that brings these actors together or that establishes relations between them. Most importantly, by means of the change in perspective that ANT makes possible, a deeper insight into the complex system of the

---

[68] Cf. Latour explains that ANT shifts the focus from net-works to work-nets: 'Work-nets could allow one to see the labor that goes on in laying down net-works: the first as an active mediator, the second as a stabilized set of intermediaries.' (2005, 132)

production of meaning in the guided tours can be achieved. Instead of looking only at interactions between the guides and the students or teachers, farther-reaching environmental and non-social factors are acknowledged as influencing some interactions.

As ANT suggests, the analysis in this Chapter will, thus, 'take seriously the beings that make people act' (Latour 2005, 236). Adopting this approach, the analysis unfolds by discussing several non-human actors including the exhibition spaces and the objects, understandings of learning, expectations surrounding the museum, working conditions and working procedures in the museums, as well as understandings of culture. These influential actors have been developed mainly from the statements of the guides in the interviews, but also from the observation protocols of the gallery sessions. Although all of these aspects can be applied to each of the three underlying principles (authority, complexity, otherness), the functions of these actors are different with respect to each principle. This chapter, therefore, considers the three principles separately and describes how the different non-social actors relate to them.

While substantial attention is given to all of these non-human actors, the analysis cannot account for all possible explanations for the performance of authority, the reduction of complexity, and the amplification of otherness. Instead, only those aspects that are deducible from the interviews and observations of the guides can be studied. A close relation to the research findings is, therefore, maintained throughout this chapter. Yet, with respect to the factors of expectations surrounding the museum as institution and understandings of culture, a broader interpretational framework has to be acknowledged because the scope of these influences is assumed to exceed the specific context of the observed gallery sessions. For example, expectations surrounding the purpose and role of museums can be found in the guides' statements and the constellations of the sessions, but these expectations also need to be related to a broader context of the functions and ideas surrounding museums in society. As an additional restriction of the elaborations below, due to the focus of the empirical research on the guides' accounts, a deeper insight into the entire organisational structure of the respective museums with all their complex historical, political, and commercial decision-making frameworks cannot be provided. For the purpose of comprehending a range of factors that affect the practices of the guides, the data from the observations and interviews are, however, sufficient because visitor-centred tasks are still often located at the margins of the organisations. The development of the gallery sessions can thus be understood as a relatively autonomous workflow within the broader museum systems.

As Latour has conceded, the study of non-social beings as a tool to arrive at social relations among human actors raises questions about the agency of the social (cf. ibid., 236f.). Yet, as he argues in relation to the perception of art objects, '[i]t is counterintuitive to try and distinguish 'what comes from viewers' and 'what comes from the object' when the obvious response is to 'go with the flow'' (ibid., 237). For the considerations in this work, this means that by following circulating entities, social agents like the museum guides, the students, the teachers, the staff of the learning departments, and the curators are not reduced to passive bystanders. Instead, their actions are perceived through the lens of their engagement with non-social actors. This framing has the benefits that on the one hand, key factors such as space and shared ideas receive more attention, and on the other, activities of human actors are portrayed in a farther-reaching system of connections and motivations. The methodology is especially helpful with regard to the gallery session because its instruction-based nature bears the danger of overemphasising the agency (and responsibility) of the guides. When levelling criticism at the communication of otherness during museum educational sessions in the respective museums, ANT hence makes it possible to acknowledge the numerous factors in the system that would have to be altered in order to change the final performance of the gallery session.

5.1 Factors Affecting the Performance of Authority

As already explained at the end of the previous chapter, the performance of authority can take a variety of forms, including the reinforcement of the cultural authority of museums, the exertion of educational authority by the guides, and the performance of ethnographic authority. These notions of authority are evident as underlying principles affecting various of the guides' ways of speaking about non-European otherness, such as Britta's or Gladys's requests for the students to be as respectful of them as Chinese or African students allegedly are of their teachers and storytellers (educational authority, ethnographic authority), to Antonia's and Feona's emphases on the originality and value of the objects (cultural authority), or to Antonia's self-presentation as an insider to the displayed cultural context by referring to her recent research trip (ethnographic authority). As already explained in Section 4.8, the problems that result from these self-authorising measures entail the construction of generalising or essentialist statements about non-European regions as facts, the representation of the museum as a mediator of objective truth, and the portrayal of the guides themselves as infallible experts. This is especially the case when, as Melinda Mayer explains, '[…] the place of factual information regarding artworks, teacher authority and responsibility, and pedagogical methods intended to create a safe learning environment [are] all in contention, thereby turning a teacher's words into a myth' (2015, 16). When such a coherent representation of non-European otherness emerges, the guided tour not only fails to stimulate critical reflections of museum representational and expository pitfalls, but also contributes to the formation of the idea that the museum's illustrations of the regional contexts were entirely truthful instead of exposing them as that which they always remain: representations.

In the following, a variety of factors that affect the guides' assertions of these forms of authority are addressed, including the working conditions of the guides, different understandings of learning, expectations surrounding the museum, as well as spaces and objects. This overview of possible influencing factors should not be understood as a set of definite causes for the guides' representations of authority, but rather as conditions and contexts that play into the guides' articulations of truth claims regarding their own credibility and the museum's alleged objectivity. For the sake of clarity, the various influencing factors are analytically separated, but it should be understood that they are closely entangled with each other and do not exist in separation. Wherever possible and logical, connections between them are indicated.

5.1.1 Working Conditions: The Performance of Authority and the Gap between Responsibility and Recognition of the Guides

The authority that the guides exert during the observed sessions can partly be related to the ambivalent roles that they occupy within the museums. The following elaborations, therefore, discuss the difficult position of the gallery educators in the museums part of this study, and problematise this position with regard to the responsibilities and representational functions that the guides occupy.

In all of the cases in this study, the guides are situated neither fully inside nor entirely outside the museum complex. On the one hand, they actively represent not only the display, but also the museums as such in front of a public audience. Even more so, they make museum meanings explicit, thereby communicating broader museum agendas and interpretations. On the other hand, they do not have their own offices in the museum buildings, are paid solely for the performance of the sessions (not for the preparation or reflection time), and do not engage in significant communication with the permanent staff members, such as the curators, gallery designers, or researchers. Although some scholars have argued that museum educators, especially those working in the Anglo-American context, are increasingly integrated into other museum-related tasks such as exhibition design (cf. Rice 2003, 16; Reeve 2010, 145), this seems to apply rather to staff of the learning departments than to the freelance guides.

In the British museums part of this study, this gap between the recognition of the freelance guides and the staff of the learning departments is especially apparent from their different working conditions. While the learning departmental staff is employed on a permanent basis, the guides are employed on zero-hour contracts.[69] They are thus not perceived as 'employees', but as 'workers', a status granting them holiday pay and maternity or paternity leave, yet no secure payment or compensation for preparation time as they are only paid for the time during which they actually perform the sessions. While it may hence be true that British museums are increasingly demonstrating a recognition of their 'key educational roles [...] and, with it, a considerable expansion of museum education departments and their activities' (cf. Black 2005, 157), this process has not affected change with respect to the marginalised positions of the guides within the museums.

---

[69] Among the six guides observed and interviewed in the two British museums part of this study, only one guide was employed as a permanent member of staff. Zero-hour contracts are comparable to freelance work, yet zero-hour contracts grant some employee rights (e.g. sick leave, maternity/ paternity leave). Furthermore, guides on zero-hour contracts are requested to work on specific days and at certain times. At the same time, the museums are not obliged to guarantee permanent work on the arranged dates. Thus, the museums could employ their guides on zero-hour contracts without assigning them any working hours (Gov.UK. 'Employment status', last accessed 14/06/2017, https://www.gov.uk/employment-status/worker).

In Germany, an integration of education with the rest of the museum is often not even implemented on the level of the learning departments. As Bystron and Zessnik argue with respect to German museums, '[…] the perception and representation of museum education within the institutions and the understandings about its tasks are mainly not up to date and develop from uninformed presuppositions' (2014, 324). In a similar vein, Susan Kamel distinguishes between smaller and larger museums, the latter often marked by 'embedded hierarchies which have previously hindered the incorporation of educators into the conceptual development of exhibitions' (2017, 118). This separation of educational from curatorial concerns can also be observed in the museums part of this study. Both of the German museums are larger museums that maintain a relatively strict distinction between curatorial and educational concerns. Furthermore, the German guides that have been interviewed work as freelancers, meaning that, besides similarly not being paid for preparation time, they do not enjoy employee rights (holiday, maternity or paternity leave, etc.). Instead of working on specific days of the week, they are 'called in' on demand. Their situation is, therefore, even more insecure than that of the British guides because they have less planning security.

The lack of appreciation of the work of the German and the British guides in terms of their employment status indicates that their work is regarded as less important or 'valuable' within the museums than that of the permanent staff, such as the learning department managers or the curators. This also echoes in the guides' reports about their problematic relationship with the curators, or about the lack of contact to them. Antonia explains, for instance, that '[…] the freelancers are kept at a distance – they are not appreciated at all and the curators work against the freelancers more than with them. It's an incredibly hierarchical thinking' (EIA, 46-51). Although other guides relativise this impression, with Doreen explaining that some curators are not interested in the educational work, but some are more open-minded (cf. EID, 442-444), almost all of the interviewed gallery educators have only very little or no contact with the curators. This concurs with studies that have described the relationship between curators and gallery educators as marked by suspicion (cf. Illeris 2009, 20) and unsettlement (cf. Rodéhn 2017, 1-2). As a result of this separation of the guides from curatorial decisions and, thus, from broader conceptual meaning-making processes in the museums, social integration through cooperation, passing on knowledge, and what Hodson and Sullivan call 'belongingness' (2012, 62) are difficult to achieve for the guides. [70] A situation that Lynn from one of the British museums describes in the interview reflects very well the uncertainty and disappointment that can result from this situation of not properly belonging:

> [At another museum where I work,] I felt very in and part of the team. And then recently, somebody left and somebody else took over. [...] And I now find myself feeling a little bit defensive because I was doing two days a week there and I suddenly got dropped to one. And then the new person is lovely, but she is inexperienced and very young. And I don't mind that at all, but she is asking to see all my sessions to learn them, to get all my expertise and I'm getting asked [to give sessions] less and less. I mean they have a very special situation [...] But I feel slightly used [...]. (Lynn, 425-445)

Lynn's experience shows that the guides can feel part of the museum, but this feeling is usually temporary and not secure or reliable. Such a lack of mutual accountability is also apparent from the guides' job insecurity. Referring to a closing and reopening process at Museum A, Doreen explains: '[...] as we are only freelancers, nobody cares what happens to us in the meantime. Once the museum is closed, we cannot do the tours anymore and if we can't do the tours, we get no money' (Doreen, 337-339). Another indicator of the marginalisation of the guides within the museum can be found in various guides' reports about delays in their

---

[70] Hodson/ Sullivan see belonging, i.e., peer support, good relations with co-workers (cf. 2012, 62), as essential factors for the achievement of self-actualisation in one's work context, i.e. drawing meaning from and identifying with one's work (cf. ibid., 58).

receipt of information regarding changes that have been made to the galleries, in some cases happening only shortly before the guided tours. Considering their employment status and the lack of teamwork with curators and other members of staff, many of the observed gallery educators are kept in a relatively unstable working situation, with little opportunity for identification with the museum as a work place.

While a separation from one's working environment can be traced in almost all forms of freelance or zero-hour employment, in the context of the work of the gallery educators, it stands in stark contrast with their representational responsibilities and workload. After all, they interpret for a wider audience not only single objects, but also the purpose of entire exhibitions. Some of the guides point to this unequal relationship between their responsibility and recognition in the interviews. For example, Doreen compares her work to that of a nurse: 'If the nurse is good, you have a good impression of the clinic, but if she is unfriendly, you would not want to be there. They are so important, but nobody acknowledges them' (EID, 393-395). Hilda also wonders whether she should invest time to improve her session and to make it more interactive although she is not paid for that kind of additional work (cf. EIH, 258-267). Most of the observed guides work more hours than they are paid for because they want their sessions to be successful. They read up on the session-related 'facts' before they arrive at the museums (cf. e.g. EIK, 100-105, EIF, 371-373) or spend their free time planning the sessions (cf. e.g. EIM, 318ff., EIA, 79ff.). Despite the lack of monetary and social appreciation they receive in the museums, they have high expectations of themselves.

In many ways, these high expectations can be seen as making the system of museum education work. For instance, as there is, often, no structured training or induction phase apart from sitting in on other gallery sessions, many guides explain that they are spending their free time preparing the sessions, learning the scripts by heart, or reading the exhibition catalogues.[71] This kind of self-initiated learning has also been described by Robin Grenier in a study on the development of expertise in museum docents. He argues that

> [w]ith demands for tours that include the most current and accurate content knowledge and changes to programming formats and structures, docents must be subject matter experts and expert facilitators. As a result, docents must use a vast array of learning to meet the needs of museums and the audiences they serve. To achieve this level of expertise participants could not depend on their museums, nor rely on chance experience. They self-initiated learning through mentors and peers, deliberate practice and an array of media to maintain an expert level of skills and subject matter knowledge. (2009, 154)

These ways in which the guides prepare themselves often remain the only form of professionalisation and are implicitly expected from the guides by the respective museums. This also becomes apparent from Britta explanations about Museum B, where guides are increasingly asked to perform sessions that are situated outside of their professional comfort zone. In order to be able to conduct guided tours about a region they are not familiar with, Britta explains that '[…] those who are interested can read up on the subject because they [the learning department] assume that with a background in ethnology […] they can read up on it, so we do this on our own, of course' (EIB, 123-126). This example shows that the fact that the guides invest much more time than they are paid for seems almost natural, not only to the gallery educators, but also to the museums that employ them.

In consequence, gallery educators are expected to function as public representatives of the museum while they themselves are never

---

[71] Allen et al. have shown that 'docent-specific training conventionally consists of occasional lectures from other members of the museum staff, readings, and perhaps briefly shadowing more experienced docents giving visitor tours […]'. Besides reading up on the subject matter on their own, some of the guides in the present study likewise report their shadowing activities and a few others mention that they receive introductions to newly designed galleries and temporary exhibitions by the curators.

really integrated with the organisation. The tension that emerges from this elevated level of public responsibility paired with the lack of appreciation for their work can be regarded as a key factor influencing the guides' performance of authority during the gallery sessions. To show how these working conditions are connected to the guides' performance of authority, an example from the observed sessions is helpful. At the beginning of her gallery session in Museum A in Germany, Antonia introduces herself:

> We will take a look at different groups, for example at New Guinea. This is a country where I work. I am a researcher, and it is my job, here in the jungle, where I have a house and a small pineapple garden, to study how people live there. (GSA-MA, 87-90)

This statement could be regarded as a method to introduce herself to the students; to tell them something interesting about herself so that they can imagine who she is and what she does. Yet, by not simply stating that she is a gallery educator, but by emphasising that she is a researcher herself, Antonia elevates her own role in the museum and, thereby, claims a kind of authority and appreciation which she is not awarded within the working environment of the museum.

According to the definitions of authority presented in Chapter 3.2.3, Antonia's performance of authority can be regarded as ethnographic authority in so far as she turns her experience of 'how people live there' into knowledge by framing this experience as a professional experience ('I am a researcher'). This transformation of personal into professional experience relates to Clifford's distinction between experiential and interpretational authority in participant-observation (cf. 1988, 127ff.). He argues that, while experiential authority derives from a '[...] "feel" for the foreign context' (ibid., 128), interpretational authority derives from a process of textualisation that 'generates sense through a circular movement which isolates and then contextualizes a fact or event in its englobing reality' (ibid., 131). Antonia's 'sense' of the region is, similarly, turned into interpretation because she isolates her experiences and contextualises them in more general terms. This becomes apparent, for instance, when she speaks about the men's clubhouses, arguing that there are no such buildings left in Palau and that it now looks like 'in America' there (GSA-MA, 301-305). In this case, Antonia's personal experience is isolated and then entangled with her description of the displayed clubhouse. By translating experience into cultural interpretation, she, thus, performs ethnographic authority.

The criticism that can be levelled at this authoritative framing is based upon the generalisation and decontextualization implicit in it. Just like the ethnographer's reformulation of specific experience to cultural reality (cf. Clifford 1988, 132), Antonia's specific experience in New Guinea is elevated to signify general knowledge of the cultural context. Her subsequent explanations of New Guinean practices thereby gain a reliability comparable to ethnographic writings: 'The data thus reformulated need no longer be understood as the communication of specific persons. [...] Instead, these texts become evidences of an englobing context, a 'cultural reality'' (ibid.). By positioning herself as an insider *and* a researcher, Antonia's experience becomes knowledge, and this transition from the personal to the allegedly objective dimension makes it difficult to doubt or challenge her statements. Her personal impression about a perceived Americanisation of Palau is valorised, and, as a consequence, nostalgic imaginations of seemingly authentic non-European cultures gain interpretational and educational currency.

Antonia's self-representation as an ethnographic authority can, at least in part, be explained by the elucidated imbalance between the responsibility of the guides and the appreciation they receive from the organisation of the museum. While this situation applies to both the German and the British museums part of this study, the German guides, in particular, refer so specifically to their ethnographic authority. This may be because, in the German museums part of this study, the guides are in a slightly more ambivalent position than those working in the British museums. Whereas the guides in the British museums are employed as educational experts rather than ethnographic experts,[72] most of the guides in the German museums are required to have backgrounds in ethnography, sinology, Islamic studies, and other area studies. This background as 'experts in the field' has an influence on the tasks that the guides are responsible for in the German museums. Officially, the learning departments conceptualise the plans for the sessions while the guides are merely called in for 'facilitating' or performing these sessions. However, this division of tasks between the learning departments and the guides is not implemented in practice. All of the German guides report in the interviews that they are responsible for, or at least significantly involved in, the conceptualisation of the sessions (cf. EIA, 79-82, EID, 392-398, EIB, 37-46, EIC, 35ff., EIM, 325ff.). Because of this disciplinary expertise and the conceptualising effort that they invest in the sessions, the German guides' may feel more responsible, flexible, and independent as ethnographic authorities.

It is this autonomy of the guides in the German museums paired with the lack of recognition of this autonomy with respect to their status in the organisation that leads to assertions of ethnographic authority. While they factually remain at the margins of the organisation from a management perspective, these guides perform a higher status and expertise during their sessions. From visitors or students, the guides can receive acknowledgment in the form of respect and interest, and perform the expertise that they are not recognised for within the museum. This expertise is also reflected in a certain pride with which the guides in the

---

[72] For instance, Feona sees her role as a guide in terms of '[...] facilitat[ing] and scaffold[ing] and lead[ing] their experience in a hopefully still quite open and enquiry-based way whilst their visiting of the museum' (Feona, 116-118). Hilda similarly describes herself as a facilitator (cf. EIH, 170-171), and Kristin explains that her role is 'somewhere in-between' a tour guide and a teacher (cf. Kristin, 132-141).

German museums speak about their role. For example, when asked about the kinds of visitors she guides through the museum, Antonia is keen to emphasise that she can guide all the groups, especially adults and academics because, as she quickly adds, she has a PhD in ethnology (cf. Antonia, EIA, 113-114). Similarly, Britta explains, '[…] so I am a little bit proud of the fact that, we as gallery educators, if you are good at it or you've gained some experience, that you can make all objects speak' (EIB, 292-295). Further, Eva states that 'I can also give you an art historical presentation [in the gallery], chronologically, about the production and meaning of the figures. I can do that. I sometimes do that with adult groups.' (EIE, 63-65). Similarly, upon being asked how she prepared for the sessions, Doreen notes that '[w]ell, I know the story. After all, I studied this at one point and I am interested in the topic. One doesn't finish the thing and then never looks at it again, but one's knowledge develops just like the galleries do, over the years' (EID, 306-309). These references of the guides to their own expertise point to, on the one hand, their self-understandings as perhaps overqualified for their roles, and, on the other hand, a simultaneous insecurity which articulates itself in a need to assert this overqualification and to position themselves as the ethnographic experts as which they are not acknowledged from an organisational perspective.

Although such an explicit performance of ethnographic authority is especially prevalent in the German sessions, the British guides also exert this kind of authority. For example, when Kate tells the 'European success story' of the retrieval of Tippoe's Tiger, she represents ethnographic authority in claiming that her story is trustworthy, without leaving room for doubt. Still, in the British gallery sessions, there are very few incidents in which the guides directly perform ethnographic authority, for instance by means of explicit, generalising statements about non-European ways of life (see Chapter 4.4). Although there are moments in which Gladys and

Hilda seem to represent ethnographic authority by speaking about 'people in Africa', these statements must be seen in a slightly different light as both guides describe themselves as being 'of African heritage'. Here, their 'insider knowledge' is turned into objective and general knowledge in some of their remarks, thus equally transforming specific insight into the claim of cultural reality. Their 'experiential authority' does not become 'ethnographic', however, but must rather be seen as part of their authority as representatives of the regions in question.[73]

In summary, the organisational marginalisation of the guides in all of the four museums stands in contrast to the various functions and responsibilities they have. As the British museum guides are understood mainly as educational experts, they predominantly exert educational authority in terms of managing groups and using appropriate teaching methods (discussed further in the next subchapter). In contrast, the German guides are employed as subject matter experts, and are thus more prone to performing ethnographic authority by turning subjective experiences or smaller-scale observations into a generalised and universal cultural description.

---

[73] This representative function of guides from the respective regions is of course ambivalent. On the one hand, a popular multiculturalist strategy of museums has been to invite representatives of the respective regions, or so-called 'source communities', to co-design exhibition spaces and to thus take part in the interpretative action. On the other hand, as Dhanjal explains, the term 'community' already suggests a unity of the respective groups that is not at all given (cf. 2012, 24). Furthermore, Christian Kravagna argues that '[...] the often conjured 'other voices' are today frequently integrated on a superficial level to give the museum a multicultural touch [...]' (2015, 99). Similarly, in the respective situations in the British museums, the authority that the guides have as ‚real representatives‘ of the displayed regions must not only be seen critical in light of the alleged unity that it suggests, but also with regard to their decorative function as multicultural employees.

5.1.2 Understandings of Learning: The Recourse to Traditional Teaching Methods and the Disciplinary Actions of the Guides

Although the working conditions and, in particular, the lack of a genuine recognition within the museum play a key role in the guides' exertion of ethnographic authority, working conditions alone cannot sufficiently explain the significance of authoritative practices in the observed guided tours. As an additional factor, different understandings of learning and teaching held by the guides, the schools, and the learning departments play a significant role. It is important to note, however, that examples of authority performance in the material can be indicative of various influencing factors at the same time. For example, when Gladys or Britta try to make the students listen to them by stating that non-European children have respect for their elders (see Chapter 4.3), this at once constructs the guides' ethnographic authority of the non-European situation and establishes their educational authority as quasi-teachers for the students. The situation can, therefore, be explained both by the marginalisation of the guides within the museums (i.e., they aim to justify and assign value to their position as guides) and by their understandings of learning (i.e., they have a clear understanding of learning that requires the students to listen to the teacher). While the two dimensions are, thus, often intertwined, their analytical separation in the previous and the present subchapter makes it possible to follow the most important threads that eventually create the complex fabric of the construction and performance of authority. The present subchapter, thus, argues that the guides tend to apply more authoritative teaching practices than they support in theory, and that these traditional learning styles contribute to the performance of authority.

Over the last several decades, a broad spectrum of learning theories and learning models for museum education have been developed and promoted by scholars such as George Hein (1998), John Howard Falk and

Lynn Dianne Dierking (2000) or and Eilean Hooper-Greenhill (2000, 2007). As this work does not aim at evaluating the teaching methods of the guides from a didactic perspective, it would be unrewarding to present a detailed overview of the varieties of fruitful approaches that have emerged from this scholarship. For the purpose of understanding the relationship between authority and understandings of learning, it suffices to note that there is a general trend, inspired by learning theories such as cognitive learning developed by Jean Piaget (1936) and experiential learning promoted by John Dewey (1938), of moving away from behaviourist and frontal learning theories to embracing and developing more constructivist museum educational models. On an imaginary scale that locates controlled learning situations at one end and free learning at the other, it is possible to clearly distinguish what Hein has called 'traditional lecture and text' (1994, 74) or behaviourist teaching practices in museums from a more recent constructivist approach that allows '[...] visitors to draw their own conclusions about the meaning of the exhibition' (ibid., 76). These constructivist ideas of learning are manifest in a variety of approaches that have been developed in the realm of museum education.[74] While all of these approaches follow different routes, they share similar goals, namely a looser interpretation of what constitutes 'learning', a shift of attention from the teacher to the learner, and an acknowledgment of learners as contributing to the making of museum meanings.

These more learner-centred approaches to museum education generally function to relativise the authority of the teacher. No longer perceived as an omniscient and objective narrator, the museum educator in this understanding of learning takes the role of a moderator or

---

[74] These include models such as the contextual learning model (Falk/Dierking 2000), the free choice learning model (Falk/ Dierking 2002), and the experiential learning model (Jacobsen 2006), as well as broader theories of aligning entire organisations with constructivist understandings of learning, such as the 'constructivist museum' (Hein 1994, 1998), the 'engaging museum' (Black 2005), or the 'participatory museum' (Simon 2010).

communicator who inspires conversation, dialogue, and shared interpretation. As Hooper-Greenhill describes this transformed function,

> communicators act as enablers and facilitators. The task for communicators – or, in the museum, curators, educators and exhibition developers – is to provide experiences that invite visitors to make meaning through deploying and extending their existing interpretive strategies and repertoires, using their prior knowledge and their preferred learning styles, and testing their hypotheses against those of others, including those of experts. (2000, 139f.)

These new ideals of collective interpretation and participation have had a considerable influence on museum practices in the 21st century. Likewise, in the four museums part of this study, the concepts of dialogical or experiential learning, as well as of visitor orientation appear either implicitly or explicitly in the mission statements and the advertised session formats. Especially in the two British museums, the learning departments are eager to represent themselves as embracing these participatory and learner-centred approaches, which becomes evident from the way in which school sessions are described on the websites or from the conversations conducted with the heads of the departments. For instance, in both of the British museums, the learning department managers mentioned the importance of developing more experiential and interactive sessions. In Museum D, these sessions are already the norm. Most of the learning processes in this museum are not entirely controlled by the guides. Instead, through methods of dialogue, deduction and hands-on experiences, the students are invited to negotiate the objects in their own ways. This methodology also has an effect on the understandings of learning held by the guides in Museum D. As Feona explains, she sees it as her task to '[...] facilitate and scaffold and lead their experience in a hopefully still quite open and enquiry-based [way] whilst their visiting of the museum' (EIF, 116-118).

Although Museum D is the only one of the four museums part of this study that has actively implemented this new learning strategy, an awareness of the desirability of such approaches can also be found in other museums; this awareness is particularly evident on the more individual level articulated in the interviews. For example, Antonia from Museum A explains that she tries to present her sessions in a dialogical fashion, with the 'Socratic approach of enabling the students to develop things by themselves if they can' (Antonia, EIA, 99-100). Similarly, Britta argues that while she is used to a frontal learning style, she thinks that for the children it is better to enter into a conversation and to make them work things out on their own (cf. EIB, 24-27). Similarly, Gladys explains that one of the most important things for her '[...] is the ownership, is for the children to feel that they have authority' (EIG, 218-219). Even Hilda, who gives a session in a lecture hall, which would seem like the least interactive framework, argues in the interview that she would like to shape the session so that '[...] the audience can have more interaction given the time and the environment' (EIH, 260-261).

While most of the guides observed during the gallery sessions show this kind of support for learner-oriented approaches in the interviews, this theoretical standpoint does not necessarily translate into their teaching practice. In Museums A, B, and C, the guides predominantly apply a more traditional learning approach that clearly positions themselves as the experts, and the children as the learners. This hierarchy is established by the guides' means of asking only factual questions, telling coherent stories about the objects, and generally 'presenting' information without focusing much on the students' perspectives. Furthermore, what the guides represent in the interviews as their idea of letting the students develop their own knowledge from the exhibition is in fact often not as open-ended as suggested. Usually, discussions or dialogues about the exhibited material or the regions on display are based upon concrete facts that the guides have in mind, while they slowly lead the students to the desired answer. There are a lot of different examples for such pseudo-dialogical practices in the observed sessions. The following situation serves to illustrate how these conversations may be intended as inclusive communication strategies, but often end up reinforcing the traditional distinction between the expert and the students. In this example, Britta from Museum B has just introduced the students briefly to the separate parts of a Chinese character. She then asks the students (S) to conclude the meaning of the whole from the parts:

B: Well, we have something like a god and a vase where food could fit in. A vessel. What does it mean in Chinese? What is when one can eat as much as one wants. What could this, well, not literally, but what could this mean, to have food every day? Yes?

S: Gratitude?

B: Gratitude would be an option, but it is not quite that. Similar, yes?

S: Well, then one is full.

B: Then one is full. And if one is full, one is? How do you feel?

S: Satisfied?

B: Almost.

S: One is happy?

B: Happy. Exactly. This is the word I've been waiting for.

S: Is it also possible to represent 'health' [as a Chinese character]?

B: No, well, we have to, health, we have to see about that. But this character means happiness.

(GSB-MB, 261-280)

The controlled nature of this dialogue is exemplary of many similar conversations between the students and the guides. In these situations, the guides usually do not ask the students for their perceptions or ideas by connecting new information with prior knowledge or by leaving room for interpretative engagement, but instead their understandings of dialogical learning situations are often restricted to making the students guess an answer until they arrive at what the guides want to hear. In the case above, Britta directs the students to the 'right' answer and does not respond to the additional student question regarding the character representing 'health'. In this way, the gallery educators maintain interpretative and educational authority by determining how the sessions unfold and what knowledge they provide.

In these cases, the understandings of learning that the guides show when reflecting upon their work and the understandings of learning that affect their practices are dissimilar. While the gallery educators aim at applying less authoritative methods, many end up exerting educational authority by speaking and 'acting' like teachers. This can again be understood in terms the 'disimprovement effect'. The guides aim at a different outcome, but do not find suitable means of translating goals into concrete methods. This confirms what Hein has explained with regard to his 'ideal' type of museums, constructivist museums, namely that that they need policies as well as practices to reach their visitors: '[o]ne of these without the other is not sufficient' (cf. 1998, 176). In the context of many of the observed cases, the disimprovement effect results from an enthusiasm for learner-centred approaches on a theoretical level, and the lack of means of implementing these ideals in practice.

There are many reasons for the guides' recourse to traditional, more authoritative teaching practices, including the lack of induction by the organisations, the easier preparation of gallery sessions that follow a clear set of facts and routines, and the lack of time to give students the chance to make their own meanings. A particularly interesting explanation can, however, be found in what Melinda Mayer has called the 'Theory-Practice Divide' (2005) in museum education. Although Mayer's considerations refer to art museum education, they can easily be applied to the cases in this study. She explains,

> [w]hen educators embrace new theoretical positions, it can be extremely challenging to reconceptualize comfortable and oft-practiced teaching methods, redefine concepts, and interrogate one's long held beliefs and values regarding what is important to teach. Layering a new set of goals and objectives on old methods does not transform teaching or learning. As a result, a widening chasm can emerge between theory and practice and the promise of exciting new learning opportunities for visitors can be lost. (2005, 16)

This dilemma also reverberates with Lauren Allen et al.'s finding that museum educators in science museums 'tend to rely on familiar epistemologies and pedagogies, which are often rooted in their own personal learning experiences in formal settings' (2014, 85). Considering the lack of educational training and carefully developed teaching methods, and in consideration of temporal constraints, it is not a surprise that the guides resort to the methods they already know when conducting guided tours. This default, however, not only establishes the guides' authority, but also reinforces the impression that the museum offers only one set of fixed meanings and that the represented cultural contexts can only be regarded from one perspective.

Besides this recourse to familiar teaching practices, the guides' more authoritative teaching styles can further be related to their responsibilities of managing the school groups during the sessions. As the guides often have a clear idea of what they want to teach and which aspects they want to include in the short duration of the gallery sessions, they are reliant on the students' compliance. Especially those guides with no prior teaching experience struggle with this task of actively disciplining the school groups, and often regard these pedagogical responsibilities as a necessary evil of their work. For instance, Maria explains that „[i]f one has to start to act as the security personnel, and tell them not to touch this and that, and then you are suddenly the bogey man and cannot fulfil your actual task properly' (EIM, 197-199). This comment shows a common perception, namely that the management of the group is separate from the task of conducting guided tours. Many guides feel uncomfortable about disciplining the students during the sessions and report that they are glad that the teachers are present for these tasks (cf. Feona, EIF, 167-169; Kate, EIK, 149-152). Yet, even though most of the guides feel uncomfortable with the disciplinary dimension of educational authority, they all eventually apply disciplinary methods. For instance, in most of the observed sessions, the students receive an instruction from the guides at the beginning of the tours that reminds them of how to behave during the sessions, including the requirement to 'listen to the guides'. They use different methods of enforcing this rule, as for instance hand gestures (Feona), singing (Britta), or raising their voice (Gladys, Antonia). The already mentioned projection of social as moral values can be seen as another means of disciplining the students. With respect to this disciplinary function of the guides, Helene Illeris has pointed out that museum education '[...] even when connected to the best intentions of social and personal empowerment, is also always related to some form of disciplining power' (2006, 18). Thus, the guides' authority derives not only from the theory-practice divide of teaching in the museum, but also from an almost inevitable disciplining power that results from the mere format of the gallery session which depends upon a clear time frame and set learning goals.

This authoritative role of the guides, in terms of their disciplining power, can also be related to the expectations and actions of the teachers. While some teachers make a considerable effort to manage the groups before and during the observed sessions, others appear less focused on the guided tours and, instead, talk to each other or walk away, leaving all educational tasks to the guides. In the interviews, the guides note that they experience such behaviour only rarely, but that they do not approve of it as they see it as a way of giving up responsibility (cf. EIB, 250-255; Feona, EIF, 178-183). In these cases, the guides feel forced into the role of the authoritative teacher.

5.1.3 Expectations Surrounding the Museum as Institution: The Museum as a Temple and the Trust in its Reliability

Besides working conditions and understandings of learning, different expectations surrounding the museum as institution are an equally important point to acknowledge when discussing factors that contribute to the performance of authority in the observed guided tours. This subchapter discusses the role of the museum as a temple and the resulting authority that is expected from the institution.

By working with the notion of 'the museum as institution', the following section calls attention to a somewhat different dimension of the museum than its perception as organisation which has been applied in the previous subchapters. In general, in this work, both conceptions play a role because the museum can be regarded in terms of an organisation as it contains conscious and regulated forms of cooperation for a specific purpose (cf. Gukenbiehl 2003, 152) as well as in terms of an institution because it subtly evokes and manifests habitualised actions based on reciprocal typifications of roles (cf. Berger/Luckmann 1966, 71f.). For the analysis in this subchapter, it suffices to distinguish the formal, structured, targeted and controlled *organisation* of action (cf. Gukenbiehl 2003, 152f.) from the more spontaneous, unplanned, and gradually objectified *institutionalisation* of action (cf. Berger/Luckmann 1966, 71-72, 76-77) in the museum. Thus, what is of interest in this chapter is connected to the modern institutionalisation of art and ethnographic objects as well as of the public behaviour towards them, which have been manifested and produced by means of the establishment of museums. As Donald Preziosi has shown, there is an inseparable relation between the way in which art and artefacts have come to be understood and the constitution of museums:

> More than simply one among many 'ideological apparatuses' in the institutional arsenal of contemporary society, museums worldwide pervade many of the social practices, both institutionalized and informal, that determine the perception and function of objects and environments, no less than of ourselves as social subjects. (2004, 3)

By conceptualising the museum 'as institution', the focus is thus shifted from the level of management and administrative processes in specific museums to habitualised actions, values, and social or cultural connotations connected to art, artefacts, and museums in a more general sense.

When reflecting upon the relationship between expectations of the museum and the performance of authority in the guided tours, a particularly pervasive connotation of the museum immediately jumps to mind, namely that of the 'temple of the arts' (Hooper-Greenhill 1989, 63) or the 'mausoleum' (Adorno 1988 [1967], 175). Adorno describes museums as holding objects '[...] which are in the process of dying. They owe their preservation more to historical respect than to the needs of the present' (ibid.). Although the evocation of these notions usually occurs in the context of 19th-century museums, the idea of the museum as a sacred place that compels respect from its visitors is still prevalent in public expectations of and associations with the museum. This expectation can be explained by the museum' still-existing functions to select, preserve and communicate to the public that what is important to remember. Through this 'museum effect', objects represented in museums acquire 'a lasting place in our visual culture' (Alpers 1991, 26). This life-sustaining measure is especially discernible in ethnographic museums, many of which have been founded with the intention to preserve 'vanishing cultures' (cf. Penny 1998, 162). Although today, most ethnographic museums are reinventing themselves as inclusive and dialogical public places, they still exert the museum effect on their exhibited objects by isolating objects from their contexts and offering them up for an attentive gaze (cf. Alpers 1991, 27).

Yet, the connotation of the museum as a temple is so pertinent not only because the museum constructs and preserves cultural memories and values, but also because the process of this active construction of meaning is not mediated or made transparent to potential visitors. The museum therefore exudes an 'aura of objectivity' (Lidchi 2006, 95) which obliterates the constructedness of the histories, values, and categories that are established by the integration of objects in museum exhibitions. Preziosi fittingly describes this apparent detachment of the museum from its narratives, which causes a peculiarly durable public trust in the institution:

> Like Moses come down from his mountain announcing with complete conviction that "it wasn't me who wrote these tablets, it was (points heavenward)," the museum could well persuade us to believe that there was a real history out there independent of our historiographies, our museographies, our devices and desires. Or to persuade us to believe in an art history independent of our museologies. (1996, 106)

In other words, neither in the organisation of the collection nor in the exhibition is a critical questioning of the fabricated reality made possible because the practices involved in this fabrication remain largely obscure to the visitors. By separating the represented reality from those who represent it, many museums can still be regarded as heterotopias, which Foucault defines as 'a place of all times that is itself outside of time' (1986 [1967], 26).

These connotations of the museum are neither all-encompassing, nor do they apply to all ethnographic museums. As already mentioned, over the last few decades, many museums have emerged as places of social debate and transformation and, hence, have developed from temples to forums (cf. Cameron 1971, Baur 2010, 43). Yet, the tenacity of the museum effect and the continuous staging of an 'aura of objectivity' is visible, for instance, in the slow revision of the nearly impervious classificatory labels that are ascribed to the objects (cf. Loren 2015, 308), in the gap between theoretical literature on participatory approaches and their realisation in museum contexts (cf. Lynch 2014, 80; Allen/Crowley 2014, 85) or in the observation that few directors and curators, at least in the German context, intensively implement current discourses in museum education and communication (cf. Bystron/ Zessnik 2014, 324). The recent debate on the newly built Humboldt Forum and its exclusion of self-referential and critical exhibitions on the artefacts' acquisition histories is another case in point.[75]

Likewise, in the observed sessions, this cultural authority of the museum as a reliable arbiter of knowledge, taste, and objective facts both affects, and is reinforced by, the guides', the teachers', and the students' actions. Expectations surrounding the museum's authority, thus, explain various statements of the guides that refer to the value of the museum and its objects. Doreen's statement that the meaning of the peace pipe cannot be found in any book, but can only be learned in the museum (cf. GSD-MA, 330-334) as well as Maria's pride in telling the students of the piece of the Kiswa that was secretly taken by a Dutch researcher and can now only be looked at in the museums (cf. GSM-MB, 489-491), are good examples. Such, and many comparable statements about the value of the museums reinforce its social and historical relevance, and at the same time reflect and are affected by understandings surrounding the authority and trustworthiness of the institution.

---

[75] A media debate about organisational and moral pitfalls of the Humboldt Forum's concept thrived when Bénédikte Savoy resigned from the advisory board of the institution, arguing that due to the conservativeness of the Stiftung Preußischer Kulturbesitz, change was happening too slowly and criticising that too little emphasis was given to provenance research (cf. Savoy qt. in Häntzschel 2017). As a response, founding director Herman Parzinger told the Rundfunk Berlin-Brandenburg that provenance research was planned, but that there was not enough money and personnel (cf. Rundfunk Berlin Brandenburg 2017). In an article in Die Welt, Viola König, director of the Ethnologisches Museum Berlin which will be integrated into the Humboldt Forum, tried to paint a more diversified picture of the question of provenance, arguing that the focus should be on object biographies rather than on provenance research for the latter's sole focus on how the objects arrived in Europe was eurocentric (cf. König 2017). Her argument was that the museum should aim at reaching a conclusive idea surrounding an object's biography before deciding whether it should be kept in a museum or given back to a community. This argument shows very well how museum discourses in Europe still work on the basis of criteria of objectivity, rationality, and factuality. By insinuating they can find a 'rational' answer to the rightful ownership of the objects, museums often still position themselves as the objective 'Brain of the Earth's Body'; as the seemingly objective referee in the world's games of ownership. But when two people quarrel, a third rejoices: Their own interests regarding the future of the artefacts are rarely made public.

In addition, by reinforcing the cultural authority of the museums, and valorising the artefacts due to their singularity, the guides perform the museum's 'civilizing ritual' (Duncan 2005). Besides expectations of the museum as a reliable arbiter of knowledge, the institution also evokes a certain hierarchy of preferred bodily practices that are presumed as appropriate in the institution. According to Duncan, this civilising ritual functions by affirming the identities of those who '[…] are best prepared to perform [the museum's] ritual – those who are most able to respond to its various cues' (ibid., 8-9). This subtle communication of accepted behaviour towards art and artefacts extends not only to the appreciation of the exhibits, but also to the habitus performed in the museum. As Susan Pearce remarks, exhibitions are classic examples of Bourdieu's concepts of habitus and cultural capital because they demand from their visitors an aesthetic appreciation that is often not otherwise justified or explained (cf. 2015, 130).

This civilising authority of the museum and the requirement of a certain habitus is also mirrored in the suspiciousness of the institution against children. As Hooper-Greenhill notes, '[s]ome visitors, particularly the young or the untidy, will be watched with extra care' (1988, 226). This 'extra care' is also reflected in the introductory instructions presented by almost all of the guides at the beginning of the sessions, which remind the students of 'appropriate' behaviour in the museum. For instance, Doreen warns the students, '[…] okay, listen, we will enter the exhibition now and remember, in the museum one is always nice and quiet and does not touch anything' (GSD-MA, 62-63). Such rehearsals of institutional constraints often precede the admission of the students to the galleries and hence function like tests of the children's eligibility to 'be' in the museum. They relate to what Helene Illeris has called the classification of visitors 'according to whether they know and have respect for ritualized practices of the museum or gallery' (2009, 19). Furthermore, such a demand for appropriate behaviour in the gallery is also evident in some of the statements regarding 'good school groups' in the interviews. For instance, Kate mentions that '[…] the school I've had in the morning were good as gold. Like they literally walked through the museum in pairs. Almost in silence. It was really weird' (EIK, 287-289). Although she acknowledges the 'weirdness' of such behaviour performed by children, she still considers it 'good as gold' and contrasts this situation with a group that she found difficult to manage. Here, pragmatic aspects such as time constraints and considerations of leading the groups through the spaces, understandings of learning, and assumptions about the museum as institution are interrelated and form a relatively authoritative ideal which prioritises the value and sacredness of the objects without questioning the origin of this alleged sacredness.

This civilising ritual of the museum is again evident in the guides' references to the value and fragility of the artefacts. Feona, as already mentioned, emphasises that '[a]nything you see in this museum is objects that are really real' (GSF2-MD, 124) and Antonia tells the students that the objects cannot be replaced if they break (GSA-MA, 47-48). Such references to the value of the objects affirm and construct expectations of the museum's cultural authority and significance, and, thereby, contribute to the formation of educated subjects who behave in conformity with the unspoken rules of the museum. The guides' performance of authority must, then, also be seen in light of an enforcement and embodiment of the desired habitus in the museum. The gallery educators perform not only the significance of the institution by alluding to the uniqueness of available experiences, but also the habitus of the museum by advising the students to be careful and quiet. In their position between the school groups and the museums, the guides thus occupy both of the functions that curator Bruce Ferguson has labelled the soft-sell (consumer-oriented) and the hard-sell (authoritative) sides of the museum (cf. 1996, 182).

What ought to be made clear is that the guides' actions are not the only ones that affirm and reinforce the authority of the museum as institution. Both the teachers' and the students' expectations of the museum also shape the situations in the guided tours. These factors are important to take into account because it would be misleading to think that the guides are in full control of the dynamics of representing the museum's cultural authority. In actuality, since the public image of the museum as a temple is extremely pervasive, it is questionable how much the guides would even be able to dismantle, challenge, or relativise the all-embracing authority that has been built into the institution from the beginnings of its existence. For instance, in a situation in Museum D, Feona hands out ceramic tiles to the children in order for them to learn what the material feels like. The tiles are not in fact museum objects, but as they are handled in the space of the museum, there is suddenly a great deal of value and preciousness in the ways in which the guide and the teachers speak about them:

F: So what I will do (.) I will hand this down. And I start on this side and
     I just want you to carefully with two hands (.) hold it. Feel it.
T: Be very sensible, okay?
                                                  (GSF2-MD, 459-461)

In this situation, the teacher also takes the perspective of the museum, and calls upon the students to handle the objects carefully. Especially with respect to using tiles as handling objects, this seems peculiar, for tiles are normally everyday objects. However, the museum effect turns these objects into artefacts – in this instance, they are placeholders for 'real artefacts', used to accustom the students to the desired behaviour towards objects that is considered to be appropriate in the museum.

Yet, it is not the case that the students come without any prior awareness of the care, silence, and self-control that is required from them by the institution. When Feona asks the students at the beginning of the gallery sessions what they already know about rules and regulations in the museum, for example, they express that they have to be mindful, sensible, and quiet. The students particularly emphasise that they need to be careful with the objects and are very aware that they cannot touch them, which the following extract exemplifies.

F: [...] can you quickly remind me what do we need to remember as we move through the museum?
S: Don't touch anything.
F: [...] What else? what else do you remember?
S: **No touching?**
F: We had that already. But I have a lot of things in my bag that you will be able to even touch. Anything else?
S: **It might break and if you touch it the others cannot see it.**
F: Alright so we take care of our hands and fingers. What else? Anything else we need to remember?
S: [...]
F: [...]
S: **And if you touch them and you'll break them (you have to make another one?)**
F: (laughs) Oh that may be many years of work. But I promise we won't break anything. We will be sensible I am sure. [...]

(GSF2-MD, 73-105)

As indicated by the repeated reference to the danger of breaking or staining the objects by touching them (see highlighted statements above), the students seem very preoccupied with damaging the artefacts. Similar concerns are evident in many other observed gallery sessions. It is not entirely clear whether the students have merely memorised these rules and regulations in class or whether they have actually internalised some of the regulations during prior museum experiences. Regardless of the reasons, this awareness of the students is available during the sessions, which shows that the students, even at an early age, are familiar with the cultural authority of the institution.

Thus, the guides' actions are not only determined by the actions and expectations of the teachers with regard to the authority of the museum, but also by the students' ideas surrounding the institution. A further group that may be equally relevant to the guides' work are the museum guards, who may possess more authoritative expectations surrounding the museum. This prospect is reflected in an example from Museum D. In the interview, Lynn elucidates an idea she had regarding lying on the floor of one of the galleries and allowing the children to bring their teddy bears. As she explains,

> [...] the housekeepers[76] will go 'there are children. And teddybears.' But I have to be strong and say "they're not damaging anything and we're using the carpet. We're engaging with the objects. You have to let us lie down." (EIL, 150-153)

This situation shows how what is accepted and not accepted in the space of the museum may not be connected to a real danger regarding the conservation of the objects, but rather to acceptable or inacceptable habitualised actions in the museum. Breaking these unwritten rules is a matter not only of asking for permission, but also of venturing into uncertain terrain. Lynn has to work up the courage to defend the method she wants to apply; she even tells herself to be 'strong'. It is remarkable how the disciplining function of the museum has a self-disciplining effect on the students *and* the guides. This has much to do with an idea of 'seriousness' that surrounds the museum. As Dicks has argued, '[...] it is this 'serious' image itself which has prevented museums, it has been argued, from properly fulfilling their public educational role' (2004, 160), which she identifies as being more relevant and more responsive to the public (cf. ibid.). This 'seriousness' can be seen in light of the museum's cultural authority as a mediator of truth and material value.

5.1.4 Spaces and Objects: Staging Authoritative Atmospheres and the Disciplinary Functions of Gallery Spaces

The expectations surrounding the cultural authority of the museum, discussed in the previous chapter, are closely related to the spatial design of the galleries in the museums. Although there are, therefore, many conceptual overlaps between the two subchapters, it is important to show in how far the design of the exhibition rooms contributes to the

---

[76] This is the word used by Lynn, but it is likely that she means guards or security personnel rather than cleaners.

performance of authority in the guided tours. In this context, particular attention is paid to the sacred atmospheres in the exhibition by discussing how they are connected both to the guides' performance of value or significance, and to their performance of discipline during the guided tours.

To discuss these aspects, it is initially important to state that spaces and objects are considered active agents within the guided tour. This approach also concurs with this chapter's attention on ANT, which focuses on the agency of objects and other non-human actors to shape the social realm (cf. Latour 2005, 72). Although possibly produced with a clear intention, both objects and spaces, once established, can develop into something new: 'An existing space may outlive its original purpose and the raison d'être which determines its forms [...]' (Lefebvre 1991, 167). Likewise, exhibition spaces are created with a clear agenda in mind, but the ways in which they are used, perceived, and signified may deviate from this original idea. This aspect is significant for the issue discussed here because it means that, while authoritative communication may not be purposefully inbuilt into the exhibitions, it may still result from the final arrangement and usage of the galleries.

In order to analyse the relationship between the authority of the exhibition spaces and the guides' performance of authority, it is further necessary to explain the relationship that exists between objects and spaces in the museum. Since the 'spatial turn' and the 'material turn', objects and spaces have come to be regarded as central agents in the formation of meaning. As Alfred Gell writes in *Art and Agency,*

> [b]ecause the attribution of agency rests on the detection of the effects of agency in the causal milieu, rather than an unmediated intuition, it is not paradoxical to understand agency as a factor of the ambience as a whole, a global characteristic of the world of people and things in which we live, rather than as an attribute of the human psyche, exclusively. (Gell 1998, 20)

He proposes that artefacts result from and reflect social agency (cf. ibid., 20) and consequently finds fault with art criticism that only refers to the 'visual-aesthetic properties of art objects much as if they had come into being by themselves' (ibid., 72). This distinction between analysing objects purely on an aesthetic level and seeing them as products of social processes is particularly relevant with respect to ethnographic objects. Their representation in museums can either unfold in the form of art or in the form of contextualised artefacts, or as Clifford has put it, in 'an ethnographic or an aesthetic milieu' (1988, 226). Clifford explains that the interpretation of objects as either authentic masterpieces or authentic artefacts is prompted by the perceived singularity and originality of art objects as against the traditional and collective nature of cultural artefacts (cf. ibid., 224). However, he also shows that, depending on the museum contexts in which they are integrated, objects can move from 'culture' to 'art' (cf. ibid.).[77] Thus, whether objects are perceived as art or ethnographica depends on the way in which they are presented within the galleries.

This mutual influence of objects and spaces may best be explained by Gernot Böhme's notion of 'atmospheres'. According to Böhme, objects must be understood not only as absorbing their environment, but also as radiating something out to it (1993, 121). He claims it is important to analyse atmospheres that '[...]' proceed from things, persons, and their

---

[77] The art/artefact debate in anthropology and visual culture studies cannot be extensively illustrated here. Arguments in favour of representing ethnographic objects as art include, for instance, the recognition of artefactual autonomy (Kirshenblatt-Gimblett 1998, 14), the acknowledgment of artistic skill of non-European artists, e.g. in case of the Benin Bronzes (Bjerregaard 2013, 250) and the attempt to recover coevalness (Bal 1992, 558). Arguments against the representation of ethnographica as art include the appropriation of objects by the art and culture market (Steyn 2006, 607) and the risk that museums may 'enhance the visual appeal of 'ethnographic' objects in order to capture the public's attention (Harris/ O'Hanlon 2013, 9). Recently, there have also been voices addressing the potential of 'ethnological art-museums' that avoid the construction of authenticity of either art or artefacts and thereby contribute to a defetishisation of ethnographica (cf. Karoline Noack 2015, 59).

constellations' (1993, 122) rather than focusing only on objects, spaces or human actors. This is because, as Böhme notes,

> [w]hat is first and immediately perceived is neither sensations nor shapes or objects or their constellations [...], but atmospheres, against whose background the analytic regard distinguishes such things as objects, forms, colours etc. (1993, 125).

When looking at the way in which the guides' performances of authority are affected by the design of the exhibition rooms and by the objects, it is similarly worthwhile to consider the atmospheres that emerge from the interplay between artefacts and the environments they are staged in. It is within these more immediately perceived atmospheres that the authority of the display is located. The combination of (often dim) lighting, secured glass display cases, scarce information on labels, lofty ceilings, old and unfamiliar objects, wall colours, and a particular soundscape creates an atmosphere of value, knowledge, truth, and reliability. As Ferguson remarks with respect to 'exhibition rhetoric', different exhibitionary procedures '[...] combine as aspects of the exhibition's active recitation. They emphasize, de-emphasize and reemphasize [...] fictions of persuasion, docudramas of influence' (1996, 181).[78]

This atmosphere of truth and value can be seen as contributing to the observed guides' performance of authority. For instance, during the instructions at the beginning of their guided tours, Antonia explicitly warns the children to be careful around the 'valuable' objects, explaining that they are irreplaceable (cf. GSA-MA, 47-48) and Feona emphasises that the

---

[78] Especially with respect to lighting, much has been said about its power in the context of exhibitions. Wilson remarks that lighting can make objects seem more authentic (cf. Karp/ Wilson 1996, 253), Charles Garoian explains that low level lighting 'subdues the body into a meditative state' (Garoian 2001, 247), Bal compares the display of art objects to watching a play in the dark (cf. 2010, 16), Ferguson connects the dramatic lighting in displays to the staging of desire (cf. 1996, 178), and Stephen Greenblatt claims that the often used 'boutique lighting' heightens the feeling of wonder which compares to the effect of commercial lighting in shops, increasing the visitors' desire, however, without a possibility for possession (cf. 1991, 49).

students cannot touch the objects because the objects need to be kept safe (cf. GSF-MD, 57-65). Britta, likewise, points to the fragility of the objects in order to explain the lack of fresh air in the museum (cf. GSB-MB, 67-71) and Kate warns the children not to touch anything because the oil on their fingers can damage the objects (cf. GSK2-MD, 78-81). Besides the relation of these disciplinary means to the reinforcement of expectations surrounding the museum as well as to the educational authority of the guides discussed in the preceding chapters, the guides' protection of the artefacts from the children's potentially damaging effects can also be explained by the authority of the exhibitions' atmosphere. The guides' statements are based upon, and reinforce, the idea that the objects are sacred, and that human contact with them can only ever take place under extremely controlled and distanced circumstances. The atmosphere of distance and significance in the exhibitions is internalised by the gallery educators and naturalised by their instructions.

These instructions are only one practice by which the guides reinforce this atmosphere. Another indicator of this correlation between the workings of the exhibition space and the guided tours can be found in the guides' way of speaking in a quiet and slow, lecturing style - comparing almost to a sermon. This can again be connected to the church-like atmosphere in the dimly lit exhibition rooms, with their high and echoing ceilings. Furthermore, the guides' references to the museum as a 'home' of the objects (cf. GSG-MC, 80) or as a place for 'looking after' foreign objects (cf. GSF2-MD, 321) corresponds to the self-assurance with which the objects are displayed, without much information on their prior biographies, the circumstances of their retrieval, and the repatriation claims of non-European nations. The space articulates expertise, self-explanatory ownership, distance, and privilege - and so do the guides.

The meditational and factual atmosphere of the exhibition rooms and objects also have an effect on actors other than the guides. As already explained, the students are often concerned about the fragility of the objects while walking through the exhibitions. For example, a student in Feona's session imagines that he will have to make another one if he breaks an object (cf. GSF2-MD, 102) and a student in Christine's session asks what would happen if the masks broke while being handled (cf. GSC-MB, 589). This awe and appreciation can also be regarded as affected by the spatial design of the galleries, for instance through the great amount of glass case displays, which make an impression of value and delicateness.

Yet, the relationship between visitors and spaces can also be inversed in so far as visitors can also have a significant effect on the atmospheres in the museums. This effect is evident, for example, from the difference between the atmospheres encountered during research in the German and in the British museums. As the two British museums are frequented by many more visitors than the German museums, they are also shaped by the presence of people, their conversations, their bodily performance, and their engagement with the objects (taking pictures, reading labels, etc.). The guided tours in Museum A and Museum B therefore appeared to be framed by a less sacred and meditational atmosphere than those taking place in the German museums. The British guides were, for instance, often difficult to understand due to the soundscape in the crowded galleries. Furthermore, the student groups attracted the attention of other visitors, who often listened in on the guides' explanations, took pictures of the school groups, or filmed the gallery sessions. In contrast, the school groups in the German museums were almost always the only visitors in the galleries. The silence and emptiness of the exhibition rooms, as well as the resulting lower voice of the guides, produced a more sacred atmosphere. This difference between empty and crowded exhibition spaces has also been pointed out by Kate Hill. She has argued that the disciplinary effect of 19th century museums must be relativised with respect to this relation between crowds and spatial atmospheres:

> [T]here is plenty of evidence to suggest that while the empty spaces look as if they could exert a disciplinary effect and could produce a certain narrative meaning, in the overcrowded state they were not infrequently in during the nineteenth century neither of these processes could function [...]. (2011, 219)

However, while it is true that the atmosphere appears less ceremonial if the spaces are filled with visitors who create a different soundscape and visual effect, in the observed sessions in the British museums, an atmosphere of truth, expertise, and self-assurance has still been observed during the session. This atmosphere persists not only because the mere presence of visitors does not change the way in which labels and text panels are written, the way in which lighting is used, the distance of the objects, and their portrayal as either art or ethnographic objects, but also because the disciplinary effects of the spaces may still function, even if there are more visitors present.

Alongside the production of value and significance through the atmospheres, this disciplinary effect of the exhibition spaces can be regarded as another way in which space affects the performance of authority during the gallery sessions. Again, the disciplinary function of the space needs to be regarded in concert with the educational authority of the guides and prior expectations of the museum as affording a certain habitus, as discussed in Chapters 5.1.2 and 5.1.3. Yet, Hooper-Greenhill has shown how this habitus is also already built into the design of the exhibition rooms: 'The clean, ordered spaces of the galleries, with their clean, well-disciplines works [...], were intended to encourage similar efforts on the part of the audience to clean, regulate and internally discipline themselves' (2000, 131). Considering the instructions of the guides regarding the preferred behaviour of the students in the galleries, this ideal of self-regulation in the museum still plays a role. The ideal is also evident in some of the guides' reflections of what they deem important as learnings for the students. As Lynn explains, the most important aspect for her is that the children enjoy their visit, however, she also remarks that she thinks that the 'experience of coming by public transport […] and being in a public space and knowing how to behave and what to touch and how to be and what level to have your voice at' (EIL, 171-173) is important 'on a wider scale.' This comment shows that the disciplinary function of the students' visit is not an implicit and unnoticed side effect, but often regarded as one of the key learnings the children are supposed to take from their experience.

This idea of the integrity of the exhibition space in terms of discipline and respect is once more evident in the example of Lynn's idea to lie down on the floor with the students, which she has to defend against the museum's security personnel. It is also evident from an episode Lynn narrates from a session she gave to art teachers with regard to visiting the museum as a group:

> [I showed them how to] [u]se the museum like a classroom […] so go off with your groups and report back. Sit in front of the objects and sketch or make (.) you can use model magic or foil or whatever it is you're trying to get out of the object. Photography, whatever it is. Sit on the floor, use the space. You don't just have to (run?) through the corridors. You're allowed to sit. And it was like a revelation for them. (EIL, 240-246)

In both cases, Lynn thinks 'outside of the box' of spatial authority and connotations. Although she expects criticism from the museum staff, she is determined to use the spaces in alternative ways as long as there is no real danger to the artefacts. In the quote above, she reports that this openness of how to move in the space was a revelation for the young teachers. This shows that, while it is possible to negotiate the authority of the space, it may not be what people tend to do in the exhibition space.

5.2 Factors Affecting the Reduction of Complexity

The second principle underlying the gallery sessions that is discussed in this chapter is the reduction of complexity. As already explained in the synthesis of Chapter 4, this term refers to the guides' strategies of shortening, circumventing, or downplaying certain aspects or information during their sessions. In the observed guided tours, this reduction can unfold in the form of generalisations, trivialisations, and categorisations. For example, it underlies recurring themes and practices in the observed sessions such as the categorisation implicit in the guides' references to the external diversity of 'cultures' as homogeneous entities (see Chapter 4.1), the generalisation evident in their condescending veneration of non-European social values (see Chapter 4.3), as well as the trivialisation perceptible in their explanations of the objects' acquisition as European success stories. It is important, therefore, to take a closer look at the factors that lead to such reductions of complexity.

At the same time, it must be conceded that any form of representing cultural realities in the form of words – in fact, any form of representation as such – is marked by a certain degree of generalisation and complexity reduction. This is not only because '[...] we are always 'making sense' of things in terms of some wider categories' (cf. Dyer 1977 qtd. in Hall, 1997, 257), but also because relations to the world can only ever unfold as 'world versions', as Goodman's theory of worldmaking has clarified: 'If I ask about the world, you can offer to tell me how it is under one or more frames of reference; but if I insist that you tell me how it is apart from all frames, what can you say?' (Goodman 1978, 3). Thus, to some extent, the reduction of complexity is a necessary strategy to understand the world, speak about it, and find common ground to negotiate meaning. This effect of generalisation in descriptions of the world has also been acknowledged in the realm of ethnography. Notably, Clifford argues that '[...] ethnographic writing cannot entirely escape the reductive use of dichotomies and essences […]' (1988, 119). He connects this concession to a desideratum, however, that also underlies the critique in this subchapter: '[ethnographic writing] can at least struggle self-consciously to avoid portraying abstract, a-historical others' (ibid.). Thus, when discussing reductions of complexity in the guided tours in the following elaborations, the critical focus is particularly on those instances in which the simplifications lead to patronising, essentialist, or passive representations of non-European people, which continue and reinforce colonial or imperialist stereotypes and hierarchies.

Perhaps Lidchi's distinction between the poetics and the politics of representation (cf. 2006, 95) is helpful to further illustrate this focus. While the reduction of complexity on the poetical level of representation would refer to the ways in which systems of signification lead to certain meanings, reduction of complexity on a political level would refer to the relationship between power and knowledge (cf. ibid.). It is this level of power and knowledge that is at the centre of attention in this work's focus on the reduction of complexity in the guided tours. When, for instance, all of the guides fail to include a critical perspective on the acquisition of objects by the museums in their explanations, and instead highlight the achievements of European explorers and collectors, this specific shaping of history must be regarded as a political act, for it marginalises the perspectives, agency, and possible resistance of the non-European groups who are merely depicted as passive and secondary characters in these European adventure stories. These are the situations whose emergence in the guided tours is articulated in the following. Including a variety of factors, ranging from the lack of time that the guides have during the sessions to the teachers' expectations and the educators' ideas surrounding culture, the chapter shows that it is not in fact the sole responsibility of the narrator – in this case the guide – to do justice to the complexity of the non-European groups' heterogeneity and agency, but that there are many other human and non-human actors implicated in all aspects of reduction of complexity.

5.2.1　Working Conditions: The Dilemma of Time, Complexity and Attention Spans

One fundamental factor that must be acknowledged when reflecting upon reasons for the guides' reductions of complexity is the role of temporal constraints. The following discussion investigates how the short amount of time that the guides have for their sessions clashes with the level of complexity of the cultural contexts to be explained.

In order to understand the influence of time constraints on the guides' actions, it is necessary to delineate briefly the temporal set-up of the observed guided tours. All of these sessions are bound to a specific time frame which is set by the individual learning departments. For most of the guided tours, an average time frame of one hour can be assumed, however, this excludes extra time that is often used for arts and crafts activities or games as additional practical components of the more formal gallery sessions.[79] While the total amount of time that school classes spend in the museums varies considerably, the information-intensive parts in which the guides explain objects and cultural practices to them are rarely longer than an hour.[80]

In the interviews, many guides speak about the effects that this limited time frame has on their work. For example, Kate notes that the job can be hard because she has only forty-five minutes to 'meet them, get

---

[79] These practical components usually happened at the end of the sessions. Due to the focus of this work on the accounts of the guides, they were not part of the analysis of recurring patterns of communicating otherness.

[80] Notable exceptions are Gladys's session in Museum C, which features almost two hours of input (three and a half hours in total, with a thirty-minute lunch break in the middle and a more loosely guided one-hour explorative part in the gallery), and Isabel's session in the same museum, which also comprises input of about two hours.

them to listen to [her], and engage with what we're talking about' (cf. EIK, 189-190) and Feona reports that 'sometimes it might be a timing thing' as to what extent she can bring in the functions of the objects as part of the tour (EIF, 232-235). Similarly, Maria mentions that some cultural phenomena or objects are more difficult to explain and whether or not she includes them in her session is a matter of time (cf. EIM, 511-513). Thus, time plays a key role in the guides' decisions regarding the information they bring in or the level of detail at which they present the objects and the represented regions. It is therefore a crucial factor determining their 'worldmaking' practices – from 'weighting' (cf. Goodman 1978, 10-12) what aspects to focus on in their accounts, through 'deleting' (cf. ibid., 14-16) information that they consider too difficult, to 'deforming' (cf. ibid., 16-17) events and information so that they can better be fitted in a short account.[81]

Consider, for instance, a brief explanation of the colonial situation in the German colony Cameroon in the beginning of the 20th century provided by Christine in Museum B. When a student asks her if a specific mask they are discussing can also have a function in times of war, Christine relates to its origin in the colonial era, but then realises that the students are not familiar with this historical period. In the interview after the session, Christine explains that in that moment, she had to find a way of explaining this era in a nutshell (cf. EIC, 132-135). Her following historical account thus emerges in between time constraints and the necessity to give some background information to answer the student's question:

> So, all of Africa, almost the whole continent, was occupied. That means, colonised by European countries. And there were also German colonies. They travelled there because they wanted

---

[81] Goodman's other two principles of worldmaking, composition and ordering, also play a role in the guides' actions – yet, the three factors mentioned in the text are the ones most closely connected to the understanding of 'reducing complexity' mentioned above. As already stated, any form of worldmaking can be regarded as a form of reducing complexity, but the reductions of interest here are those that more directly concern the politics of representation.

natural resources, the valuable resources that were there, naturally only for themselves. They played the boss there. They could do that because they had better weapons. This went on for some time in Africa, in Cameroon it was initially the Germans. And they forced the people to work for them. And it was brutal and therefore the people at some point said "we no longer put up with this. We will rise up against our occupiers." They tried to. The problem was that the others had better weapons and that turned into a bloody matter. And therefore the people laid down their work and escaped. Yes, and because they had to come back to their villages at some point, they brought Obasinjom. As a sort of instrument to defend themselves from those attackers who perhaps had better magic. And it did not work to chase the colonisers away, but it sometimes helps within the society to deal with bad things and to make sure that everybody followed the rules that are considered morally right here. (GSC-MB, 478-496)

In this case, the complexity of the colonial situation is reduced, for instance by *weighting* the fact of colonisation and the failed revolt instead of contextualising aspects such as the broader reasons for Europe's 'occupation' of Africa. Reduction is further evident in the *deformation* of information that is practised by reducing the variety of revolts against the German occupation to a single event. Thus, by shaping this narrative into a brief and seemingly simple account, the situation is rendered much more straightforward than it was, thereby making it seem less significant as a whole, and further preventing empathy or a critical perspective from emerging. This lack of identification or affect in the account is also achieved through the distanced perspective that Christine takes: She speaks of both the Cameroonians[82] and the Germans in the third person, and the way in which she uses language (i.e., 'they played the boss', 'it turned into a bloody matter') adds a layer of distance and detachment to the account. These strategies contribute to a reduction of complexity on a broader level, namely with respect to the reactions it facilitates: As the narrative remains objective and factual, further questions about

---

[82] Obviously, many different groups were involved in revolts in the colony of Cameroon. The revolt that Christine's statement refers to is, according to information in the gallery, the Anyang revolt of 1904.

responsibility, long-term effects, and power hierarchies are not aroused by it. A discussion about this difficult period is apparently not desired, and so a critical perspective on colonialism as a whole does not unfold from this statement. In its brevity, distance, and simplicity, it predominantly remains a piece of context information, and after Christine has completed this account, there is no further discussion about it, which she facilitates by explicitly indicating the limitation of time that the group should spend at that station: 'So, two more questions' (ibid., 498).

This situation shows the lack of time that the guides feel they have during the sessions, paired with expectations of the school groups to integrate the sessions in their curriculum (which is discussed in the next section), may lead to reductions of culturally and historically significant information, which as a consequence are turned into mere anecdotes as in the case above.[83] Furthermore, as in this particular example, the spontaneous conflation of history into anecdote can lead to a problematic reduction not only of the significance and scope of colonialism, but also of the agency of the non-European groups. Although Christine refers to the Cameroonians' rising up against the German colonisers, she does not refer to the multiple attempts to do so, or to the significance of these revolts as signs of the involved groups' resistance and capacity. A similarly problematic case of 'presenting history in a nutshell' can be found in the previously discussed accounts regarding the acquisition of the objects in the museums' collections which come off as European success stories. Just as in the case above, due to time constraints, some important pieces of information, particularly 'their' perspectives are deleted or deformed in these accounts.

Some of the educators realise this imbalance between complexity and the available time in their reflections in the interviews. On the way from

---

[83] As already mentioned, such individual situations cannot be explained by only one factor, which is why this example will be taken up in the following sections to show which other factors may play into this case of reducing complexity.

the session to the coffee shop where the interview is conducted, Feona explains that the collecting history of one of the objects she has addressed in her session is very complex and that she had to shorten the colonialism aspect, which she always finds difficult to do. Similarly, when Maria reflects upon her way of dealing with the students' questions about terrorism in her gallery session, she concedes that it is, to some extent, her responsibility as a guide to negotiate such questions (cf. EIM, 296-298), but she explains that it is difficult to '[…] address this only briefly in passing. I mean, you can say five commonplaces that everyone has heard already. But you can't address it comprehensively.' (EIM, 300-303). These guides realise that they would need more time to do justice to the complex issues discussed in the galleries.

The question of the appropriate amount of time that should be scheduled for a gallery session leads to a dilemma. On the one hand, it would be desirable to allocate more time to the explanation of historical events, social differences in the countries represented, and diachronic changes of cultural practices. On the other hand, as many of the interviewed guides agree, it is already challenging for them to uphold the young students' attention for the duration of an hour. For example, Britta indicates that it is difficult to keep up the interest of younger students when spending a lot of time at one position (cf. EIB, 308-311), Gladys notes that the attention span of the students is not very flexible (cf. EIG, 142-143), and Doreen mentions that one has only one minute in the beginning of the session to get the students interested in the topic of the tour and to thereby motivate them to participate (cf. EID, 135-137). This confirms the results of other studies, for instance that of Cecilia Rodéhn who has recently conducted research on museum educators' articulations of their work. She has found that 50 minutes is already a long time to sustain visitor attention (cf. 2017, 9). Just as the guides in the study at hand, her respondents explain that it is difficult to keep their audience focused on the tour for a long time and to retain 'a total presence in the moment' (cf. ibid.).

This concern about keeping the students' focused also affects the ways in which the guides structure the time of their sessions. In most of the observed sessions, the guides change the stations they pass with the children rather often so as to keep them engaged. Britta explains that she has to move between different objects with the students so that they don't lose interest (cf. EIB, 308-311) and Eva also describes how she changes from explaining things to doing yoga with the students when they appear restless to her (cf. EIE, 227-229). Thus, the guides feel they cannot 'afford' to stay put at one point of the exhibition for a very long time because they need to cover various stations within the one-hour slot in order to uphold the students' attention. This dilemma of wanting to explain various objects and topics while only having a short amount of time leads to the reduction of complexity through the guides' shortening of information and their foreclosure of longer discussions.

Resolving the dilemma of complexity and time by reducing the complexity of the described non-European contexts can be especially problematic if it causes the guides to overlook or bypass sensitive issues. This is the case, for instance, in the previously discussed example featuring a student in Britta's session who explains that what he does not like about the Chinese is that they torture their animals (cf. GSB-MB, 517). Britta simply answers by saying 'You probably mean that the Chinese eat animals that we do not eat and that they kill them in cruel ways. That's right. You're right. This is a different culture from ours' (cf. ibid., 519-521). In the interview, Britta explains her reaction to this comment of the student as follows:

> I tend to respond to this too much, I think. And I also realised this with the education of my own children and I have learned or I have received feedback that it is sometimes better to let it rest and not to constantly explain everything. And in this case, it was also the time, I had the time factor. I was confused because I did not know

exactly until when they had booked the tour, this happens to me sometimes, and I did not want to get caught at this point. And if one starts, one knows this and the other knows that. That is quite interesting that the students speak, but often it gets to a point where everyone explains what their grandmas have eaten at a Chinese restaurant and such things, and of course I try to keep the focus on the here and now and on what I want to tell them. And this is why I kept that rather short. (EIB, 213-226)

This statement shows very well that Britta restricts herself to a brief comment in response to the student's remark in order to avoid 'getting caught' at a specific part of the exhibition. Her desire not to lose valuable time in which to convey all the information she has planned for the tour is a main factor that contributes to her bypassing the essentialist and generalising comment of the student. In so doing, however, she affirms a very limited perspective that denies any form of negotiation and understanding. Almost certainly, this shut-down is not what Britta intends, but her time-consciousness, among other factors, dictates that she keep a clear focus and, thus, hinders a genuine discussion about cultural practices and constructions of difference. The lack of discussion once again causes the disimprovement effect to emerge: While Britta explains in the interview that she aims at broadening the children's horizons and working against 'this typical rejection that we see very often in students' (cf. EIB, 95-97), what she does in this situation is nothing but confirm the student's rejection. Although Britta argues that it was her conscious decision not to elaborate the issue, in this particular situation, time pressure and the brevity of the moment seem more likely as explanatory factors. Relatedly, in the end of her reflection on the situation, Britta adds: '[…] It is not something one has much time to think about, but one continues speaking and the others have perhaps already wandered off and (.) then, [what to answer] is often a very spontaneous decision' (EIB, 229-231).

5.2.2 Understandings of Learning: Learning Styles, Goal Orientation, and the School-Museum Relationship

The aforementioned temporal limitations of the guided tours and the guides' inclination to cover a range of envisaged stations in the galleries so as to retain the students' attention are necessarily entwined with the guides' understandings of learning. This subchapter explains how the lecture and text teaching style, the goal orientation of the sessions, the scriptedness of a part of the sessions, as well as the catering of the guided tours to the school curriculum affects a reduction of complexity during the gallery sessions.

As explained in Chapter 5.1.2, these guides' understandings of learning are marked by an ambiguity between their theoretical support for learner autonomy and their recourse, in practice, to the more traditional 'lecture and text' teaching style. This teaching style can be regarded as an influential factor in the reduction of complexity because it is based upon an idea of knowledge that is objective, structured, and factual: As Hein has defined the 'lecture and text' teaching style:

> Within this traditional view of education, the teacher has two responsibilities. First, s/he must understand the structure of the subject, the knowledge that is to be taught. [...] The second responsibility of the traditional teacher is to present the domain of knowledge to be taught appropriately so that the student can learn. Thus, there is a logical order of teaching dictated by the subject to be taught that would make it easiest to learn. The concept of a linear textbook, a great 19th century invention, is predicated on this view of learning. (Hein 1994, 74)

Although there are moments of experiential learning in the observed sessions,[84] most of the guides' teaching practices are based upon the understandings described in the above definition.[85]

As the guides often have a clear structure of the teaching process planned for their gallery sessions, with specific stations to visit, objects to focus on, and information to include, they do not usually take into account spontaneous questions, remarks, and interests of the students. A case in point is Britta's brief answer '[y]es, you're right, this is a different culture to ours' (cf. GSB-MB, 521-522). Besides being determined by time constraints, this reaction can also be regarded as a result of the strict session plan that Britta has in mind. If she allows a longer debate over the student's idea about Chinese 'culture' to unfold, she fears the focus of the session will get lost (cf. EIB, 224-226). Such a strict conception of what is to be 'achieved' in the guided tour not only causes a self-restriction in terms of the extent to which the guides answer student questions, but it can also result in their restriction of input from the students. Accordingly, Britta notes that while it is interesting when the students participate, it can become problematic for her when 'everyone explains what their grandmas have eaten at a Chinese restaurant' (ibid., 221-224). In a similar vein, Kate notes in the interview that some questions of the students are difficult to manage because 'if you were to go into it you would be there for another half an

---

[84] This is not to argue that experiential learning is unproblematic. As is explained in Chapter 5.3.3, the focus on experience can be equally problematic for it disregards information and only immerses the students in an experience of otherness. However, this statement is to show that the lecture-and-text style is not the only style applied by the guides. A constructivist understanding of learning, in contrast, would be more desirable because of its focus on multiple 'truths', but it is not applied in the observed sessions.

[85] The only exception to this is Museum D, where discovery learning is more widely practiced and integrated with the session formats developed by the learning departments. Here, the students are encouraged to think about the materiality of the objects and discuss it amongst themselves. Although the guides still often 'lecture' about certain aspects and equally apply the practice of leading the students to the foreseen answers by asking them questions, this learning approach is more experiential than those of the other museums.

hour' (EIK, 298-299). In this case, the usually desirable participation of the students turns into a problem with regard to the lecture and text teaching style. If the guides feel obliged to stick to their original session plans, contributions of the students cannot be discussed in depth, often causing potentially meaningful observations to be dismissed and subject matters to be reduced to a mere factual level.

Besides the previously discussed theory-practice divide and recourse to familiar teaching practices, a significant explanation for the application of the lecture and text teaching style, and the concomitant reduction of complexity, is the goal-orientation of the sessions. As George Hein has argued, learning goals in museums usually focus on 'simple concrete 'outcomes' for visitors [...] chosen from a much larger domain because they appear to be attainable in a short time with a limited exposure' (1998, 92). There are several reasons for the predominance of this focus on learning outcomes in the guided tours.

First, this goal-oriented understanding of learning is connected to the ephemeral nature of the gallery sessions. While it is difficult to measure the effects of learning in the museum because, as Karp and Kratz conclude, '[i]f an exhibition affects a visitor, it may take time and other experiences to activate that effect' (2014, 62), in practice, such immediately measurable results may be more desirable for the guides. This is because they only interact with the students for a brief moment and will otherwise not be able to 'reap the fruit of their labour'. This wish to measure the outcomes of the sessions is reflected especially in the British museums. In these museums, the guides often include a repetition practice at the end of the guided tours in order to review what the students have learned.

Second, the goal-orientation of the guided tours is also affected by the learning departments.[86] These departments, in part, determine the strict structure and goal-orientation of the guided tours, especially when they devise a script-like plan for the sessions that the gallery educators are asked to implement, as is the case in most of the observed British session. If the tours are planned according to fixed formats so as to be predictable for teachers and reproducible by different guides, it is more difficult for the guides to make longer departures from planned materials or to conduct the sessions in a way that proceeds spontaneously from the students' interests or the topics' complexity. Museum-education scholars Barbara Piscitelli and Katrina Weier have argued, '[...] if a particular object generates a great deal of interaction or discussion, the guide should focus on the teachable moment, restructuring the rest of the program as necessary' (2002, 125). This may, however, not be feasible in scripted sessions.

Admittedly, all of the British guides explain in the interviews that they do not have to stick entirely to the script that the learning departments provide for them. Yet, even if smaller stations can be left out spontaneously, the broader concepts signalled in the script need to become apparent in the guides' performances. As Kate notes, 'well, it's kinds of a finished script [...]. But within that there's some things that you can switch with something else that interests you. They kind of have got the main points that they want to get across' (EIK, 69-71). Even though there is the possibility of switching topics, a solid goal-orientation is thus built into this process of scripting the sessions. Moreover, as most of the British guides are trained in museum studies or education rather than

---

[86] Another factor is the lack of hands-on engagement with the objects in the museums and the guided tours, which render a more experiential approach rather difficult to implement. Many scholars have criticised that this prevention from touching the objects is detrimental to the learning experience (cf. Golding 2012, 173; O'Neill 2006, 102).

cultural studies, art history, or ethnology, and are not paid for any preparation time, it is difficult for them to digress from the script and to bring in additional, complexifying information, for instance on transcultural entanglements. As Lynn notes with respect to the reduction of complexity,

> I'm being very honest here in that I don't have an expertise in the classics. I'm a jack of all trades, so for me, I don't have a depth of knowledge about anything in particular. My first degree was biology. So, I don't have any depth of knowledge about any particular area. So, for me, I find that I'm always going 'What do I need to find out? How deep do I have to go?' So, I'm working from knowing nothing to knowing enough rather than going 'How can I simplify this?' Because I don't know much. (EIL, 486-492)

Yet, although it is especially difficult for the British guides to spontaneously digress from the provided script so as to add multiple perspectives or critical discussions to some of their explanations, this cannot be the only or dominant explanation for a reduction of complexity. The observed German sessions, which are designed by the guides and often much less strict in terms of contents than their British counterparts, are not more responsive or elaborated by comparison. In most of the sessions, the digressions that are made by the German guides amount to nothing more than short question and answer sessions with the students or the narration of brief anecdotes from their own experience. While some of the guides do adjust the session contents more spontaneously than the British guides, this is usually not because of student comments, topic affordances or interests, but because of the teachers' intentions and wishes.

As a third explanatory approach to understand the guided tours' goal orientation and the reduction of complexity is related to the teachers: Measurable outcomes may also be expected by the school teachers who see the museum as an *alternative* learning space, but a learning space nevertheless. A close relationship between the schools' requirements and the learning experiences provided by the museums is not surprising, considering that the learning departments' success is largely dependent on the teachers' utilisation of museum educational programmes.

Furthermore, in the British case, museums have been encouraged through political incentives to cater to the national curriculum, while the national curriculum has likewise been adjusted to the museums' collections.[87] Therefore, in the British museums part of this study, the link between the school programmes developed by the learning departments and the national curriculum is rather strong. For instance, the session formats of Museum C and Museum D contain information on 'national curriculum links', which make it easier for teachers to integrate their visits with work done at school. In Germany, on the other hand, the federal state curricula merely recommend field-trips to museums, but they are not a prescribed part of school education (cf. Dhanjal 2012, 25). Although this means that the sessions of the German museums are not officially expected to mirror the curricula, a general connection is still implemented by the museums in order to maintain their relationships with the schools. As Christine explains in the interview, the team of educators in Museum B has conceptualised some tours that respond to the curricula for specific age groups, that are then also advertised to the local schools (cf. EIC, 33-37).

The fact that there is this content overlap between school and museum education also implies that teachers may regard the school trip as a component of the work done at school, which is why they may expect clear-cut information and the achievement of specific learning goals. Alison Grinder, in her sourcebook for interpreters and docents, has already indicated this divergence between understandings of learning held by teachers and museum representatives: 'Teachers may be most interested in measurable progress in learning; museums do encourage learning

---

[87] As explained in Chapter 2, in 1988, a new British national curriculum emphasised the role of artefacts and museums in formal school education (cf. hereto Hooper-Greenhill 2007, 5ff.), making it easier for teachers to integrate school field trips into their learning agendas. Furthermore, during Labour government from 1997, the financial support of Britain's National Museums was increasingly connected to a demand for an increased provision of learning within museums (cf. ibid., 6).

specific knowledge, but they may place greater emphasis on the discovery of general principles [...]' (1985, 65). Bystron and Zessnik also note that in a project they conducted at the Ethnological Museum in Berlin to develop support materials for students, which integrated perspectives of students, guides, and teachers, the teachers part of the project insisted on a close relation between the learning materials and the curriculum (cf. 2014, 344). Similarly, in some of the observed sessions of this study, teachers have students fill out worksheets during the sessions or ask the guides to concentrate on a specific aspect discussed at school. For instance, in the interview, Christine complains about the fact that the teachers brought worksheets to her session and had the students fill them out while Christine was talking: 'if they only tick their boxes [....] they can do this on their own. [...] And afterwards I heard how they said, "ah that [piece of information] wasn't part of the tour"' (Christine, 210-215). Furthermore, the projects that the teachers work on with the students are usually rather superficial, including such topics as 'designing African masks' or 'Australia'. Therefore, more complex issues such as colonialism, object biographies, and cultural heterogeneity, may not 'fit' with what the teachers have in mind, making such issues seem irrelevant for the teachers and the guides.

While many scholars have argued in favour of an integration of guided tours in the school context (e.g. Xanthoudaki 2003, Tran 2007), this situation of the teachers' goal-orientation and demands for clear-cut, factual 'school' topics indicates a main problem of the school-museum relationship. Ben Garcia has equally criticised this perspective of seeing the museum solely in terms of an addition to formal learning at school:

> Museum school programs are generally designed to support K-12 content standards, because many schools will visit only if they see a fit with their academic goals. Many of us (myself included) have designed school programs that do this, and have — in ways small and large — sold out our collections in the process. (2012, 48)

Similarly, a sole orientation of guided tours toward the expectations and demands of schools may be detrimental to encouraging discussions about broader concepts, which may be particularly significant in the context of describing non-European cultural practices. While presumed facts about objects, history, and non-European cultural practices may be easier to connect to facts learned at school, it is especially the informal learning environment that can unravel student perceptions about otherness and facilitate a more genuine negotiation process.

Here, the mentioned 'disimprovement effect' becomes visible again. The guides often explain in the interviews that they aim at much broader goals than the confirmation or illustration of school content. For instance, Feona argues that she wants to use the objects in the exhibition to inspire further thought and discussion about where they come from (cf. EIF, 361-368), and Antonia notes that she does not only want to deliver facts but also, more importantly, to destabilise clichés (cf. EIA, 30). During the sessions, however, because of the discussed reasons of a recourse to familiar teaching strategies, goal orientation, and scriptedness of some of the sessions, these aims are rarely put into practice. A similar result has been found by Lynn Tran (2007) in a study on science education in museums. She argues that while gallery educators want to achieve 'affective gains' and contribute to life-long learning, their sessions resemble school lessons in discourse and design (cf. 294). While Tran traces this back to the lack of 'a distinct educational agenda of its own, rooted in its own educational values—values which it needs to explicitly articulate and enact in its daily practice' (ibid.), this study rather points to a variety of factors that play into the guides' recourse to the 'lecture and text' learning style. In particular, the similarities of reductions of complexity in the two German and the two British museums despite differences in the guides' training and in the organisation of museum education point to more immediate factors such as the short amount of time that the guides have at their disposal, their concerns surrounding teacher expectations, and the easier preparation of sessions with a clear structure and content.

5.2.3   Spaces and Objects: Spatial and Design-related cues of the Reduction of Complexity in the Exhibitions

This subchapter is concerned with the extent to which the reduction of complexity in the guided tours is affected by the ways in which the exhibitions are designed. The following elaborations first briefly discuss the link between curatorial intentions and the guides' accounts, and subsequently address the ways in which the structure of the galleries and the means of storytelling in the exhibition rooms may have an effect on the reduction of complexity in the gallery sessions.

The extent to which there is a link between the intentions of the curators and the accounts of the guides is not easy to define. In the German cases, curators usually give introductory tours in the temporary exhibitions to provide the gallery educators with the facts that they need to translate the exhibitions for visitors. Other than that, however, there is almost no contact between the two actors. The curatorial decisions in relation to the permanent galleries that are at the centre of attention in this work are usually not repeatedly communicated to the guides, and, from the guides' statements in the interviews, it appears that they are relatively free in choosing what to tell the students about these exhibitions. As Doreen explains in the interview, the curators provide introductions to the galleries for the guides, but the guides then need to adjust this rather complex introduction to the target group of younger students (cf. EID, 62-64). This preparation of the exhibition contents for children can lead to a reduction of complexity, especially if this process is carried out using strategies of simplification based on typification of categorisation. In the British museums, whereas there is no direct contact between the curators and the guides, the scripts or session plans developed by the learning departments are co-designed or informed by the curators. That means that the curatorial interpretations play a more important role in these sessions.[88] In general, however, regardless of the extent of the curators' influence in the development of the sessions, the guides always adjust their accounts to the individual situations and students they encounter during the sessions.

From this short description of the contact between the curators and the guides, it would seem that the curators provide information in a sufficiently complex and reflective manner while the gallery educators abridge and simplify the facts, thereby causing essentialist and generalising representations of otherness. However, as the following remarks show, this is not entirely true. Although the guides certainly make abbreviations and apply simplifications, the information presented in the exhibitions are not always balanced, culturally sensitive and heterogeneous. Instead, within the organisation of spaces and objects, it is possible to find spatial and textual cues that point to a reduction of complexity which is already inbuilt into the visual and verbal narratives available in the exhibition spaces. These reductions can, to some extent, have an influence on the guides' ways of framing their sessions, which is explained in the following.

The first means by which a reductive framing in the gallery sessions is already inscribed in the spaces of the museums is manifest in the visual narratives and the gallery texts in the four museums part of this study. As already mentioned before, in all of the museums part of this study, relatively fix and generalising regional categories are used to separate different galleries, which suggests that culture was identical with location. Correspondingly, education scholar William Gaudelli has explained the

---

[88] Gladys's session, however, is an exception to this rule because she has co-designed the session and feels more independent in her communication as a gallery educator.

educational pitfalls that such an arrangement of 'cultures' can have within exhibitions by analysing *the American Museum of Natural History* as a pedagogical space. Based on one of his university student's (Raisa) observations, he compares the museum's arrangement with an amusement park:

> One of Raisa's observations typifies this idea as she observed a young girl quickly walking through the various cultural exhibits, saying, 'And these are the African people and these are the Indian people [Indus Valley, not Native American Indian], these are the prehistoric people' and so on—skipping through all the sections just to be able to name them. This child's strategy was not unlike having one's passport stamped at an amusement park to claim that she had been there, done that on her day at the museum, collecting a Maori here, a Gikuyu there. [...] This moving through spatiality, coupled with the sheer enormity of the museum, suggests a pedagogical approach that might easily lead away from complexity and towards oversimplification and surface readings. (2014, 163)

This analysis shows that, due to the spatial separation, the ethnographic museum can be regarded by visitors as a synopsis of different 'cultures'. Although the exhibitions may not be interpreted in a similarly superficial way by all the students in this work, this 'been there, done that' connotation is also, in part, suggested by those gallery sessions that give the students an overview of three different galleries or 'cultures' in the framework of one hour (e.g. GSF-MD). Furthermore, the neat separation of cultural regions in different rooms or galleries may also affect the expectations of the museum that are held by the guides, teachers, and students. This aspect is further discussed in the section on expectations surrounding the museum (Chapter 5.2.4), but it is important to note here that such expectations are partly evoked and reinforced by the spatial design of museums that arrange cultural regions neatly separated and side by side.

A further way in which reductions may already be inbuilt into the museum as institution can be found in the ways in which information is presented. Although all museums part of this study usually use more experimental modes of interpretation in their temporary exhibitions, their permanent galleries are predominantly designed in a more traditional style that is marked by an authoritative, academic, and factual tone. In so far as this form of mediating knowledge is generally less open to visitor contributions, critical questions, and the emergence of unintended meanings, the permanent galleries often only allow for and acknowledge one perspective or lens through which the objects and regions are seen. In order to give an example for the way in which the museum's knowledge is represented in the galleries, the following gallery text from a text panel in Museum A is insightful:

> The Iatmul of the Middle Sepik region initiate young boys in the age of twelve to sixteen into the world of the male adults. After the ritual the adolescents are accepted as full members of the adult community. (Gallery text, Museum A)

Seemingly omniscient, presented with zero focalisation, factual, all-encompassing, and dissociated, this short contextual description on the text panel compares to a transcendent voice-over rather than to an actual human being having written an explanatory text as a result of research and prior knowledge. In this context, Lidchi's reference to the exhibition as a myth (cf. 1997, 182) is particularly suitable, for the museum's myth of objectivity and truth appears to its visitors like 'innocent speech', in Barthes' words, and this is, as he claims, 'not because its intentions are hidden – if they were hidden, they could not be efficacious – but because they are naturalized' (1957, 130). In a similar vein, the reductions of complexity in the above statement do not appear as such. Neither in this extract nor in the remainder of the text panel does the implied visitor learn about the Iatmul as a group, its social make-up, its history, contact with European colonisers or ethnologists, let alone the group's self-understanding. Furthermore, besides the fact that the perspective available to the visitor is only that of the ethnologist speaking *about* the group, never that of members of the group representing themselves, it is unclear from the ethnographic present adopted in this description whether the addressed ritual of initiation is still practised, whether the group is still intact, and in how far the ritual has been transformed over the years. But even more basic than these points, the mere unquestioned and not contextualised use of the term 'latmul' can be seen as a process of reducing complexity that creates entities where there are none, considering that Gregory Bateson 'invented' the term as a standardising measure in the 1930s, as Ulrike Claas has explained in detail:

> Even before Bateson's arrival in 1929, the area was being recognized as a 'style area' (Reche 1911), but it was his seminal research that gave the inhabitants the name by which they are now known among Papua New Guineans and Westerners alike, the 'latmul'. Bateson, as it happens, was far from happy with the term he had chosen and his misgivings were well placed. He had visited less than half of the villages he united under the term, leaving out the western group completely [...]. Furthermore, he had visited only one of the many neighboring villages from which he was differentiating 'the latmul'; [...]. In naming the 'latmul', in other words, Bateson drew a boundary line that defined the extent of Western knowledge rather more than it did any actual 'tribe'. (Claas 2009, 217)

Especially considering this historical context, adopting this categorical term for a cultural group without providing information on its emergence casts the 'latmul' as a holistic group in the eyes of potential visitors. The objective and persuasive style of the text further marks it as reliable. Within the dynamics of this discursive mode, there is no room for the visitors to ask further questions, make meaning by themselves, or ask critical questions. Especially for non-experts, the question of the heterogeneity of what are labelled the 'latmul' does not even pose itself.

This brief analysis of one statement from a text panel in Museum A is presented here in order to show a possible connection between the guides' communication and the communication style evident in the exhibitions. As many of the galleries part of this study are already designed in ways that favour the previously discussed lecture and text learning style rather than active participation (e.g. through the distance of the objects, the factual and seemingly omniscient gallery texts, and the authoritative design), the guides are not specifically encouraged by the exhibition environment to ask open questions, engage in critical debates with the students, or let them construct meaning on their own. Graham Black has similarly pointed to a similarity between education and gallery design, arguing that both the museum and its museum education are 'didactic' in nature because it is easier to refer to artefacts "[...] based on the transmission of information relating to particular collections or fields of knowledge, and to structure this knowledge into manageable chunks suitable for display' (2005, 130). This easier mode of a more predefined and didactic communication may be one of the reasons for the guides' reductions of complexity. Although some of the gallery educators *complexify* the exhibitions by relating to the situation in the respective countries today, or by speaking about their own experiences, when it comes to categorising 'cultures', relating to their rituals, and describing artefacts, often, the same seemingly objective and reductive style as evident in the gallery design and texts is applied. While it is important to note that these reductions are also closely related to the guides' understandings of culture discussed in the next section, their continuation of an objective, normalising narrative style in combination with the portrayal of generalised knowledge devoid of references to the ways in which information, labels, and categories have been developed, points to a process of inheriting or mimicking a reductive mode of communication which is normalised in the galleries.

Besides these implications of authority and factuality that are manifest in the gallery texts and the gallery design, another aspect related to the reduction of complexity that is connected to representations available in the museum is the perspective through which history and culture are presented in these museums. Admittedly, it is impossible to accommodate all possible perspectives within museum representations, but, in European museums representing non-European artefacts, the perspectives of those who have used and made the objects often seem particularly underrepresented. Yet, as previously argued, the recovery of

342

perspectives of past informants is difficult because of the limited records that exist about them (cf. Clifford 1997, 198). Despite this problem of the availability of information, what could be done is to include contemporary perspectives from a range of regions in the mediation of the objects.

Such alternative or critical voices are difficult to find in the museums part of this study, and instead a certain process of euphemising history can be observed. This is apparent, for instance, in the abstract examination and representation of the objects on display as well as in the lack of sufficient criticism of colonial practices of 'collecting' visible in the museums. For example, in one of the German museums, a throne from King Njoya[89] originating in today's Cameroon is still described in the gallery text as a present from the king to the German emperor, while what is excluded is that prior to its donation, the German colonial authorities had increasingly demanded the bestowal of this 'gift' (cf. Mirzoeff 1999, 142). The gallery text's framing of the donation revolves around its intended function to establish diplomatic relations with the Germans, which suggests a gesture at eye level. Yet, as Nicholas Mirzoeff explains, King Njoya's efforts to maintain good relations with the Germans were based on fears of persecution, and must thus be seen as strategies of acculturation:

> This strategy of acculturating colonialism provided a space for Africans and Europeans to coexist in the uneasy cold war of colonial settlement. For Europeans, the visual documentation of Africa was central to their transculturation of the continent into a land fit for colonization. Africans aided this process as an alternative preferable to the kind of violence that led to an international outcry over conditions in the Congo from 1897 onwards. (Ibid., 143).

This situation shows how certain histories are favoured in the museum, and how this process is governed by a European perspective on history. In the case above, the respective museum can thus be regarded as writing a history that justifies the museum's existence. As Preziosi writes, '[t]he

---

[89] A definition is provided in the glossary.

past is what the present needs to legitimize, naturalize, and sustain itself; in and by museography the past becomes a monument in the present' (1996, 102).

This focus on a European perspective in the gallery can also partly explain a focus on such perspectives in the guided tours. For example, when Johan explains the story of the King Njoya's throne in the guided tour, he similarly refers to the throne as a present, not reflecting upon or further addressing the debates surrounding the artefact (cf. GSJ-MA, 83-85). Thus, such reductions of complexity may be taken up by the guides not necessarily because they automatically share them, but because these are the only ones available in the museum. This may also explain, at least in part, the categorically positive rendering of acquisition histories in the guides' accounts. For instance, Maria's story of a Dutch collector's theft of a piece of the Kiswa suggests that stealing the object was ultimately a good thing. In this case, the same historical perspective that euphemises the history of King Njoya's throne is applied to the representation of collection history. In so doing, the complexity not only of the actual historical event, but also of its implications is considerably reduced, leading to a narrative that represents the European agents as rightful owners, and the Other as passive bystanders. Such a reconstruction and reinforcement of political binaries and a 'history of winners' compares to what Eric Wolf criticises in *Europe and the People without History* regarding narratives that turn interconnected phenomena into 'static things': 'History is thus converted into a tale about the furtherance of virtue, about how the virtuous win out over the bad guys' (1982, 5).

5.2.4 Expectations Surrounding the Museum: Order and Repose

One of the explanations for the described optimistic and uncritical representation of the past in both the exhibitions and the guided tours can also be found in the public role of the museum as an informative, entertaining, pleasurable, and affirmative place. These expectations of order and repose are discussed in the following.

The museum as institution is known for its function to put the world in order and to, thereby, provide guidance in a world that is increasingly complex and incomprehensible. Among others, Dicks has argued that '[visitors] do not, on the whole, expect to find reflexivity, hybridity and fragmentation' (2004, 149) in exhibitions.[90] This expectation has further been postulated and explained by Rounds:

> [Museums] provide vantage points from which the order that's invisible in quotidian life becomes intensified and visible in the space of an exhibition. Outside is the blooming, buzzing confusion of everyday life, an endless flow of one thing after another. Inside the museum, the visitor finds a world laid out in order, in which everything has its proper place in a meaningful system, in which everything is neatly labeled. The museum shows us a world that makes sense, and that is a world in which we can believe that our lives make sense. (2006, 140)

A reduction of complexity may, with regard to this association of the museum as a mechanism of systematising and ordering of the world, be firmly inbuilt in workings and self-understandings, as well as public expectations of the institution.

In this form of expectations of order and structure, these reductions may similarly become integrated into the guided tours. In a relatively short amount of time, the students are familiarised with a region or 'culture': A deeper and critical reflection of identity ascriptions and constructions of otherness is not suggested by the short session formats about 'voyages'

---

[90] This understandings of the museum as a provider of truth and order are still pervasive, so that, despite the recent discourse on a participatory opening-up of the institution, visitors not always like to 'participate', but prefer to listen and learn in the 'traditional' way. This is an observation that has, for example, been made by Elisabeth Timm who has looked at participation and visitor movement in museums. In an exhibition of the *Museum der Dinge* in Berlin, which encouraged visitors to unravel the meaning of objects by themselves, she observed that visitors were sometimes reluctant to interpret the objects, but initially expected someone to tell them a story (cf. 2014, 5).

through the museums or 'African masks'. The teachers, the parents, but also the guides may expect that the museum can facilitate a holistic, but brief, insight into non-European worlds. Asked about the relation of the guided tour to the learning goals of the teachers, Britta reckons that '[...] they come to learn about a tribe or an ethnic group, or the people. About the culture in the wider sense' (EIB, 325-328). Considering the contexts in which the guided tours are embedded (e.g. project weeks on entire regions or continents), Britta's anticipation of the teachers' intention seems plausible. Yet, regardless of its plausibility, this expectation, as she explains, motivates her to focus less on specific objects and more on general information about China. In this case, the teachers' expectations and the guides' expectations surrounding the museum interact. Both actors interpret the guided tour as a means of introducing the students to the represented cultures, and they thereby, as Riegel has argued in the context of general visitor expectations, '[...] grant the museum a certain authority to accurately document and depict those cultures' (1996, 87).

Besides this idea of the ethnographic museum as a place where non-European culture is mediated in an orderly fashion, the museum is further associated with entertainment, relaxation, and pleasure. This expectation can be seen to affect the reduction of complexity in so far as it, for instance, leads to the avoidance of elaborated discussions about controversial issues, such as colonialism, acquisition histories, repatriation, racism, or war. These aspects almost never appear in the guides' accounts, and if they do, they are usually dismissed rather quickly. This observation concurs with studies in visitor research. Danielle Rice has found, for instance, that the idea of being controversial is often 'counter to the expectations of museum visitors that the museum environment is a place of recreation and repose' (1995, 20). Similarly, Riegel notes that visitors expect a cognitive distance from exhibits, hoping to separate personal emotions from their educational experience (cf. 1996, 87).

346

Judging from the observations of the gallery sessions that are marked by a lack of critical engagement with social and cultural problems, these visitor expectations evidently also affect museum educational practice. Confirming this idea, Allen et al. have similarly found that many docents tend to '[...] avoid potentially uncomfortable or political topics' (2014, 94), and John Reeve explains that '[...] teachers and museum educators worldwide often express a lack of confidence in dealing with controversial topics such as Islamic history and art, or the less positive aspects of Christianity' (2010, 151). Some of the reductions of complexity in the observed guided tours can, then, be regarded as means of maintaining and guaranteeing uncontroversial visits.

While these elaborations may suggest that reductions of complexity derive only from the guides' and the teachers' expectations of the museum as a place providing ordered and uncontroversial knowledge, it is important to consider that these expectations are partly evoked and reinforced by the actual structures of the museums. As already mentioned in the section on space (Chapter 5.2.3), some conceptual reductions of complexity may already be inbuilt into the spatial design of exhibitions that arrange cultural regions like a theme park. Furthermore, museum agendas can actually include indications of an uncontroversial direction of museum communicative measures. This is apparent, for example, in Gladys's explanation of her role as a guide with an African migration background. She explains that she has worked on an art project on the Benin Bronzes[91], relating to her position in-between the local and the official narrative of the artefacts' history:

G: I have to do the research on the story. And so, I go from the object and then I come to the subject. So, you cannot be there. It will never be quite right. but you can begin to imagine what the object might be saying. And then you bring your own interpretation. But you never never forget the kind of official narrative. But you also need to understand, and this doesn't always rest very well with the establishment, that this is, this is narrative. There is also, this is

---

[91] A definition is provided in the glossary.

> where anthropology comes in, there's a local narrative. And sometimes the two can be in contradiction. But obviously I have to represent the museum. But as an African, I also want to bring in these other stories.
>
> [...]
>
> KW: Has that been a problem?
>
> G: It is not a problem but there have been, kind of, sometimes when it's been interesting. Because I have actually been told to not say this. Because obviously it comes very political. It's a debate, isn't it.
>
> (EIG, 260-273)

Gladys's explanations show that it is not only the mere *expectation* of the museum as an uncontroversial place that keeps her from including alternative or local narratives into her guided tour, but this kind of political action is *in fact* not approved by the museum as institution. Her reduction of complexity is, therefore, induced by the institution, for the sake of a less political and instead 'unthreatening' museum experience. This again explains the 'disimprovement effect' or what Robert Janes has called 'the widespread disconnection between individuals who work in a museum and the manner in which the museum functions as an organization' (2009, 19). When Museum C only appreciates and authorises educational experiences that are affirmative and unpolitical, even those guides that want to discuss controversial aspects are discouraged from doing so. In this case, a reduction of complexity in terms of social issues and historical ambiguities seems almost unavoidable.

5.2.5 Understandings of Culture: Culturalism and Multiculturalism as Frameworks for the Reduction of Complexity

In the context of this work, the term 'understandings of culture' refers to shared conceptions of what defines or delimitates 'culture', what makes 'a culture', and what is assumed about non-European 'culture'. These ideas can influence the accounts of the guides, the expectations of the teachers, but also the experience of the students. As in the context of expectations surrounding the museum, a comprehensive analysis of all available understandings of culture can clearly not be accounted for. Consequently, the two most salient understandings of culture that affect the performance of the guided tours are discussed in the following. At first, culturalistic understandings of the guides and the teachers are presented. Subsequently, multiculturalism is presented as an important underlying concept in the guided tours.

As defined in Chapter 3.1.5, culturalism leads to the loss of the *social* in social discourse when, for example, social inequality is relabelled as cultural difference (cf. Kaschuba 1995, 15). As Kaschuba argues, this reduction of all social phenomena to cultural traits exacerbates the comprehension of social situations and problems (cf. ibid.). This process of obscuring social complexity through culturalistic explanations is apparent, for instance, in the previously discussed situation in Museum B, in which a teacher tries to connect a Cameroonian cultural practice explained by Christine to a situation the teacher knows from school. While Christine describes a system of mutual dependencies between families in Cameroon, which she identifies as a form of 'social insurance', the teacher tells the students about a boy described by her as 'having the same tradition', who spends more time with his German friend's family than with his own because allegedly, 'in Africa, everyone takes care of each other' (GSC-MB, 665-666). As explained in Chapter 4.7, with this comment, the teacher reduces the complexity of the 'social insurance system' described by Christine, and merely summarises the guide's explanations in terms of a preconceived stereotype of 'African solidarity'. In this situation, the communication of non-European otherness is affected by the teacher's culturalistic understandings of 'African culture'. The social practice described by Christine is overshadowed by these more general ideas about Africanness.

Interestingly, in this situation, culturalism can only affect the session in this way because Christine does not oppose this comment of the teacher. Christine reacts to the teacher's reductive comment by saying '[…] that's right, this is a good example' (GSC-MB, 672). Furthermore, in the interview, Christine claims that she appreciated the comment:

> This was thankfully a very nice, good comment that also suited the situation well. Otherwise I try, if I don't consider a comment suitable - sometimes teachers also explain something wrong because they have heard that somewhere - well, then one has to turn it around: 'Ah, good comment. This leads to an important topic, which is…', and then I can relate to the teacher's comment, somehow like that. (EIC, 159-165)

Apparently, Christine does not admit or realise the problematic dimension of the culturalistic comments of the teacher. What she also explains, however, is that, even if she deemed the comment inappropriate, she would not set it right. As she argues, if she thought a comment was unsuitable, she would still commend it at first and then subtly revise it later on. This again shows that the avoidance of controversial debates in the guided tours can be detrimental to a more diversified explanation of non-European objects and practices.

Christine's reflection indicates that not only the teachers or visitors, but also the gallery educators may be affected by culturalistic understandings. Not even in the interview does Christine problematise the teacher's generalising statement that 'in Africa, everyone takes care of each other', mainly because it is a positive culturalistic generalisation. Such positive stereotypes adopted uncritically by gallery educators are also evident in statements like 'in Africa the door is always open' (GSG-MC, 218-219) or 'it's not all wrapped up in cotton wool as it is here' (GSD-MA, 772-786). These statements suggest that specific practices or constellations in the non-European regions can be explained by an all-encompassing 'culture', which not only generalises these regions, but also ignores social factors that may affect these practices. Furthermore, what is obscured in these cultural translations is the degree to which these observations are informed by their translators. Such positive reductions are, as already explained in Chapter 4, common in the guides' accounts, and they work specifically because of their positive and optimistic nature.

It is this positive connotation of 'culture' that needs to be discussed further, and that is closely related to the second understanding of culture addressed in this subchapter: multiculturalism. In the previously described comments of Britta and Eva, 'this is a different culture to ours', and 'other countries, other manners' respectively, such positive culturalistic explanations are used to avoid possibly negative debates during the gallery sessions. Considering these statements' outward openness (i.e., their focus on tolerance) and restriction to inner homogeneity (i.e., culturalism), these comments seem to be informed by a multiculturalist understanding of culture. As previously mentioned, when multiculturalism is used to describe a certain idea of culture underlying the guides' accounts in this work, the concept is interpreted in terms of what Kymlicka has called the 'misleading model' of multiculturalism. This type of multiculturalist understanding ignores political and economic factors, suggests that groups are hermetically sealed, and can lead to a struggle of authority and power within groups if they are pushed to decide which traditions are 'authentic' (cf. 2012, 4-5). This idea of culture has been adopted widely in the public discourse, as Anderson has argued, because of its '[...] intuitive appeal: it evokes familiar sayings such as 'variety is the spice of life' or 'it takes all sorts to make a world' (2011, 528). This framework implies a cultural relativism that highlights the decorative aspects of culture and downplays its more serious discourses such as secularism versus religious symbols and cultural values versus individual preferences. Reductions of complexity based upon this multiculturalist understanding cannot only be seen in the aforementioned quotes of Britta and Christine, but also in the previously discussed references of various guides to the apparent 'diversity' of cultures (see Chapter 4.1) or in Antonia's references to an 'Americanisation' of non-European regions (cf. GSA-MA, 309-310).

Kymlicka's perhaps most striking point regarding this model of multiculturalism with regard to the statements of the guides is related to good intentions and problematic outcomes:

> Even with respect to the (legitimate) goal of promoting greater understanding of cultural differences, the focus on celebrating 'authentic' cultural practices that are 'unique' to each group is potentially dangerous. [...] To avoid stirring up controversy, there's a tendency to choose as the focus of multicultural celebrations safely inoffensive practices — such as cuisine or music — that can be enjoyably consumed by members of the larger society. But this runs the opposite risk of the trivialization or Disneyfication of cultural differences, ignoring the real challenges that differences in cultural and religious values can raise. (ibid., 5)

This definition bears a striking resemblance to the reduction of complexity practised by the guides during the sessions. As already explained, the idea to deliver uncontroversial contents and facilitate a positive museum experience subtly runs through all the observed sessions. The previously discussed lack of accounts about struggle, exploitation, and power relations in the guided tours can then not only be explained by expectations surrounding the museum as a place of pleasure and entertainment but must also be seen as a result of a multiculturalist understanding of culture. The achievements of non-European 'cultures', their 'diversity', their ostensibly 'authentic' traditions and their (stereo)typical appearance is almost continuously at the centre of attention in the guided tours, while politics, social inequality, and internal heterogeneity are usually omitted from the accounts. In that way, culturalism, as the reduction of social to cultural issues, is at the basis of this multiculturalist framework of understanding that then celebrates these 'cultural' traits, and campaigns for tolerating them.

This publicly still accepted superficial, separating, and homogenising celebration of culture affects both the understandings of the teachers and the understandings of the guides. Multiculturalism can, however, also be seen as embedded in the advertising logics of museums, as von Bose has explained with reference to the planned *Humboldt Forum*

352

in Berlin (cf. 2015, 33). The mission statements of Museums A, B, C, and D in this work are similarly marked by references to cultural dialogue, respect, and notions of learning about the 'cultures of the world', which again hints at multiculturalist ideas of an unspecific tolerance, acceptance, and the identification of clearly defined cultural entities. The resonance of multiculturalist concepts in museum agendas is not overly surprising, considering that these institutions are publicly funded organisations. Accordingly, Harris and O'Hanlon have alluded to the requirement of museums to respond to wider political agendas, visible in the idea that '[...] ethnographic museums offer a perfect setting for the enactment of key terms in the vocabulary of liberal governments such as social inclusion, multiculturalism and diversity' (2003, 12).

The interplay of these multiculturalist mission statements and publicly shared understandings of culture-as-identity can be regarded as affecting the reduction of heterogeneous and controversial cultural realities to broad and decorative cultural types in various of the observed sessions. Because an approach to culture that is decorative rather than critical, holistic rather than individual, and culturalistic rather than socio-economic is both widely accepted in the social realm and compatible with the separate, difference-based, uncontroversial representation in the observed museums, such multiculturalist accounts come to be neatly embedded in the rhetoric of the guided tours. Hence, when Antonia makes a comment on the development of Polynesians while 'we were still living in caves'; when Britta explains that a museum of contemporary culture in China would consist of plastic toys; when Christine explains that 'the people there are much more economical'; when Doreen notes that the Native American Indians are strong and courageous; when Eva explains that there are completely different greeting practices in India; when Gladys states that 'in Africa the door is always open', and when Maria changes the subject of terrorism by saying that this does not affect the students –

these statements can all be understood as reductions of complexity both informed by the guides' ideas surrounding culture and by the museum's multiculturalist agendas.

Two final qualifying comments must be made to relativise the elaborations above. First, in all these considerations, Museum D has not been featured with examples of culturalistic or multicultural framings. While the guides in Museum D sometimes promote tolerance and respect by alluding to the achievements of the non-European regions, the communication in Museum D is very much focused on the objects, their materiality, and their design rather than on their contexts or the broader cultural regions connected to them. Therefore, although there are reductions of complexity observable in the guides' accounts, for instance with respect to the uncritical ways in which object histories are mediated, these situations are not as frequently observable in the communications of these guides.

Secondly, with regard to Museum C, what has to be noted is that this museum includes the only two guides who problematise representations of identity and culture, either in the interviews or in the guided tours. Interestingly, these are the two guides who feel that they are representing 'themselves', i.e., Gladys and Hilda who both describe themselves as being of 'African heritage'.[92] As already stated, Gladys would like to include alternative local narratives in her guided tour, but is advised not to do so by the museum. Still, she brings in minor controversies on the side, if only to raise awareness on the part of the parents and the teachers. For instance, at one point of the session she states: 'Many adults don't know

---

[92] Among the observed guides in all museums, there is only one other guide who identifies himself with the exhibition by means of his own migration background, explaining the exhibition in terms of an internal focalisation and thus speaking of 'us' when addressing the region represented in the section of the museum. This is Johan in the Africa gallery of Museum A. However, unlike Hilda and Gladys, he does not articulate criticism of the objects and history on display during his session.

that Africa is a continent, especially those who run for the vice presidency in America' (GSG-MC, 129-130). Hilda, similarly, actively changes the script of her session and the power point presentation that has been prepared by the learning department because she feels uncomfortable with the representation of 'African' life. In the interview, she explains this change of the script as follows:

KW: [...] [t]here was one picture coming up in the very beginning. and the second one was the picture with the traditional houses. and you said: We've got this. But we also have very modern architecture. So, is this something that you are bringing into session?

H: Yes. So, I have issues with those pictures because people, children, see Africa as that. They don't see it in terms of any modernity. and they don't even show urban (-) people driving cars. streets. young people you know. at the market places. you see people building a mud hut. they'll call that a mud hut. you know this is how Africans live. And that's why I am trying to make the link between African (facts?) and also trying to say that this is what we do as humans worldwide. [...]

(EIH, 178-187)

These examples show that broad culturalistic generalisations and reductions of complexity can be relativised by the guides, by way of their introductions of different perspectives or more comprehensive explanations. This fulfils a criterium for change that Karp and Wilson have articulated: 'Museums become sites where one not only asserts things but where there is also the possibility of questioning those very assumptions' (1996, 267). They claim that this was the only way to arrive at a multicultural polity that allows people to be part of many cultures at the same time (cf. ibid.). With her statement, Hilda makes clear that various realities exist in Africa, and that these are all equally valid. Thereby, she brings in the complexity that the format has ignored.

However, while this complexifying strategy is evidently possible, it is interesting that it does not occur very often in the gallery sessions. In order to explain this lack of diversifying or complexifying measures in the guided tours, the next chapter offers further insights.

5.3. Factors Affecting the Amplification of Otherness

While the links between the observed recurring themes in the guided tours and the two previous factors of the performance of authority and the reduction of complexity are quite distinctive, the final factor addressed in this chapter is much more subtle, indirect, and equivocal. This is because what is described in the following as the 'amplification of otherness' cannot simply be regarded in terms of the construction of cultural difference during the gallery sessions. Instead, it addresses a more complex process which entails the embracement, reinforcement and showcasing of a categorical, distinct otherness of holistic 'cultures'. This principle is thus concerned with the peculiar appeal of 'otherness' as a status that seems to underlie both the teachers' and the gallery educators' actions and statements. In the observed sessions, a 'pleasure' of speaking about, experiencing and thereby maintaining categorical otherness can be observed. This desire for the existence and evidence of otherness; this conviction and defence of non-European cultural distinctiveness, helps to explain various of the described recurring patterns of communicating otherness.

The amplification of otherness should not be confused with the aforementioned culturalism. While public understandings of culture that conflate social with cultural explanatory frameworks must be seen as influencing the guided tours both in terms of the reduction of complexity and in terms of an emphasis on otherness, the amplification of otherness as an underlying factor of the communication in the guided tours is more overarching and cannot only be understood in terms of culturalism. Culturalism describes how social, religious, political, and economic phenomena are reduced to broad notions of culture and (Kymlicka's 'misleading model' of) multiculturalism points to the superficial celebration of this notion of culture as long as it remains on a decorative, non-threatening level. In contrast, the amplification of otherness described here is not limited to a superficial celebration of cultures as entities and to the application of culturalistic explanations, but it points to means of communication and performance in the gallery sessions that reproduce, configure and cling to distinctive otherness as a fact, not necessarily in the sense of 'other' cultures, but in more general terms in the sense of 'the unfamiliar', 'the unknown', and 'the exotic'. It is thus the fascination and desire for clearly defined and visible non-European otherness that is at stake in this subchapter.

As already explained in the synthesis of Chapter 4, many different concepts play into this amplification of otherness in the guided tours, including Ahmed's stranger fetishism, Said's orientalism, or Barthes' exoticism. It can be understood as an effect of establishing the boundaries of the self or of seeking authenticity. While many of these aspects are addressed on the following pages, none of them explains alone what is alluded to here. In the context of this work, it is the unique combination of a postulated still widely accepted exoticisation and celebration of visible and commensurable otherness together with the museum's presentation of ordered, remote Others to indulge in without the nuisance of real life experiences of messiness, confrontation and guilt, that makes possible this specific amplification and showcasing of otherness.

5.3.1 Expectations Surrounding Museum as Institution: Visitor Expectations and the 'Core Competence' of Remote Otherness

In relation to the amplification of otherness, the role of expectations surrounding the museum is particularly noteworthy as ethnographic museums are still often linked to the desire for and pleasurable experience of cultural otherness. This subchapter discusses the relation between the amplification of otherness in the gallery sessions and the expectation of the museum as a place offering experiences of distinct cultural otherness in the form of scientific education. Furthermore, this expectation is connected to an increasing focus on 'experience' in museum communication and the related correlation between cultural encounters in tourism and in the museum. Finally, these expectations of ethnographic museums are explained by the museum's 'core competence' of exhibiting remote, and therefore ordered and distinguishable, otherness.

Although much has changed in terms of museum representational strategies over the last decades, it is questionable whether the already-mentioned multiculturalist agendas of museum communication, revolving around diversity, dialogue and exchange, actually prevent an amplification of otherness in contemporary ethnographic museums. A genuine change of the categories by which otherness is understood seems improbable because, as has been shown in this work, the cultural diversity that is promoted in the museum's mission statements and the guided tours is marked by the celebration of seemingly authentic, coherent cultures, which lacks a deeper historical and social contextualisation. Similarly, Riegel has criticised that

> [u]nder the guises of philanthropy, value-free knowledge and a certain patina of 'culture' and 'civilization', museums have made it their business to reproduce other cultures for the visual consumption of their visitors (1996, 84).

As non-European groups are still often represented in museum communication as distinct cultures, the amplification of otherness seems to be a pervasive function of the ethnographic museum. The lure of the exotic and unfamiliar must, thus, still be seen as a key factor of the museum's public appeal.

This ongoing public expectation of the museum as facilitating seemingly pristine and visible otherness is, to a great extent, not merely an unfortunate by-product of the museum's work. While it goes back to the modern invention of ethnographic museums as 'windows into the authentic', where, as Geurds has framed it, '[...] subjective viewers, in studying the objects on exhibit, could contemplate a "true" view of the distant and exotic' (2013, 4), the continuation of this distance and exoticism cannot simply be regarded as the result of a 'slippery slope' of historical development, or a projection of visitor expectations onto the representations in the museums. Today, the maintenance of compartmentalised and categorised non-European Others in ethnographic museums also needs to be seen as an effective 'marketing' strategy.

While it is true that the still-existing representation of clearly distinguishable cultural entities in ethnographic museums is also affected by financial, organisational, and historical factors, it would be naive to disregard the function of the museum's facilitation of experiences of well-organised, visible otherness as a 'unique selling point'. Such an ordered and distinct, as well as unthreatening otherness can rarely, if ever, be found outside of the museum's walls. The museum thus works to draw visitors in by offering up an exotic non-European world for consumption. As Sturge frames it, '[a]s an ordered whole, the exhibition claims to represent a people or peoples in translated form: they are offered for "reading" in a familiar idiom – the idiom of scientific taxonomy born of wondrous strangeness' (2006, 431f.).

This combination of offering strangeness together with scientific 'truth' is key to the appeal of the museum. The institution not only satisfies a desire for difference, but it also convincingly establishes the displayed cultural artefacts and traditions as 'heritage' to be commemorated. The museum, therefore, not only offers an experience of otherness, but also an experience of science and education. This process of assigning scientific value can be compared to Kirshenblatt-Gimblett's framing of heritage as a 'valued added industry' (cf. 1998, 150):

> Heritage organizations ensure that places and practices in danger of disappearing because they are no longer occupied or functioning or valued will survive. It does this by adding the value of pastness, exhibition, difference, and, where possible, indigeneity. (ibid.)

In the museum, the marketing of values of pastness or material significance are, interestingly, articulated much more explicitly than the values of difference and exoticness. This explicit emphasis on science rather than on the experience of otherness is evident, for instance, from the seemingly objective communication in the museums, as found in object labels that contain information on the materiality and the time of collecting, but do not explicitly refer to the objects' visible distinction from a perceived norm. As previously described with reference to the spatial design, an atmosphere of difference may predominantly be generated implicitly, for example, by the dimly lit exhibition rooms and their usage of 'boutique lighting' to stage the objects.

The guides, in contrast, refer more openly to the exoticness and difference of the represented cultural regions, which is evident from their references to 'strange objects' (cf. GSF2, 155), 'unmodern behaviour' (cf. GSE-MB, 112), or typical ways of sitting down in the respective regions (cf. GSE-MB, 229). In guided tours for school classes, it thus seems, expectations of the museum as a place that offers experiences of otherness are more openly met than in the exhibition spaces.

Considering these experiences of otherness, expectations surrounding the ethnographic museum can, to some extent, be compared to expectations of tourist experiences. Especially the focus on 'experience' has been described by Kirshenblatt-Gimblett as a process both observable in museums and in tourism (cf. 1998, 138). She argues that the shift of the museum towards visitor orientation has caused a movement away from a product-orientation towards market-led strategies, which are increasingly guided by active notions of doing rather than passive notions of seeing (cf. ibid., 137). Thus, the already discussed immersion of visitors in the 'world' that is represented in the museum is increasingly preferred to more passive and cognitive visits. Similarly, Pieterse notes that 'exhibitions are substitute tourism, feeding the hunger for difference, recreating the travel experience [...]' (2005, 166). Avoiding the trouble of travelling to distant countries, museum visitors can experience otherness as a fact, as an aesthetic product, as a comprehensive depiction – on their doorstep. The marketing of touristic experiences in the museum is not only visible in the variety of in-situ displays in the galleries, but also in the session formats that immerse the students in imaginations of 'being' in the countries represented in the exhibitions (see Chapter 4.6), for example by pretending to go on a journey through the world, or by dressing the students in non-European traditional costumes. In these instances, cultural difference becomes an experience for its own sake, a 'tourist destination' in Kirshenblatt-Gimblett's framing.

In order to understand the appeal of such experience-centred offers, the museum's focus on remote otherness, briefly mentioned in Chapter 3, may be an important starting point. As Akhil Gupta and James Ferguson have argued, distinct 'peoples' and 'cultures' are increasingly difficult to identify on the map, which is why ideas of culturally distinct regions become more salient (cf. 1992, 10). In competing with touristic experiences, museums may provide the advantage of offering more holistic, coherent, and distinct cultural experiences. In contrast, travelling to faraway countries may not provide the desired experience of cultural wholeness. As Kirshenblatt-Gimblett notes,

> [v]iewers might prefer the panorama of Naples to Naples itself because it is 'even more pleasant to look upon in Leicester Square, than is the reality with all its abominations of tyranny, licentiousness, poverty, and dirt'. (1998, 134)

Experiences in the museum may, thus, be preferred over 'real-life' tourism because only the museum's remote 'cultures' can meet still-existing public expectations or desires of cultural coherency, order, and distinct or visible otherness. Although the students in the guided tours cannot be expected to search for holistic, cultural experiences unavailable in tourism, the guides' communication of distinct otherness, visible in the practices mentioned above, can be connected to this expectation in so far as the development of the session formats might be partly informed by public ideas of the museum.

Finally, this expectation of remote and coherent cultural environments can also be connected to the framing of cultural life in the form of a tableau vivant: '[I]t is not enough, from the industry's perspective', writes Kirshenblatt-Gimblett, 'to open the bus and release tourists into the lifespace of their destination. [...] The industry prefers the world as a picture of itself – the picture window, cultural precinct, and formal performance' (ibid., 144). The argument that a picture of the world satisfies the desire for otherness again relates to the expected coherence of remote 'cultures'. This aspect has been addressed by Timothy Mitchell in *The World as Exhibition*. Related to colonialism and the practices of imagining the colonial Other, he argues that '[t]here was a contradiction between the need to separate oneself from the world and to render it up as an object of representation, and the desire to lose oneself within this object-world and to experience it directly' (1989, 231). In order to illustrate this point, a short anecdote he relates is inserted here:

> On his first day in Cairo, Gerard de Nerval met a French 'painter' equipped with a daguerreotype, who 'suggested that I come with him to choose a point of view.' Agreeing to accompany him, Nerval decided 'to have myself taken to the most labyrinthine point of the city, abandon the painter to his tasks, and then wander off haphazardly, without interpreter or companion.' Within the labyrinth of the city, where Nerval hoped to immerse himself in the exotic and finally experience, 'without interpreter,' the real Orient, they were unable to find any point from which to take the picture. [...] In the end they found themselves outside the city, 'somewhere in the suburbs, on the other side of the canal from the main sections of the town.' Here at last, amid the silence and the ruins, the photographer was able to set up his device and portray the Oriental city. (ibid.)

Corresponding to this ideal framing of cultures as remote and undisturbed by the messiness of everyday life, the museum as institution is expected, and often achieves, to provide at the same time an immersive experience in the represented non-European contexts as well as a distant 'viewpoint' from which 'cultures' can be comprehensively understood in safe abstraction and categorisation. Such a desire for a viewpoint may also affect the amplification of otherness in the guided tours, not only because the guides may cater to the ideas of otherness they anticipate, but also because this production of authentic, safely remote and ordered cultural experiences may affect their own understandings of the objects and exhibitions.

5.3.2 Spaces and Objects: Spatial Cues of Otherness and the Immersive Power of Gallery Spaces

Many of the aforementioned considerations surrounding the ways in which ideas about the museum as institution affect the amplification of otherness in the guided tours are closely related to spatial and object-related factors. While the previous section has predominantly focused on immaterial associations with museums as well on as self-understandings of the institution, the following elaborations discuss how the specific spatial design, the arrangement of the objects as well as the aesthetic function of the objects can affect the amplification of otherness in the guided tours.

As explained in the discussion of objects and spaces as factors in the performance of authority, it should be clear that the interpretation of meanings in museums and the experiences that visitors have in them are highly dependent on their individual prior knowledge and conceptions. However, objects and spaces, and particularly the atmospheres they constitute, can still highlight specific meanings. As Sandell explains, exhibitions

> contain spatial cues, deploy spatial strategies that, while unable to guarantee a given, preordained response in all visitors, can nonetheless privilege certain readings, and offer ways of thinking that can play a part in tackling prejudice. [...] These cues [...] must be understood not in isolation but in relation to the individual and social practices of the visitor and the multiple ways in which diverse audiences can draw on them to generate their own (prejudiced? liberal? contradictory?) accounts and meaning. (2005, 186)

While Sandell points to the positive agency that exhibition spaces can have in the provocation of visitor debates about social inequality and prejudice, this agency of the space can also be looked at from a more problematic perspective if these 'spatial cues' lead to an exoticising and distancing gaze in the ethnographic museum. This is especially noteworthy in so far as museum atmospheres are constituted by a variety of factors, not limited to exhibition rooms and objects, making it difficult to 'plan' or anticipate the impressions that result from them. For example, as already briefly mentioned, an exhibition room can have a completely different atmosphere depending on the number of visitors wandering through it, which is why the less frequented German museums in this study appeared much more like 'sacred spaces' than the two British museums.

The particular concern in this section is with the production of atmospheres of otherness. Such an atmosphere can be evoked not only by the emptiness of the buildings, but also by the use of dim lighting, the silence or the whispering of voices, the distance between the viewers and the objects, and the hall-like architecture of the galleries. In that sense, the staging of atmospheres of otherness is closely connected to the authority of the museum. For example, museum objects are rendered in a way that causes a desire for them, but this desire of possession, as Greenblatt has explained, is never fulfilled (cf. 1991, 49). This distance that is upheld between desire and possession – the impossibility of owning, of using the object – makes it 'other': Museum objects cannot be domesticated, appropriated and included in one's own life, which consequently marks them as 'different' from one's lifeworlds. However, in the ethnographic museum, this experience of object otherness can be turned into an experience of cultural otherness. A case in point is Fred Wilson's account of his experiment of arranging contemporary art in an ethnographic-looking gallery:

> When I placed the work in the ethnographic space, I would have visiting curators say with surprise, 'Oh, you have a collection of

> primitive art.' [...] The environment really changed the work; the labels just had the materials, not the names, because in most ethnographic museums [...] the labels don't have any names because the works were collected at a time when the names of the people who made the objects were not important. [...] The works became exotic, they looked like something made by someone you could never know; the works in many instances were dehumanized because of the way they were installed.' (Karp/ Wilson 1996, 252f.)

Of course, the artists that created the objects exhibited by Wilson had also worked on objects that, in his words, 'seemed to fit in an ethnographic museum' (ibid.). However, his experiment still shows that the museum's spatial as well as curatorial measures can assign 'otherness' to the objects (i.e., their unfamiliarity, their non-ordinary status, their value as evidence of history) and hence contribute to the perceived otherness of the people they are associated with.

Additionally, however, his experiment also shows that there seems to be an internalised 'feel' for what constitutes ethnographic objects – not only in terms of their staging but also in terms of their appearance. While this may be 'learned' in the museum, it is difficult for curators, for the same reasons as Wilson's visiting curators mistake contemporary art for ethnographica, to avoid repeating and reinforcing such preconceived mental images. This is not only because of visitor expectations, but also due to the objects' own social agency and presence. As Lidchi explains, '[t]heir physicality delivers a promise of stability and objectivity; it suggests a stable, unambiguous world' (1997, 162). In the atmosphere of the ethnographic museum, the objects' evidential and referential character contributes to the impression of cultural difference as static and clearly categorisable. This is, of course, further heightened by the logical and clear-cut arrangement of the artefacts. However, even this arrangement cannot be ascribed entirely to the agency of the curators. Accordingly, Peter Bjerregaard refers to an exhibition room he planned with a curatorial team, for which they had determined 'chaos' as its overarching principle. However, unintentionally and caused by time-pressure, '[...] we started to make up categories on the spot as we faced the thousands of objects taken out of the storage and brought into the exhibition hall' (2015, 55). In museums holding large amounts of non-European artefacts, it can hence be difficult to avoid strategies of ordering and compartmentalising.

As a result of these complex material and spatial dynamics, atmospheres of ordered and visibly distinct otherness can often be found in museums holding non-European objects. In the guided tours, these atmospheres affect the amplification of otherness when, for example, exhibition rooms are equated with cultural regions. In Feona's session, the students are supposed to find out '[…] how do we know that this is China' (GSF2-MD, 536), meaning that they are asked to find markers that show them that this exhibition room represents 'Chinese culture'. While this question already speaks to the translation of the gallery's focus on visible otherness to the guided tour, one student's answer is particularly telling. She points to a gate that is located on the second floor of the museum, which, due to the open architecture of the building, can be seen from the Chinese exhibition room. Feona answers: 'Do you know what, I think that's just a gate from the galleries upstairs. But it does look a bit Chinese' (ibid., 540-542). Here, on the one hand, the agency of the space becomes observable as the objects visible in (and from) the gallery are all marked as Chinese due to the labelling of the entire room. On the other hand, the social agency of objects is at play: The gate, normally functioning as a simple decorative element and not as an ethnographic artefact, evokes familiar ideas about 'Chinese' culture due to its ornate appearance. Thus, this situation also relates to the 'museum effect' that turns all objects in the museum into art (Alpers 1991, 27). As admitted by Feona, the gate *could* be part of the gallery, revealing that perceptions of non-Europeanness are not only intrinsic to the objects themselves (just like in Wilson's experiment), but go back to both spatial cues and general, internalised ideas about 'cultural style'.

Besides this dimension of the staging of cultural difference by means of spatial and object 'cues', another effect of spaces and objects on the amplification of otherness in the guided tour is the immersive experience that the spaces make possible. This is, for instance, achieved by means of the previously discussed in-situ displays. As Kirshenblatt-Gimblett explains, 'in situ displays are immersive and environmental. They privilege "experience" and tend to thematize rather than set their subject forth' (1998, 3). When, for instance, students walk through the reconstructed Oriental bazar street in Museum B, they not only 'see' otherness, but 'experience' it. Such experiences are staged to appear 'real', suggesting that the bazar street is more than just a representation. The in-situ display, thus, offers an experience of the world of the Other in a nutshell. Distinct otherness in a condensed and consolidated form 'comes alive' by means of the gallery design.

Another example of how atmospheres can be immersive and therefore lead to an elevation of difference can be found in Johan's session in the Africa section of Museum A. Having a Nigerian migration background, Johan refers to 'us' when he describes religion or cultural practices to the students in the African gallery. In the conversation before the start of the session, he explains that he likes to activate the students by dancing or singing with them. At various points of the sessions, he implements this, for instance, by comparing praying in Nigeria to 'rapping' and rapping a prayer for the students, or by performing a call-and-response with them (cf. GSJ-MA, 73, 92ff., 107ff.). On the one hand, besides activating the students and catching their attention, some of these practices, especially the performance of 'rapping', contribute to destabilising associations of African 'rituals' with past life, backwardness, and fixity. Johan shows the contemporaneity of Africa while the exhibition illustrates its past. Furthermore, by means of the students' active involvement, they not merely gaze passively at the African context, but take on another role and perspective.

One the other hand, while Johan's actions can thus be regarded as dedicated attempts to de-mystify representations of 'Africa', the atmosphere that frames these performances might again enmesh them in exoticness and difference. The exhibition room in the African gallery of Museum A is dark, the wall colours are black – the only light seems to come from the objects themselves. This visual impression already mediates fascination, peculiarity, and difference. As a further sensorial influence, unusual sounds of drums and percussions come from an exhibition room nearby and can be heard quietly in the background. The gallery is empty except for the school group and a museum guard. This entire atmosphere immerses the students in an experience of otherness which may overshadow and influence the meaning of Johan's actions. His performances of speaking melodically in Nigerian become part of the already present atmosphere and might, therefore, add to the experience of distinct otherness.

Sensory impressions that result from the spaces and the objects can hence be very powerful in immersing visitors in atmospheres of difference. Because such sensory means '[...] prompt physical memories and emotions' (Austin 2012, 108), they can reinforce and facilitate ideas of otherness that are already deeply embedded in collective understandings. Accordingly, some gallery educators carry spices for the students to smell in the India or Orient galleries of the museums. In a similar vein, the performance of 'traditional' greeting practices, practices such as 'sitting like the Chinese would sit', and the dressing up in all sorts of non-European traditional costumes reproduces common stereotypes of otherness – not only on a cognitive, but also on a bodily and sensorial level. The feeling of 'being' in the place that is exhibited thus becomes even stronger, and so does the encounter of a whole world of easily distinguishable otherness –

with its own scents, sounds, and visuality. While many education scholars have argued in favour of addressing the various senses in the museum (cf. e.g. Hein 1998, 165; Hooper-Greenhill 2000, 5; Golding 2012, 173ff.), these reflections raise the question to what extent there is a dilemma between the demand for more experiential and immersive educational offers and the requirement for a less exoticising and orientalising representation and mediation of non-European regions. This is particularly so as Bjerregaard points to the power of atmosphere over the spoken word: 'In fact, one may wonder whether audiences are more affected by the atmospheres in the museum than by what they are supposed to learn' (2014, 75). Is the experience-centred 'solution' of museum education really the best option for museums that offer up experiences of categorised, clearly demarcated otherness? This question will again be taken up in the next section.

5.3.3 Understandings of Learning: Authoritative Speech about the Other, Experiential Methods, and Intercultural Education

Understandings of learning have previously been discussed in this work with respect to the sessions' goal orientation that leads to a reduction of complexity, and with regard to the performance of authority by the guides through their disciplinary and seemingly omniscient self-representation. In addition, understandings of learning can be connected to the amplification of otherness in the guided tours. This is because, as Anthony Shelton has rightly argued, '[e]ducation is never disinterested, and museums transmit central fictions, on which a 'reality' is predicted and core institutional values, distinctions and identities are rationalized' (1995, 7). This rationalisation of identities, in particular non-European identities, unfolds through the guides' factual speaking about otherness, through the immersive methods they apply, and through the approach of intercultural education that their actions are based upon. These three influences are outlined in detail below.

The lecture-and-text learning style has been described in this work as a means of performing and substantiating not only educational, but also ethnographic authority. Due to the guides' factual and objective way of speaking, their statements about non-European contexts often seem unequivocal and certain. This performance of ethnographic authority can amplify the otherness of non-European groups by means of the positionalities of 'us' and 'them' that are subtly reinforced during the act of 'speaking about the Other'. As Alcoff remarks, '[w]ho is speaking to whom turns out to be as important for meaning and truth as what is said; in fact what is said turns out to change according to who is speaking and who is listening' (1992, 12). She explains that there is an inbuilt problem when 'First World persons' speak about a group in 'the Third World':

> For example, in a situation where a well-meaning First World person is speaking for a person or group in the Third World, the very discursive arrangement may reinscribe the 'hierarchy of civilizations' view where the United States lands squarely at the top. This effect occurs because the speaker is positioned as authoritative and empowered, as the knowledgeable subject, while the group in the Third World is reduced, merely because of the structure of the speaking practice, to an object and victim that must be championed from afar, thus disempowered. (ibid., 26)

In the observed guided tours, the situation is comparable, yet, even more problematic. The guides as speakers are already in a dominant position due to their 'First World' status and privilege. This dominance increases due to their function as gallery educators and due to the specific discursive situation of speaking to young, less-informed, but equally privileged students. Neither are the students in a position to criticise or even doubt the guides, nor is the constructed, dominant 'us' position apparent to the in-group of the guides and the students as it is not confronted and critically reflected as such.[93]

Following this argumentation, authoritative and holistic statements that the guides make about non-European regions may amplify non-European otherness especially because of these positionalities involved in speaking about Others. This is blatant in generalising statements of the guides, as, for example Eva's explanation that '[...] all Asians are floorsitters, by nature' (GSE-MB, 249-250) or Doreen's statement that '[w]hen the Indians are hit by a raindrop, they don't start crying like we do' (GSD-MA, 177-178). In these cases, the guides' authoritative position causes the above 'information' to appear 'true' while they in fact simply recreate broad stereotypical distinctions that have been learned and re-learned repeatedly. In these cases, it is mainly the lecture-and-text understanding of learning that positions the guide in an atmosphere of expertise. If the guides' accounts were not presented with zero focalisation, suggesting that they have complete insight in the life of the Other, there would be less room for self-contained statements about non-European groups and their amplified otherness.

Besides this traditional teaching style, other understandings of learning can also be problematic with regard to the amplification of otherness. Experiential learning is, for instance, closely connected to what has been described with respect to the immersive functions of exhibitions. Guides who use methods of experiential learning design their sessions by activating the students and thereby encouraging them to bodily engage with the represented reality. For instance, Johan's performance of rapping,

---

[93] This positionality is different in Gladys's, Hilda's, and Johan's sessions as the guides themselves are part of the represented non-European group. The positionality in these cases is less problematic with regard to Europeans speaking about non-Europeans. Yet, Alcoff's 'problem of speaking for others' is still apparent in these cases as the guides as individuals represent entire African countries. When they make seemingly omniscient and objective statements about Africa during their sessions, they, therefore, still amplify otherness.

Kate's provision of a variety of materials for the students to touch, as well as Maria's dressing-up-session with 'Muslim' and 'oriental' clothing, are cases in point. In these situations, the students are invited to 'absorb' the fabrics, the materials, and the soundscapes of the non-European worlds that are presented to them. Although widely proposed as a more active, cognitively engaged way of learning than the lecture-and-text style, this experiential learning can sometimes lead to the amplification of otherness. As the clothes that the students are asked to dress up in are, as previously discussed in Chapter 4.6, mainly 'traditional' in nature, the cultural experience is essentialising and causes distinction rather than negotiation.

The reason for the facilitation of such experiences in the guided tours is connected to the idea of confronting visitors or students with something new and exotic, giving them the chance to imagine what it would be like to 'be there':

> Many museum experiences offer opportunities to learn about alternative ways of living, and of making sense of the world, without the risks that might be involved in actual immersion in those alternatives. The visitor can maintain the present boundaries that define his or her personal identity, while becoming familiar with the fact that other people see things very differently. The museum visitor can act as an 'objective' observer, without risking being tainted by participation. This is a first step toward imagining the possibility that you might be different. (Rounds 2006, 146)

The problem implicit in Rounds' statement is that such experiences rest upon the assumptions that first, there are clearly definable 'alternative ways of living', and second, visitors will feel 'empathy' with the non-European contexts simply by 'experiencing' the exhibits. The first assumption refers to the issue of essentialism that has been discussed widely in this work. Although specific practices and 'ways of living' are certainly different from the ones the students are familiar with, the offered-up experience suggests that the entire region or group is categorically different from them. The second assumption refers to the question of whether a genuine change of perspective and the development of empathy is facilitated through the sensorial experience of non-European worlds. In relation to dressing-up, Julia Petrov argues that '[...] seeing the discarded clothes of another sparks also a desire to wear them, with the implication that one could almost become them by so doing' (2012, 237). She claims that the potency of museum display of dress consists in its communication of 'the intimate specifics of the past' rather than generalities (cf. ibid.). However, in relation to the educational practice of dress-up in the ethnographic museum, the relation between past and present is often unclear, and, as mentioned, the garments represent a general depiction of the respective region rather than historical and 'intimate' specifics. It is not that a variety of social identities become represented via these performances of clothing, but in most of the cases in question, traditionality and perceived typicality are highlighted. It is, therefore, doubtful whether a change in perspective will actually unfold via this type of experiential learning which often only confirms visual stereotypes and ideas about non-European otherness.

While it is, thus, possible to facilitate feelings of cultural empathy by means of education, the pitfall of a holistic and temporally indeterminate experiential learning process consists in its immersion of the students in a world of otherness that is already imagined before the encounter; a world which they may already know from Orientalist stories, media representations, and films. While such practices evoke a kind of empathy, this empathy is directed at fictional, romanticised, decorative Others, rather than real and diversified human beings. This is problematic because of the previously mentioned truth claim in the museum regarding a link between representation and reality: The students are told that the decorative figures whose perspective they take are in fact representative of the 'culture' represented. Students thus experience, feel like, and thus internalise the often generalised and essentialised non-European characters *as if* they were real.

This issue of experiencing a distinct and decorative otherness that is rendered as a fact is once again a matter of remoteness and immediacy. As long as romanticised, remote Others are experienced in a place devoid of immediate otherness, the imagination works. Yet, such imaginations may not be feasible once people associated with the represented regions may confront and make visible these generalising and essentialising practices. This imbalance becomes most visible when imagining that a student wearing a head scarf would be encouraged to dress up in different typically 'Oriental' headscarves as provided in Maria's session. While such a specific situation does not occur in the observed sessions, a previously mentioned conversation between the students and Gladys points to a similar paradox between the performative experience of distinct otherness and the actual identities of 'real' people: Gladys wants to hear 'foreign' words for 'grandma' and 'grandpa' from '[...] those of us who have grandmas and grandpas from cultures where we use that language like babushka or amma' (GSG-MC, 113-114). When the students do not provide the answers Gladys is looking for, she claims she *knows* that some of the students have these words in their 'own culture'. In this situation, students whom Gladys (visually) identifies as having a non-European background are asked to contribute 'their expertise' to the session, thereby functioning as representatives of the non-European regions. This is already problematic because, as Barbara Lutz-Sterzenbach, Ansgar Schnurr, and Bernd Wagner explain with reference to similar educational situations, '[…] whenever a divergent cultural identity of migrants appears unquestionable, cultural-ethnic otherness is powerfully produced as 'othering', the production of the Other' (2013, 18-19). But besides this dimension of 'othering', the described situation also reveals the incongruity of remote and immediate otherness. Most of the students in Gladys's session say 'grandma' and 'grandpa' instead of more foreign-sounding words, disappointing Gladys's expectation of distinct otherness. In this situation, immediate otherness reveals itself in its ambiguity, stratification, and complicatedness – which stands in stark contrast to the remote otherness offered in the museum. This may also be why Britta explains that it is a 'moment of shock' for her initially when she sees that many 'Asian students' participate in a session (cf. EIB, 340-341) or when Maria explains, after she has asked the children whether anyone in the group was 'Muslim', '[...] No-one? Okay, but then it is good, then we can engage with the topic collectively today' (GSM-MB, 158-159).

Thus, while experience-centred approaches can lead to a negotiation of meaning, as is the case in Feona's and Kate's facilitation of experiencing different materials of objects and relating these back to geographic and artistic conditions, this learning style can also again reinforce the production of stereotypes and the immersion of the students in a 'disneyfied' otherness. Once again, the disimprovement effect is at play: The guides aim at understanding and active experience, yet the result is often an essentialist construction of otherness. As Gorski explains, when he was young, 'Taco Nights' were held at his school in order to immerse the students in the experience of Mexico. He states:

> I am certain, all these years later, that the educators at Guilford did not intend to inflate the stereotypes about Chicana/os and Latina/os into which the media and my parents and church had been socializing me since birth. I am equally certain that they did not intend to reify my growing sense of racial and ethnic supremacy by essentializing the lives and diverse cultures of an already-oppressed group of people, then presenting that group to me as a clearly identifiable 'other.' But that is exactly what they did. (2008, 3)

In a similar vein, the guides do not intend to reinforce stereotypes by means of experiences such as dressing-up and performing distinct otherness. But that is exactly what happens.

Besides the focus on experience and immersion, another reason for this disimprovement effect can also be found in the intercultural education approach that some of the guides take. For the purposes of this work, it suffices to state that 'intercultural education' is understood as an approach that focuses on the mediation of knowledge, tolerance and respect for non-European people. Implicit in these notions are inbuilt problems of power and control, as Gorski describes: '[A]n intercultural education constructed on the basis of these visions becomes a tool for the maintenance of the very marginalization that progressive educational movements ought to dismantle' (Gorski 2008, 7). As explained above, this is due to the fact that 'visions' of cultural dialogue and diversity suggest an equal or balanced relationship between 'us' and 'them', thereby obscuring actual and still-existing power relations and an imbalance of authority.

Similarly, if the guides in the observed sessions use intercultural methods of teaching by celebrating non-European diversity or emphasising the achievements of the Other, cultural difference is neither analysed in a farther-reaching sense nor questioned as a fact. As already explained with respect to Eva's statement of 'different countries, different manners', such a promotion of tolerance is predicated on a cultural relativism that denies a genuine examination and discussion of specific practices. Instead, as Mohanty mentions, '[t]he goal is to overcome ethnocentrism and to promote tolerance, to 'gaze in wonderment' at the other, unwilling to judge – hastily or otherwise' (1995, 112). Thus, such intercultural learning strategies are informed by the demand for evoking positive ideas of otherness, for seeing non-European otherness as something colourful and unthreatening. Accordingly, Eva explains in the interview that she would like to promote 'openness for different cultures' (EIE, 324-325), Antonia wants to achieve a greater 'intercultural understanding' and tolerance (cf. EIA, 31ff.), and Britta wants to mediate 'a better understanding of the cultures' (EIB, 364-366). These vague and positive conceptions of their teaching goals point to the intercultural conception of learning and to the use of intercultural methods that avoid conflict and obscure continuing power relations. This is closely connected to what has been explained in relation to the expectations surrounding the museum as institution, which are guided by visitor desires to '[...] go to learn about other cultures rather than about themselves' (Rounds 2006, 107). This desire for learning about 'happy otherness', i.e. easily distinguishable but tolerable or commensurable otherness, can, for instance, be seen in the lack of discussions of repatriation claims in the exhibitions[94] and in the underrepresentation of social, temporal, and political stratifications and conditions of perceived otherness. Together with the guides' interculturally informed goals of promoting tolerance and positive understandings of otherness, this 'happy' focus of exhibitions can support the amplification of otherness in the guided tours.

Another feature of the guides' intercultural education methods, besides the concentration on tolerance and positive associations of otherness, consists in the idea that learning about the Other will have a positive effect on the students' perceptions of the Other. For instance, Britta explains that the reason for the school groups' interests in learning about the groups and the people (rather than about the objects) is that

> [...] one wants to show the students that there are different life forms. And we have, for example, here in [city name] so many people without a German passport [...]. This is our life world and actually one knows very little about one's neighbour who is Muslim, and there is the opportunity here in the museum to mediate this to some extent. (EIB, 329-335).

Once again, a relationship between immediate and remote otherness is established in the self-understandings and aims that Britta articulates. This idea of tackling 'one's own ignorance' and 'one's own fears of contact' through the encounter of the 'cultures of the Other' has been criticised by Evelyn Johnston-Arthur (cf. 2009, 16). She claims that such a focus on

---

[94] In this context, Kravagna makes the insightful point that a widely propagated 'inclusion of different voices' is only partially implemented in the museums: 'Today, the often invoked 'different voices' are integrated on a superficial level in order to render the museum in a multicultural light, by means of performing folklore, fashion shows or cooking [...]. Other 'different voices' that, for instance, make demands for repatriation or protest against exhibitions, are often oppressed in an arrogant way, just like it used to be the case before [...]' (2015, 99).

one's own lack of knowledge implies a naturally unmarked and neutral construction of 'us' as reference point – and a seemingly natural and visible otherness of those marked as 'them' (cf. ibid., 17): 'Being white is so supernatural, so self-explanatory, so normal, that it never has to be stated. In this light, the otherness of the always marked Other gains an extreme and simultaneously natural visibility' (ibid.).

Similarly, in Britta's statement, the assumption is that one knows more about neighbours not marked as 'Other' than one knows about the 'Other' neighbour. The feelings of distance and strangeness that the non-European neighbour evokes are regarded predominantly as a result of a lack of information. However, as Bauman has already clarified, '[t]he phenomenon of strangerhood cannot be [...] reduced to the generation of – however vexing – hermeneutic problems' (1991, 58). The marking of people as strangers would not be avoided if '[...] only I learned that languages [...], I studied those strange customs' (ibid.), but is tied to questions of social discourse, representation, power, and history. Moreover, in Britta's case, the assumption is even more problematic as she suggests that learning about remote Others in the museum could be a way of better understanding immediate Others in one's lifeworlds. However, the knowledge that is mediated in most of the museums part of this study is often not self-critical and self-conscious with respect to its own emergence and to the construction of the non-European Other as a category. Accordingly, Kravagna argues that the knowledge that has been produced on a colonial basis today still does more harm than good if neither the agents of knowledge production nor its interests are openly acknowledged in the museum (cf. 2015, 98). This lack of a self-critical engagement with the Other renders the methods of intercultural education and the promotion of tolerance in the observed sessions superficial and often involuntarily essentialist, thereby amplifying and compartmentalising otherness rather than mediating and negotiating perceptions related to it.

5.3.4 Understandings of Culture: Multiculturalist Othering and the Fascination with the Other

The final factor that is considered in the analysis of possible explanations for the amplification of distinct otherness in the observed gallery sessions revolves around understandings of culture held by the teachers, the guides, and even the students. In this section, many points that have already been addressed regarding culturalism, multiculturalism, and the desire for remote and ordered otherness would have to be repeated because these all amount to underlying understandings of culture that affect the gallery sessions. In order not to be repetitive, this subchapter only mentions these relations briefly and then places more attention on the broader question about a general public fascination with the non-European Other that might inform the formats and the performance of the guided tours.

As discussed in previous chapters, in the gallery sessions, cultures are often mediated as homogeneous entities. India is represented in terms of traditional and respectful greeting practices, saris or dhotis, as well as Hindu gods. Africa is framed in terms of masks, solidarity, and the poor-but-happy stereotype. This portrayal of clearly defined cultural distinction, however, stands in stark contrast to experiences of the transculturation, messiness, and heterogeneity of culture in the outside world. Pieterse concludes, therefore, that ethnographic museums now seem 'quaint' themselves, as they exhibit an idea of otherness left over from the past (cf. 2005, 164). Yet, it is questionable to what extent museums that still present distinct otherness are really 'outdated'. Certainly, ethnography and anthropology have long moved away from territorial, all-encompassing, 'authentic' or 'pure' fantasies of otherness: In academic discourse, the relegation of non-European groups to an unspecific time and to clearly categorisable identities is outmoded. Public representations and discourses, in contrast, still often market cultures as holistic entities, thereby portraying cultural identity as a given set of specific and unalterable traditions, values, and ideas – not to mention appearances. With respect to social discourse, the ethnographic museum's portrayal of categorical Others can thus be seen as 'right on time'. Dicks has shown that this disparity between academic and public discourse presents a problem for the ethnographic museum:

> Herein, however, lies a source of tension for museums. For, although the cultural mosaic view remains culturally dominant in popular touristic discourse, it has been subjected to thorough-going critiques within the world of anthropology over the past 20 years or so. [...] Yet, for many visitors, the belief that places and cultures are specifiably distinct from each other remains central to their idea of 'how the world is' (or should be). (2004, 149)

This 'idea of how the world is', which is based upon the idea of clearly defined cultures, can be regarded as one of the reasons for the uncritical reactions of the teachers and the students to culturalistic comments of the guides. As far as the mainstream public discourse is concerned, cultures with definite boundaries do exist.[95]

This apparently widespread understanding of distinguishable cultural identity in the public discourse must again be seen as affected by the dominance of multiculturalist frameworks of speaking about non-European culture. Not only in media representations, but also in self-representations of institutions and public festivals, representations and statements of colourful, traditional, and distinct otherness can be found. From the celebration of Holi festivals to cultural theme parks where visible difference is happily 'consumed' – the celebratory multiculturalist utopia of 'variety without antagonism' (Anderson 2011, 529) is still broadly enacted and performed. In this context, the focus on consumption is crucial. In the

---

[95] Again, in this context, it is important to note that the unambiguous cultural affiliations were also not questioned during the guided tours, either because there were no participants who identified themselves as non-European, or because these clear affiliations were regarded as a means of empowerment (i.e., in Gladys's session).

discourse on multiculturalism, cultural practices related to consumption and experience (cuisine, arts and crafts, festivals, clothing, rituals) are acknowledged and treated as part of a positive discourse about 'cultural diversity' while less easily appropriable dimensions of values and norms (religious requirements, gender relations, understandings of hygiene and beauty, economic differences) are not considered or treated as part of this discourse. This selective celebration has much to do with the superficially and additive 'consumable' nature of the 'misleading' model of multiculturalism. In order to celebrate Indian culture in the sense of cuisine, arts, and festivals, it is not necessary to abandon or question one's own values. Instead, cultural practices marked as decoratively 'Other' are added to the realm of the self. Norms and values, however, are more mutually exclusive and are, therefore, often omitted from multicultural celebrations.[96] Ahmed criticises this conception of difference in multiculturalism:

> The claiming of difference as that which 'we' have involves the erasure of differences that cannot be absorbed into this 'we'. Furthermore, differences become immediately defined in terms of 'lifestyles', ways of being in the world that find easy commodification in terms of an aesthetics of appearance [...]. (2000, 96)

Not only are 'cultural differences' reduced to easily accessible and a 'not so different at all' logic, but in the course of that process, a discourse on the more critical dimensions of 'otherness' that would necessitate a questioning of oneself is also avoided and prevented. In this sense, ethnographic museums can be seen as places fulfilling the public ideal of

---

[96] At this point, one could argue that the guides' references to the moral superiority of the Other object this model of celebratory multiculturalism. However, due to their selective appropriation of non-European social values, the guides can project 'our' overarching moral values, such as respect for one's elders and solidarity, onto the Other. Their explanations are thus not to be understood as a deeper reflection of the respective non-European values, but again as a decorative consumption of what is imagined as 'their culture'. Such a celebration of easily appropriable 'values' can also be seen in the widespread 'adoption' of Buddhist 'mindfulness' as a stress-releasing practice in Europe and the US.

being confronted with otherness without being confronted with one's own views and norms: once again, to learn 'about other cultures rather than about [oneself]' (Lidchi 2006, 107).

In the guided tours, this lack of controversial or self-reflective discussions has already been addressed. Despite all the references to 'their' culture, 'we' are rarely mentioned. A genuine change of perspectives can, therefore, not unfold. This observation has also been made by Heidi Layne and Amikeng Alemanji in their analysis of children's literature in Finland. They have found that, while children's books can be used as a tool for handling topics like racism and exclusion, there is a danger of ignoring key issues, such as the 'us/ them boundaries' by representing and offering a 'positively happy but somewhat naïve perspective of the world' (2015, 192).

The amplification of distinct and celebratory otherness in the guided tours is not exclusively connected to such multiculturalist understandings of culture, but can also be explained by a more general fascination with the non-European Other in public discourse. While this fascination and exotisation may also play into the celebratory function of multiculturalist agendas, it is here regarded as a separate aspect because it is not related to an actual presence or confrontation with the Other, but rather to the preceding imagination of and desire for conspicuous otherness.

This fascination with the Other is difficult to grasp because it is not predominantly evident from the explicit statements that the guides or the teachers make, but it is more closely connected to their implicit ways of speaking about non-European regions and people, and from their body language and habitus. Antonia and Doreen, for instance, often lower their voices when they speak about remarkable aspects of the Other, Gladys and Eva euphorically perform the Other by doing yoga (Eva) or changing their accent (Gladys), and Maria is wearing so-called 'harem trousers'

382

while performing her session in the Orient gallery of Museum B. Obviously, these are all extremely vague markers: Harem trousers are rather popular today and are worn outside conspicuously 'Other' environments. However, these aspects may serve as a hint to the factor that is so difficult to circumscribe and to describe comprehensively: The guides themselves find pleasure in the otherness they mediate.

This pleasure of otherness is connected to the proposition of commensurability and celebration that multiculturalism puts forward. But it is also more than that. As is argued here, this pleasure derives from a triad of nostalgia, exoticism, and stranger fetishism.   Nostalgia can be regarded in this context as connected not only to the perceived 'authenticity' of non-European worlds, but also to the pleasure of indulging in imaginations of a bygone time, an ordered reality, something definitely 'Other'. This argument has, for instance, been brought forward by MacCannel, who relates the quest for authenticity in tourism to increasing anxieties about the authenticity of social relationships in modern society (cf. 1999, 93). In the museum, such an illusion of authenticity can be consumed and imagined, seemingly offering an order in the chaos of constant transformation and fast-paced lifestyles. This nostalgia for authenticity is, therefore, not least informed by an availability of such 'imagined pasts'. As Appadurai has argued, '[...] Americans themselves are hardly in the present anymore as they stumble into the megatechnologies of the twenty-first century garbed in the film-noir scenarios of sixties' chills, fifties' diners, forties' clothing, thirties' houses, twenties' dances, and so on [...]' (1996, 30). In a similar vein, Ahmed refers to the BBC show *The Happiness Formula*, in which the narrator explains that we need to 'put glue back into communities' (cf. 2007, 122). The show thus depicts '[...] a world where people are less physically and socially mobile as a happier world, offering a romantic image of a French village, where people stay put over generations, as if happiness itself resides in staying put' (ibid.). Hence, nostalgia for the life of the Other is predicated on a perceived loss or shortcoming perceived on the part of one's own life, but also on the impression that these 'Other' lives, or at least that which is considered enviable, are available for consumption.

While exoticism equally '[...] evokes a sensibility, and uses objects to construct a conceptual line of escape out of Western culture into a titillating, yet manageable other', as Root has argued (1989, 78), it is inspired not only by ideas of escape and orderliness, but also by perceptions of mystery and opacity. This fabrication of mysteriousness is already apparent in traditional practices of ethnographic museums to make the objects seem more mysterious and 'tribal', such as photographing newly arrived objects from non-European regions in front of red backgrounds (cf. Deliss/ Mutumba 2014, 147). This pleasure of experiencing the exotic is also evident from the teachers' desired focus on 'masks' in the Africa section, or when the students are spellbound while watching an ethnographic film about African mask dances in Johan's session (cf. GSJ-MA, 150-153). Mystery and secrecy are also implied by the lowering of the guides' voices, or by Antonia's explanation of the concept of initiation, including her statement that 'I will tell you this when you are older in more detail [...]' (GSA-MA, 255). In this situation, the lure of the unknown and secret is performed, and exoticness is created. This desire for exoticness, however, is nothing new. As Kirshenblatt-Gimblett notes, '[...] we have long valued the inscrutable strangeness of the exotic as an end in itself [...], and many multicultural festivals today still feed this appetite while at the same time encouraging understanding and reflection by offering 'interpretation'' (1998, 72). The same can be applied to museums. They feed this peculiar 'appetite' for the mysterious, however, under the guise of knowledge and comprehension.

Finally, both exoticism and nostalgia are predicated on the conviction that there is indeed a 'culture' or 'group' that is Other. This idea of the Other as a clearly definable and bounded 'figure' compares to Ahmed's notion of stranger fetishism. Although her concept of the 'stranger' is much broader than this work's focus on the construction of non-European otherness, the workings of stranger fetishism can be applied to the analysis in the sense of an 'otherness fetishism'. Translating Marx's commodity fetishism to a 'fetishism of figures', Ahmed argues that stranger fetishism displaces social relations of labour in the course of transforming objects into figures:

> What is at stake is the 'cutting off' of figures from the social and material relations which over- determine their existence, and the consequent perception that such figures have a 'life of their own'. Stranger fetishism is a fetishism of figures: it invests the figure of the stranger with a life of its own insofar as it cuts 'the stranger' off from the histories of its determination. (2000, 5).

Through detaching 'strangers' from the processes that turn them into 'strangers', even more so by *forgetting* these processes (cf. ibid., 9), it is possible to fixate strangeness unquestionably onto 'their' bodies. In a similar vein, the guided tours as well as the museum spaces proceed from the idea of an existence and distinctiveness of otherness that is always already presupposed. The discursive strategies of 'othering' that initially produce this presupposition are neither laid bare nor reflected upon. Thus, when Feona dresses a student in a turban and thus recreates a common image of Oriental otherness, this otherness is taken for granted. The socio-historical reasons and usages or functions of turbans, their emergence of a symbol of the 'Oriental' in the West, and their embeddedness in transcultural production processes and capitalist marketing are not addressed. Sure, it may not be possible to comprise this complexity during a five-minute stay at one station of the guided tour, however, in its illustrative and performative workings, the method is informed by the perceived clarity of the figure of the Oriental Other. Likewise, once the student is dressed in a turban, other classmates shout out: 'You look like a genie' (GSF2-MD, 409). The evocation and naturalisation of the figuration of the Other is, thus, also inspired by and reflected in visitor expectations. As Wagner explains with respect to the North American Indian exhibition in the *Ethnological Museum* in Berlin, '[...] parents often complain that the exhibition does not live up to their expectations of a representation of North American Indians, but overstrains the children with ambiguous meanings. Perhaps it is predominantly the adults who value coherent boundaries [...]' (2010, 196). The publicly accepted premise that there are distinct non-European Others in the first place, hence, underlies much of the museum's communication and is often expected by parents and teachers. Its integrity is not merely constructed in the guided tours, but a prerequisite for an interest in and demand for these gallery sessions.

In its interplay, this triad of nostalgia, exoticism, and stranger- or otherness fetishism that amounts to the aforementioned pleasure of speaking about, describing, explaining, and performing the non-European Other. The fact that there are repeating patterns of communicating non-European otherness in the guided tours suggests that this pleasure not only rests upon stereotypes of Others communicated in capitalist and media discourses, but also relies upon a publicly imagined, concrete, not arbitrary figuration of the Other. The amplification of otherness in the guided tours is then dependent on the production and reproduction of an easily commensurable, ordered, happy, mysterious, and clearly definable, unquestioned non-Europeanness, which is socially accepted and desired. This kind of 'happy otherness', closely interrelated with social and political agendas of cohesive communities, is made visible and brought to life in the ethnographic museum. The remote otherness that is presented here can remain as remote as necessary, but can also be approached and embodied if needed. The guided tour then facilitates the familiarisation of students with an otherness that is 'made safe' – which, of course, implies that immediate otherness can be dangerous and unpleasant.

6 Reflections: Main Findings, Contributions, and Suggestions for Future Research

The previous two chapters have intensively discussed how and why a 'status of otherness' is assigned to the people and regions illustrated during school guided tours in museums holding non-European objects. The concluding chapter of this work serves to synthesise and contextualise the main findings and to discuss whether ethnographic museums can avoid the pitfalls of communicating non-European otherness that have been outlined.

The chapter begins by acknowledging once again the two different European contexts in which research has been conducted. Because of the similarities in the accounts of the guides in the British and the German museums, the differences between the two countries' museum landscapes have not been considered extensively in the analytical chapters. To explain in more detail in how far local and national variances may still cause different ways of communicating otherness in the German and the British museums, the reflection pays special attention to these aspects.

Subsequently, the similarities of the analysed cases and the common patterns of speaking about non-European regions that have been found are again summarised. In so doing, the broader findings of this work that relate to overarching dynamics of constructing non-European otherness are presented and reflected upon. One of the main findings in this regard is that the communication of otherness in the gallery sessions cannot only be explained by organisational and contextual factors, but is also affected by socially accepted understandings of distinct and commensurable non-European otherness. This demand for and supply (as well as marketing) of remote, uncontroversial, and decorative otherness in the ethnographic museum is regarded in light of a consumption-oriented, experience-centred, and authenticity-driven relationship with otherness under the guise of multiculturalist discourses surrounding diversity, tolerance, respect, and cultural celebration.

From this line of argumentation, the question of the possibility for change and intervention emerges as a concluding debate in this work. Can educators in ethnographic museums avoid the illustrated 'disimprovement effect' and what could be strategies to achieve this? In relation to this question, the importance of a more comprehensive scholarship on museum communication is emphasised. While museum education scholars have focused mainly on educational methods, and scholars criticising museum representations have largely bypassed the topic of education and mediation, this work argues in favour of a more inclusive take on the communication of otherness in museums. In so doing, the argument is made that new educational methodologies, such as the previously mentioned free choice learning or experiential learning, may not necessarily be sufficient to avoid essentialist identity ascriptions in guided tours for school classes.

Despite this critical argumentation, the elaborations do not end on a negative note. By referring to and introducing examples of moments in the guided tours that contribute to more genuine processes of cultural negotiation and hybridity, the work argues that essentialist, generalising, decorative, and uncritical accounts about non-European regions can be reduced. Suggesting that a transcultural approach can be used as a method to critically reflect upon taken-for-granted views of seemingly static non-Europeanness, the work concludes by providing recommendations for further research in the areas of museum representation and transcultural education.

6.1 Disparities in the Research Results of the German and British Guided Tours: Organisational, Methodological, and Historical Reasons

What may have fallen short in the analysis of patterns of communicating non-European otherness and their reasons is a detailed differentiation of observations in the German and in the British museums. This is because all of the described themes and practices of speaking about otherness and the factors influencing these ways of speaking can be traced, at least to some extent, in both the German and British museums part of this case study. Due to the focus of the analysis on communicative patterns, the focus has been placed on these broader similarities rather than on smaller-scale differences. Nevertheless, as observations of several guided tours only took place in four museums, it is important to explain in more detail the distinctions between the observed phenomena. While this is not directly relevant in order to present overarching ways of communicating otherness in guided tours for school classes (because the quantity of observed patterns is not as important as their repeated occurrence in connection to different non-European contexts and in statements of different guides), a reflection of differences between the case studies helps to provide a more comprehensive framework to understand the findings of the analysis as well as their implications.

With regard to the documented themes and practices of communicating non-European otherness, there is a slight imbalance of occurrences of these patterns in the German and the British museums. Whereas all of the seven principles of communicating otherness can be found in the British museums, they are often more frequently and more distinctly evident in the German cases. This is also visualised in Figure 6.1 (see next page) which shows the number of guided tours in each of the two countries that contain the respective patterns. As the graph shows, compared to the German sessions, fewer of the British guided tours contain references to the described principles.

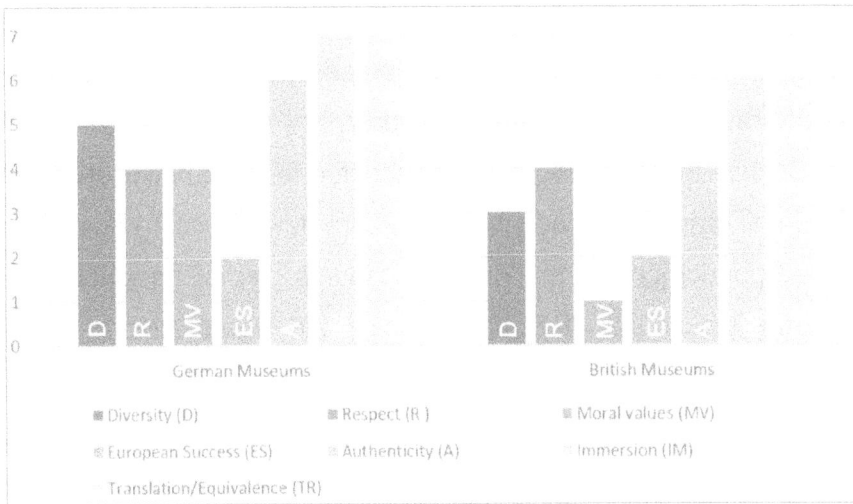

Fig. 6.1. Distribution of patterns of communicating otherness in the observed sessions, differentiated according to the German and British museums part of this study. The diagram shows the respective number of guided tours in which the specific pattern could be observed. In each of the countries, seven different guided tours had been observed.

Although the graph indicates that there is a slight imbalance of occurrences, this visual representation cannot really account for a deeper understanding of the differences that exist between the two case studies. Firstly, this is because the graph only tracks whether or not a certain principle appears in the guided tours – *not* the frequency of occurrences within the individual sessions. This is due to the issue of quantifying qualitative observations. Within each session, ambiguous as well as unambiguous occurrences of the phenomena can be found. It would thus be difficult to decide which of the guides' explanations 'count' as separate occurrences of the phenomena. Secondly, the graph does not acknowledge the context and the conditions of the sessions. Hence, two corrections have to be added. On the one hand, within each of the sessions that contain the described principles, there are numerous examples of the same principle to be found. On the other hand, due to the scripted nature of the British sessions, two sessions that were observed in the British museums followed the same format, meaning that the two occurrences of the European success story in the British museums refer to the same historical information in the same guided tour format which is, however, presented by two different guides.

Despite these inadequacies connected to the quantification of the results in a graph, the fact that there are fewer occurrences of the described phenomena in the British museums cannot be ignored. This discrepancy results both from differences in the organisation of the case studies and from diverging organisational and institutional conditions in Germany and Great Britain. These are briefly discussed below.

First, due to reasons described in Chapter 2, the process of selecting guided tours to observe was more restricted in the British cases than in the German ones. As a result of a lack of flexibility of observing British sessions (due to the organisation of separate research stays instead of spontaneous visits like in the German museums) and of a greater determination of the selection process by the British learning departments, the students in these sessions were younger than those in the German case study. Furthermore, in Museum D, organisational challenges resulted in the observation of only two guides who taught sessions with the appropriate thematic focus on non-European regions. As guides in Museum D have to be able to teach all available session formats for Key Stages 1 and 2, the observations of Feona and Kate included many different sessions, but the criterion of observing three guides with three different focuses was not fulfilled in this case. Although a third guide, Lynn, was observed in Museum D, she delivered a session that addressed European and British history, which is why this session was excluded from the analysis (yet, the interview was included). These problems of sampling partially explain the lower number of occurrences of the described patterns in the British sessions. For instance, it is possible to argue that sessions for younger students are more focussed on games and activities rather than entailing descriptions of non-European lifeworlds, which is why these guided tours show not as much evidence for the described motifs and practices.

These organisational reasons can, however, not solely explain the differences in the findings. Even though Gladys's session is catered to younger students, it contains much evidence of the presented patterns of speaking about non-European otherness. A more convincing explanation for the disparity between German and British museums can be found in the conceptions of the British sessions and the organisation of museum education in the British museums. As explained in Chapter 5, the sessions in the British museums are generally more standardised because they are developed by the learning departments, often to cater specifically to the British national curriculum. For instance, one of the sessions in Museum C is specifically catered to explain the history of the kingdom of Benin on the basis of the Benin plaques and another session has been developed to combine the use of digital devices with information about clothing in North America. Instead of providing a general introduction to an entire region or 'culture', as is the case in most of the German guided tours, the British sessions are more thematically focused. In addition to this thematic focus, in Museum D, the distinctiveness and specificity of the sessions is further related to the agenda of the museum. As an arts and design museum, its educational goals centre around the exploration of artistic practices and materials rather than on learning about 'different cultures'.

Despite these implications, this factor should not be overestimated. It would be misconceived to assume that broader cultural statements are entirely prevented by a more specified thematic orientation of the gallery sessions. As the graph shows, the British sessions still include occurrences of the recurring patterns. However, these occurrences are more frequent in the German sessions than in the British ones. Especially in the context of Museum D, conclusions about cultural practices always derive from an engagement of the school group with the objects and their materiality, which focuses cultural statements on a specific artefact rather than generalising it. Because of its potential to avoid broad cultural generalisations, this focus on the objects is taken up again later on in this reflection.

A final reason for the disparity between the British and the German cases is connected to the disciplinary background or training of the guides. As discussed in Chapter 5, the gallery educators in the German museums were usually trained in ethnology or in a connected discipline whereas the British guides were predominantly trained as teachers, museum studies professionals or storytellers. Especially in Museum D, where two of the three interviewed guides saw themselves as educational experts, and the third identified herself as having a background in arts, the gallery educators almost never made additional comments regarding the beliefs, cultural practices or 'ways of life' of non-European groups unless such insights were connected to specific objects or to a historical context. The same is true for Isabel in Museum C as she always situated her statements about non-European practices in the historical framework addressed in the session. Some of the guides' comments nevertheless fit the described patterns (e.g., evoking respect, performing otherness, translating the Other), however, they usually do not amount to the kind of broad and generalised cultural narratives often included as a side note in the German sessions.

In general, it seems that, while a certain amount of constructing otherness can be observed in all of the sessions (i.e., the dressing up in non-European garments was practised in the German and the British museums alike), more essentialist statements about the everyday and contemporary lifeworlds of the groups exhibited in the museums can predominantly be found in those sessions that are led by guides who perceive themselves as ethnographic experts. This observation is true for both Hilda and Gladys (as cultural 'insiders'), as well as for the German guides who, due to their knowledge and field experience in the respective regions, consider themselves capable and eligible to describe the regions in broader terms. This point is controversial. What it does not mean to suggest is that ethnologists are more prone to making essentialist statements than educators. The described difference is not so much about actual expertise and training as it is about self-perception and seeming entitlement. Guides who perceive themselves as knowledgeable with respect to a certain region may dare to make more assertive statements about it. As a consequence, their accounts include more references to 'cultures' as wholes, simply because these guides have a more holistic understanding of these regions due to their personal experience and prior knowledge.

Besides these organisational differences between the case studies, there is another possible set of explanatory factors that may be related to the presented disproportions of the findings. Local varieties of the communication of non-European regions can also be explained by the differences of the ways in which ethnographic museums and museum education have emerged and developed in Great Britain and in Germany.

Clearly, there are various differences between the development of ethnographic museums and museum education in Germany and Great Britain. For instance, in the 19th century, due to the focus in German ethnography on 'saving vanishing cultures' (as against the British focus on evolutionary approaches), ethnographic museums and collections in Germany grew much more extensively than their British counter parts. As Shelton concludes from an estimation of a curator at the British museum, '[…] in 1898, the collections of the Berlin Museum alone were "six or seven times as extensive" as those in London' (2006, 69). Furthermore, after World War II, the development of museums in both countries took different paths. Due to decolonisation and the ensuing crisis of representation in anthropology, which caused a reorientation of anthropology in terms of a more dialogical, inclusive, and self-critical approach (cf. Brenner 2014, 49f.), ethnographic museums in Great Britain slowly replaced evolutionist with functionalist representations (cf. Shelton 2006, 72) whereas museums in Germany included sociological perspectives, debating contemporary global issues in order to stay relevant (cf. ibid., 73). Relevance was also a problem for ethnographic museums In Great Britain: The *Imperial Institute* had to close due to a decline in public interest. The crisis that had thus befallen ethnographic museums in the 1970s and 80s was negotiated by museums in similar ways. For example, aesthetic approaches, though criticised by anthropologists, were introduced by some museums both in the German and in the British context (cf. ibid., 75). Still visible differences between the museums in both countries that can be regarded as a result of this crisis are located on the level of the organisational structure of the museums. Whereas in Germany, ethnographic museums are mainly public institutions funded by the state or federate states, in the British context, funding has been increasingly ensured by means of a cooperation with private investors and interest groups. Hence, the British non-European galleries are still often funded by private investors or, as Shelton notes, foreign national organisations (cf. ibid.).

Although these differences with regard to the development of ethnographic museums in Germany and Great Britain explain, for instance, why there are more such museums in Germany, why aesthetic approaches coexist with anthropological approaches in both contexts, and why renovation and refurbishment was possible more extensively in the British context, these differences are only loosely linked to the slight disparities in the results of the findings of this work. One could argue that the thematic orientation of Museums C and D is connected to the lower number of specifically ethnographic museums in Great Britain as a whole. If a larger number of ethnographic museums was distributed across Great Britain, it would have been possible to observe sessions in a more specifically ethnographic museum. However, this is only a very weak link, especially as Museums C and D do contain artefacts from ethnographic and colonial expeditions and further categorise them according to regional categories. Although both museums adopt a more aesthetic approach, such approaches can partially also be found in Museums A and B. Thus, differences between the organisational contexts described above can, to some extent, be explained by the development of ethnographic museums in Great Britain and in Germany, but these developments are neither absolutely consistent within the countries not can they serve as clear differentiating markers.

Another interesting aspect is the influence of the development of museum education on the differences in the research results. In Great Britain, there has been a more intensive development of learning in the museum, not least because of the government's 'Museum and Gallery Education Programme', launched in 1999, which supported institutions in the structural development of educational projects (cf. Black 2005, 157). This support has not only promoted the establishment of learning departments as key components of the museum, but also facilitated the provision of additional spaces available for education. Although such a coordinated effort to foster museum education has not been implemented in Germany, learning in museums is also increasingly valued as an important aspect of museum work in the German museums. This is apparent, for example, from the 'Survey of Museums in Germany' of 2014.[97] According to the museums participating in this survey, the second most important factor contributing to an increase in visitor numbers is the extension of museum educational and public programmes (cf. Institut für

---

[97]Original: Statistische Gesamterhebung an den Museen der Bundesrepublik Deutschland. The survey is conducted every year by the Institute of Museum Studies (Institut für Museumsforschung) of the SMB. The most recently published issue 69 presents data collected in 2014.

Museumsforschung 2015, 16).[98] Annette Noschka-Roos and Doris Lewalter have summarised this increasing awareness of the necessity to address and invite visitors to engage with museums as the result of an advancement of 'visitor-orientation' in German museums (cf. 2013, 202). However, due to a less specified funding of museums (i.e., state support is not connected to museum educational expansion), the learning departments as well as the spaces available for education are less well-equipped than in the British cases.

This organisational difference with respect to museum education can be connected to what has been explained regarding the more specified, curriculum-oriented, and educational sessions in the British museums. The British sessions are conceptualised predominantly in terms of educational criteria (i.e., inquiry-based learning, experiential learning, discovering materials) while the German sessions often seem to prioritise information (i.e., mediation of facts about non-European regions). This disparity can further be related to a farther-reaching history in the British context of efforts to professionalise museum education. For instance, the so-called Rosse Report of 1963 has led to the early formation of school-museum partnerships (cf. Hooper-Greenhill 2007, 25). In addition, the School of Museum Studies at the *University of Leicester* has already been established in 1966. As stated in the beginning, many of the guides observed in the British museums have a degree in this or similar programmes related to museum studies. In contrast, in Germany, gallery educators are still recruited from (regional) subject disciplines (cf. Bystron/ Zessnik 2014, 323). Although there are many universities that offer programmes in museum studies and museum education in Germany, the heads of the learning departments of Museums A and B reported that they prefer employing facilitators with a disciplinary background in ethnology or

---

[98] The most important factor is considered to be the realisation of large special exhibitions.

area studies. Furthermore, with regard to the school-museum-relationship, due to the lack of a specific curriculum link between the sessions and the work done at school, a visit to the ethnographic museum is not a common and oft-practised activity in German school contexts.

These disparate ways in which museums and museum education have developed in Great Britain and in Germany, thus, affect the slightly lower number of occurrences of the seven principles of communicating non-European otherness in the British sessions. However, what becomes apparent when comparing these conditions with the research results is that, regarding the organisational and thematic varieties in the German and British museums (fewer decidedly ethnographic museums in Great Britain, differences in the disciplinary backgrounds of museum educators, a clearer focus on educational approaches in the British cases, a more coordinated curriculum-link of the British sessions), there are not 'enough' disparities between the guides' ways of communicating non-European otherness. In contrast, while there are differences in terms of the frequency of occurrences, all of the described phenomena can be found in both the British and the German museums. Why is it that, despite the historical, methodological and organisational differences, ways of communicating otherness are still so similar? This aspect is discussed in the next section.

6.2 Similarities of the Case Studies Despite Conceptual Differences: Trustworthiness, Happy Otherness and Multiculturalism

Despite the various differences in terms of the history, organisation and educational methodologies of the German and the British guided tours, many similarities can be found in the ways in which gallery educators communicate non-European otherness.

Firstly, as ways of communicating non-European regions, such as playing dress-up, telling fictional stories, and pretending to go on a journey, recur in different guides' accounts with varying regional focuses, it appears that there are overarching modes of constructing and reproducing non-European otherness among the 14 observed sessions. Furthermore, similar characterisations of non-European contexts can be found in accounts about varying geographical regions. Descriptions of non-European moral superiority, for instance, appear in British and German sessions about China, Africa, India, and North America. In a similar vein, references to the diversity of broader regions can be found in almost all of the observed sessions. This similarity of motifs in British and German accounts about varying non-European contexts indicates that the non-European Other is, at least to some extent, maintained as a unified figure which serves as a projection surface for nostalgic imaginations of authenticity and community. This still-existing typification and figuration of non-European otherness confirms Bowman's argument that '[i]n today's anthropology the other still remains culturally 'in place' despite the evidence on the thoroughfares of any First World metropolis that his or her locale now overlaps spatially with our own' (2007, 41f.). Even though a fixation and consequent 'othering' of non-European contexts is increasingly questioned and avoided in anthropology, this development has not yet reached the guided tour as a segment of communicating anthropological knowledge to the public.

As a second similarity and continuity of the observed sessions, the underlying factors of the performance of authority, the reduction of complexity, and the amplification of otherness can be traced in both the British and the German sessions. Differentiations exists on a lower level, as has been shown with respect to ethnographic authority, which is more prevalent in the accounts of the German than in those of the British guides. Yet, these core factors play a crucial role in all of the sessions; be it in the form of time constraints that cause a reduction of complexity, or in the form of understandings of culture that evoke an amplification of difference.

A final similarity of the German and the British sessions consists in the disimprovement effect. In most of the conducted interviews, the guides explain that they aim at fostering mutual understanding, awareness of diversity and explorative potentials. Yet, in promoting diversity and respect for the non-European contexts, they often 'end up' reinforcing stereotypes, constructing ideas of authentic otherness, and repeating expectations of the museum as a reliable and infallible narrator. The disimprovement effect can be observed at different levels of the guided tours, for instance, on the level of cultural translation, on the level of expectations of the museum as institution, or on the level of teaching methods. The common denominator of all the sessions lies in the dilemma that the guides explicate their open-minded, antiracist, constructivist agendas while finally communicating authoritative and essentialist messages.

This disimprovement effect is not specific to the guided tour, but can be interpreted as one of the main pitfalls of intercultural communication, and, in particular, of museum communication in the ethnographic museum. For example, with respect to developing museum representations that avoid casting anthropology as the 'science of strange peoples' (Antweiler 2015, 120), Christoph Antweiler has proposed a focus in exhibitions on patterns of diversity and on cultural comparisons (cf. ibid.). While he argues that this method should not overemphasise strangeness, he does hold that it should draw on an interest in exoticism (cf. ibid.). The challenge lies exactly in this focus on the appeal and celebration of the exotic. While approaches that work with positive stereotypes of otherness may serve to evoke affirmative perceptions of non-European groups and may, thus, avoid eurocentrism, these communicative methods also work to establish ethnocentrism by suggesting that 'cultures' can be ascribed to specific, self-contained, static, and internally homogeneous traits of identity and practices.

Such more overarching pitfalls of conceiving of non-European contexts have been shown to affect the gallery sessions considerably. While the working conditions of the guides, the spatial design of the galleries, and the understandings of learning embedded in the guided tours are significant influencing factors, broader social ideas surrounding the representation of non-European culture have emerged in the analysis as especially noteworthy. The importance of these broader social expectations, including ideas surrounding the museum as institution and understandings of non-European culture, derives, for one thing, from the fact that these ideas are also traceable in the more immediate factors of the working conditions, the gallery design, and the teaching practices. The gallery design, for instance, echoes certain expectations of the museum and understandings of culture. Even the working conditions of the guides can be connected to expectations of the museum as a research-intensive, collection-based institution rather than as an educational space. For another thing, the role of the factors of understandings of culture and expectations surrounding the museum is especially significant because, while specific differences between museums can be traced with respect to the spatial organisation, working conditions, and teaching practices, these expectations of museums and distinct culture are more widely shared across different museums and national borders.

In the following, three aspects, that are considered the most important findings with respect to conceptions of ethnographic museums and culture, are briefly summarised. These include the role of the museum as a reliable mediator of knowledge, the marketing of easily commensurable and remote otherness, and multiculturalist frameworks of celebrating non-European culture. With respect to the third research question of this work, which is based upon the reconstruction of influences of the guides' accounts, these three notions are considered as the core findings. The preference of these core findings in terms of more abstract notions of shared understandings can be explained by the argument that will be made in Chapter 6.3, namely that an improvement of the guides' working conditions and an adoption of new teaching methods is not sufficient to avoid the typification and generalisation of non-European otherness in guided tours for school classes in ethnographic museums.

First, the expectation of the museum as a reliable, trustworthy institution has been discussed in relation to its cultural authority and its offer of neatly framed, ordered, and uncontroversial experiences of non-European otherness. Just as Preziosi explains that '[m]useums put us in the picture by putting us together as centered, unique, selfidentical subjects' (ibid.), this reassurance, equally alluded to by Rounds as a form of using the museum for purposes of 'identity maintenance' (2006, 147), can still be observed in museums today. The continuous appeal of these ordered and coherent representations can again be connected to the authority of logical narratives. Due to the process of emplotment (White 1980, 20), coherent accounts that suggest a shared moral and a certain completeness appear more convincing (cf. ibid., 20ff.). More specifically applied to the museum context, Bal has similarly explained that unified discourses appear much more 'real' (cf. 1992, 594): 'If the visual and verbal interaction between exhibits and panels corroborates the repression of the conflicts in the museum's endeavor, then it will convey a sense of unity that contributes to the shaping of social reality' (ibid.). This prevention of conflict has also been traced in the guided tours. In this sense, the guided tours provide trustworthy (because coherent) experiences of otherness, which are labelled as education. As Pieterse frames it,

> Indeed, colonialism as a subject is excluded from ethnological museums: it enframes the ethnological museum, but is not addressed by it. [...] But when it comes to power, museums and exhibitions tend to reproduce the charms of power. 'Treasures of', 'Gold of', 'Splendour of' exhibitions invite the public to luxuriate in the aura of power, moonstruck by the accumulated glitter of palaces turned inside out. Under the head of education, museums provide gratification. (2005, 176)

In turn, the persuasion that forms of gratification and luxuriation implied by such experiences are in fact instances of 'education' is made possible by the perceived reliability of the institution.

This marketing of such coherent experiences of otherness in the museum is another key factor that explains the actions of the guides. To argue that consumerist notions underlie the ways in which non-European otherness is communicated in the exhibitions and the guided tours is not to suggest that all of the available information and experiences in the museums are solely determined by the notion of consumption. Yet, it should be clear that the work of the museum is not exempt from the dynamics of the market. As Dicks has explained, the turn of museums towards visitor orientation can be regarded as an effect of the museums' increasing dependency on visitor numbers and similarly market-driven considerations (cf. 2004, 32). While an orientation of museums on matters of supply and demand can, thus, also democratise the institution, there is a danger that exhibitions of non-European regions become annexed by the consumerist world, thereby being reduced to mere decorative experiences instead of being seen as complex, critical, and negotiational contact zones. Dicks has accordingly argued that commodification can turn culture '[...] into essentialized images of 'otherness' seemingly frozen in time' (ibid., 33). Such processes have likewise been traced in the guided tours and can be observed, for instance, when the guides dress the students in traditional clothes of the represented regions without contextualising and complexifying such acts. It is the peculiar interplay of experience-centred pedagogy and the reduction of non-European culture and history to decorative symbols, traditional buildings, and stories of adventures and exploration that casts the identities represented as 'products' to be consumed without a necessity for deeper reflection.

Yet, it is not only the offer of such decorative experiences itself, but also the easily commensurable nature of them that turns the non-

European regions into *Disneyworld*. As Kirshenblatt-Gimblett remarks with reference to an example of the *American Museum of Natural History* which had visitors get their 'passport' stamped at stations in five galleries: '[s]uch tropes form an archive of historical understandings that go uncontested. Their playfulness insulates them from the very critiques that [...] have brought museums themselves to task for their historic role in grand projects of discovery and conquest' (1998, 136). A similar playfulness of the marketed experiences can be found in the stories that the guides in this study tell the students about the achievements of European collectors. These stories remain uncontroversial and 'happy' in nature. When Cristina Lleras argues that heritage sites are often marked by a reassuring and reconciliatory narrative, thus being used to '[...] soothe away our individual and collective stresses, leaving only contented and well-balanced people in an all-inclusive harmonious society' (2013, 456), this harmony can also be found as an underlying message in all of the observed guided tours. The experiences of otherness provided by the museums and the guided tours, thus, turn out as means of marketing a commensurable and generally 'happy' otherness that is devoid of conflict and social struggle. As has already been explained, this harmony is only possible because of the remoteness of the otherness represented: The distance in time and space facilitates the consumption of visible differences without the need to deal with the pitfalls that a confrontation with such differences would entail. It is only in the museum where such a happy celebration of otherness can be practised as well as 'taught' to children.

Finally, this demand or desire for a 'happy' and decorative otherness has been connected in this work with a continuing persistence of multiculturalism as a socially accepted framework to conceptualise cultural differences. Multiculturalism as the promise of Anderson's 'variety without antagonism' is often reduced to the celebration of secular and easily commensurable differences such as food, festivals, cultural rituals, and dress. This form of multiculturalism has also been adopted in the museum. In this context, the analysis of the accounts of the guides and the mission statements of the museums suggests that the museums part of this study have rebranded modernist anthropological representations of non-European Others (as relegated to an unspecific time and tied to cultural 'niches') in terms of multiculturalist notions of cultural diversity respect, tolerance, and cultural dialogue. In this sense, 'saving vanishing cultures' becomes 'respecting cultural differences', 'rendering the Other as passive' becomes 'cultural dialogue' in which power imbalances are obscured, and 'exoticism' becomes 'the celebration of cultural diversity'. These dynamics are not as easy as these formulas suggest. The workings of multiculturalism are different from narratives of extinction, primitivity, and purity. However, the partial comparability of multiculturalist discourses with these early anthropological categories shows that such static ideas of multiculturalism may hinder a more genuine and self-critical engagement with notions of otherness. Similarly, Lleras argues that a fundamental challenge for museums is how to instigate a more critical instead of a celebratory multiculturalism (cf. 2013, 464). This is especially crucial because empty signifiers such as diversity and respect, when not filled with meaning, amount to a form of 'zoological multiculturalism' which renders diversity as a 'national possession' (cf. Bennett quoting Hage, 2006, 61).

These three notions, the reliability of the museum as institution, the marketing of 'happy' otherness, and multiculturalism, are regarded as key in understanding the recurring patterns and practices of communicating non-European otherness in the guides accounts. Considering the wide-ranging scope of these factors, the question is whether these pitfalls of communicating non-European otherness can be overcome or reduced at all. The final part of this chapter draws on examples in the material that shows how transcultural encounters, cultural hybridity and negotiation can be embedded in the guides' accounts, thereby exploring starting points for change and alternative narratives.

6.3   Speaking about Others without 'Othering'?

As alluded to before, this work and the analysis in Chapter 5 have shown that there are several factors that influence the guides' accounts and the messages conveyed during their explanations and performance. This variety of determining factors suggests that the guides alone cannot be made responsible for an ongoing prevalence of essentialist or condescending accounts about non-European otherness in the observed sessions. A more far-reaching system of interactions and expectations co-creates the contents of the guided tour. This complexification of responsibility, however, also means that it is not easy to identify strategies that can be applied to change the guides' accounts. Regardless of this difficulty, the following remarks still reflect upon possible ways in which the figuration and essentialist reproduction of non-European otherness in gallery sessions can be eschewed. The elaborations first address the pitfalls of exclusively museum educational or curatorial models that have been brought forward to effect change in terms of representations of non-European contexts in museums. As an alternative, this subchapter subsequently briefly shows a more holistic ideal of a range of influential factors that would need to be considered for a more in-depth and long-term redevelopment of the communication of non-European in ethnographic museums. Because of the complexity and scope of this ideal, the final part of this subchapter again focuses on the agency of the gallery educator and points to three concrete practices, found rudimentarily in the observed sessions, that avoid essentialist ascriptions of identity. By highlighting these dynamics, the potential of the format of the guided tour is highlighted, and transculturality is suggested as an approach to the communication of non-European otherness.

While museum education scholars have developed and documented ways of museum learning that are democratic, subjective, and participative, meant to counter racism and social exclusion (cf. Golding 2012, Simon 2010, Trofaneko/ Segall 2014), and while art historians and curators have equally contributed strategies of designing critical and less authoritative exhibitions (cf. Kazeem et al. (eds.) 2009, Kravagna 2015, Bjerregaard 2015), these conceptions may both be too broad and too narrow to effect change with regard to the communication of otherness during gallery sessions. On the one hand, the suggested approaches are too broad because they entail general demands for participative learning processes in museums (Simon 2010) or for the integration of different voices in museums (Golding 2012). While such demands are justified, they are only implicitly applicable to concrete educational measures such as the guided tour, and usually do not offer explicit strategies for concrete situations of mediating non-European contexts. On the other hand, such suggestions are too narrow because they consider changes of museum meanings solely to be affected by new museum educational methods or curatorial techniques.

In this work, in contrast, a specific segment of the museum has been at the centre of attention, and due to this focus on a concrete educational measure and concrete employees who work in real-life-situations, it is possible to acknowledge influencing factors not only connected to educational methods and curatorial strategies, but also to the guides' working conditions, their positions within the organisations, their responsibilities, different understandings of learning, expectations surrounding the institution, spatial features, as well as cultural understandings. In consideration of these numerous factors, it has become clear that alternative ways of speaking about non-European otherness in gallery sessions can only be realised if attention is paid both to detail (i.e., by focusing on the messages that specific museum representatives articulate) and by acknowledging the entanglement of influences that affect these specific messages. Instead of reifying the artificially imposed museum structure of separate curatorial, educational, administrative and conservational departments[99] in suggestions for alternative ways of speaking about non-European otherness, it is important to keep in mind this more specific, yet bigger contextual picture of museum work when proposing changes or novel approaches. It is certainly possible for museums to promote new teaching styles when training their guides, or for the curators to adopt more subjective and multidimensional strategies of representation. It is, however, questionable whether such isolated measures will bring about change and prevent culturalistic, essentialist, or distancing accounts about otherness to emerge. For example, if the working conditions of the guides are not improved, how can the guides be encouraged to adopt new methods – with only a few hours of their day dedicated to the freelance job as a facilitator? Furthermore, if more learner-centred methods of teaching are established, this purely methodological change does not mean that cultural essentialism is prevented, as becomes apparent, for instance, from the critical reflections on experiential learning in Chapter 5.3.3.

These reflections show that a more holistic approach would need to be taken if museums sought to avoid an essentialist communication of non-European otherness in guided tours. Besides improving the working conditions and the embeddedness of the guides in the museums, the spatial design of the exhibition rooms would need to enable a critical

---

[99] Slam has shown that „[c]riticism of the traditional departmental structure of museums which separates curatorship, conservation, education, administration and exhibition is not a new phenomenon. As early as 1942, in the American Association of Museums/Metropolitan Museum of Art report, *The Museum as Social Instrument*, it was recognized that the departmental structure in museums needed adjustment, the usual structural pattern having been developed long before people recognized, for example, that public education had any part to play in museum missions' (2005, 62).

408

engagement with the museum's history as well as a more interactive and self-reflective discourse on interpretative theories. The separation of 'foreign cultures' in different rooms, for instance, would need to be revised for the sake of a more permeable and exchange-based representation of non-European *and* European groups. In the course of these approaches, museums would need to distance themselves from visitor expectations of coherent non-European 'cultures', thereby perhaps risking disappointing some visitors.

Because of the complex interrelation between public understandings of non-European culture, visitor expectations, the market-orientation of museums, and not least the financial challenge that such an all-inclusive ideal of change would mean, this suggestion remains, at least in the museums part of this study, a utopia.[100] In order to still suggest some more practical and immediate strategies of avoiding stereotypical framings in gallery sessions, it is worthwhile to again go back to the agency of the gallery educators. Due to the criticism offered in the analysis, it might seem as if this work suggested that the gallery session be abandoned as an educational format in museums. To the contrary, the concern of the analysis with culturally essentialist accounts in guided tours derives from an acknowledgment of a potential of the guided tour to complement and complexify the exhibition is. Especially as a more holistic redevelopment of exhibitions is not always possible, the guides are seen here as theoretically able to add layers of meaning, pose critical questions, and use the exhibition for a self-reflective deconstruction of perceived otherness. Despite being determined by a variety of influencing factors, gallery educators are, eventually, those individuals that stand in front of

[100] There are museum projects and designs that do oppose a static representation of cultures, evoke critical debates, and integrate museum education more deeply. Yet, as can be argued, these projects are more widely visible in smaller museums or exhibitions, and not very often in long-established national museums or large public institutions.

diverse school groups, trying to negotiate prior ideas with new information. By means of their ways of speaking and negotiating cultural contexts, they can affect the representation of non-European groups in the museum.

This agency can, as the analysis has shown, play out one way or the other, but the following remarks concentrate on those practices of the guides that contribute to a genuine negotiation of identities. As described in some instances in Chapter 4, there are moments in which the guides facilitate a balanced and self-critical reflection of cultural identities. In this work, these moments are regarded as starting points for the redevelopment of the gallery session as a transcultural 'contact zone' where, as Mary Louise Pratt has argued, the trajectories of previously separated subjects intersect, leading to interactive and improvisational encounters (cf. 1992, 7). While Pratt as well as Clifford, in his appropriation of the concept in 'Museums as Contact Zones' (1997), both conceptualise this zone as marked by the movement of people, the contact zone that the gallery educators can generate is a contact zone of ideas. Through the confrontation of visitors or, in this work, student groups, with discontinuities, historical or social contexts, and relations to contemporary experiences of immediate otherness, the guided tour can provide multiperspectival encounters of cultural identities presented as constantly changing, interactive, heterogeneous, and, therefore, negotiational. In this sense, the communication in gallery sessions could apply transculturality not only as an analytical lens, but also as a proactive approach.

To adopt this approach would not mean to conceptualise culture, as Welsch's concept of transculturality partly does, as the happy and well-balanced picking and choosing of affiliations (cf. 1999, 205), but to translate a transcultural analytical lens into descriptions of ethnographic artefacts. As Juneja has explained in her conception of transculturalism, a focus on assertions of difference and cultural contestations is necessary to understand the transcultural formation and construction of identities (cf.

2013, 32). Ethnographic artefacts can be seen as perfect starting points for such transcultural histories. Instead of regarding them as representatives of one 'culture', these objects can be used to show multidimensional processes of a transformation of ideas in materiality, the continuous appropriation of meanings by different owners, and the conflicts through which cultural identity emerges. These transcultural object biographies could, implicitly and explicitly, point to the constructedness of national or cultural identity, and to crucial entanglements between what is considered 'us' and what is considered 'them'. One precondition for the telling of such stories is that the guides abandon their avoidance of uncontroversial topics. This is because controversy is at the bottom of processes of cultural encounter and assertions of identity. Juneja, for instance, refers to the paradoxical nature of warfare to show that conflict evokes both dynamics of negotiation and dynamics of alterity:

> [W]arfare presents us with the paradox of bringing together men (and in specific historical contexts entire families) of different ethnicities, religious faiths, and linguistic identities (often fighting across these lines), thereby promoting, in the long run, the practice of cosmopolitan exchange and at the same time of producing discourses of irreconcilable alterity, articulated through innumerable textual and visual representations, and practices such as iconoclasm or looting. (2013, 32)

With regard to these reflections, the following three observations of means by which the communication of non-European regions is diversified must be regarded as mere starting points. The guides' emphasis on discontinuities, the contextualisation of the objects, and the reference to immediate otherness cannot be interpreted as elaborate methods of implementing a transcultural approach to ethnographic museum education. They do, however, point to the potential of the gallery session, and to the availability of alternatives to the patterns described in Chapter 4. A further development of these three starting points in terms of transcultural discontinuities, histories, and assertions of difference would, therefore be desirable in the future.

6.3.1   Emphasising Discontinuities

The first strategy observed during the sessions is the guides' reflection and deconstruction of seemingly apparent meanings concerning non-European contexts. For instance, when Hilda points out to the students that a picture of traditional houses does not adequately represent Africa and emphasises that there is a large film and fashion industry in urban centres (cf. GSH-MC, 114-118), she actively addresses the shortcomings of the stereotypical representation and adds another dimension to the cultural reality 'displayed', thereby diversifying meaning. Another example is Kate's explicit focus on the glass display cases when the students explore different materials of the objects in an exhibition room (cf. GSK-MD, 314-317). By drawing the students' attention not only to the exhibited artefacts but also to the material that is used by the museum display them, Kate opens up a space for a meta-level of experiencing the museum in which not only the artefacts, but also the ways in which they are represented becomes 'visible'. Finally, another example can be found in Doreen's session when responds to a students' repulsed reaction to an account about the Inuit's use of seal's intestines to make waterproof clothes by explaining that the students frequently eat intestines in the form of sausages (cf. GSD-MA, 855-857).

These are only three very different examples in which the guides engage in some form of critical reflection and meta-level discourse by highlighting discontinuities. This call for the integration of self-critical and reflexive narratives in museum communication is not new. Similar strategies have already been discussed in relation to museum studies and curating, for instance by curator Joachim Baur, who has argued in favour of acknowledging and showcasing the messiness of the museum and its objects (cf. 2013, 375ff.), or by Bjerregaard who develops the concept of montage to be applied in exhibitions as a way of highlighting the fluidity of objects and their 'continuous reactivation' in different settings (cf. 2013, 243). These notions of messiness and montage could also be adopted as principles to be highlighted gallery sessions, thereby 'undoing' what Bal has called the 'sense of unity' (1992, 594) that results from self-affirming messages in the exhibitions.

While the demand for self-reflection has, thus, been a common and repeated suggestion for change in museums, these propositions often seem very broad. For instance, Shelton has claimed that '[m]useums require a new honesty, generous, reflexive and open [...] to provide the essential bridges of understanding within and between local, national and international communities (1995, 12). In a similar vein, Karp and Wilson have identified the potential of the museum as places in which the construction of value can be negotiated and countered (cf. 1996, 264). This is also related to general demands of critical ethnologists to contest essentialist knowledge. Appadurai has argued, accordingly, that ethnographers must remain aware of the fact that what appear to be 'essences' are 'temporary localisations of ideas from many places' (1988, 46). Although these recommendations are important, it is difficult to translate them into concrete practices. To engage more specifically in self-reflective and critical discourse in gallery sessions, the guides would need to be paid for preparation time and be enabled to discuss possible discontinuities on all levels of the exhibitions with the curators. Such a cooperation would also necessitate a rethinking on the part of the curators, who would need to regard the education as complementing their work. In comparison to the holistic changes suggested above, these small-scale transformations do seam feasible. Even if this organisational change is not possible, however, the examples above show that the guides can already point out discontinuities of common stereotypes and ways of using ethnographic exhibitions.

Finally, the communication of such discontinuities is again dependent on the previously stated courage to be controversial. To connect this general demand to more concrete practices, Gorski's statements about paradigmatic 'shifts' in intercultural education can be applied to the guided tours. First, he argues that understanding differences is not sufficient, but that the exploitation of differences by the hegemonic norm must be exposed (cf. 2008, 10). This exposure of hegemonic norms would, for instance, prevent celebratory accounts about the 'success stories' of acquiring the objects. Gorski further suggests that educators should not primarily focus on conflict resolution, but on justice (cf. ibid.). Instead of avoiding conflicts during the gallery sessions, guides should aim at dismantling discrimination and stereotypes. This is done, for instance, by Doreen when she disagrees with the students' reactions to the story about Inuit. Thirdly, Gorski holds that intercultural educators must accept a 'loss of likeability' (2008, 11). While the guides may want to achieve consensus between themselves, the students, the teachers, and the parents, in order to prevent essentialism, they need to hazard the consequences of criticising or questioning understandings of culture. In the example of a teacher's comment about solidarity in Africa, Christine would, thus, need to challenge the teacher, thereby accepting a loss of consensus.

The application of these measures in the realm of museum education may also require a genuine reflection of the guides on their roles as authority figures. By, for instance, discussing contributions of the students in more detail, or else, by using conditional clauses or offering different theories about certain aspects, guides could destabilise the idea of the educator as more knowledgeable and objective. Elizabeth Ellsworth has argued in a compelling piece about the lack of empowerment in measures of critical pedagogy, acknowledgment of the power involved in authoritative teaching methods has not led to the development of concrete programmes and methods targeted at its deconstruction: 'In the absence of such an analysis and program, their [the educators', KW] efforts are limited to trying to transform negative effects of power imbalances within the classroom into positive ones' (1989, 306). As has been shown, such a reframing of negative disciplinary practices into positive ones, such as Britta's relation to the Chinese respect for teachers as a means of alluding to her own authoritative position, does not question the authority of educators. If the guides distance themselves from the idea of having to mediate concrete, coherent, and factual accounts, but rather focus on discontinuities and deconstructions through discussions with the students, an authoritative position is no longer necessary.

6.3.2   Making Concrete Statements about Objects and History

Another strategy that can work to avoid generalising statements about non-European regions is the focus on concrete objects and historical contexts. Instead of speaking broadly about 'their culture', guides can counter culturalistic accounts by offering explanations that closely revolve around the object at hand or a specific historical event. This is evident especially in Museum D that, as already explained, follows a decided focus on materiality and design. For instance, in her session, Feona asks the students to think about the shapes of a specific objects and to compare these with similar looking shapes: 'How else can we describe these forms? What do they remind you of?' (GSF-MD, 269). Similarly, Kate works from the objects' materiality to explaining how they were made: 'Why is stone a really good material to make sculptures?' (GSK-MD, 281-282). Furthermore, in Isabel's and Hilda's sessions in Museum C, concrete statements about objects or historical contexts can frequently be found. For example, Hilda is keen to limit her explanations to the depictions on the Benin plaques and to what they reveal about the old Kingdom of Benin. She thereby avoids making statements about African 'culture' for the most part of her session.

This formalist approach to museum education that takes as a starting point the 'communicative capacity of objects' (Auslander 2012, 358) can be compared to the so-called 'Visual Thinking Strategies' (VTS) developed by Abigail Housen and Philip Yenawine (cf. e.g. Housen 2007, Yenawine 2013). This strategy entails discussion-based reflections of aesthetic experiences of visitors, which leads to the development of multiple meanings of objects and artworks. As Blume et al. explain in their research on aesthetic education,

> This technique begins with general questions that motivate observation, proceeds to questions that extend the process of observation and interpretation, and leads to questions that encourage reflection on observations. [...] The success of this method is dependent on the skill of the discussion leader, who must follow up the viewer's visual observation with an appropriate question that extends the discussion and leads to a new observation. (2008, 92)

VTS has been described as a constructivist learning method (cf. Mayer 2005, 14) and can, if carried out properly, lead to meaning-making processes that are closely attached to the objects on display and at the same linked to the prior knowledge of the students or visitors.

However, this strategy of starting out from the objects and extrapolating meanings is not without challenges. On the one hand, this is such a distinguished and wide-reaching methodology of art education that it cannot simply be adopted by gallery educators in museums. The strategy of posing questions which enable visitors to make their own meaning and develop these meanings without imposing 'facts' from the outside must be studied and practised intensively. Accordingly, even though Feona and Kate do use comparable strategies in their work, they still often aim at arriving at a previously anticipated meaning of an objects and guide the students toward it. Due to its open-ended and subjective nature, VTS may appear more suited to contemporary art than to ethnographic artefacts. While this is a misconception connected to the idea that history is unidimensional and 'objective', it may still be challenging for the guides to avoid introducing 'correct' answers, especially when teachers and parents expect the students to gain knowledge about the displayed objects and regions.

A second issue of VTS consists of its exclusive focus on the objects and not to the ways in which, as Bjerregaard maintains, atmospheres in the museum that result from the staging of the artefacts, the spatial dimension, the objects' agency, and the interaction with the objects, shape the ways in which the objects are perceived (cf. 2014, 80). Thus, while VTS does consider the multiple impressions that visitors may have when encountering artefacts in museums, it does not regard the museum's power to create meaning. Especially with regard to non-European objects, this dimension is, however, important. While contemporary art objects can be 'simply about art', a similar perspective on ethnographic objects would, if not paired with self-critical observations and historical information, take for granted the objects' representation in European museums, the reasons for their collection, and the power imbalance that still exist between the European and non-European regions as well as within the European art market. VTS could hence be a way of introducing the objects to the students, of making it possible to see multiple meanings and to discuss these within the group, or of showing the same objects with different ways of lighting, in different object ensembles or with different labels. Once the students have thereby realised that these artefacts are fluid and unstable, subject to prior knowledge, experience, staging, and material qualities, theories about the previous contexts of the objects (best explained in the form of longer-term 'object biographies' that also include references to a transcultural exchange of ideas as well as to historical discontinuities wherever possible) and the conditions and reasons for their collection and representation in Europe could be added. Without providing general information about holistically perceived 'cultures', such object-based encounters would facilitate an experience of artefacts marked by open-endedness, multiple connections, and genuine discourse.

6.3.3   Connecting Remote and Immediate Otherness

A final way of countering constructions of non-European otherness that the guides in the observed sessions already use to some extent, but that could be elaborated, is to establish a link between remote and immediate otherness. As already discussed at length in this work, it is particularly the remoteness of the represented Others that makes it possible to celebrate 'variety without antagonism' and to construct an order of the world that is affirmative and coherent. But just like the European worlds of the students, non-European worlds are confusing, multi-layered, and never comprehensible as a whole. By denying non-European worlds this density of meanings and instead providing easily commensurable facts, some of the observed sessions relegate these worlds not only to a place distant from 'us', but also distant from contemporaneity altogether. The experiences of non-European groups, their complex lifeworlds, the similarities between 'us' and 'them', contextual social systems, and diverse historical narratives are thereby flattened and obscured. The remote Other becomes, in contrast to the immediate stranger, a utopian figure marked by authenticity, exoticism, and essential distance.

Some of the guides in the observed sessions work against this distance by explaining that non-European practices and lifeworlds are not remote, but are enmeshed with the immediate everyday experience of the students. For example, in her session on various kinds of clothing in different regions, Isabel shows traditional North American slippers to the students and then makes the connection to 'moccasins', explaining that these are worn by many people all over the world today (cf. ibid., 42-46).

Similar examples that show a connection between what is represented and the experienced reality of the students have already been discussed in Chapter 4.7, as, for instance, Antonia's comparisons of Palauan outrigger boats to seaplanes, or Feona's comparison of tiles used in Iranian houses to the tiles on the museum's floor and in the students' bathrooms. There are many such instances to be found in the gallery sessions. Almost all of the observed guided tours contain connections between the represented regions and the students' lifeworlds.

Although links between immediate and remote otherness have the potential to not only make the Other *present*, but also to question prior ideas that picture Others as essentially different, these comparisons often unfold on a rather superficial level, with the point of comparing being to enhance learning and meaning-making by connecting new information with information the students already know (cf. Hein 1994, 77). While such strategies work well to relativise the distance between 'us' and 'them', they are often only based upon similar objects and similar practices, and not upon values, social norms, and aspects of identification or exclusion. Yet, particularly this correlation between the guides' explanations of social realities in the respective regions and the students' encounters of non-Europeanness in their everyday lives would be a leverage point for discussing and refuting common stereotypes or misconceptions about Others. The student-induced round of questions about terrorism in Maria's session can be seen as a positive example in this regard. Although it is problematic to discuss terrorism in a session about the 'Orient' as if it was an intrinsic part of the represented region, the situation still leads to a crucial process of reflection on the part of the students. Thus, Maria explains to the students that terrorists are politically motivated and that terrorism is not connected to Islam and should not be equated with the majority of Muslims. Thereby, Maria explicitly counters common associations about Islam and terrorism. As this example shows, if students raise problematic questions, guides can base their explanations on such student comments in order to diversify and complexify situations and perceptions.

Such forms of making connections and critically addressing issues of discrimination, stereotyping or the negotiation of identity may not be perceived as the task of the ethnographic museum or of the guided tours. Accordingly, as explained, Maria argues in the interview that the museum cannot tackle such issues. In contrast to this statement, this work argues in favour of making aspects of cultural understanding and transculturation the primary concern of gallery sessions in ethnographic museums. If these issues are not addressed in spaces that explicitly deal with non-European regions, it is questionable where else they could be addressed. No other public institution or organisation has the same expertise and material resources to engage in debates about transcultural negotiation, essentialism, and 'othering'. Although schools may address such issues in different subjects, it is the ethnographic museum that holds material objects from these places and thus provides a suitable place for the introduction to transcultural histories, the complexity of non-European regions past and present, and processes of asserting difference. In the four museums part of this study, notions of 'learning about different cultures' or 'cultural contact zones' remain firmly embedded in mission statements and self-representations. However, without facilitating actual debates about the meaning of 'otherness', the workings of stereotypes, and the connections between 'us' and 'them', these concepts remain empty signifiers and, often, marketing terms.

A final comment on the connection between immediate Others, or 'strangers', and remote Others: As has been explained in the beginning of this work, these are not the same. As Fabian has rightly emphasised, alterity should not be 'sociologised' by turning Others into strangers (cf. 2006, 146). This means that, while it is important to counter ideas of non-

Europeanness as remote and inaccessible by showing the immediateness of non-European groups, this process of 'presenting' should not lead to a relabelling of Others as strangers. The construction of strangers can be seen as a result of the constitution of the self, which, in the case of the regions displayed in the ethnographic museum, would not be a sufficiently complex model to understand the production of otherness. It is, therefore, still important for the guides to emphasise the historical and political production of non-European Others in terms of a hegemonic discourse.

Having explained these three suggestions of how the guides could effect change without a larger restructuring of the museums, it is necessary to ask in how far the guides would be 'allowed' by their institutions to integrate such comparatively political messages in their accounts. There are two possibilities in this regard. If the guides can be integrated better in the structure and organisation of the museum, for instance by intensifying contact with curators, these measures of the guides can be promoted as additions to the exhibitions and developed in concert with the curators. If a better integration is not possible, however, it is possible to turn the marginalised positions of the guides into a productive element. As the gallery educators, as of now, do not fully belong to the organisation, but take an in-between position between the museum and the public, they can both utilise the authority that the institution bestows on them and their relative independence as employees to question the museum's messages. As has been argued in this work, despite much planning and session formatting, there are always moments in which the guides bring in their own ideas, anecdotes and personality. This subjective gap could be used to tell transcultural histories in the guided tours. In general, it is important that museum education in ethnographic museums becomes more political, which is concurrent with Gorskis' argument that intercultural education must be political: 'In fact, the very act of claiming neutrality is, in and of itself, politically value-laden and supportive of the status quo' (2008, 11).

As gallery educators can, likewise, not be neutral, they may as well make transparent the various political dimensions of the exhibitions and discuss them with the students. After all, the simultaneity of dissimilar political accounts is more neutral than the empty claim of neutrality.

6.4. Limitations of this Work and Research Outlook

While the previous subchapters have summarised and highlighted the main findings and contributions of this work, some important aspects could not be discussed or adequately represented. The following remarks therefore show where the limitations of the analysis and the results lie, and in what ways further research could take this work as a starting point.

First, what is missing from the analysis is a more comprehensive engagement with the museums part of this study. As explained in the introduction, museum education can be regarded as a relatively separate division in most of the museums in so far as it is often coordinated independently. Even if there is contact between curators, learning managers, and guides, the educational programmes are often developed after curatorial decisions have been made. For this reason, but also for reasons of manageability of the empirical research, focus was placed on the guides, the exhibition spaces, the learning managers, as well as on the reactions of the students, teachers, and accompanying parents. As has been specified in Chapter 5, factors that influence the guided tour are not limited to these actors. Although expectations of the museum as institution and the working conditions of the guides have been discussed in detail, deeper organisational aspects, such as the financial set-up of the museums or intricate hierarchical relationships between the museum management and the staff could not be included in the analysis because this would have exceeded the scope of the project. It would have been desirable, however, to gain a better understanding of the management processes in the museums part of this study in order to be able to explain

422

how machineries in the 'backstage' facilitate and lead to certain impressions and performances during the sessions. Yet, it is questionable whether such a deep insight into museums can be achieved if researchers come from the outside. Similar to corporations or companies, well-established and larger museums are not keen on being investigated inside-out. This problem of accessibility becomes apparent already from this study in so far as some museums declined granting access to their guided tours. Still, deeper insights into the institutions, in the form of organisation sociology, would be necessary in order to get a better idea of the multiple processes involved in formulating and translating mission statements or learning (or experience) goals into practice.

The difficulty to gain access is closely connected to another limitation of this research. It would have been desirable to choose museums in the English context that are more comparable to the German museums, that means, museums with a clear focus on ethnography. Yet, on the one hand, for reasons discussed in Chapter 6.1, there are not many decidedly ethnographic museums in the British context, and, on the other hand, the few that there are rejected the offer to participate. Although it was not feasible in the time frame dedicated to this research to incorporate more than four museums, this difficulty of an imbalance between ethnographic museums in German and Great Britain would have presented a challenge if the inclusion of more museums had been planned. Considering the different focuses of the museums (i.e., decidedly ethnographic museums in Germany and universalist or design museums in Great Britain), it is especially interesting that similar patterns of communicating otherness emerged in the guided tours. The unplanned conceptual distinction between the institutions has thus facilitated an even farther-reaching interpretation of the research results in so far as ways of speaking about non-European otherness can be seen to go beyond the immediate institutional and organisational dependencies. Nevertheless, more research about the contents of museum educational accounts in ethnographic museums all over Europe would contribute to a better understanding of how similar 'worlds of otherness' become reinforced in these and comparable situations.

As a third limitation of this present study and suggestion for future research, a comparison of the research results to intercultural communication in educational (schools, nurseries, children's literature) or experiential contexts (culture festivals, theme parks) would be an interesting additional step. As ways of speaking about non-European regions seem to be informed, among other factors, by socially accepted cultural understandings and public expectations, it would be interesting to investigate whether issues such as the disimprovement effect, the marketing of remote otherness, and the multiculturalist idea of celebratory culture also appear in different situations of communicating non-European contexts. Layne's and Almanji's study on the promotion of imperial stereotypes in children's books (2015) and Diekman's and Kay Smith's anthology *Ethnic and Minority Cultures as Tourist Attractions* (2015) are notable examples of such research. Particularly interesting in these fields would be an even more microscopic analysis of what it is that educators or performers say about non-European lifeworlds and what types of accounts imply essentialism and distance.

As a fourth leverage point for further research, this study has not placed its focus on the provision of an all-encompassing model for the decolonisation or demystification of museum education and museum communication. Instead, at the centre of attention was the work of pointing to the existence, the types of, and the reasons for frequently repeated accounts of otherness in an ostensibly trustworthy and objective environment. Nevertheless, in the reflections in this chapter, transcultural theory has been proposed not only as a lens, but also as an approach to facilitate negotiation instead of an ascription of identities. In the framework of this work, this suggestion of transculturality as an approach could, however, only be briefly mentioned as a possible alternative. More research should be undertaken in fields of transcultural art and museum education by developing concrete educational practices that point to the hybridity, historical complexity, and coevalness of the groups and people on display. Lutz-Sterzenbach et al.'s concept of remix, that can be promoted in art education (2013), and Arata Takeda's suggestions about transculturality at school (2010) are inspiring starting points although the alternatives they give could be even more concrete and exemplary.

Finally, new models for organising museums in a less culturalistic way have not been provided. This clearly results from the sociological perspective that this study takes, which does not entail a full-fletched offer of a new system as part of the critique of the old system. It was, thus, not the intention of this work to provide a solution for the issue that has been raised. However, as has been argued in this chapter, a more holistic approach to museum communication that combines education and curation and, thereby, prevents a separation of these fields, could contribute to critically scrutinising stereotypical or essentialist representations instead of merely relabelling them in terms of cultural diversity. Villeneuve's and Love's concept of edu-curation (2017) and Mörsch's et al.'s book on *Contemporary Curating and Museum Education* (2016) show that such comprehensive frameworks are, in fact, possible and fruitful. This suggestion for further research does not mean that participative curating or edu-curation answer all questions of essentialism and celebratory otherness that have been raised in this work (in contrast, visitors may expect holistic ideas of cultures to emerge in museum representations and thus curate even more fixed notions into the galleries), but such approaches can serve to destabilise the often-unquestioned authority of the institution.

7 Final notes: The Show Never Stops

Gladys changes her accent to sound more 'African' in a guided tour about Africa – this has been the starting point of this work, which has classified, analysed, interpreted, and partially explained recurring ways of communicating non-European otherness in gallery sessions. The point of this work was to reveal which tropes about non-European objects, cultural practices, beliefs, and lifeworlds are articulated in such educational measures. A main concern was to discuss, thereby, which recurring problems persist in the educational communication of non-European groups, and, to some extent, also to explain why these communities are still 'othered' in these situations. In the context of these questions, the specific framework of the guided tour allowed for an investigation of concrete ways of speaking about non-European regions, some of which could be connected to shared understandings and more overarching accepted ideas about remote, cultural otherness. It was specifically this small-scale dissection of moments in which stereotypes or essentialist framings of non-European people emerge that was intended in this work. Not the question of how to avoid cultural otherness as an experience as such, but the question of why the same stories about non-European otherness are repeated over and over, was of utmost concern in the analysis.

Indeed, confirming the initial hypotheses of this work, common myths and patterns of communicating non-European regions have been found in the material. It is still largely acceptable, in the observed sessions, to represent non-European regions as homogeneous, culturally authentic, and coherently ordered entities. Children are dressed up in saris or turbans, are asked to 'sit like an Indian', are, thus, familiarised with non-European otherness in the form of a cultural show. These performances of otherness emerge despite good intentions, such as the idea to produce positive associations or to introduce children to unfamiliar objects and cultural practices in a playful way. The outcome of this playful and celebratory performance of non-European culture is, however, the powerful continuation of static, homogenising, and sometimes condescending ideas about what constitutes Africa, Asia, China, North America, or the Middle East. The problem that has been raised in relation to this outcome is that these cultural regions are not, in fact, merely imaginary projection screens on which to illuminate happy stereotypes of easily consumable, remote otherness. The countries really exist. The people in these regions have everyday lives that are more complex and heterogeneous in order for them to be even rudimentarily understood in terms of the images that are commonly associated with the categories of 'Africa' or 'South Asia'. The artefacts in ethnographic museums contain stories and histories of possession and appropriation that are obscured when these objects merely serve as symbols for always already pre-imagined sets of decorative culture. Role-playing and pretending can be fruitful ways of learning, but what if the show never stops? What if culture remains a neatly ordered image of exotic strangeness, and is not presented in its heterogeneity and complexity? The reductive, authoritative, multiculturalist, and celebratory modes of communication observed in the guided tours often reinforce and reproduce the Other as a typified and 'culturalised' figure.

Yet, as has become apparent from the analysis, the guides are not the only actors in the field that facilitate these static figurations of non-European identities. Instead, a variety of factors influence the performances and ways of speaking in the gallery sessions. Gallery educators' accounts are thus affected by the lack of content-related contact between curators and guides, by the insecure working conditions that exacerbate a more intensive and critical development and preparation of the sessions, by the goal-orientation of the teachers, by the scriptedness of the sessions, by common understandings of museums as arbiters of uncontroversial and coherent knowledge, as well as by the dominant lenses of culturalism and multiculturalism that shape understandings of non-European 'cultures' as bounded, distinct, and authentic entities. Regarding these diverse influences, it seems difficult to effect change in this complex system of meaning-making.

Taking a step back, however, one critical question is whether such broader changes are even asked for, demanded, and perceived as necessary in the public and in the institutions. From the discussed expectations and understandings of museums, and from the conversations with the guides, teachers, and learning department managers, the question of how to appropriately negotiate non-European worlds and identities does not seem to be the most relevant to these focus groups. Most of the observed school classes and teachers, for instance, appeared to be rather comfortable with the multiculturalist, celebratory, distinct conception of non-European culture offered in the guided tours. Yet, as this work has shown, the ways in which African, Indian, or 'Oriental' worlds are too often uncritically presented as marked by social authenticity, communal solidarity, colourfulness, segmented diversity, or traditional craftsmanship, contribute to an ongoing denial of non-European coevalness and modernity. Such representations must not be taken for granted, naturalised, and considered as meaningless activities for children. While some of the criticism in this work may seem exaggerated, especially in consideration of the fact that most of the young students will not be deeply affected by the sessions, it is in such apparently inconsequential activities that underlying power imbalances become apparent. For, if the described ways of speaking about non-European regions are acceptable in public museums specialised in ethnology, where are they unacceptable?

In this work, this question has been turned into a more optimistic request: Where, if not in the ethnographic museum, could students be

428

confronted with matters of representation, cultural identity, and otherness? By directing academic attention to the format of the guided tour in the ethnographic museum, this work has emphasised both the potential of the gallery session to become a 'third space' where seemingly incommensurable identities are negotiated (cf. Bhabha 1994, 218), and the necessity of redeveloping its contents so that gallery sessions can provide more meaningful, anti-racist, and self-reflective encounters of the concept of cultural otherness and its pitfalls.

In order to implement such changes on the smaller scale of the guides' individual practices, the work has suggested that a transcultural approach to ethnographic gallery sessions be further developed academically, and adopted by the guides. By applying such a transcultural framework, guides could raise awareness for the continuous shaping of identities, cultural practices, and social values. They could also demonstrate that identification specifically works through the encounter of what is perceived as 'other'. Philipp Schorch has made the insightful argument that only if cross-cultural dialogue was deconstructed as interpersonal dialogue, could the Other be freed from its abstract cage (cf. 2013, 76). In the guided tour, such interpersonal dialogues could be facilitated by diverting attention back to the students' own cultural practices and traditions when explaining non-European cultural practices.

Not presented as authentic master pieces, but as materials shaped into form and attached with different meanings over time, museum objects could, then, be used as windows, not into the authentic, but into the heterogeneity, complexity, sociality, and subjectivity of history and culture.

Works Cited

Ackermann, Andreas. 2012. "Cultural Hybridity: Between Metaphor and Empiricism." In *Conceptualizing Cultural Hybridization: A Transdisciplinary Approach*, edited by Philipp Wolfgang Stockhammer, 5–23. Berlin, Heidelberg: Springer.

Adams, Ruth. 2010. "The V&A: Empire to Multiculturalism?" *Museum and Society* 8 (2): 63–79.

Adick, Christel. 2010. "Inter-, Multi-, Transkulturell: Über Die Mühen Der Begriffsarbeit in Kulturübergreifenden Forschungsprozessen." In *Interkultur – Jugendkultur. Bildung Neu Verstehen*, edited by Alfred Hirsch and Ronald Kurt, 105–34. Wiesbaden: VS Verlag.

Adorno, Theodor W. 1988. *Prisms, Translated by Samuel and Shierry Weber*. Cambridge, MA: MIT Press.

Augé, Marc. 2002 [1986]. *In the Metro*, Translated and with an Introduction and Afterword
by Tom Conley. Minneapolis: University of Minnesota Press.

Ahmed, Sara. 2007. "Multiculturalism and the Promise of Happiness." *New Formations* 63: 121–37.

Ahmed, Sara. 2000. *Strange Encounters - Embodied Others in Post-Coloniality*. London and New York: Routledge.

Ahmed, Sara. 2006. "The Nonperformativity of Antiracism." *Meridans* 7 (1): 104-126.

Ahmed, Sara. 2010. "Embodying Diversity: Problems and Paradoxes for Black Feminists." In *Black and Postcolonial Feminisms in New Times: Researching Educational Inequalities*, edited by Heidi Safia Mirza and Cynthia Joseph, 41-52. London, New York: Routledge.

Ahrens, Jörn. 2012. *Wie Aus Wildnis Gesellschaft Wird. Kulturelle Selbstverständigung Und Populäre Kultur Am Beispiel von John Fords Film The Man Who Shot Liberty Valance*. Wiesbaden: Springer VS.

Albano, Caterina. 2014. "Narrating Place: The Sense of Visiting." *Museum and Society* 12 (1): 1–13.

Alcoff, Linda. 1992. "The Problem of Speaking for Others." *Cultural Critique* 20: 5–32.

Allen, Lauren B., and Kevin J. Crowley. 2014. "Challenging Beliefs, Practices, and Content: How Museum Educators Change." *Science Education* 98 (1): 84–105.

Alpers, Svetlana. 1991. "The Museum as a Way of Seeing." In *Exhibiting Cultures. The Poetics and Politics of Museum Display*, edited by Ivan Karp and Steven D. Lavine, 25–32. Washington, D.C.: Smithsonian Institution Press.

Anderson, Gail. 2004. "Introduction: Reinventing the Museum." In *Reinventing the Museum: Historical and Contemporary Perspectives on the Paradigm Shift*, 402. Lanham, MD: Altamira Press.

Anderson, Perry. 2011. *The New Old World*. London, New York: Verso.

Ansgar Nünning. 2013. "Wie Erzählungen Kulturen Erzeugen: Prämissen, Konzepte Und Perspektiven Für Eine Kulturwissenschaftliche Narratologie." In *Kultur - Wissen - Narration: Perspektiven Transdisziplinärer Erzählforschung Für Die Kulturwissenschaften*, edited by Alexandra Strohmeier, 15–54. Bielefeld: Transcript.

Antweiler, Christoph. 2015. "Welche Ethnologie Für Das Museum? – Welches Museum Für Die Ethnologie?" In *Quo Vadis, Völkerkundemuseum? Aktuelle Debatten Zu Ethnologischen Sammlungen in Museen Und Universitäten*, edited by Michael Kraus and Karoline Noack, 111–32. Bielefeld: Transcript.

Appadurai, Arjun. 1988. "Putting Hierarchy in Its Place." *Cultural Anthropology* 3 (1): 36–49.

Appadurai, Arjun. 1996. *Modernity at Large. Cultural Dimensions of Globalization*. Minneapolis: University of Minnesota Press.

Appiah, Kwame. 1993. "Thick Translation." *Callaloo* 16 (4): 808–19.

Augé, Marc. 2002. *In the Metro, Translated and with an Introduction and Afterword by Tom Conley*. Minneapolis: University of Minnesota Press.

Auslander, Leora. 2012. "Material Culture and Materiality." In *Travelling Concepts for the Study of Culture*, edited by Birgit Neumann and Ansgar Nünning, 353–69. Berlin, Boston: Walter de Gruyter.

Austin, John Langshaw. 1997. *How to Do Things with Words*. Edited by J.O. Urmson and Marina Sbisà. 2nded. Cambridge, MA: Harvard University Press.

Austin, Tricia. 2012. "Scales of Narrativity." In *Museum Making: Narratives, Architectures, Exhibitions*, edited by Suzanne McLeod, Laura Hourston Hanks, and Jonathan Hale, 107–18. Abingdon, Oxon: Routledge.

Bachmann-Medick, Doris. 2012. "Culture as Text: Reading and Interpreting Cultures." In *Travelling Concepts for The Study of Culture*, edited by Birgit Neumann and Ansgar Nünning, 99–118. Berlin, New York: de Gruyter.

Bachmann-Medick, Doris. 2014. "From Hybridity to Translation. Reflections on Travelling Concepts." In *The Trans/National Study of Culture: A Translational Perspective*, 119–36. Berlin, Boston: de Gruyter.

Bal, Mieke. 1992. "Telling, Showing, Showing off." *Critical Inquiry* 18 (3): 556–94.

Bal, Mieke. 1997. "Introduction." In *Narratology. Introduction to the Theory of Narrative*, 3–15. Toronto, Buffalo, London: University of Toronto Press.

Bal, Mieke. 2010. "Guest Column: Exhibition Practices." *PMLA* 125 (1): 9–23.

Barry, Brian. 2001. *Culture and Equality: An Egalitarian Critique of Multiculturalism*. Cambridge, MA: Harvard University Press.

Barthes, Roland. 1957. *Mythologies*. New York: The Noonday Press.

Barthes, Roland. 1977. "The Death of the Author." In *Image, Music, Text*, 142–48. New York: Hill Publications.

Bauman, Zygmunt. 1991. *Modernity and Ambivalence*. Cambridge, Malden, MA: Polity Press.

Baur, Joachim. 2010. "Migration – Kultur – Integration. Und die Rolle des Museums? Vorläufige Vermessungen eines unwägbaren Terrains." *Museumskunde* 75 (1): 12–19.

Baur, Joachim. 2013. "Messy Museums. Über Ordnung und Perspektiven des Museums." In *Kultur_Kultur. Denken, Forschen, Darstellen*, edited by Reinhard Johler, Christian Marchetti, Bernhard Tschofen, and Carmen Weith, 369–77. Münster: Waxmann.

Bench, Raney. 2014. *Interpreting Native American History and Culture at Museums and Historic Sites*. Lanham, Boulder: Rowman & Littlefield.

Benjamin, Walter. 1963. *Das Kunstwerk Im Zeitalter Seiner Technischen Reproduzierbarkeit*. Frankfurt am Main: Suhrkamp.

Bennett, Tony. 2006. "Exhibition, Difference, and the Logic of Culture." In *Museum Frictions: Public Cultures/ Global Transformations*, edited by Ivan Karp, Corinne A. Kratz, Lynn Szwaja, and Tomás Ybarra-Frausto, 46–69. Durham, London: Duke University Press.

Berger, Peter L, and Thomas Luckmann. 1966. *The Social Construction of Reality. A Treatise in the Sociology of Knowledge*. London: *Penguin* Books.

Bertram, Jutta. 1995. *Arm, aber glücklich: Wahrnehmungsmuster im Ferntourismus und ihr Beitrag zum (Miss-)Verstehen der Fremde(n)*. Münster: Lit Verlag.

Bhabha, Homi K. 1983. "The Other Question." *Screen* 24 (6): 18–36.

Bhabha, Homi K. 1994. *The Location of Culture*. London, New York: Routledge.

Bjerregaard, Peter. 2013. "Assembling Potentials, Mounting Effects. Ethnographic Exhibitions Beyond Correspondence." *Transcultural Montage*, 243–61.

Bjerregaard, Peter. 2014. "Dissolving Objects: Museums, Atmosphere and the Creation of Presence." *Emotion, Space and Society* 15: 74–81.

Bjerregaard, Peter. 2015. "Disconnecting Relations: Exhibitions and Objects as Resistance." In *Objects and Imagination: Perspectives on Materialization and Meaning*, edited by Oivind Fuglerud and Leon Wainwright, 45–63. New York, Oxford.

Black, Graham. 2005. *The Engaging Museum: Developing Museums for Visitor Involvement*. Abingdon, New York: Routledge.

432

Blume, Nancy, Jean Henning, Amy Herman, and Nancy Richner. 2008. "Looking to Learn: Museum Educators and Aesthetic Education." *Journal of Aesthetic Education* 42 (2): 83–100.

Blumer, Herbert. 1969. *Symbolic Interactionism: Perspective and Method.* Edited by Prentice Hall. Upper Saddle River.

Böhme, Gernot. 1993. "Atmosphere as the Fundamental Concept of a New Aesthetics." *Thesis Eleven* 36: 113–26.

Bose, Friedrich von. 2015. "Paradoxien Der Intervention: Das Humboldt Lab Dahlem." *FKW // Zeitschrift Für Geschlechterforschung Und Visuelle Kultur*, no. 58: 28–40.

Bowman, Glenn. 2007. "Identifying versus Identifying With 'the other.' Reflections on the Siting of the Subject in Anthropological Discourse." In *After Writing Culture: Epistemology and Praxis in Contemporary Anthropology*, edited by A. James, J. Hockey, and A. Dawson, 34–50. New York: Routledge.

Brenner, Carena. 2014. "Verräumlichung Der Macht." In *Die Ethnologie und die Politik des Raums. Bedeutungsproduktion Im Ethnographischen Film*, 21–88. Bielefeld: Transcript Verlag.

Broekhoven, Laura N.K. Van. 2013. "Authenticity and Curatorial Practice." In *Creating Authenticity: Authentication Processes in Ethnographic Museums*, edited by Alexander Geurds and Laura N.K. Van Broekhoven, 151–62. Leiden: Sidestone Press.

Bruner, Edward M. 1994. "Abraham Lincoln as Authentic Reproduction: A Critique of Postmodernism." *American Anthropologist* 96 (2): 397–415.

Bruner, Jerome. 1991. "The Narrative Construction of Reality." *Critical Inquiry* 18 (1): 1–21.

Burke, Peter. 2009. "Varieties of Terminology." In *Cultural Hybridity*. Cambridge: Polity Press.

Butler, Judith. 1993. "Critically Queer." *GLQ: A Journal of Lesbian and Gay Studies* 1: 17–32.

Butler, Shelley Ruth. 2000. "The Politics of Exhibiting Culture: Legacies and Possibilities." *Museum Anthropology* 23 (3): 74–92.

Bystron, Daniela, and Monika Zessnik. 2014. "Kulturzentrum oder Museum? Vermittlungspraxis im Ethnologischen Museum Dahlem und Hamburger Bahnhof - Museum für Gegenwart - Berlin." In *Experimentierfeld Museum. Internationale Perspektiven auf Museum, Islam und Inklusion*, edited by Susan Kamel and Christine Gerbich, 319–52. Bielefeld: Transcript.

Cameron, Duncan. 1971. "The Museum, A Temple or a Forum." *Curator: The Museum Journal* 141: 11–24.

Caputo, Richard K. 1988. *Management and Information Systems in Human Services: Implications for the Human Services.* London, New York: The Haworth Press.

Charmaz, Kathy. 2003. "Grounded Theory." In *Qualitative Psychology: A Practical Guide to Research Methods*, edited by J.A. Smith, 81–110. London: Sage.

Charmaz, Kathy. 2006. *Constructing Grounded Theory: A Practical Guide*. London: SAGE Publications.

Claas, Ulrike. 2009. "'Fish, Water, and Mosquitos': The Western Invention of Iatmul Culture." In *Form, Macht, Differenz: Motive Und Felder Ethnologischen Forschens*, edited by Elfriede Hermann, Karin Klenke, and Michael Dickhardt, 215–26. Göttingen: Universitätsverlag Göttingen.

Clifford, James. 1985. "Objects and Selves - An Afterword." In *Objects and Others. Essays on Museums and Material Culture*, edited by George W. Stocking, 236–46. Madison, WI: University of Wisconsin Press.

Clifford, James. 1986. "Introduction: Partial Truths." In *Writing Culture: The Poetics and Politics of Anthropology*, edited by James Clifford and George E. Marcus, 1–26. Berkeley, London: University of California Press.

Clifford, James. 1988. *The Predicament of Culture: Twentieth-Century Ethnography, Literature, and Art*. Cambridge, MA: Harvard University Press.

Clifford, James. 1997. *Museums as Contact Zones. Routes: Travel and Translation in the Late Twentieth Century*. Cambridge, MA, London: Harvard University Press.

Clifford, James, and George Marcus. 1986. *Writing Culture: The Poetics and Politics of Ethnography*. Berkeley: UCB Press.

Coombes, Annie E. 1988. "Museums and the Formation of National and Cultural Identities." *Oxford Art Journal* 11 (2): 57–68.

Coombes, Annie E. 1994. *Reinventing Africa: Museums, Material Culture and Popular Imagination in Late Victorian and Edwardian England*. New Haven, London: Yale University Press.

Crane, Susan A. 2006. "The Conundrum of Ephemerality: Time, Memory, and Museums." In *A Companion to Museum Studies*, edited by Sharon Macdonald, 98–110. Malden, MA, Oxford, Carlton: Blackwell Publishing.

Crossley, Émilie. 2012. "Poor but Happy: Volunteer Tourists' Encounters with Poverty." *Tourism Geographies* 14 (2): 235-253.

Deliss, Clémentine, and Yvette Mutumba. 2014. *Ware & Wissen, or the Stories You Wouldn't Tell a Stranger*. Zürich: diaphanes.

Derrida, Jacques. 1988. *Signature Event Context*. Evanston, IL: North Western University Press.

Derrida, Jacques. 2005. *Wrting and Difference, Translated, with an Introduction and Additional Notes, by Alan Bass*. London, New York: Routledge.

434

Dewdney, Andrew, David Dibosa, and Victoria Walsh. 2012. "Cultural Diversity. Politics, Policy and Practices. The Case of Tate Encounters." In *Museums, Equality and Social Justice*, edited by Richard Sandall and Eithne Nightingale, 114–24. London and New York: Routledge.

Dewey, John. 1938. *Logic: The Theory of Inquiry*. New York: Henry Holt and Company.

Dhanjal, Sarah. 2012. "Ethnizität, Kulturelles Erbe Und (Die Funktion von) Museen Aus Britischer Perspektive." *Museumskunde* 77 (2): 23–28.

Dicks, Bella. 2004. *Culture on Display: The Production of Contemporary Visitability*. Berkshire, England: Open University Press.

Diekmann, Anya, and Melanie Kay Smith, eds. 2015. *Ethnic and Minority Cultures as Tourist Attractions*. Bristol: Channel View Publications.

Dipesh Chakrabarty. 2000. "Provincializing Europe." Princeton: Princeton University Press.

Dominguez, Virginia R. 1994. "Invoking Culture: The Messy Side of 'Cultural Politics.'" In *Eloquent Obsessions: Writing Cultural Criticism*, edited by Marianna Torgovnick, 237–59. Durham, NC: Duke University Press.

Douglas Kellner. 2001. "Cultural Studies and Philosophy: An Intervention." In *A Companion to Cultural Studies*, edited by Toby Miller, 139–53. Malden, Oxford: Blackwell.

Dresing, Thorsten, and Thorsten Pehl. 2013. *Praxisbuch Interview, Transkription & Analyse*. Marburg: Eigenverlag.

Duensing, Sally. 2002. "The Object of Experience." In *Perspectives on Object-Centered Learning in Museums*, edited by Scott G. Paris, 317–28. Mahwah: Lawrence Erlbaum Associates.

Duncan, Carol. 2005. "The Art Museum as Ritual." In *Heritage, Museums and Galleries. An Introductory Reader*, edited by Gerard Corsane, 78–88. London, New York: Routledge.

Durkheim, Emile. 1984. *The Division of Labour, with an Introduction by Lewis Coser, Translated by W.D. Halls*. Houndmills, London: Macmillan.

Durrans, Brian. 1988. "The Future of the Other: Changing Cultures on Display in Ethnographic Museums." In *The Museum Time-Machine*, edited by Robert Lumley, 144–69. London, New York: Routledge.

Ellsworth, Elizabeth. 1989. "Why Doesn't This Feel Empowering? Working Through the Repressive Myths of Critical Pedagogy." *Harvard Educational Review* 59 (3): 297–324.

Eriksen, Thomas Hylland. 2006. "Diversity versus Difference: Neo-Liberalism in the Minority-Debate." In *The Making and Unmaking of Difference. Anthropological, Sociological and Philosophical Perspectives*, edited by Richard Rottenburg, Burkhard Schnepel, and Shingo Shimada, 13–26. Bielefeld: Transcript.

Fabian, Johannes. 1983. *Time and the Other: How Anthropology Makes Its Object*. New York: Columbia University Press.

Fabian, Johannes. 1991 [1985]. "Culture, Time, and the Object of Anthropology." In *Time and the Work of Anthropology: Critical Essays 1971-1981*, 191–206. London, New York: Routledge.

Fabian, Johannes. 2006. "Critical Afterthoughts." *Anthropological Theory* 6 (2): 139–52.

Falk, John Howard, and Lynn D. Dierking. 2002. *Lessons Without Limit: How Free-Choice Learning Is Transforming Education*. Walnut Creek, CA: AltaMira.

Falk, John Howard, and Lynn Diane Dierking. 2000. *Learning from Museums: Visitor Experiences and the Making of Meaning*. Lanham, MD: Rowman & Littlefield.

Feldmann, Doris. 2010. "Differenzen Ohne Ende? Möglichkeiten Und Grenzen Der Differenzkategorie Aus Kultur- Und Literaturwissenschaftlicher Sicht." In *Identität Und Unterschied: Zur Theorie von Kultur, Differenz Und Transdifferenz*, edited by Cristian Alvarado Leyton and Philipp Erchinger, 59–72. Bielefeld: Transcript.

Ferguson, Bruce W. 1996. "Exhibition Rhetorics: Material Speech and Utter Sense." In *Thinking about Exhibitions*, edited by Reesa Greenberg, Bruce W. Ferguson, and Sandy Nairne, 175–90. London: Routledge.

Flick, Uwe. 2000. "Episodic Interviewing." In *Qualitative Researching with Text, Image and Sound: A Practical Handbook for Social Research*, edited by Paul Atkinson, Martin W Bauer, and George Gaskell, 75–92. London: Sage Publications.

Flick, Uwe. 2009. *An Introduction to Qualitative Research*. London: Sage Publications.

Forster, E.M. 1962. *Ansichten Des Romans*. Frankfurt am Main: Suhrkamp.

Foucault, Michel. 1986. "Of Other Spaces: Utopias and Heterotopias." *Diacritics*, no. 16: 22–27.

Fraser, Annabel, and Hannah Coulson. 2012. "Incomplete Stories." In *Museum Making: Narratives, Architectures, Exhibitions*, edited by Suzanne Macleod, laura Hourston Hanks, and jonathan Hale, 223–31. New York, London: Routledge.

Freud, Sigmund. 1930. "Das Unbehagen in Der Kultur." In *Studienausgabe Bd. IX*, 191–270. Frankfurt am Main: S. Fischer.

Friedman, Jonathan. 1990. "Being in the World: Globalization and Localization." In *Global Culture: Nationalism, Globalization and Modernity*, edited by Mike Featherstone, 311–28. New York: Sage.

Fritsch, Juliette. 2011. "'Education Is a Department Isn't it?' Perceptions of Education, Learning and Interpretation in Exhibition Development." In *Museum Gallery Interpretation and Material*

Culture, edited by Juliette Fritsch, 234–48. New York: Taylor & Francis.

Gadamer, Hans-Georg. 1975. *Truth and Method*. London, New York: Continuum.

Garcia, Ben. 2012. "What We Do Best Making the Case for the Museum Learning in Its Own Right." *Journal of Museum Education* 37 (2): 47–56.

Garoian, Charles R. 2001. "Performing the Museum." *Studies in Art Education* 42 (3): 234–48.

Gaudelli, William. 2014. "An Ethnology Museum as Pedagogical Space." In *Beyond Pedagogy: Reconsidering the Public Purpose of Museums*, edited by Brenda Trofaneko and Avner Segall, 155–68. Rotterdam: Sense Publishers.

Geertz, Clifford. 1973. *The Interpretation of Cultures: Selected Essays*. New York: Basic Books.

Gell, Alfred. 1998. *Art and Agency: An Anthropological Theory*. Oxford, New York: Clarendon Press.

Geurds, Alexander. 2013. "Culture Sketching: The Authenticity Quest in Ethnographic Museums. An Introduction." In *Creating Authenticity: Authentication Processes in Ethnographic Museums*, edited by Alexander Geurds and Laura Van Broekhoven, 2013:1–11. Leiden: Sidestone Press.

Glover Frykman, Sue. 2009. "Stories to Tell? Narrative Tools in Museum Education Texts." *Educational Research* 51 (3): 299–319.

Goffman, Erving. 1965. *The Presentation of self in Everyday Life*. Edinburgh: University of Edingburgh Social Sciences Research Centre.

Golding, Viv. 2012. "Towards a New Museum Pedagogy: Learning, Teaching and Impact." In *Learning at the Museum Frontiers: Identity, Race and Power*, 165–91. Farnham: Ashgate Publishing.

Goncalves, Susana. 2013. "Seen at a Distance: How Images, Spaces and Memories Shape Cultural Encounters." In *Diversity, Intercultural Encounters, and Education*, edited by Susana Goncalves and Markus A. Carpenter, 1–40. Abingdon: Routledge.

Goodman, Nelson. 1978. *Ways of Worldmaking*. Indianapolis: Hacket Publishing Company.

Gorski, Paul C. 2008. "Good Intentions Are Not Enough: On Decolonizing Intercultural Education." *Intercultural Education* 19 (6): 515–25.

Greenblatt, Stephen. 1991. "Resonance and Wonder." In *Exhibiting Cultures. The Poetics and Politics of Museum Display*, edited by Ivan Karp and Steven D. Lavine, 42–56. Washington, D.C.: Smithsonian Institution Press.

Grenier, R. S. 2009. "The Role of Learning in the Development of Expertise in Museum Docents." *Adult Education Quarterly* 59 (2): 142–57.

Griffiths, Gareth. 1995. "The Myth of Authenticity." In *The Postcolonial Studies Reader*, edited by Bill Ashcroft, Gareth Griffiths, and Helen Tiffin. London, New York: Routledge.

Grinder, Alison A., and E. Sue McCoy. 1985. *The Good Guide: A Sourcebook for Interpreters, Docents, and Tour Guides*. Winter Haven, Fl: Ironwood Publishing.

Gupta, Akhil, and James Ferguson. 1992. "Beyond 'Culture': Space, Identity, and the Politics of Difference." *Cultural Anthropology* 7 (1): 6–23.

Gukenbiehl, Hermann L. 2003. "Institution Und Organisa." In *Einführung in Hauptbegriffe Der Soziologie*, edited by Hermann Korte and Bernhard Schäfers, 143–60. Wiesbaden: Verlag für Sozialwissenschaften.

Häntzschel, Jörg. 2017, "Das Humboldt Forum ist wie Tschernobyl, Interview mit Benedicte Savoy," in Süddeutsche Zeitung Online, 20/07/2017, last accessed 26/09/2017. <<http://www.sueddeutsche.de/kultur/benedicte-savoy-ueber-das-humboldt-forum-das-humboldt-forum-ist-wie-tschernobyl-1.3596423-2?reduced=true>>

Hall, Stuart. 1997. "Introduction." In *Representation: Cultural Representations and Signifiying Practices*, edited by Stuart Hall, 1–15. London, Thousand Oaks, New Delhi: SAGE Publications.

Hallam, Elizabeth. 2000. "Texts, Objects and 'Otherness': Problems of Historical Process in Writing and Displaying Cultures." In *Cultural Encounters: Representing "Otherness,"* edited by Elizabeth Hallam and Brian V. Street, 260–83. London, New York: Routledge.

Harris, Clare, and Micheal O'Hanlon. 2013. "The Future of the Ethnographic Museum." *Anthropology Today* 29: 8–12.

Hein, George E. 1994. "The Constructivist Museum." In *The Educational Role of the Museum*, edited by Eilean Hooper-Greenhill, 73–79. London, New York: Routledge.

Hein, George E. 1998. *Learning in the Museum*. London: Routledge.

Hein, George E. 2006. "Museum Education." In *A Companion to Museum Studies*, edited by Sharon Macdonald, 340–52. Malden, MA, Oxford, Carlton: Blackwell Publishing.

Heinen, Sandra. 2009. *Narratology in the Age of Cross-Disciplinary Narrative Research*. Edited by Sandra Heinen and Roy Sommer. Berlin, New York: Walter de Gruyter.

Herman, David. 2009. "Narrative Ways of Worldmaking." In *Narratology in the Age of Cross-Disciplinary Narrative Research*, edited by Sandra Heinen and Roy Sommer, 71–87. Berlin: Walter de Gruyter.

Hill, Kate. 2011. "Thinking About Audience and Agency in the Museum: Models from Historical Research." *Current Issues in European Cultural Studies* June 2011: 217–22.

438

Hodson, Randy and Teresa A. Sullivan. 2012. *The Social Organization of Work*. Belmont, CA: Wadsworth.

Hooper-Greenhill, Eilean. 1988. "Counting Visitors or Visitors Who Count?" In *The Museum Experience*, edited by Robert Lumley, 213–32. London, New York: Routledge.

Hooper-Greenhill, Eilean. 1989. "The Museum in the Disciplinary Society." In *Museum Studies in Material Culture*, edited by Susan M. Pearce, 66–72. Leicester: Leicester University Press.

Hooper-Greenhill, Eilean. 1994. *The Educational Role of the Museum*. London: Routledge.

Hooper-Greenhill, Eilean. 2000. *Museums and the Interpretation of Visual Culture*. London and New York: Routledge.

Hooper-Greenhill, Eilean. 2007. *Museums and Education: Purpose, Pedagogy, Performance*. London: Routledge.

Hourston Hanks, Laura. 2012. "Writing Spatial Stories. Textual Narratives in the Museum." In *Museum Making: Narratives, Architectures, Exhibitions*, edited by Suzanne MacLeod, Laura Hourston Hanks, and Jonathan Hale, 21–34. London, New York: Routledge.

Housen, Abigail. 2007. "Art Viewing and Aesthetic Development: Designing for the Viewer." In *From Periphery to Center: Art Museum Education in the 21st Century*, edited by Pat Villeneuve. Reston, VI: National Art Education Association.

Illeris, Helene. 2006. "Museums and Galleries as Performative Sites for Lifelong Learning: Constructions, Deconstructions and Reconstructions of Audience Positions in Museum and Gallery Education." *Museum and Society* 4 (1): 15–26.

Illeris, Helene. 2009. "Visual Events and the Friendly Eye: Modes of Educating Vision in New Educational Settings in Danish Art Galleries." *Museum and Society* 7 (1): 16–31.

Jackson, Michael. 1996. "Phenomenology, Radical Empiricism, and Anthropological Critique." In *Things as They Are. New Directions in Phenomenological Anthropology*, 1–50. Bloomington, Indianapolis: Indiana University Press.

Jacobsen, John W. 2006. *Experiential Learning Museums*. Marblehead, MA: White Oak Associates.

Janes, Robert R. 2009. *Museums in a Troubled World: Renewal, Irrelevance or Collapse?* London, New York: Routledge.

Jenkins, Tiffany. 2011. "Inverting the Nation at the British Museum." In *Great Narratives of the Past. Traditions and Revisions in National Museums Conference Proceedings from EuNaMus, European National Museums: Identity Politics, the Uses of the Past and the European Citizen*, edited by Dominique Poulot, Felicity Bodenstein, and José María Lanzarote Gurial, 387–94. PAris.

Johnston-Arthur, Araba Evelyn. "»… um die Leiche des verstorbenen M[..]en Soliman …« Strategien der Entherzigung, Dekolonisation und Dekonstruktion österreichischer Neutralitäten." In *Das Unbehagen im Museum. Postkoloniale Museologien*, edited by Belinda Kazeem, Charlotte Martinz-Turek, and Nora Sternfeld, 11-42. Wien: Turia + Kant.

Joyce, Rosemary. 2013. "When Is Authentic? Situating Authenticizy in Itineraries of Objects." In *Creating Authenticity: Authentication Processes in Ethnographic Museums*, edited by Alexander Geurds and Laura N.K. Van Broekhoven, 39–58. Leiden: Sidestone Press.

Juneja, Monica. 2011. "Global Art History and the 'Burden of Representation.'" In *Global Studies: Mapping Contemporary Art and Culture*, edited by Hans Belting, Jakob Birken, and Andrea Buddensieg, 274–97. Stuttgart: Hatje Cantz.

Juneja, Monica, and Christian Kravagna. 2013. "Understanding Transculturalism. Monica Juneja and Christian Kravagna in Conversation." In *Transcultural Modernisms*, edited by Fahim Amir, Eva Egermann, Moira Hille, Jakob Krameritsch, Christian Kravagna, Christina Linorter, Marion von Osten, and Peter Spillmann, 22–33. Wien: Sternberg Press.

Kamel, Susan. 2017. "How Access-Iting? Museums as Cultural Educators or Shelters of Knowledge." In *Contemporary Curating and Museum Education*, edited by Carmen Mörsch, Angeli Sachs, and Thomas Sieber, 117–30. Bielefeld: transcript.

Karp, Ivan, and Fred Wilson. 1996. "Constructing the Spectacle of Culture in Museums." In *Thinking about Exhibitions*, edited by Reesa Greenberg, Bruce W. Ferguson, and Sandy Nairne, 251–67. London, New York: Routledge.

Karp, Ivan, and Corinne A. Kratz. 2014. "Collecting, Exhibiting, and Interpreting: Museums as Mediators and Midwives of Meaning." *Museum Anthropology* 37 (1): 51–65.

Karp, Ivan, and Corinne A. Kratz. 2000. "Reflections on the Fate of Tippoo's Tiger: Defining Cultures through Public Display." In *Cultural Encounters: Representing "Otherness,"* edited by Elizabeth Hallam and Brian V. Street, 194–228. London, New York: Routledge.

Kaschuba, Wolfgang. 1995. "Kulturalismus: Vom Verschwinden des Sozialen im gesellschaftlichen Diskurs." In *Kulturen - Identitäten - Diskurse. Perspektiven Europäischer Ethnologie*, edited by Wolfgang Kaschuba, 11–30. Berlin: Akademie-Verlag.

Kaufmann, Thomas Dacosta. 2008. "The Geography of Art: Historiography, Issues, and Perspectives." In *World Art Studies: Exploring Concepts and Approaches*, edited by Kitty Zijlmans and Wilfried van Damme, 167–82. Amsterdam: Valiz.

Kazeem, Belinda, Charlotte Martinz-Turek, and Nora Sternfeld, eds. 2009. *Das Unbehagen Im Museum. Postkoloniale Museologien*. Wien: Turia + Kant.

440

Kershow, Baz. 1994. "Framing the Audience for Theatre." In *The Authority of the Consumer*, 154–74. London, New York: Routledge.

Keurs, Pieter Ter. 1999. "Things of the Past? Museums and Ethnographic Objects." *Journal Des Africanistes* 69 (1): 67–80.

Kidd, Jenny. 2012. "The Museum as Narrative Witness. Heritage Performance and the Production of Narrative Space." In *Museum Making: Narratives, Architectures, Exhibitions*, edited by Suzanne McLeod, Laura Hourston Hanks, and Jonathan Hale, 72–82. Abingdon, Oxon: Routledge.

Kirshenblatt-Gimblett, Barbara. 1998. *Destination Culture. Tourism, Museums, and Heritage*. Berkeley, Los Angeles: University of California Press.

Kjell, Olsen. 2002. "Authenticity as a Concept in Tourism Research: The Social Organization of the Experience of Authenticity." *Tourist Studies* 2 (2): 159–82.

Kohl, Karl-Heinz. 2000. *Ethnologie - Die Wissenschaft vom kulturell Fremden. Eine Einführung*. München: C.H. Beck.

König, Viola. 2017. „Die Ethnologen sind keine Täter." *Welt Online* 22/08/2017. Last accessed 06/10/2017. <<https://www.welt.de/kultur/article167880505/Die-Ethnologen-sind-keine-Taeter.html>>

Kopytoff, Igor. 1986. "The Cultural Biography of Things: Commoditization as Process." In *The Social Life of Things. Commodities in Cultural Perspectives*, edited by A, 64–91. Cambridge: Cambridge University Press.

Korff, Gottfried. 2002. "Fremde (the Foreign, Strange, Other) and the Museum." *Journal of the Society for the Anthropology of Europe* 2 (2): 29–34.

Kravagna, Christian. 2015. "Vom ethnologischen Museum zum Unmöglichen Kolonialmuseum." *Zeitschrift für Kulturwissenschaften* 1: 95–118.

Kristeva, Julia. 1991. *Strangers to Ourselves*. New York: Columbia University Press.

Kuckartz, Udo. 2010. *Einführung in die computergestützte Analyse qualitativer Daten*. Wiesbaden: VS Verlag.

Kymlicka, Will. 2012. *Multiculturalism: Success, Failure, and the Future*. Washington, D.C: Migration Policy Institute.

Lacan, Jacques. 1988. *The Seminar of Jacques Lacan, Book I: Freud's Papers on Technique [1953-1954]*. New York: W.W. Norton.

Laclau, Ernesto. 1996. *Emancipation(s)*. London and New York: Verso.

Lang, Caroline, John Reeve, and Vicky Woollard. 2016. "The Impact of Government Policy." In *The Responsive Museum: Working with Audiences in the Twenty-First Century*, 19–28. Abingdon, New York: Routledge.

Latour, Bruno. 2005. *Reassembling the Social. An Introduction to Actor-Network-Theory.* Oxford: Oxford University Press.

Laukötter, Anja. 2007. *Von der "Kultur" zur "Rasse" - Vom Objekt zum Körper?: Völkerkundemuseen und ihre Wissenschaften zu Beginn des 20. Jahrhunderts.* Bielefeld: transcript Verlag.

Laukötter, Anja. 2013. "Das Völkerkundemuseum." In *Kein Platz an Der Sonne: Erinnerungsorte Der Deutschen Kolonialgeschichte*, 231–43. Frankfurt am Main: Campus Verlag.

Lavine, Steven D. 1991. "Museum Practices." In *Exhibiting Cultures. The Poetics and Politics of Museum Display*, edited by Ivan Karp and Steven D. Lavine, 151–58. Washington, D.C: Smithsonian Institution Press.

Layne, Heidi, and Amikeng Alemanji. 2015. "'Zebra World': The Promotion of Imperial Stereotypes in a Children's Book." *Power and Education* 7 (2): 181–95.

Lefebvre, Henri. 1991. *The Production of Space.* Oxford, Cambridge, MA: Blackwell.

Levinas, E. 1981. *Otherwise than Being, Or, beyond Essence, Translated by Alphonso Lingis.* Pittsburgh, PY: Duquesne University Press.

Lidchi, Henrietta. 1997. "The Poetics and the Politics of Exhibiting Other Cultures." In *Representation: Cultural Representations and Signifiying Practices*, edited by Stuart Hall. London: SAGE Publications.

Lidchi, Henrietta. 2006. "Culture and Constraints: Further Thoughts on Ethnography and Exhibiting." *International Journal of Heritage Studies* 12 (1): 93–114.

Littler, Jo. 2005. "Introduction: British Heritage and the Legacies of 'Race.'" In *The Politics of Heritage. The Legacies of "Race,"* edited by Jo Littler and Roshi Naidoo, 1–20. Abingdon, Oxon: Routledge.

Lonetree, Amy. 2012. *Decolonizing Museums : Representing Native America in National and Tribal Museums.* Chapel Hill: University of North Carolina Press.

Loren, Diana DiPaolo. 2015. "Seeing Hybridity in the Anthropology Museum: Practices of Longing and Fetishization." *Journal of Social Archaeology* 15 (3): 299–318.

Lozanski, Kristin. 2010. "Defining 'real India': Representations of Authenticity in Independent Travel." *Social Identities* 16 (6): 741–62.

Lueger, Manfred. 2000. *Grundlagen Qualitativer Feldforschung: Methdologie, Organisierung, Materialanalyse.* WUV-Univer. Wien.

Lutz-Sterzenbach, Barbara, Ansgar Schnurr, and Ernst Wagner. 2013. "Remix der Bildkultur - Remix der Lebenswelten. Baustellen für eine transkulturelle Kunstpädagogik." In *Bildwelten Remix. Transkultur, Globalität, Diversity in kunstpädagogischen Feldern*, edited by Barbara Lutz-Sterzenbach, Ansgar Schnurr, and Ernst Wagner, 13–26. Bielefeld: Transcript Verlag.

Lynch, Bernadette. 2014. "'Generally Dissatisfied': Hidden Pedagogy in the Postcolonial Museum." In *Thema. La Revue Des Musées de La Civilisation*, edited by Mathieu Viau-Courville and Mélanie Lanouette, 79–92. Québec: Les Musées de la civilisation.

MacCannel, Dean. 1999. *The Tourist: A New Theory of the Leisure Class*. Berkeley, Los Angeles: University of California Press.

Macdonald, Sharon. 2003. "Museums, National, Postnational and Transcultural Identities." *Museum and Society* 1 (1): 1–16.

Macdonald, Sharon. 2006. "Collecting Practices." In *A Companion to Museum Studies*, edited by Sharon Macdonald, 81–97. Malden, MA, Oxford, Carlton: Blackwell Publishing.

MacGregor, Neil. 2004. "The British Museum." *ICOM News* 1: 7.

Marcus, George E. 1998. "Ethnography In/of the World System. The Emergence of Multi-Sited Ethnography." In *Ethnography Through Thick and Thin*, 79–104. Princeton, NJ: Princeton University Press.

Mayer, Melinda M. 2005. "Bridging the Theory-Practice Divide in Contemporary Art Museum Education." *Art Education* 58 (2): 13–17.

Mayer, Melinda M. 2015. "Looking Outside the Frame: 'Demythifying' Museum Education." *Art Education* 65 (4): 15–18.

Mirzoeff, Nicholas. 1999. *An Introduction to Visual Culture*. London, New York: Routledge.

Mitchell, Timothy. 1989. "The World as Exhibition." *Comparative Studies in Society and History* 31 (2). Cambridge University Press: 217–36.

Mohanty, Satya P. 1995. "Epilogue Colonial Legacies, Multicultural Futures : Relativism, Objectivity, and the Challenge of Otherness." *PMLA* 110 (1): 108–18.

Mörsch, Carmen. 2011. "Über Zugang hinaus. Nachträgliche einführende Gedanken zur Arbeitstagung 'Kunstvermittlung in der Migrationsgesellschaft.'" In *Kunstvermittlung in der Migrations-gesellschaft/ Reflexionen Einer Arbeitstagung – 2011*, 10–12. Berlin, Stuttgart.

Mörsch, Carmen, Angeli Sachs, and Thomas Sieber, eds. 2016. *Contemporary Curating and Museum Education*. Bielefeld: Transcript.

Nietzsche, Friedrich Wilhelm. 1987 [1969]. *On the Genealogy of Morals*. New York: Vintage Books.

Nitz, Julia. 2012. "The Reconstruction of the Past in Museums: A View from Narratology." In *The Museal Turn*, edited by Sabine Coelsch-Foisner and Douglas Brown, 173–88. Heidelberg: Universitätsverlag Winter.

Noack, Karoline. 2015. "Museum und Universität: Institutionen der Ethnologie und Authentizität der Objekte. Rückblicke, Gegenwärtige Tendenzen und zukünftige Möglichkeiten." In *Quo Vadis, Völkerkundemuseum? Aktuelle Debatten zu ethnologischen*

Sammlungen in Museen und Universitäten, edited by Michael Kraus and Karoline Noack, 41–68. Bielefeld: transcript.

Noschka-Roos, Annette, and Doris Lewalter. 2013. "Lernen im Museum – Theoretische Perspektiven und empirische Befunde." *Zeitschrift für Erziehungswissenschaft* 16 (S3): 199–215.

Nünning, Ansgar. 2009. "Narrativist Approaches and Narratological Concepts." In *Travelling Concepts for the Study of Culture*, 145–84. Berlin, Boston: Walter de Gruyter.

Nünning, Ansgar. 2010. "Making Events - Making Stories - Making Worlds: Ways of Worldmaking from a Narratological Point of View." In *Cultural Ways of Worldmaking: Media and Narratives*, edited by Ansgar Nünning, Vera Nünning, and Birgit Neumann, 191–214. Berlin, New York: Walter de Gruyter.

O'Neill, Mark. 2004. "Enlightenment Museums: Universal or Merely Global?" *Museum and Society* 2 (3): 190–202.

O'Neill, Mark. 2006. "Essentialism, Adaptation and Justice: Towards a New Epistemology of Museums." *Museum Management and Curatorship* 21 (2): 95–116.

Ortiz, Fernando. 1995. *Cuban Counterpoint. Tobacco and Sugar*. Durham. London: Duke University Press.

Parmentier, Michael. 2005. "Evaluation von Schulklassenbesuchen im Museum." *Zeitschrift für Pädagogik* 51 (6): 774–85.

Pearce, Susan M. 2015. "Authority and Anarchy in a Museum Exhibition." *Cultural Dynamics* 7 (1): 125–40.

Petrov, Julia. 2012. "Playing Dress-Up. Inhabiting Imagined Spaces Through Museum Objects." In *The Thing About Museums. Objects and Experience, Representation and Contestation*, edited by Sandra Dudley, Amy Jane Barnes, Jennifer Binnie, Julia Petrov, and Jennifer Walklate, 230–41. Abingdon, New York: Routledge.

Phillips, Anne. 2008. *Multiculturalism without Culture*. Princeton, NJ: Princeton University Press.

Piaget, Jean. 1936. *Das Erwachen Der Intelligenz Beim Kinde*. Stuttgart: Klett.

Pieterse, Jan Nederveen. 1995. "Globalisation as Hybridization." In *Global Modernities*, edited by Mike Featherstone, Scott Lash, and Roland Robertson, 45–68. London: Sage.

Pieterse, Jan Nederveen. 2005. "Multiculturalism and Museums. Discourse about Others in the Age of Globalization." In *Heritage, Museums and Galleries. An Introductory Reader*, edited by Gerard Corsane, 163–83. London, New York: Routledge.

Pierroux, Palmyre. 2010. "Guiding Meaning on Guided Tours." In *Inside Multimodal Composition*, edited by A. Morrison, 417–50. Cresskill, NJ: Hampton Press.

Piscitelli, Barbara, and Katrina Weier. 2002. "Learning With, Through, and about Art: The Role of Social Interactions." In *Perspectives on*

444

    Object-Centered Learning in Museums, edited by Scott G. Paris, 121–51. Mahwah: Lawrence Erlbaum Associates.

Pratt, Mary Louise. 1992. *Imperial Eyes: Travel Writing and Transculturation. Imperial Eyes: Travel Writing and Transculturation*. London, New York: Routledge.

Preziosi, Donald. 1996. "Brain of the Earth's Body: Museums and the Framing of Modernity." In *The Rhetoric of the Frame. Essays on the Boundaries of the Artwork*, 96–110. Cambridge: Cambridge University Press.

Preziosi, Donald. 2003. *Brain of the Earth's Body: Art, Museums, and the Phantasms of Modernity*. Minneapolis: University of Minnesota Press.

Preziosi, Donald. 2004. "General Introduction: What Are Museums For?" In *Grasping the World: The Idea of the Museum.*, edited by Donald Preziosi and Claire Farago, 1–9. London, New York: Routledge.

Ravelli, Louise J. 2006. *Museum Texts: Communication Frameworks*. London, New York: Routledge.

Rectanus, Mark W. 2006. "Globalization: Incorporating the Museum." In *A Companion to Museum Studies*, edited by Sharon Macdonald, 381–97. Malden, MA, Oxford, Carlton: Blackwell Publishing.

Reeve, John. 2010. "Material Religion, Education, and Museums: Introduction." *Material Religion: The Journal of Objects, Art and Belief* 6 (2): 142–55.

Rice, Danielle. 1995. "Museum Education Embracing Uncertainty." *Art Bulletin* 76 (1): 15–20.

Rice, Danielle. 2003. "Balancing Act: Education and the Competing Impulses of Museum Work Linked References Are Available on JSTOR for This Article: Balancing Act: Education and the Competing Impulses of Museum Work." *Art Institute of Chicago Museum Studies* 29 (1): 6–19.

Riegel, Henrietta. 1996. "Into the Heart of Irony: Ethnographic Exhibitions and the Politics of Difference." In *Theorizing Museums*, edited by Sharon Macdonald and Gordon Fyfe, 83–104. Oxford: Blackwell.

Roberts, Lisa. 1995. *From Knowledge to Narrative: Educators and the Changing Museums*. Washington, DC: Smithsonian Institution Press.

Rodéhn, Cecilia. 2017. "The Job That No One Wants to Do? Museum Educators' Articulations about Guided Tours." *Museum & Society* 15 (1): 1–15.

Rodman, Margaret Critchlow. 1993. "A Critique of 'Place' through Field Museum's Pacific Exhibits." *The Contemporary Pacific* 5 (2): 243–74.

Rogers, Richard. 2006. "From Cultural Exchange to Transculturation: A Review and Reconceptualization of Cultural Appropriation." *Communication Theory* 16 (4): 474–503.

Root, Deborah. 1989. "Conquest, Appropriation, and Cultural Difference."
In *Cannibal Culture: Art, Appropriation, and the Commodification of
Difference*, 79–80. Boulder: Westview Press.

Rounds, Jay. 2006. "Doing Identity Work in Museums." *Curator: The
Museum Journal* 49 (2): 133–50.

Rundfunk Berlin-Brandenburg. 2017. „Parzinger wehrt sich gegen Kritik
am Humboldt Forum." *Rbb 24 Kultur* 28/07/2017. Last accessed
06/10/2017. <<
https://www.rbb24.de/kultur/beitrag/2017/07/parzinger-wehrt-sich-
gegen-kritik-am-humboldt-forum.html>>

Rutherford, Jonathan. 1990. "The Third Space. Interview with Homi
Bhabha." In *Identity: Community, Culture, Difference*, 207–21.
London: Lawrence and Wishart.

Said, Edward W. 1978. *Orientalism*. New York: Pantheon.

Sandell, Richard. 2005. "Constructing and Communicating Equality. The
Social Agency of Museum Space." In *Reshaping Museum Space.
Architecture, Design, Exhibitions*, edited by Suzanne McLeod, 185–
203. London, New York: Routledge.

Schöfthaler, Traugott. 1983. "Kultur in der Zwickmühle. Zur Aktualität des
Streits zwischen kulturrelativistischer und universalistischer
Sozialwissenschaft." *Argument* 139 (25): 333–47.

Schorch, Philipp. 2013. "Contact Zones, Third Spaces, and the Act of
Interpretation." *Museum and Society* 11 (3): 68–81.

Schwab, Raymond. 1984. *The Oriental Renaissance. Europe's
Rediscovery of India and the East 1680-1880, Translated by Gene
Patterson-Black and Victor Reinking*. Edited by Columbia University
Press. New York.

Searle, John R. 1976. "A Classification of Illocutionary Acts." *Language in
Society* 5: 1–23.

Sedgwick, Eve Kosofsky. 2003. "Introduction." In *Touching Feeling:
Affect, Pedagogy, Performativity*, 1–25. Durham: Duke University
Press.

Sfard, Anna. 1998. "On Two Metaphors for Learning and the Dangers of
Choosing Just One." *Educational Researcher* 27 (2): 4–13.

Shelton, Anthony. 1995. "Introduction: Object Realities." Edited by
Anthony Shelton. *Cultural Dynamics: Insurant Scholarship on
Culture, Politics and Power* 7 (1). London: SAGE: 5–14.

Shelton, Anthony. 1997. "My Others' Others Other: The Limits of
Museum Ethnography." *Antropologia Portuguesa*, no. 14: 37–62.

Shelton, Anthony. 2006. "Museums and Anthropologies: Practices and
Narratives." In *A Companion to Museum Studies*, edited by Sharon
Macdonald, 64–80. Malden, Oxford, Carlton: Blackwell Publishing.

Simmel, Georg. 1908. "Exkurs über den Fremden." In *Soziologie.
Untersuchungen über die Formen der Vergesellschaftung*, 509–12.
Berlin: Duncker & Humblot.

Simon, Nina. 2010. *The Participatory Museum*. San Francisco, CA: Museum 2.0.

Simpson, Moira G. 2001. *Making Representations. Museums in the Post-Colonial Era*. 2nd ed. London: Routledge.

Slam, Deirdre C. 2005. "The Informed Muse. The Implications of 'The New Museology' for Museum Practice." In *Heritage, Museums and Galleries. An Introductory Reader*, edited by Gerard Corsane, 54–70. London, New York: Routledge.

Spencer R. Crew, and James E. Sims. 1991. "Locating Authenticity: Fragments of a Dialogue." In *Exhibiting Cultures. The Poetics and Politics of Museum Display*, edited by Ivan Karp and Steven D. Levine, 159–75. Washington, D.C: Smithsonian Institution Press.

Spivak, Gayatri C. 1985. "The Rani of Sirmur: An Essay in Reading the Archives." *History and Theory* 24 (3): 247–72.

Spock, Daniel. 2006. "The Puzzle of Museum Educational Practice: A Comment on Rounds and Falk." *Curator: The Museum Journal* 49 (2): 167–80.

Steiner, George. 1998. *After Babel. Aspects of Language and Translation*. Oxford: Oxford University Press.

Steyn, Juliet. 2006. "The Museums' Future." *Futures* 38 (5): 606–18.

Sturge, Kate. 2006. "The Other on Display: Translation in the Ethnographic Museum." In *Translating Others Vol II*, edited by Theo Hermans, 431–39. Manchester: St. Jerome.

Sturge, Kate. 2007. *Representing Others. Translation, Ethnography and the Museum*. Manchester: St. Jerome.

Takeda, Arata. 2010. "Transkulturalität im Schulunterricht. Ein Konzept und vier 'Rezepte' für grenzüberschreitendes Lehren und Lernen." In *Schule Gestalten: Vielfalt Nutzen! Die schulpraktische Bedeutung der spezifischen Ressourcen von Lehrerinnen und Lehrern mit Migrationshintergrund. Beispielsammlung*, 1–6. Stuttgart: Stabsabteilung Integrationspolitik.

Taylor, Charles. 1994. "The Politics of Recognition." In *Multiculturalism: Examining The. Politics of Recognition.*, edited by Amy Gutman, 25–73. Princeton: Princeton University Press.

Timm, Elisabeth. 2014. "Partizipation. Publikumsbewegungen im modernen Museum." *Perfomap.de* 5 (Juni): 1–11.

Tran, Lynn Uyen. 2007. "Teaching Science in Museums: The Pedagogy and Goals of Museum Educators." *Science Education* 91: 278–97.

Tulving, Endel. 1992. "Episodic and Semantic Knowledge." In *Organization of Memory*, edited by Endel Tulving and Wayne Donaldson, 381–402. New York, London: Academic Press.

Turner, Ralph. 1962. "Role-Taking: Process vs. Conformity." In *Behavior and Social Processes*, edited by Arnold Rose, 20–40. Boston, MA: Houghton Mifflin.

Vannini, Philipp, and J. Patrick Williams. 2016. *Authenticity in Culture, self, and Society*. Abingdon, New York: Routledge.

Vergo, Peter. 1989. *The New Museology*. London: Reaktion Books.

Villeneuve, Pat, and Ann Rowson Love. 2017. *Visitor-Centered Exhibitions and Edu-Curation in Art Museums*. Lanham, Boulder, New York, London: Rowman & Littlefield.

Wagner, Bernd. 2010. "Kontaktzonen im Museum. Kindergruppen in der Ausstellung 'Indianer Nordamerikas.'" *Paragrana* 19 (2): 192–203.

Wallman, Sandra. 1997. "Appropriate Anthropology and the Risky Inspirations of 'Capability' Brown: Representations of What, by Whom, and to What End?" In *After Writing Culture: Epistemology and Praxis in Contemporary Anthropology*, 244–63. London, New York: Routledge.

Walz, Markus. 2016. "Einleitung." In *Handbuch Museum*, edited by Markus Walz, 1–7. Stuttgart: J.B. Metzler Verlag.

Welsch, Wolfgang. 1999. "Transculturality: The Puzzling Form of Cultures Today." In *Spaces of Culture: City, Nation, World*, edited by Mike Featherstone and Scott Lash, 194–213. London: Sage.

Welz, Gisela. 1996. *Inszenierungen Kultureller Vielfalt*. Frankfurt am Main, New York, Berlin: Akademie-Verlag.

White, Hayden. 1980. "The Value of Narrativity in the Representation of Reality." In *On Narration*, 1–23. Chicago: University of Chicago Press.

Wolf, Eric R. 1982. *Europe and the People Without History*. Berkely, Los Angeles, London: University of California Press.

Xanthoudaki, Maria. 2003. "Museums, Galleries and Art Education in Primary Schools. Researching Experiences in England and Greece." In *Researching Visual Arts Education in Museums and Galleries. An International Reader*, edited by Maria Xanthoudaki, Les Tickle, and Veronica Sekules, 105–16. Dordrecht, Boston, London: Kluwer Academic Publishers.

Yap, Yee-yin. 2014. "Ethnographic Representations of Self and the Other in Museums: To Whom Do They Speak, and What Do They Say?" *Glocal Times* 21: 1–12.

Yenawine, Philip. 2013. *From Periphery to Center: Art Museum Education in the 21st Century*. Cambridge, MA: Harvard University Press.

Appendix

Transcription System

The rules for the transcription of the material are based upon Dresing and Pehl's simplified transcription system (2013), but some aspects have been omitted and modified to suit the purpose of this research project. The following table gives an overview of the applied transcription rules.

Element of speech	Transcription rule	Adaptation Dresing/Pehl
Anacoluthon	flattened if redundant	
Half sentences / interruption	'And I knew it was /' - 'bad?' 'Exactly.'	Dresing/ Pehl only mark half sentences by '/'
Contractions	flattened ("hats = hat es")	
Pauses	(.) 1 second pause (..) 2 second pause (...) 3 second pause (4) 4 second pause	Dresing/ Pehl only use (...) as a marker of a short pause
Signals of understanding ('ehm', 'mhm')	omitted unless the statement consists only of these signals	
Highlighted words	CAPITAL LETTERS	
Emotional non-verbal utterances	(laughs)	
Situation descriptions	(a member of staff interrupts us)	This is an addition to the model of Dresing/ Pehl

incomprehensible words or phrases	German transcripts: "(unv.)" English transcripts: '(incompr.)' reasons for incomprehensibility are provided in brackets	
Statements that are difficult to understand, guesses at statements due to incomprehensibility	'And then we (went into?) the museum.'	
Abbreviations of interviewer and interviewees	Interviewer: KW Interviewees: First letter of anonymised name	Dresing/ Pehl use A and B as abbreviations
Comments of interviewer added during the transcription	[anonymized]	This is an addition to the model of Dresing/Pehl.

Selbstständigkeitserklärung

Ich erkläre: Ich habe die vorgelegte Dissertation selbständig, ohne unerlaubte fremde Hilfe und nur mit den Hilfen angefertigt, die ich in der Dissertation angegeben habe. Alle Textstellen, die wörtlich oder sinngemäß aus veröffentlichten Schriften entnommen sind, und alle Angaben, die auf mündlichen Auskünften beruhen, sind als solche kenntlich gemacht. Bei den von mir durchgeführten und in der Dissertation erwähnten Untersuchungen habe ich die Grundsätze guter wissenschaftlicher Praxis, wie sie in der 'Satzung der Justus-Liebig-Universität Gießen zur Sicherung guter wissenschaftlicher Praxis' niedergelegt sind, eingehalten.

Gießen, Oktober 2017

Katja Kirsten